All Things Ancient Egypt

All Things Ancient Egypt

An Encyclopedia of the Ancient Egyptian World

VOLUME 2: L–Z

Lisa K. Sabbahy, Editor

All Things

GREENWOOD™

An Imprint of ABC-CLIO, LLC
Santa Barbara, California • Denver, Colorado

Library of Congress Cataloging-in-Publication Data
Names: Sabbahy, Lisa, editor.
Title: All things ancient Egypt : an encyclopedia of the ancient Egyptian world / Lisa K. Sabbahy, editor.
Description: Santa Barbara, California : Greenwood, An Imprint of ABC-CLIO, LLC, 2019. | Includes bibliographical references and index.
Identifiers: LCCN 2018039678| ISBN 9781440855122 (set : alk. paper) | ISBN 9781440869839 (volume 1 : alk. paper) | ISBN 9781440869846 (volume 2 : alk. paper) | ISBN 9781440855139 (ebook)
Subjects: LCSH: Egypt—Civilization—To 332 B.C.—Encyclopedias.
Classification: LCC DT61 .A49875 2019 | DDC 932/.0103—dc23
LC record available at https://lccn.loc.gov/2018039678

ISBN: 978-1-4408-5512-2 (set)
978-1-4408-6983-9 (vol. 1)
978-1-4408-6984-6 (vol. 2)
978-1-4408-5513-9 (ebook)

23 22 21 20 19 1 2 3 4 5

This book is also available as an eBook.

Greenwood
An Imprint of ABC-CLIO, LLC

ABC-CLIO, LLC
147 Castilian Drive
Santa Barbara, California 93117
www.abc-clio.com

This book is printed on acid-free paper ∞

Manufactured in the United States of America

Contents

VOLUME I

Entries A–K

VOLUME 2

Entries L–Z

Guide to Related Topics

BEFORE AND AFTER PHARAONIC EGYPT

Predynastic Period (ca. 5300–3000 BCE)
Ptolemaic Egypt (305–30 BCE)
Roman Egypt (30 BCE–395 CE)

BEYOND THE BORDERS

Ethnicity
Foreign Relations and Treaties
Foreigners
Gebel Barkal
Kerma
Kush
Nubia
Punt

CITIES AND SITES

Abu Ghurab
Abusir
Abydos
Beni Hasan
Bubastis
Cities and Villages
Dahshur
Deir el-Medina
Dendera
Edfu
Elephantine
Giza
Hawara
Heliopolis
Hierakonpolis
Lahun
Lisht
Meidum
Memphis
Philae Island
Sakkara
Tanis
Tell el-Amarna
Tell el-Dab'a
Thebes, East and West

FAMILY AND COMMUNITY

Childbirth
Dance
Ethics
Families
Houses
Marriage and Divorce
Music and Musical Instruments
Sports and Games
Women

FUNERARY PRACTICES

Book of the Dead
Canopic Jar and Box
Coffin Texts
Coffins and Sarcophagi
Mummies, Royal
Mummification
Tomb Models
Tombs, Private
Weighing of the Heart

JOBS, SKILLS, AND MATERIALS

Art
Basketry and Cordage
Beads
Color Symbolism
Faience
Furniture and Woodworking
Glass
Gold
Iron
Labor
Leather
Mining
Pottery
Pyramid Construction
Quarrying
Sculpture and Sculptors
Ships and Shipping
Silver
Sledge
Transportation
Weaving and Looms

LEARNING AND THE SCIENCES

Astronomy
Calendar
Education
Language and Script
Mathematics

MONUMENTS

Abu Simbel
Colossi of Memnon
Obelisk
Pyramids

NATURE AND THE ENVIRONMENT

PERSONAL BELONGINGS

POLITICS AND WAR

RELIGION, PRACTICES, AND EXPRESSIONS

Karnak
Magic
Myth
Myths, Creation
Offerings, Votive
Opening of the Mouth
Oracles
Osiris
Priestesses
Priests
Ptah
Ra
Religion, Personal
Scarab
Temples, Mortuary
Temples, Ptolemaic-Roman
Temples, State
Thoth

THE STATE

Administration
Crime and Punishment
Crowns
Harem
King Lists
Kingship
Kingship Myths
Law
Nomes and Provincial Administration
Officials
Opet Festival
Palaces
Police
Queens
Royal Regalia
Royal Titulary
Sed Festival
Seth
State Formation
Taxation
Tomb Robbery
Vizier

STUFF OF LIFE

Agriculture
Beer
Bread
Dental Health
Disease
Food
Gender and Sex
Jewelry
Medicine and Doctors
Wine

THE WRITTEN WORD

Autobiographical Inscriptions
Decipherment
Graffiti
Libraries
Literacy and Orality
Literature, Fiction
Scribes and Scribal Equipment
Seals and Sealing
Wisdom Literature

L

Labor

Labor, also called corvée labor, was a form of taxation in ancient Egypt, because like being taxed and turning over a percentage of their harvest or other produce, peasants could also expect to be called up to work unpaid for the state. It might be agricultural projects, clearing canals and carrying sand, building projects such as the king's pyramid, mining or quarrying expeditions, or even taking part in a military expedition. It is not clear exactly how picking people for state labor was done or whether there was a set amount of time a picked person had to work for the state every year. Textual evidence points to local officials, such as nomarchs or provincial mayors, being in charge of mustering workers when the king or his officials requested them. The main official who requested and supplied workers for the king was the "overseer of all the works of the king."

It appears that all the people of Egypt theoretically owed work to the crown, but only people without titles; therefore, no officials of any kind ended up being taken. The men taken are often referred to as *nfrw*, which mean "young men," which makes sense if hard work was to be done. The possibility of being called upon for state labor was so pervasive that by the end of the Middle Kingdom, about 1650 BCE, small figures known as *shabtis* were put into tombs to magically come alive and do the labor the tomb owner might be called upon to do. Certain people were granted an exemption by the king, and no official could take them for work for any reason. These people were generally workers attached to a royal institution, such as a chapel or a temple.

There is a well-known decree of the Old Kingdom that King Pepi I (2321–2287 BCE) set up in his mother's mortuary chapel at Coptos, in Upper Egypt. On it, the king exempts all the people and animals attached to the chapel from taxation and forced labor. Another decree like this, from the New Kingdom, was carved on the wall of a small temple King Seti I (1294–1279 BCE) built in the Wadi Mia in the Eastern Desert. The king also dug a well at this spot so that the workers mining and processing gold for Seti's Temple of Abydos had water. The decree states that the gold washers are exempted and protected, and the king will put a curse on any official who interferes with them or their work.

There is a Middle Kingdom papyrus, Papyrus Brooklyn 35.1446, that lists 76 men and women who had fled from their state labor, and it gives a short description of their case and their punishment (Hayes 1955). Punishment could also be extended to the entire family of the guilty person, which was probably meant to be a deterrent from their running away in the first place. The typical punishment for not showing up for state labor or running away while working was "permanent commitment as an unpaid laborer to the government farms and workhouses" (Hayes 1955, 65).

There were also skilled workers who were certainly treated somewhat better. The Fourth Dynasty (2613–2494 BCE) village of Heit el-Ghorab at Giza was built for the workmen who seem to have been sent from the king's royal estates to help build his pyramid. Graffiti has been found on stone blocks in Khufu's pyramid with the name of one group of men who must have been transporting the stones as "the Followers of the Powerful White Crown of Khufu" (Lehner 2015, 417). Similar graffiti naming groups of workers of the king has been found on the stones of the later pyramid of Menkaura. These work gangs must have been assigned to live in the blocks of galleries found at the Heit el-Ghorab site, where 40–50 men could sleep in each separate gallery. There were four gallery complexes, each with 8–10 separate long sleeping galleries. Food production areas were next to them, especially on the east and the south, including storage magazines for grain and bakeries. Animal bone remains from the main streets and dump areas showed a daily diet of protein, particularly beef, along with sheep, goat, and also fish. These men were doing their rotation of state labor, but they were well fed and housed while doing it. The impression of the excavators of Heit el-Ghorab was that the men in these galleries were not common workers, but specialized crews brought from various estates of the king when needed.

Lisa K. Sabbahy

See also: Animals; Deir el-Medina; Giza; Nomes and Provincial Administration; Pyramid Construction; Taxation

Further Reading

Caminos, Ricardo. 1990. "Peasants." In S. Donadoni, ed. *The Egyptians*. Chicago and London: University of Chicago Press, pp. 1–30.

Cooney, Kathlyn. 2007. "Labour." In T. Wilkinson, ed. *The Egyptian World*. London and New York: Routledge, pp. 160–174.

Eyre, Christopher. 2010. "Who Built the Great Temples of Egypt?" In B. Menu, ed. *L'organisation du Travail en Égypte Ancienne et en Mésopotamie*. Cairo: French Institute, pp. 117–191.

Hayes, William. 1955. *A Papyrus of the Late Middle Kingdom in the Brooklyn Museum*. Brooklyn, NY: Brooklyn Museum.

Lehner, Mark. 2015. "Labor and the Pyramids: The Heit el-Ghurab 'Workers Town' at Giza." In P. Steinkeller and M. Hudson, eds. *Labor in the Ancient World*. Vol. 5. Dresden: ISLET-Verlag, pp. 397–522.

Lahun

Lahun (El-Lahun, Illahun) is a modern village south of the Nile Delta, near the mouth of the Fayum. King Senusret II (1877–1870 BCE) chose this location for his burial complex, the structures of which included a mudbrick pyramid, originally cased in stone, and a nearby mortuary temple for the continued worship of the deceased king as a god. During excavations undertaken near the pyramid around the turn of the 20th century, Sir William Flinders Petrie discovered a walled town, which he called Kahun. The town, founded by Senusret II and inhabited for approximately 100 years, was originally called *Hotep-Senusret* ("Senusret is

Satisfied"). While Kahun today generally refers to the ancient town and Lahun refers to the modern village and pyramid complex, the names are often used interchangeably, and it is becoming common to just call the entire site Lahun.

The Lahun pyramid complex was surrounded by a brick and stone enclosure with a row of trees planted and maintained outside the southern and eastern walls. Inside the northeast corner of the enclosure, a much smaller pyramid was constructed for the burial of one of Senusret II's queens. Among a row of shaft tombs cut along the south side of the pyramid base, Petrie found the burial of Senusret II's daughter, Princess Sat-Hathor-Yunet (or Sithathoriunet). Although plundered in antiquity, a cache of royal jewelry had been overlooked in a niche in this princess's tomb. The "Lahun Treasure," as it is known today, contains exquisitely crafted jewelry in gold and precious stones and is representative of the highest level of technical skill ever reached by ancient Egyptian jewelers. Except for a few pieces held in the Egyptian Museum in Cairo, the bulk of the Lahun Treasure is currently in the collection of New York's Metropolitan Museum of Art.

East of Senusret II's pyramid was the town of Kahun, a deliberately planned settlement. The site housed construction workers for the king's building projects, soldiers, priests, and other temple personnel, as well as administrative officials who managed the town and its activities. Its physical layout followed a grid pattern surrounded by an unfortified wall with only one surviving gateway, therefore suggesting centralized control over the movements of the townspeople. Kahun was internally divided into two major sections separated by a thick wall. The reason for this physical barrier is unknown; the western section might have been a later addition to the town or the separation may relate to the status of its residents. The eastern section contained at least one temple (unrelated to the king's mortuary temple at the edge of the town), workshops, and nine large mansions complete with courtyards, offices, living quarters, and storage spaces, including large grain silos. The western section, nearest the king's mortuary temple, was made up entirely of rows of smaller houses with two to seven rooms, some of which possessed small grain silos.

Excavated papyrus records retrieved from both the western and eastern sections of the town provide valuable information about the daily life and administration of Kahun and its associated temples. These records constitute the largest collection of surviving Middle Kingdom papyri from a single location. Dating from the reign of Amenemhat III (1831–1786 BCE) through that of Sobekneferu (1777–1773 BCE), these documents are generally categorized by scholars as a temple archive, related to the functioning of the king's mortuary cult, and an administrative group of miscellaneous records pertaining to activities in the town. In addition to the names and titles of people living or working in the town and the projects in which they were involved, these documents include important medical and religious texts. The Kahun Medical Papyrus (UC 32057), also known as the Gynaecological Papyrus, is one of the oldest known medical texts in the world addressing women's health issues, including pregnancy and contraception. The Kahun Veterinary Papyrus (UC 32036) is recognized as the oldest veterinary text, mostly concerning eye diseases afflicting cattle, fish, dogs, and birds. Another fragmentary papyrus from Kahun (UC 321919) lists one year of festivals and

Mummy Portraits

In Roman Egypt, the faces of the mummified dead were sometimes represented with impressionistically painted, lifelike portraits. These depicted elite men and women of various ages on rectangular panels of wood or linen shrouds. Whether these were produced during the subject's life or posthumously is not known. The portraits were cut down into irregular shapes and fitted into the mummy wrappings of their subjects. Unlike earlier Egyptian mummies, no jewels or amulets were included inside the wrapping, but the visible surface was beautifully decorated. It is likely that portrait mummies were kept on display and visited for a period of time in homes or funerary chapels before burial. Many of the approximately 900 surviving mummy portraits were found in the Fayum region, where they were first excavated by William Flinders Petrie at the Roman necropolis of Hawara. These objects are therefore often known as Hawara or Fayum mummy portraits, although they were in use throughout Egypt from the first through the third centuries CE.

Mummy portraits were executed in either tempera (pigment mixed with a water-soluble binding agent) or encaustic (pigment mixed with beeswax that, depending on the technique used, could be applied hot or cold). The subject is not usually presented frontally but positioned at a slight angle, with the head turned or tilted to face the viewer. Although some male subjects appear nude, most portraits represent individuals in formal clothing with hairstyles that reflect fashions popular in Rome. At an unknown point after the paintings were finished, some were treated with gilded crowns applied over the hair, as well as golden accents on the face, clothing, or background. Along with the gilding, the inclusion of garlands or vessels in the hands of some subjects may indicate initiation into the cult of Isis.

Jennifer Ruth Butterworth

records the singers and dancers who performed, many of whom were explicitly described as Asiatic or Medjay (pastoral nomads from the Eastern Desert and Lower Nubia) in origin. Foreigners documented in the papyri also worked at Kahun as priests, letter carriers, doorkeepers, temple guards, domestic servants, and group leaders of small workforces.

The presence of Asiatic men and women in Kahun is also attested by the excavation of various personal artifacts, such as torques, or simple necklaces popular in the northern Levant, and decorative hair combs, such as found in Jericho, which suggest some members of the Kahun population adorned themselves in Asiatic styles. Proto-Canaanite script incised on the surface of a loom demonstrates the presence of Asiatic textile technology, likely associated with foreign domestic labor in a private household. Pottery sherds from Nubia, Cyprus, and Crete, as well as weights calibrated to Palestinian and Phoenician standards found in the town, suggest the presence of foreign merchants or commercial contact with external markets. Kahun's non-Egyptian inhabitants, numbering approximately 130 or more individuals (Petrik 213–215), would have been a small minority in the town; however, estimates for the general population size range from 8,500 to 10,000 (Kemp 2007, 216).

Kahun was abandoned during the Thirteenth Dynasty (1773–1650 BCE), although parts of the town and the surrounding desert were later used sporadically as burial sites. Stone from the Lahun pyramid complex and Kahun temples was removed for the temple of Ramses II at Ihnasya el-Medina, or Heracleopolis, farther to the south. A small cemetery in the desert between the Lahun pyramid and Kahun town dates to the Third Intermediate Period and Late Period, but almost all of these burials had reused earlier tombs. During the Late Roman Period, a Coptic monastery was located at the site, which Petrie examined but did not document.

Jennifer Ruth Butterworth

See also: Cities and Villages; Foreigners; Houses; Jewelry; Pyramids

Further Reading

Brunton, Guy. 1920. *Lahun I: The Treasure*. London: British School of Archaeology in Egypt University College and Bernard Quaritch.

David, A. Rosalie. 1997. *The Pyramid Builders of Ancient Egypt: A Modern Investigation of Pharaoh's Workforce*. London and New York: Routledge.

Griffith, F. Ll. 1898. *The Petrie Papyri: Hieratic Papyri from Kahun and Gurob (Principally of the Middle Kingdom)*. London: Bernard Quaritch, pp. 1–90.

Horváth, Zoltán. 2009. "Temple(s) and Town at el-Lahun: A Study of the Ancient Toponyms in the El-Lahun Papyri." In D. Silverman, W. K. Simpson, and J. Wegner, eds. *Archaism and Innovation: Studies in the Culture of Middle Kingdom Egypt*. New Haven, CT: Yale University; Philadelphia: University of Pennsylvania Museum, pp. 171–203.

Kemp, Barry J. 2007. *Ancient Egypt: Anatomy of a Civilization*. New York: Routledge, pp. 211–221.

Petrie, Sir Flinders, Guy Brunton, and M. A. Murray. 1923. *Lahun II*. London: British School of Archaeology in Egypt University College and Bernard Quaritch.

Petrie, W. M. Flinders. 1890. *Kahun, Gurob, and Hawara*. London: Kegan Paul, Trench, Trübner, and Co.

Petrik, M. 2011. "Foreign Groups at Lahun during the late Middle Kingdom." In E. Bechtold, A. Gulyas, and A. Hasznos, eds. *From Illahun to Djeme: Papers Presented in Honour of Ulrich Luft*. Oxford: Archaeopress, pp. 211–226.

Quirke, Stephen. 1998. *Lahun Studies*. Reigate, UK: SIA Publishing.

Szpakowska, Kasia. 2008. *Daily Life in Ancient Egypt: Recreating Lahun*. Malden, MA: Blackwell Publishing.

Language and Script

The ancient Egyptian language flourished in the northeast corner of Africa, along the northern Nile valley and delta, from about 3300 BCE through the Middle Ages, about 1200 CE. Linguists generally classify the language of ancient Egypt as belonging to the "Afroasiatic" family, which includes dozens of related languages from North Africa and Southwest Asia. Thus, ancient Egyptian shares some features with modern North African languages, such as Berber and Chadic. At the same time, Egyptian also shares certain features with the Semitic branch of the Afroasiatic family, including modern Hebrew and Arabic, as well as the ancient languages of Aramaic and Akkadian, among others. However, most of these similarities appear to be even more ancient than the Egyptians' native writing system, suggesting that their language had already diverged from its Afroasiatic parents in prehistory. Because of this early split and the many differences that it produced, "Egyptian" is usually classified as its own branch within the Afroasiatic language family.

As a spoken language, Egyptian is "dead," meaning that there are no living native speakers who might verify precisely how the language worked, how it was pronounced, or why one construction was preferred over another in a particular context. Although Egyptian is today a dead language, it was a vibrant and living tradition in Egypt for more than 4,500 years. Consequently, Egyptian may be regarded as the longest-surviving language attested in writing. Given its incredibly long history as a living language, it is not surprising that Egyptian went through many changes in both its writing system and grammar. Egyptologists usually divide this history broadly into Earlier Egyptian, characterized by its "synthetic" verbal system, and Later Egyptian, characterized by a more "analytic" verbal system. The synthetic verbs of Earlier Egyptian signaled changes in meaning primarily through pronunciation, similar to the English verb "run" (present tense) versus "ran" (simple past). Unfortunately for us, such changes in pronunciation were not originally reflected in the ancient Egyptian script, which did not write vowels, so tense and other possible features of the verb often appear to us as ambiguous and must be deduced through context. The analytic verbs of Later Egyptian, on the other hand, signaled changes in meaning primarily through the addition and combination of short words, similar to English "I run" (present tense) versus "I have run" (past perfect). As a result, features such as tense are much easier to identify and interpret in the later phases of the language.

Within the broad categories of Earlier and Later Egyptian, scholars recognize six major subdivisions: the "Earlier" phase is divided into Archaic, Old, and Middle Egyptian, while the "Later" phase is divided into Late Egyptian, Demotic, and Coptic. Each of these subdivisions possessed its own peculiarities of script (writing system), grammar (rules for sentence formation), syntax (word order), and vocabulary (word choice). Archaic Egyptian texts, attested from the terminal Predynastic Period through the Second Dynasty (ca. 3300–2593 BCE), consist almost entirely of nouns and adjectives, which were employed as labels for goods and as captions to figural images in art. The emergence of Old Egyptian in the Third Dynasty (ca. 2592–2543 BCE) constitutes the first fluorescence of the fully productive written language, with a rich system of verbal and nonverbal sentence constructions, capable of expressing the full range of Egyptian thought and experience. This phase of the language also coincided with the introduction of three text genres that would remain in use for the rest of pharaonic history: magical-religious texts, autobiographical or self-presentation texts, and administrative texts. By the Eleventh Dynasty (ca. 2080–1940 BCE), Middle Egyptian had more or less replaced Old Egyptian. This change coincided with the reestablishment of kingship over the entire country following more than a century of disunity, during the First Intermediate Period. The new royal family, which ushered in these changes, hailed from the southern city of Thebes. Significant in this regard, some linguistic evidence suggests that Middle Egyptian might represent a southern/Theban dialect, as opposed to the northern dialect of Old Egyptian from Memphis (Edgerton 1951). However, the extent (if any) to which political maneuvering may have played an active role in the change from Old to Middle Egyptian is unknown. The emergence of Middle Egyptian also ushered in an important new literary genre, which took the form of tales, poems, wisdom texts, and lamentations, all of which might also serve as vehicles for royal propaganda. Middle Egyptian thrived as a living language until the early New Kingdom and survived as the preferred "classical" dialect of monumental inscriptions and religious texts for the remainder of pharaonic history. The latest known hieroglyphic inscription, dating to 394 CE, on the island of Philae, still employed this classical dialect.

Over the course of the early Eighteenth Dynasty (ca. 1539–1292 BCE), Middle Egyptian texts began to show greater influence from the contemporary spoken language. These changes culminated in the emergence of Late Egyptian during and immediately after the reign of the heretic king Akhenaten (ca. 1352–1336 BCE). Seven centuries later, Demotic superseded Late Egyptian in administrative texts and day-to-day correspondence, with Demotic literary texts also attested from the Ptolemaic era of Greek dominance in Egypt (332–30 BCE) (Johnson 1976, 1). From the second half of the Ptolemaic era, Egyptian scribes began to experiment with writing native words in the foreign Greek alphabet. These experiments ultimately led to the emergence of Coptic, the final phase of the Egyptian language and the only phase to be written with a nonnative script (modified Greek), during or shortly after the first century CE. Coptic continued to be spoken and written as a living language until around 1200 CE, when it was replaced by Arabic. Nevertheless, Coptic—and therefore ancient Egyptian—survives to the present day as the liturgical language of the Coptic (Egyptian Christian) church, in much the same way that Latin survives as the liturgical language of Catholicism.

For most of their history, the ancient Egyptians employed two main writing systems, or "scripts": hieroglyphic and hieratic. The hieroglyphic script was inscribed primarily on monuments made of stone, but it also appears on artifacts of wood and metal and, rarely, on papyrus (a precursor to paper, made of dried papyrus-reed stalks). The hieroglyphic script is what immediately comes to mind when most people imagine Egyptian writing: groups of individual "hieroglyphs"—images of people, gods, animals, plants, and inanimate objects—arranged in compact rows or columns of text, which might be written from the right or left. Signs in the hieroglyphic system were of four varieties: ideograms, which wrote words for things using simplified images of the things themselves (for example, in depicting the floor plan of a simple one-room building, one might write the word for "house"); phonograms, which spelled out words using either one, two, or three consonants of the Egyptian language; phonetic complements, which repeated the sound values of an accompanying phonogram but were not pronounced as separate sounds; and determinatives, which provided a clue as to the general sense of a word.

Alongside their monumental script, the Egyptians also employed the cursive hieratic writing system, which was written mainly on papyrus and flakes of limestone or pottery, known as *ostraca*. Unlike hieroglyphs, which were usually carved with a hammer and chisel, the hieratic script was usually drawn with a brush and ink. In addition, hieratic texts were written exclusively in rows, from right to left.

A great many, although certainly not all, preserved examples of the ancient Egyptian language are carved in stone in the hieroglyphic script. In fact, durability and preservation were precisely the reasons why Egyptians used stone as a medium for writing in the first place. However, this accident of preservation

This small sheet of papyrus has a short letter written on it in hieratic script, the hand-written cursive script of the ancient Egyptians. Black ink was used to draw the characters. Hieratic script was written from right to left. (Rogers Fund, 1927/The Metropolitan Museum of Art)

creates a false impression that Egyptians mainly wrote in hieroglyphs, when the cursive hieratic script was far more common in daily use. In fact, most ancient Egyptian scribes—the literate minority of Egypt's population—*only* knew how to write in hieratic; relatively few went on to learn the hieroglyphic script.

Over time, the hieratic script became ever more cursive, as the individual signs bore less and less resemblance to their hieroglyphic counterparts. In Late Egyptian documents of the Twentieth Dynasty (ca. 1190–1077 BCE), for example, whole words might be written with only one or two distinct signs followed by simple lines or dots to give the general impression of the rest of the word. This tendency toward ever more cursive writing eventually led to a splinter tradition of "abnormal hieratic" in the Twenty-Fifth Dynasty (ca. 722–655 BCE), from which developed the distinctive Demotic script, employed exclusively for that phase of the language, from Dynasty 26 and later.

Joshua Aaron Roberson

See also: Decipherment; Scribes and Scribal Equipment

Further Reading

Allen, James P. 2013. *The Ancient Egyptian Language: An Historical Study*. Cambridge: University Press.

Collier, Mark, and Bill Manley. 2008. *How to Read Egyptian Hieroglyphs: A Step-by-Step Guide to Teach Yourself.* London: British Museum.

Edgerton, William F. 1951. "Early Egyptian Dialectical Relationships." *Bulletin of the American Schools of Oriental Research* 122: 9–12.

Johnson, Janet. 1976. *The Demotic Verbal System*. Studies in Ancient Oriental Civilization 38. Chicago: Oriental Institute. https://oi.uchicago.edu/sites/oi.uchicago.edu/files/uploads/shared/docs/SAOC38.pdf.

Wilson, Penelope. 2003. *Sacred Signs: Hieroglyphs in Ancient Egypt*. Oxford: Oxford University Press.

Law

The king of Egypt's most important responsibility was to uphold *Maat*, which translates as "justice" and "truth" as well as "world order." *Maat* was in existence at the time of creation. In upholding it, the king satisfies the god and goddesses, and the Egyptian world functions and is in order. In fact, in offering ceremonies, the king of Egypt hands a figure of *Maat* to the god. The vizier, the most important figure, just under the king, held the title of High Priest of *Maat*, also showing his responsibility to uphold order. Practically, that hat placed the vizier in the position of being the chief judge, and he functioned as such at any important trial. The "Instructions to the Vizier" found in the Theban tomb of Thutmose III's vizier, Rekhmire, make this clear. The king speaks to Rekhmire, saying that he must carry out his job very carefully as "it is the pillar of the whole land." Rekhmire must see that everything is done correctly, and "done according to law" (Lichtheim 1976, 22).

The ancient Egyptian word *hep* is translated as "law," but it can also mean "rule" or even "custom." There is no evidence that Egyptian law was codified before the time of the Twenty-Seventh Dynasty, when the Persian king Darius I ruled over Egypt and ordered that all laws in Egypt be collected and written in Demotic, the dialect of ancient Egyptian used at that time, and Aramaic, the administrative language of the Persian Empire. It is clear, however, that records were kept of trial verdicts and that precedent was later followed in similar cases. In the reign of Seti II (1200–1194 BCE), when the lady Herya of the village of Deir el-Medina is taken to court for stealing, the case is recorded on a limestone ostracon, probably to be copied on papyrus, as it is to be sent to the vizier. The text mentions a similar earlier case, in the reign of Ramses II (1279–1213 BCE), in which another woman was charged with theft.

By the Middle Kingdom, the word, *kenbet* is used for "court." There were local courts, such as the one in the village of Deir el-Medina, and Great Courts, which seemed to be only in Memphis and Thebes. They were not "sitting courts," but were put together when needed, just as there were not career judges, but simply important people who were picked to judge when there was a case. When there was a case, the panel of judges would question the plaintiff and the defendant, or if it was a criminal case, like tomb robbery, just the defendant or defendants, and hear testimony from witnesses if needed. The people questioned could be given an oath, referred to as the "oath of the lord" or sometimes the "oath of the lord and god" (McDowell 1990, 36–37), which basically says that as long as the king and the god exist the person taking the oath is telling the truth. It is not actually clear what the penalty for lying under oath was, although some Egyptologists have suggested it brought the death penalty. If needed, defendants were "questioned by the stick."

Most noncriminal cases and legal documents that have been preserved from ancient Egypt deal with property: buying, selling, owning, and inheriting. Unless social practice was different than what was written, men and women both seemed to be equal in all these situations. Both women and men could buy and own property in their name and will it to whom they wished. Both males and females inherited equally, and wives and husbands equally split communal property. In terms of a court case, both men and women could bring cases in court and also serve as witnesses. They were also punished with the same punishments if found guilty.

Courts not only had the power to declare a verdict but also the power to order the verdict carried out. If someone owed someone else money and it was proved in court, they had to pay it. If they were accused of stealing something and were found guilty of it, they had to return it and probably also got beaten. The punishments for serious crimes were more harsh. Standard punishment was 100 blows and 5 pierced wounds (which is not entirely understood but could not have been pleasant). If the crime was serious enough to be exiled from Egypt, the criminal also had their nose cut off. The death penalty, applied for crimes against the state, which would include anything against a deity as well as the king, in Ramesside (1295–1069 BCE) times was being impaled on a sharp stick.

In Ramesside times, the court system had become so inefficient or corrupt that many cases were solved by going to an oracle. On festival days, when a god or goddess came out in procession in the sacred barque carried by the priests, questions could be asked of him or her, and the answer would come from the way the barque moved, left or right, back or forth. If someone had to be picked out, for example, as the thief, the barque would go up to the person, pointing him or her out. The decision of the oracle was accepted as the will of god.

Lisa K. Sabbahy

See also: Crime and Punishment; Deir el-Medina; Kingship; *Maat*; Oracles; Tomb Robbery; Vizier

Further Reading

Bierbrier, Morris. 1984. *The Tomb-Builders of the Pharaohs*. New York: Charles Scribner's Sons.

Lichtheim, Mariam. 1976. *Ancient Egyptian Literature: A Book of Readings*. Vol. 2. Berkeley: University of California Press.

McDowell, A. G. 1990. *Jurisdiction in the Workmen's Community of Deir el-Medineh*. Leiden: Nederlands Instituut voor het Nabije Oosten.

Tyldesley, Joyce. *Judgement of the Pharaoh: Crime and Punishment in Ancient Egypt*. London: Phoenix.

Leather

The use and importance of leather and skin products throughout Egypt's history fluctuated. It reached a peak in the New Kingdom (1550–1069 BCE), probably accelerated by the invasion of foreign people who brought their own expertise in leatherwork, especially associated with footwear and chariots. Another reason for the change in importance seems to have been a change in slaughterhouse practices, with more attention being paid to hides and skins as products in themselves. Until the New Kingdom, the leather industry in ancient Egypt, though handled with considerable skill and confidence, had remained basically unchanged since earliest times. The "Pan-Grave" culture is associated with many types of leather products; this culture was brought into Egypt by a seminomadic tribe of Nubian cattle herders, who arrived during the Middle Kingdom (2055–1650 BCE) and the Second Intermediate Period (1650–1550 BCE). The Nubian people probably influenced the Egyptian leather industry as well; the Nubian C-group people may have been skilled leatherworkers who were integrated into Egyptian society because of those skills. Interpretation of the use of leather after the New Kingdom is problematic due to the paucity of data. From the Roman Period (30 BCE–395 CE) relatively more finds are recorded, showing a change in technology that was due to the Romans bringing in their own tradition in leatherwork. In Roman times, an overall increase in the level of technological skill can be seen.

The term *leather* is generally used in literature, but, technically speaking, this term only refers to vegetal tanned or tawed skins rather than cured skins. Keeping a lack of possible evidence in mind, in Egypt, tanning or tawing did not occur in pharaonic times; oil curing, that is, working oil into skins to make them more durable, was preferred. However, oil curing is reversible; if the oil is washed out by water, the hide is no longer protected from rotting. Vegetable tanning, a technology that was probably introduced in postpharaonic times, possibly in the Ptolemaic Period (332–30 BCE), although there is still some debate, is irreversible and a better protection of the skin against decay. Before making a skin durable, however, a number of actions are needed, which starts, of course, with flaying the skin. Removal of the underlying fat and the hair was also part of the preservation process, although sometimes it was partially left. Removal was probably done by rubbing urine, ash, or a mixture of flour and salt into the haired surface to loosen the hairs and scrape them off. Next, the skin needed to be made durable. After this process, the leatherworker took the skin and made it more supple by pulling it back and forth across a beam, a method called staking, and the remaining oil was worked into the skin before the skin was finally dried on a wooden stretching frame.

In pharaonic Egypt, skins from cows, sheep, goats, and gazelles were commonly used from the earliest times onward. The choice of skin was at least partially based on what its use would be. Besides those listed, more exotic animal skins were used, such as lion, panther, cheetah, antelope, leopard, and crocodile. Skin products were used for a large range of objects, with a peak in the variety of applications in the New Kingdom, such as lashings, which were usually made of rawhide, as it shrinks upon wetting, making a tight binding; parts of musical instruments; furniture; clothing; chariots; horse harnessing; footwear; and cordage. The objects were stitched together with simple seams, and stitches were mainly done with thread of sinew or, to a lesser extent, flax. Before the New Kingdom, leather thongs were often used for stitching. The Tano Chariot leather of the later New Kingdom indicates more economic use of materials and improved technological skills, exemplified by a wider variety of finishings and application techniques.

Pair of sandals from the earlier Eighteenth Dynasty, found with a child's burial in a private tomb on the West Bank of the Nile at Thebes. The leather has been stained with a red color, and the straps and tops of the soles have designs cut into them. (Rogers Fund, 1936/The Metropolitan Museum of Art)

Leather was often enhanced with color and other decoration techniques. Before the New Kingdom, mineral dyes predominated. In the later New Kingdom, vegetable dyes such as indigo (blue) and pomegranate (yellow and black) appear. Most commonly used to stain leather, however, were red, from madder with alum as a fixant, and green, from copper compounds, combined. The color was confined to the surface, and the complete skin was usually dyed after curing. Gilding became popular in the Coptic Period, although some of Tutankhamun's (1336–1327 BCE) leather footwear and chariots had been gilded or covered with gold sheets. By far the most common decoration technique in pharaonic times is multicolored appliqué. Less common, but still seen regularly seen, is openwork, done by the cutting out of figures. Stamped decoration becomes very common in the later Christian Period, but it is already seen in some examples from the Pharaonic Period.

Texts and imagery in tombs and temples are of little value for the study of leather in ancient Egypt. There are only a small number of depictions, and they offer incomplete narration of the leatherworking process. As well, interpretation of some words and texts related to objects that involve leatherworking are problematic. Equally little is known about the status of leatherworkers. This makes it difficult to recognize the value of leather. It has been suggested that it is important to keep the value of an animal in mind when discussing the monetary value of a skin, as a direct correlation between the value of the animal and its hide/skin is to be expected. This would mean that hides from cattle would have been most expensive, except for exotic skins, such as leopard, but these were used only rarely and restricted to the royals and certain members of the clergy.

The leatherworking trade in ancient Egypt, as well as in its neighboring countries, is still barely understood, which is, among things, due to lack of research carried out on this subject. Fortunately, in the last two decades, interest has greatly increased, resulting in growing knowledge and understanding of the many aspects of this versatile material and the leatherworker's craft, including the organization of the trade, its technological development, and its place within ancient Egyptian society.

André Jacques Veldmeijer

See also: Chariot; Clothing; Footwear

Further Reading

Driel-Murray, Carol van. 2000. "Leather and Skin Products." In Paul T. Nicholson and Ian Shaw, eds. *Ancient Egyptian Materials and Technologies*. Cambridge: Cambridge University Press, pp. 299–319.

Veldmeijer, André J. 2011. *Amarna's Leatherwork*. Part 1, *Preliminary Analysis and Catalogue*. Leiden: Sidestone Press.

Veldmeijer, André J. 2011. *Sandals, Shoes and Other Leatherwork from the Coptic Monastery Deir el-Bachit: Analysis and Catalogue*. Leiden: Sidestone Press.

Veldmeijer, André J. With Contributions by Felix Arnold and Cornelius von Pilgrim. 2016. *Leatherwork from Elephantine (Aswan, Egypt): Analysis and Catalogue of the Ancient Egyptian & Persian Leather Finds*. Leiden: Sidestone Press.

Veldmeijer, André J. With Contributions by Daniel Polz and Ute Rummel. 2017. *Sailors, Musicians and Monks: The Leatherwork from Dra Abu el-Naga*. Leiden: Sidestone Press.

Veldmeijer, André J., and Salima Ikram. With Contributions by Ole Herslund, Lisa K. Sabbahy, and Lucy Skinner. 2018. *Chariots in Ancient Egypt: The Tano Chariot: A Case Study*. Leiden: Sidestone Press.

Veldmeijer, André J., and Lucy-Anne Skinner. 2018. "Nubian Leatherwork." In Dietrich Raue, ed. *Handbook of Ancient Nubia*. Berlin: De Gruyter (in press).

Libraries

Tracing libraries in ancient Egypt is not straightforward and would need a classification different than the modern understanding of this institutional phenomenon. By applying a functional approach and looking beyond the modern idea of the public access and the purpose as a service provider, we are able to detect ancient Egyptian libraries and define them as places for the storage, preservation, and circulation of written knowledge. In this way, libraries are bound into the formation and upkeep of the "cultural memory" of a society by ensuring the continued availability of the knowledge and skills inherent in the stored texts.

Archaeologies of memory contribute to the understanding of the past and reveal strategies how past societies observed, presented, and interpreted their own ideas. Insofar as we can follow their constructed social and cultural memory in the archaeological record, the past is remembered or forgotten according to the needs of the contemporary present. This indicates that the formation of memory is an active, controlled, and ongoing process either incorporating direct links to ancestors as remembered past or going beyond that by providing general associations with a mythical time. Both areas are important within the Egyptian cultural memory. By constructing memory in this way, the ancient Egyptians were able to create the story of Egypt, the unified culture characterized by *Maat* as the right order. This helped to overcome times of disunity, such as the Intermediate Periods. Memory aided identity and legitimized authority.

The ability to preserve wisdom and knowledge via writing is expressed in several ancient Egyptian texts. One often cited example is a passage called "Eulogy of Dead Writers" from Papyrus Chester Beatty IV (British Museum EA10684). This text describes how authors of wisdom texts were remembered as their words were written down. Writing materialized cultural memory.

It was long doubted that a system of libraries existed in ancient Egypt, as we can only prove two libraries for certain in the archaeological record, Edfu and Philae. A closer look revealed a variety of institutions established to store written texts and preserve the inherent knowledge, as attested in more than 300 textual and archaeological resources. All these types seem to have served slightly diverse purposes. These institutions and their respective responsibilities changed over the time. Looking at them with today's eyes would classify some as libraries, others as archives.

Several ancient Egyptian phrases were used to describe what we could translate as "library" or "archive." Terms depended on the specific function this institution would fulfill for the Egyptians, which is difficult to pin down in detail, as well as the time. Many Egyptian idioms can be translated as "library," such as *per-medjat*, which means "house of books/book rolls." These terms could sometimes be used synonymously, so it is nearly impossible to find useful translations that can explain the differences and specific features of a single institution. These words were used in different sources in diverse frequency and at different times. However, it seems that they can be differentiated from a slightly different type of institution, which could be translated as "archives," and for which there are also a wide variety of terms with slightly different meanings denoting somewhat differing functions.

All of these institutions dealt with two different ways of remembering: orality and literacy. Speaking words and writing them down constituted knowledge and created cultural memory. High culture in ancient Egypt was characterized by writing and literacy as well as by oral language as a parallel medium of communication. By the Fifth Dynasty (2494–2345 BCE), it became necessary to give words authority by placing them in writing to overcome the speaking situation defined by time and space. At this moment, Egypt had already seen 800 years of predynastic and dynastic history connected with some forms of writing, as the turn from speech to writing took place around 3300 BCE. Tomb inscriptions that copied royal decrees were used to convey royal authority. In the tomb of Rawer (Giza G5270; Cairo, Egyptian Museum JE 66682, lines 7–11), we read about the favor Rawer received from King Neferirkara: "His Majesty decreed that (it will be) put in writing on his tomb which is in the necropolis. His Majesty caused that there should [be made for him] an authorization in respect of it, written beside the king himself on the stone-workshop of the palace, to write what was said in his tomb in the necropolis" (Eyre 2013, 80). The translation of "authorization" reflects the word "a," which literally means "the king's document." This way to store important documents—in the case of the tomb for all eternity—already indicates the differences to the modern understanding of libraries.

Learning to write and to read was restricted. The percentage of the population thought to have been literate is estimated at 1–10 percent, depending on the period and the definition of literacy. Despite the low percentage of literacy, ancient Egypt was a literate society due to the enormous influence the word—written and spoken—had on culture, both in the sense of individual literacy in different levels as well as through the phenomenon I like to call "collective literacy." The writing and storing of texts reiterated different potencies of the word: some revealed their strength due to being written down (magical texts, oracles); others were meant to be used as orally recited (ritualistic texts); and many stand between orality and literacy (letters where both communicants grammatically engaged in speech acts).

Privately owned book collections existed as evidence of specific and individual literacy. In contrast to modern private libraries, their content was less literary than magical or professional. The following are often cited examples of privately owned libraries. The Ramesseum Library was found with professional magical equipment in a Middle Kingdom (2055–1650 BCE) tomb situated under the mortuary temple of Ramses II (Ramesseum). The so-called Berlin Library consists of four literary papyri. Their connection is not proven for the pharaonic past, as they were very likely grouped together by the first collector in modern times. The third example is the very heterogeneous Collection Deir el-Medina of the scribe Qenherkhepshef. Other private collections are described in literary texts. In the Westcar Papyrus, the magician Djedi calls his children to bring his books, as he needs to solve tasks set by the king. The artistic representation of bringing books is shown on the Stela of Jekj (Rijksmuseum van Oudheden AP 25), where a musician is accompanied by a helper carrying book chests. Papyri found in tombs could also be counted as evidence for privately owned books.

When going beyond the individual level of literacy and privately owned book collections, we are entering the sphere of collective literacy as institutionalized literacy. Texts that were useful for and needed by the society as a whole were stored as collections. That could be on temple walls, as described below, or in libraries and archives. Only two libraries are preserved in architecture. The temple libraries in Edfu and Philae (both are characterized as *per-medjat*, "house of book rolls") were small special libraries used for the daily cult ritual. The small room in Edfu, which was only about 20 square feet, was inscribed with a book catalog. In scenes accompanying the catalog, we see the king offering book chests to Horus the Behdet—the main god of the temple. In the east and west walls of this room, there were several niches, which may have contained similar wooden book chests as shown in the offering scenes. This library was an integral part of the daily cult ritual. When performing the ritual, the priests cleansed and robed themselves as preparation in the adjacent Morning House—in Edfu situated over the central axis as a mirror image of the *per-medjat*. When proceeding into the temple inner, they picked up the books needed for the ritual in the library. The papyri were needed to make the incantations and recitations while proceeding toward the sanctuary. In Philae, we see a similar picture. Even though the actual setting of the rooms is different—here the room called *morning house* is right next to the room labeled *per-medjat* at the inscription over the entrance—the functional spatial arrangement of the library as part of the procession with the books into the temple is the same.

Another important institution is the *per-ankh*, the "House of Life." While the House of Books was a small special library, the House of Life was an institution within temple precincts or close by that included a large library. Associated with kingship, the *per-ankh* acted as a place for the creation, use, and preservation of cultural knowledge. Although *per-ankh* appears frequently in writings from the end of the Old Kingdom, the only confirmed archeological example we have is in Tell el-Amarna. This mudbrick building is classified by a stamped inscription with the term *per-ankh* on top. The stamp, which functioned as builders' mark needed to deliver the correct bricks to the correct building site, only came to light during the excavation; it could not have been seen when the building was intact. The House of Life in Tell el-Amarna was very close to the state chancellery (*ta-set-(naw)-shaswt-per-aa*) where the correspondence of the Pharaoh was stored. Having such similar institutions so close together shows their difference in functionality and purpose.

A few relief blocks indicate a library in the Montu-temple in el-Tôd, in Upper Egypt. In the Dela at Tanis, excavators uncovered a brick building that contained bits of papyri, limestone potsherds, and other fragments of objects; this structure could have been either an archive or a library. Furthermore, small rooms were found in the Ramesseum on the West Bank of Thebes, which might have been used as offices. They are situated between the palace and the northern repository and were identified as *per-ankh* by the excavators.

Archaeologically or textually evidenced libraries are not the only way to store texts and create cultural memory. We need to take into consideration the mythological function of the temple as part of an idealized place to store knowledge—a huge library in stone of important texts. Jan Assmann called this phenomenon "the temple as book" (Assmann 2011, 156–170), characterizing the temple as a three-dimensional and monumental translation of a book into space. *Book* is here understood as an ideal corpus of cultural texts and images comprised from all sorts of writings and decorations covering a wide knowledge in the sense of a monumental library, while passages are often only indicated by title or in part. Handling texts in this way ensures an extended audience mediated through literacy.

One example is the account of the Battle of Megiddo, fought by Thutmose III (1479–1425 BCE). We find the report about the siege and victory on the walls in the Hall of Annals of Karnak Temple. Despite being on the stone temple wall, the actual inscription mentioned that it should be stored on a leather roll in the Temple of Amun, very likely in a library or archive. The same text was therefore adapted to different audiences. The monumental version set in stone was directed to the gods and as such fixed the event in time, while the archival copy on a leather roll was kept elsewhere in or nearby the temple, likely in a *per-ankh*, the "House of Life."

Katharina Zinn

See also: Edfu; Language and Script; Literacy and Orality; Philae Island; Scribes and Scribal Equipment; Tell el-Amarna

Further Reading

Assmann, J. 2001 "Libraries in the Ancient World—with Special Reference to Ancient Egypt." In S. Bieri and W. Fuchs, eds. *Building for Books: Traditions and Visions.* Basel: Birkhäuser, pp. 50–67.

Assmann, J. 2011. *Cultural Memory and Early Civilization: Writing, Remembrance, and Political Imagination.* Cambridge: Cambridge University Press

Baines, J., and C. Eyre. 2007. "Four Notes on Literacy." In J. Baines, ed. *Visual and Written Culture in Ancient Egypt.* Oxford: Oxford University Press, pp. 63–94.

Eyre, C. 2013. *The Use of Documents in Pharaonic Egypt.* Oxford: Oxford University Press.

Jay, J. E. 2016. *Orality and Literacy in the Demotic Tales.* Leiden: Brill.

Pestman, P. 1982. "Who Were the Owners, in the 'Community of Workmen,' of the Chester Beatty Papyri." In R. Demaree and J. Janssen, eds. *Gleanings from Deir el-Medina.* Leiden: Nederlands Instituut voor het Nabije Oosten, pp. 155–172.

Ryholt, K. 2013. "Libraries in Ancient Egypt." In J. König, K. Oikonomopoulou, and G. Wolf, eds. *Ancient Libraries.* Cambridge: Cambridge University Press, pp. 23–37.

Van Dyke, R. M., and S. E. Alcock. 2003. "Archaeologies of Memory: An Introduction." In R. M. Van Dyke and S. E. Alcock, eds. *Archaeologies of Memory.* Oxford: Oxford University Press, pp. 1–13.

Zinn, K. 2011. "Temples, Palaces and Libraries—a Search for Their Alliance between Archaeological and Textual Evidence." In K. Spence and R. Gundlach, eds. *Palace and Temple—Architecture, Decoration, Ritual.* Wiesbaden: Harrassowitz, pp. 181–202.

Zinn, K. 2018. "Literacy in Pharaonic Egypt: Orality and Literacy between Agency and Memory." In A. Kolb, ed. *Literacy in Ancient Everyday Life—Schriftlichkeit im antiken Alltag.* Berlin: De Guyter, pp. 67–97.

Lisht

The ancient Egyptian site of Lisht is situated on the west bank of the Nile about 30 miles south of the modern city of Cairo. The important ancient remains at the site are two Middle Kingdom pyramids of the early Twelfth Dynasty: those of kings Amenemhat I, in the north part of the site, and his son, Senusret I, a mile to the south. King Amenemhat I founded a new royal residence at a place called Itja-tawy, which has never been found, but it is assumed that Itja-tawy was opposite Lisht on the east bank of the Nile. Itja-tawy remained the center of royal rule throughout the Middle Kingdom and was known to have been a center for the training of scribes and artists.

Today, the pyramid of Amenemhat I "has been reduced to a sand covered mound" (Arnold 2015, XIII). It had largely been built by his son, Senusret I, when Amenemhat I died in his 30th year of reign. It was constructed with many reused blocks brought from earlier buildings at Giza and Sakkara, including decorated blocks from the pyramid temples of Kings Khufu and Khafre. The architecture of the complex seems to have been influenced by Theban royal tombs of the First Intermediate Period, as it had a wide, open causeway leading up to a temple for a cult statue of the king on one level and the pyramid behind, on a terrace above. Amenemhat I was Theban and had ruled from Thebes in the first 10 years of his reign. The stone was largely taken from the pyramid in the Second Intermediate Period, the period following the Middle Kingdom.

The pyramid of Senusret I was more traditional and constructed in the style of Old Kingdom pyramids, with a causeway leading up to a mortuary temple and then the king's pyramid, surrounded by smaller pyramids for the king's female family. It was also built from local limestone quarried nearby. There was an outer enclosure wall around all of these pyramids, with an inner enclosure wall just around the pyramid of the king. On the inner and outer sides of this inner wall were 100 tall panels with the king's Horus name, alternating with recesses holding standing statues of the king as the god Osiris. Some of these panels and statues can be seen in the Metropolitan Museum in New York. The Metropolitan Museum of Art had excavated at these two pyramids from 1906 to 1934 and returned to work there again in 1984 (Emery 1993, 207).

Lisa K. Sabbahy

See also: Pyramid Construction; Pyramids

Further Reading

Arnold, Dieter. 1988. *The Pyramid of Senwosret I*. New York: Metropolitan Museum of Art.

Arnold, Dieter. 2015. *The Pyramid Complex of Amenemhet I at Lisht: The Architecture.* New York: Metropolitan Museum of Art.

Edwards, I. 1993. *The Pyramids of Egypt*. London: Penguin Books.

Goedicke, Hans. 1971. *Reused Blocks from the Pyramid of Amenemhet I at Lisht*. New York: Metropolitan Museum of Art.

Jánosi, Peter. 2016. *The Pyramid Complex of Amenemhet I at Lisht: The Reliefs*. New York: Metropolitan Museum of Art.

Literacy and Orality

Ancient Egypt was, alongside Mesopotamia, the inventor of one of the world's first writing systems, and the importance of literacy among the ruling elite was heavily stressed. Writing was a critical element of ancient Egyptian society, used both as a tool to administer the complex economy and as a means by which the literate elite could mark and legitimize its authority. Recent scholarship has, however, begun to place a much greater emphasis on the nonliterate majority of the population of ancient Egypt and on the ways in which the mind-sets and modes of communication characteristic of fully oral societies ("orality") continued in Egypt long after the invention of writing. As a result, an important current area of research within Egyptology is the intersection between the spheres of literacy and orality.

The earliest attestations of the hieroglyphic writing system date to roughly 3300 BCE and take the form of inscriptions on ivory and bone labels found in a late Predynastic Period ruler's tomb, tomb U-j at Abydos. These labels seem to indicate quantities of goods and the names of the locations from which those goods came. In the first two dynasties (3000–2686 BCE), writing was primarily used to record the names of kings and high officials. Another early indicator of the importance of literacy as a marker of prestige is the blank piece of papyrus found in the tomb of a

First Dynasty official named Hemaka. Similarly, intricately carved wooden panels from the tomb of the Third Dynasty (2696–2613 BCE) official Hesy-Ra depict the tomb owner with the tools of the scribal trade: ink pots and brush.

It was important for the king to be able to read and write, even though most practical writing would have been produced by administrators of the lower elite; the highest officials had secretaries to take dictation. By the Fifth Dynasty (2494–2345 BCE), a wide variety of text types had appeared in writing: tomb biographies of the high officials, Pyramid Text spells in the tombs of the kings (intended to guide the ruler into the afterlife), and more mundane spreadsheet-like tables recording daily activities in the temple. As a group, these texts speak to the ways in which the literate elite used writing to control Egypt's economy and shape its culture.

The possibility of female literacy in ancient Egypt remains an open question. We have no evidence that women attended the scribal schools, and they were certainly not part of the scribal administration. We have letters addressed to and from women that could have been written by the women themselves, but they could also have been written by men. However, it is possible that women were taught to read and write at home, for purposes such as keeping household accounts. The female counterpart to the male title "scribe" does occur, although rarely, and might not have the same meaning.

Despite the clear importance of writing in ancient Egypt, surviving written texts exhibit numerous indicators of the continued significance of the spoken word and oral communication, even at the highest levels of society. For example, a phrase that literally translates "saying words" is frequently used to introduce religious spells and rituals, clearly showing that they were intended to be spoken out loud. Texts written on funerary monuments often take the form of a first-person address from a deceased individual, as though the dead person were literally speaking to the living. In general, the phenomenon of "silent reading" is a very recent development, and an ancient Egyptian approaching a written text would have processed it by reading it out loud to himself. Since the Egyptian writing systems record neither word divisions nor vowels (the latter with the exception of the very late Coptic, written in the Greek alphabet), reading out loud would have been an essential aid to comprehension.

There are cases in which the use of written documentation increased with the passage of time. The village of Deir el-Medina, in the New Kingdom (1550–1069 BCE), was the home to the workers who built the tombs in the Valley of the Kings. There, the Twentieth Dynasty saw a rise in the number of both formal administrative documents and of written records of private business transactions, suggesting that the villagers increasingly exploited the potential usefulness of writing once they had been introduced to it. However, the formulae used in private documents likely derive from statements spoken out loud before witnesses, with the action of speaking being what actually confirmed the transaction. The production of a written record would have augmented such practices rather than replacing them. Overall, such documents record just a fraction of the exchanges that must have occurred at Deir el-Medina, and a recent study has concluded that such records of transactions were of very limited value at the site. In fact, Eyre argues that documents in general, that is, contracts, orders, and reports, were not used in a way fully separate from oral discourse until the Greco-Roman Period (332 BCE–495 CE) and that they played a relatively small role in the country's administration, which was carried out for the most part by face-to-face personal communication (Eyre 2013, 349–354).

Texts from Egypt clearly reveal how orality impacted the lives and written records of the literate elite. In contrast, our access to the world of the nonliterate majority is obviously limited. We do, however, possess a few hints of how this segment of the population communicated. Two specific avenues of research will be explored here: traces of oral storytelling techniques in the surviving written literature and nontextual systems used by illiterate and semiliterate workers.

One of the earliest literary narratives that we possess from ancient Egypt, in the early Middle Kingdom, roughly around 1985 BCE, the *Tale of the Shipwrecked Sailor*, contains a number of elements reminiscent of oral folktales. It uses repetition frequently, it incorporates a number of proverbs, and its characters are anonymous. In fact, quite a few ancient Egyptian stories read like folktales or fairy tales, key examples being the Middle Egyptian stories of the Westcar Papyrus and the Late Egyptian *Tale of Two Brothers*, likely reflecting the influence of oral storytelling techniques on the literate scribes who composed these stories. Structurally, the *Tale of the Shipwrecked Sailor* takes the form of a story-within-a-story-within-a-story and is thereby a literary account of the act of oral storytelling itself. The reoccurrence of this device in a number of Egyptian stories of different periods highlights the importance of oral performance in the culture as a whole.

When looking for traces of orality in the Egyptian tradition of written literature, it is also useful to consider fictional stories composed by professional oral storytellers across the globe, which tend to draw on the same stock phrases and scenes, making the task of composition during performance easier. These elements have been studied in most extensive detail for Homer's *Iliad* and *Odyssey*. In Egypt, stories composed in writing, even during the Ptolemaic-Roman Period (332 BCE–495 CE), contain may of the same repeated phrases and scenes, revealing the continued influence of orality at that late date.

Turning to nontextual markings, New Kingdom workers at Deir el-Medina devised a system of recording that was clearly inspired by formal Egyptian writing systems. Lists of workers were produced in which each worker was represented by his own unique individual sign; workers' signs also appear in graffiti and as identifying marks on a variety of objects. Some signs were inspired by hieroglyphic or hieratic signs, while others were purely pictorial, geometric, or abstract. The workers also adapted from the formal system their own nonstandard way of recording dates.

Miners quarrying for stone in the dry valleys extending into the desert perpendicular to the Nile left their mark as well. One group of quarry marks dating to the Ptolemaic-Roman Period has been discovered at a sandstone quarry in the south of Egypt called Gebel el-Silsila. There, the workers etched into the rock numerous representations of harpoons, altars, offerings tables, and figures of humans and animals—all images that have parallels in contemporary magical papyri and amulets. The most common mark is the harpoon, which can be connected to the god Horus and his defeat of his uncle Seth. In general, it is assumed that these marks had a religious/magical connection and were made by specific individuals for protection or to achieve a certain desired result. Such traces provide invaluable insight into the lives and mind-sets of those ancient Egyptians who could not read and write.

Jacqueline E. Jay

See also: Deir el-Medina; Education; Literature, Fiction; Officials; Scribes and Scribal Equipment

Further Reading

Allon, N., and H. Navratilova. 2017. *Ancient Egyptian Scribes: A Cultural Exploration.* London: Bloomsbury.

Baines, J. 1990. "Interpreting the Story of the Shipwrecked Sailor." *Journal of Egyptian Archaeology* 76: 55–72.

Baines, J. 2007. "Orality and Literacy." In J. Baines, ed. *Visual and Written Culture in Ancient Egypt.* Oxford: Oxford University Press, pp. 146–178.

Eyre, C. 2013. *The Use of Documents in Pharaonic Egypt.* Oxford: Oxford University Press.

Haring, B. 2003. "From Oral Practice to Written Record in Ramesside Deir El-Medina." *Journal of the Economic and Social History of the Orient* 46: 249–272.

Haring, B. 2009. "Workmen's Marks on Ostraca from the Theban Necropolis: A Progress Report." In B. Haring and O. Kaper, eds. *Pictograms or Pseudo Script? Non-textual Identity Marks in Practical Use in Ancient Egypt and Elsewhere.* Leiden/Leuven: Peeters, pp. 143–167.

Jay, J. 2016. *Orality and Literacy in the Demotic Tales.* Leiden: Brill.

Nilsson, M. J. R. 2012–2013. "Quarry Marks in Partition B, Main Quarry at Gebel el Silsila: Remarks on their Meaning and Function." *Journal for the Society of the Study of Egyptian Antiquities* 39: 139–177.

Redford, Donald B. 2000. "Scribe and Speaker." In Ehud Ben Zvi and Michael H. Floyd, eds. *Writings and Speech in Israelite and Ancient Near Eastern Prophecy.* Atlanta: Society of Biblical Literature, pp. 143–218.

Robins, G. 1993. *Women in Ancient Egypt.* Cambridge, MA: Harvard University Press.

Literature, Fiction

The earliest Egyptian literature recorded in writing appears relatively late in Egyptian history, in the early Twelfth Dynasty, which begins the period called the Middle Kingdom in 1985 BCE. There must have been a tradition of oral storytelling in earlier periods, but the Egyptians clearly felt no desire to preserve these stories in writing. The emergence of written literature at the beginning of the Middle Kingdom likely reflected the need of the newly recentralized government to educate and enculturate its scribes. However, performances of written literature must also have served to entertain an audience. Additionally, many texts contain a subversive element and so may well have enabled the literate elite to question aspects of Egyptian society, including the king himself, in ways not permitted in more formal and overtly practical monumental texts.

Modern scholars have debated at length the very definition of "Egyptian literature." Should this category be restricted to obviously fictional texts that are relatively open in their function, or should it also include texts with a specific purpose, such as religious hymns or narrative biographies that exhibit literary qualities? (For the question of definitions, see Loprieno 1996; for a collection of texts exhibiting a broader perspective, see Simpson 2003.) While the broader approach certainly has value, this entry will focus on Egyptian literature in the narrower sense. Into this category fall three main genres: (1) narrative stories, sometimes given the very loose designation "sedjed" by the Egyptians, from a verb meaning "to relate, recount"; (2) instructions or teachings, a literal translation of Egyptian "sebayet"; and (3) lamentations. Here we will trace the evolution of these three main genres from the Middle Kingdom to the Ptolemaic-Roman Period (332 BCE–495 CE). Up until the Ptolemaic-Roman Period, literary texts were written in the cursive hieratic script on papyrus, wooden writing boards, or flakes of limestone called *ostraca*; under the Ptolemies, the newer cursive, Demotic, was used instead. It should be noted that the titles of specific literary works discussed below are modern and not ancient designations.

Four largely complete tales have survived from the Middle Kingdom and Second Intermediate Period (1650–1550 BCE), alongside a few far more fragmentary examples: the *Tale of the Shipwrecked Sailor*, the *Tale of Sinuhe*, *The Eloquent Peasant*, and the tales of the Westcar Papyrus. Although these tales are all written in a phase of the ancient Egyptian language called "Middle Egyptian," they vary dramatically in their structure and style, revealing a high degree of experimentation as stories first began to be composed in writing. The *Tale of the Shipwrecked Sailor* possesses elements borrowed from oral folktale and from written reports of real royal expeditions, while the *Tale of Sinuhe* takes the form of a high official's tomb biography. *The Eloquent Peasant* begins as a stylistically simple story of a man who loads his donkey with goods to sell in the Nile valley. When the peasant's goods are unfairly confiscated, this simple narrative becomes the frame for a series of highly stylized petitions spoken out loud by the peasant in his quest for justice. The Westcar Papyrus, named after its first modern owner, is set in the time of King Khufu, the builder of the Great Pyramid during the Fourth Dynasty, and consists largely of a series of embedded stories told by the king's sons to entertain him.

Texts of the instructional genre are typically framed as advice given by a man, usually a high official, to his son. The Middle Kingdom *Instruction of Ptahhotep*, for example, is presented as the wisdom of a vizier of the Fifth Dynasty of the Old Kingdom. The advice given in such texts reveals the concerns and goals of elite male Egyptians, both in the public and the private sphere; advice ranges from how to deal with superiors, equals, and inferiors in the administration, to good table manners, to how to treat your wife. The texts promote important values such as humility, self-control, and honesty. Two instructional texts have also survived that are presented as advice from a king to his son: the *Instruction for Merikare* and the *Instruction of Amenemhat*. These both give insight into challenges and desires specific to the office of kingship.

Texts classified as "lamentations" are more pessimistic in nature than the instructions. The *Dialogue of a Man and His Ba* depicts a man in deep anguish who addresses his own *ba*, for the Egyptians, one of the soul-like aspects of an individual, typically depicted as a human-headed bird. The man feels "impelled toward death before his time" (Simpson 2003, 179), a phrase often interpreted to mean that he is considering suicide. His *ba*, however, attempts to dissuade him with descriptions of what is good in life as compared to the difficulties of death. The text ends on an ambiguous note, with the man's final decision left unclear. In the *Admonitions of Ipuwer*, a wise man named Ipuwer addresses an unnamed king with a series of complaints about the topsy-turvy world he sees around him, in which, for example, "paupers have become men of affluence" (Simpson 2003, 191), and the withdrawal of the creator god from his creation. *Ipuwer* thus contains clear criticism of both the king and the god and has been described as a "theodicy," a type of text that explores the contradiction between divine goodness and the existence of evil. Unfortunately, *Iupwer*'s ending is lost, making it difficult to know how or even if the text reached some kind of resolution. In contrast, the similar descriptions of chaos in the *Prophecy of Neferti* conclude on a more positive note, foretelling the coming of a strong king who will restore order. This "prophecy" was most likely designed to legitimize the king who was actually on the throne at the time of its composition.

Classics of Middle Kingdom/Middle Egyptian literature, especially the *Tale of Sinuhe*, continued to be recopied in the New Kingdom (1550 BCE–1069 BCE), often for the purposes of scribal education. In fact, recent arguments have suggested that many key Middle Egyptian texts, including the *Instruction for Merikare*, the *Instruction of King Amenemhat*, *Ipuwer*, and the *Prophecy of Neferti*, were actually composed in the Eighteenth Dynasty (1550–1295 BCE) or, in some cases, perhaps the Second Intermediate Period (1550–1650 BCE). The Nineteenth Dynasty (1295–1186 BCE) witnessed the emergence of a tradition of literature written in a more contemporary form of the language called Late Egyptian. Nine Late Egyptian stories survive. Some, such as *The Capture of Joppa*, set in the time of Thutmose III of the preceding Eighteenth Dynasty, can be categorized as historical fiction, while others, such as the *Tale of Two Brothers*, draw on fairy tale and mythology. Two major instructional texts also survive from the later New Kingdom: the *Instruction of Any* and the *Instruction of Amenemope*. Both emphasize the same basic values expressed in Middle Kingdom examples of this genre.

In contrast, a group of Ramesside Period (1295–1069 BCE) Late Egyptian poems, typically termed "love songs," represent a genre with no known written precedents. Many of the poems take the form of first-person speeches by unmarried young men and women suffering the pangs of love. They are highly elaborate in their imagery, which often invokes elements of nature. The poems may have served purposes of entertainment, and they may also have been used in religious contexts to pacify the goddess Hathor in her more dangerous aspects. Although written copies of this love poetry survive only from the Ramesside Period, examples must have been performed orally in earlier and later periods. The short-lived appearance of the genre in writing likely reflects societal changes immediately following Akhenaten's failed religious revolution at the end of the Eighteenth Dynasty.

There is a sizable gap in the literary tradition from the end of the New Kingdom to the beginning of the Ptolemaic Period, with very few texts that could be classed as literature surviving from the first half of the first millennium. The political fragmentation of the country and the rule of foreigners certainly contributed to this lack of documentation, although literature must have been produced in forms that have not survived. In contrast, a wealth of material exists from the Ptolemaic-Roman Period, which produced a rich tradition of literature written in the newer cursive script Demotic.

Most examples of narrative literature from the Ptolemaic-Roman Period fall into three main groups of stories. The Inaros Cycle takes its name from the character Inaros, ruler of the Delta city of Athribis in the late Third Intermediate Period. It concerns the military activities of Inaros and his contemporaries, including their rebellion against the Assyrians. The Setna Cycle revolves around a priest-magician named Setna Khaemwase, loosely based on a real son of Ramses II; one Setna story served as an inspiration for the modern franchise of mummy movies. A third cycle also deals with priests, involving a number of priests of Heliopolis. The emphasis on priests in the last two sets of stories likely reflects that with the rising use of Greek for administrative and economic purposes, the production of texts in Egyptian languages and scripts was increasingly becoming an activity of the native Egyptian priesthood.

Two extensively preserved instructional works survive in Demotic: the *Instruction of Onchsheshonqy* and the Papyrus Insinger. The advice given in these texts shows clear continuity with earlier examples of the genre, with the importance of moderate behavior remaining an important theme. Certain new emphases may, however, reflect the changed circumstances of Egypt in the Ptolemaic-Roman Period. For example, it is possible that the distrust expressed toward masters, outsiders, and greedy merchants is a reflection of the political and social fragmentation experienced by Egypt in the first millennium BCE, when many different foreigners were entering and living in Egypt. In terms of structure, these Demotic wisdom texts differ significantly from their Middle and New Kingdom predecessors. Instead of being arranged in extended stanzas dealing with a single theme, the Demotic texts take the form of single-line/single-sentence sayings, a format that has precedence earlier in the first millennium BCE. The *Instruction of Onchsheshonqy* has an extended explanatory frame story in which a priest named Onchsheshonqy is imprisoned for failing to report a plot against Pharaoh; from prison, he writes this advice to his son on potsherds.

While Demotic narrative and instructional texts show a high degree of continuity with the earlier literary tradition, the apocalyptic lamentations of the Ptolemaic-Roman Period represent a stronger departure and obviously reflect their historical context. The Middle Egyptian *Prophecy of Neferti*, most likely written under the newly instituted native rule of the kings of the early Eighteenth Dynasty, created the fiction of a coming savior king who would restore order out of chaos to legitimize the king already on the throne. A number of texts of the Ptolemaic-Roman Period describe society in a similar state of chaos: the *Oracle of the Lamb*, the *Potter's Oracle*, and the *Demotic Chronicle*. These later texts, however, were written under foreign rulers, and as a result, their focus is on the future return of *native* Egyptian rule, and hence their designation as "apocalyptic," a term adopted from the Jewish and Christian tradition of prophetic revelations concerning future destruction and the ultimate victory of good over evil. This late genre of apocalyptic literature serves as a clear example of the Egyptians' continual ability to adapt traditional literary forms to remain meaningful in new circumstances.

Jacqueline E. Jay

See also: Language and Script; Literacy and Orality; Literature, Fiction; Wisdom Literature

Further Reading

Dieleman, J., and I. S. Moyer. 2010. "Egyptian Literature." In J. Clauss and M. Cuypers, eds. *A Companion to Hellenistic Literature*. Malden, MA; Oxford: Wiley Blackwell, pp. 429–447.

Enmarch, R. 2008. *A World Upturned: Commentary on and Analysis of the Dialogue of Ipuwer and the Lord of All*. Oxford and New York: Published for the British Academy by Oxford University Press.

Hollis, S. T. 2008. *The Ancient Egyptian "Tale of Two Brothers": A Mythological, Religious, Literary, and Historico-Political Study*. 2nd ed. Oakville, CT: Bannerstone Press.

Lichtheim, M. 1973, 1976, 1980. *Ancient Egyptian Literature*. 3 vols. Berkeley: University of California Press.

Loprieno, A. 1996. "Defining Egyptian Literature: Ancient Texts and Modern Theories." In A. Loprieno, ed. *Ancient Egyptian Literature: History and Forms*. Leiden: Brill, pp. 39–58.

Manassa, Colleen. 2013. *Imagining the Past: Historical Fiction in New Kingdom Egypt*. Oxford: Oxford University Press.

Parkinson, R. B. 1999. *The Tale of Sinuhe and Other Ancient Egyptian Poems, 1940–1640 BC*. Oxford: Oxford University Press.

Parkinson, R. B. 2002. *Poetry and Culture in Middle Kingdom Egypt: A Dark Side to Perfection*. London and New York: Continuum.

Simpson, W. K., ed. 2003. *The Literature of Ancient Egypt: An Anthology of Stories, Instructions, Stelae, Autobiographies, and Poetry*. 3rd ed. New Haven, CT: Yale University Press.

Stauder, A. 2013. *Linguistic Dating of Middle Egyptian Literary Texts*. Hamburg: Widmaier Verlag.

Primary Document—Excerpt from the Tale of the Shipwrecked Sailor

One of the most famous pieces of literary fiction of the Middle Kingdom (2055–1650 BCE) is the *Tale of the Shipwrecked Sailor*, who is washed up on an island after a storm. When he settles in on the island, he meets its only inhabitant:

> Then I heard the noise of a storm cloud. I thought it was a wave of the sea. The trees broke and the earth shook. I uncovered my face and found that a snake was coming. It was thirty cubits long, and his beard, it was as great as two cubits. His skin, it was overlaid with gold, and his eyebrows were actual lapis lazuli. He was bent up in front, and he opened his mouth to me, while I was on my belly before him. He said to me: Who brought you?
>
> Source: Translated by Lisa K. Sabbahy from Blackman, Aylward. 1972. *Middle-Egyptian Stories*. Bibliotheca Aegyptiaca 2. Bruxelles: Édition de la Fondation égyptologique Reine Elisabeth, p. 43, lines 5–11.

Lower Egypt

Today, Lower Egypt, or the Nile Delta, is a fertile floodplain, 106 miles long by 149 miles wide at its Mediterranean coastline. Until the building of the Aswan High Dam, the alluvial buildup was regulated by the depth of the annual inundation over the floodplain, which varied from 1 to 10 feet. Slightly north of Cairo, the Nile splits into two major branches, the Rosetta in the west and the Damietta in the east, before flowing into the sea. However, the delta has not always had its present form; during the last glacial period, there was a broad, sandy, minimally vegetated plain, with many seasonally dry anastomosing channels. This started to change in the postglacial warming period as sea levels rapidly rose, and by the early to mid-Holocene, ca. 8,900 cal BP and more rapidly from 7,000 to 6,000 cal BP, the rich alluvium that is today characteristic of the delta landscape started to be deposited. There was a deceleration in sea level rise that occurred during the seventh millennium cal BP. This initiated further changes in the delta, with a transition to a meandering riverine landscape during the sixth millennium cal BP, when the delta consisted of a floodplain dominated by woodland, shrubland and grassland, and wetlands and marshes, and brackish-water lagoons in the outer part of the delta. As the alluvium started covering the dry, sandy plains between the former anastomosing channels, some areas of high ground were left. These islands of Pleistocene sand are today referred to as "turtlebacks." Most of the permanent ancient settlements were placed on these geziras, but also on levees of the water channels, out of the way of the raging waters of the annual inundation. The settlement pattern of the delta was also dictated by the river branches and channels, although as the river moved, some sites were left miles away from a water course.

Although the apex of the delta is now located north of Cairo, this has moved due to changes in the sea level, for when the base of a river channel reaches sea level, the channel bifurcates into two smaller and shallower channels. During the Old Kingdom and New Kingdom, the head of the delta was in the Memphite region, but in the Middle Kingdom, it had moved south to near Lisht. The number of Nile branches reaching the Mediterranean has also changed over time. In the Predynastic Period, there were seven branches; these dwindled to five after the Old Kingdom, but they were back up to seven by Ptolemaic times: from east to west, the Pelusiac, Tanitic, Mendesian, Phatnitic, Sebennytic, Bolbitine, and Canopic.

The timing, amount, and characteristics of the sediment load of Nile water depended on the relative contributions from the White Nile, Blue Nile, and other East African tributaries. This in turn was dependent on the amount of rain falling in this region, which was governed by the movement of the Intertropical Convergence Zone (ITCZ). Responding to fluctuations in the flood discharge of the Nile, incursion and retreat of the Mediterranean shoreline, and subsidence of the land, the floodplain of the delta is a showcase of how climate change and geological processes can shape landscapes. It was in the context of this moveable, changeable, and dynamic landscape that Egyptian civilization was forged. The rich environment of the Nile Delta provided a large amount of agricultural land and also pasturage for cattle and other domesticates. From the Early Dynastic Period, there were many royal domains or estates located in the Delta, providing food for the workers engaged in the royal projects, such as building the royal tomb complexes.

From the First Dynasty, the capital of Egypt was located at the apex of the delta, with Narmer credited as founding *Ineb-hedj*, the "White Walls" or "White Fortress." Located at the edge of the floodplain at North Sakkara, the monumental mudbrick tombs of the Early Dynastic Period were situated on the escarpment overlooking the city. During the Old Kingdom, the royal residence moved several times—following the location of the pyramid—and by the time of King Pepi I (2321–2287 BCE) of the Sixth Dynasty, his pyramid town called *Men-nefer* ("Established and Beautiful") was located just east of what is now termed South Sakkara. *Memphis*, the name this ancient capital is known by today, is a Greek word stemming from the hieroglyphic name *Men-nefer* (Smith and Jeffreys 1986, 88). The reasons for locating the capital at the apex of the delta were to control the trade and travel routes that converged on the Nile valley from the Nile Delta, Levant, Red Sea, and Saharan oases.

Farther north, the Old Kingdom is represented at several sites, such as the Fifth and Sixth Dynasty mastabas at Tell el-Ruba (Mendes) and those of the Fourth to Sixth Dynasties at Tell el-Basta (Bubastis). The earliest mastaba tomb found so far is at Quesna, dating to the Third Dynasty. Other sites found with domestic or sacred remains include Tell el-Farkha, Tell Awalad Dawood, Tell el-Dab'a, and Tell Faraun. Tell Ibrahim Awad boasts the remains of an early temple sequence, in addition to settlement and cemetery remains dating to the First, Second, and Fourth to Sixth Dynasties. The Fifth and Sixth Dynasty settlement and cemetery remains have been excavated at Kom el-Hisn, whereas Sixth Dynasty tombs are known from Kom Abu Billo. Textual evidence suggests that Busiris (Djedu) was an important religious center in the Old Kingdom, and it was a center of Osiris worship from the Sixth Dynasty onward.

After the division of the country in the First Intermediate Period, the kings of the Middle Kingdom reunified the country, allowing the major sites of Athribis, Bubastis, Busiris, Buto, Kom el-Hisn, Heliopolis, Mendes, Sais, and Tell el-Dab'a to flourish. Although Memphis remained an important center, the capital was moved south to Lisht (Itja-tawy). At the end of the Middle Kingdom, the delta broke away from the Thirteenth Dynasty rulers and formed several smaller kingdoms with Avaris as their capital. This is termed the Fourteenth Dynasty (1720–1650 BC), with the names of several of the kings revealing Canaanite heritage. In 1650 BCE, a politically weak Lower Egypt was invaded and ruled by a group of people from Western Asia known as the Hyksos. This group of invaders made Tell el-Dab'a their capital (Avaris). The sphere of rule of the six Hyksos kings of the Fifteenth Dynasty seems mainly limited to the East Delta, encompassing the sites of Tell el-Basta, Tell el-Yahudiya, and, in the Wadi Tumilat, the sites of Tell el-Ku'a and Tell el-Maskhuta.

Around 1550 BCE, Ahmose I, the first king of the Eighteenth Dynasty, expelled the Hyksos and again unified the country, starting the New Kingdom. As the empire expanded, the traditional center of the delta, such as Athribis, Bubastis,

Buto, Imu (Tell el-Hisn), Mendes, Sais, and Xois, grew into large cosmopolitan centers, with newer center established at Pi Ramses and Tell Muqdam (Leontopolis). Pi Ramses was a harbor town, a royal residence, and a seat of government during the reign of Ramses II. There was also a strengthening of the defenses with a line of fortresses in the West Delta stretching from Zaweiyet Umm el-Rakham in the northwest through Tell el-Abqa'in, with another line, the Way of Horus, in the East Delta, such as Tell Habouh, Tell el-Borg, and Bir Al-Abd, and in the Wadi Tumilat, Tell er-Rataba.

In the first millennium BCE, the region was home to many thriving cities, including Alexandria, Bubastis, Busiris, Mendes, Naukratis, Sais, Tanis, and a burial ground for the kings of the Third Intermediate Period. Recent underwater discoveries in the area of Alexandria are revealing the splendors of the delta in the Greco-Roman Period: the western harbor of Alexandria contains a wonder of the ancient world, the Pharos lighthouse, and the eastern harbor shelters the palaces of Anthony and Cleopatra. The seaboard became a major focus for trade in the Greco-Roman Period, as the long-lost cities of Nicopolis, Taposiris, Canopus, Menouthis, and Herakleion are now being refound. Even the name "delta" was given by the Greeks because of its resemblance to the triangular Greek letter *delta*.

Geoffrey John Tassie

See also: Memphis; Nile River; Ptolemaic Egypt; Tanis; Tell el-Dab'a; Upper Egypt

Further Reading

Bietak, M. 2010. "From Where Came the Hyksos and Where Did They Go." In M. Marée, ed. *The Second Intermediate Period (Thirteenth-Seventeenth Dynasties): Current Research, Future Prospects*. Leuven: Peeters, OLA, pp. 39–181.

Blouin, K. 2014. *Triangular Landscapes: Environment, Society, and the State in the Nile Delta under Roman Rule*. Oxford: Oxford Studies on the Roman Economy, Oxford University Press.

Blue, L., and E. Khalil, eds. 2010. *Proceedings of the International Conference on the Archaeology of the Mareotic Region Held at Alexandria University, Egypt 5th–6th April 2008*. University of Southampton Series in Archaeology 2. Oxford: Archaeopress.

Jucha, M. A., and A. Mączyńska. 2011. "Settlement Sites in the Nile Delta." *Archéo-Nil* 21: 33–50.

Pennington, B. T., J. Bunbury, and N. Hovius. 2016. "Emergence of Civilization, Changes in Fluvio-Deltaic Style, and Nutrient Redistribution Forced by Holocene Sea-Level Rise." *Geoarchaeology: An International Journal* 31, no. 3: 194–210.

Rowland, J., and G. J. Tassie. 2014. "Prehistoric Sites along the Edge of the Western Nile Delta: Report on the Results of the Imbaba Prehistoric Survey 2013–14." *Journal of Egyptian Archaeology* 100: 49–65.

Stanley, J.-D., F. Goddio, T. F. Jorstad, and G. Schnepp. 2004. "Submergence of Ancient Greek Cities Off Egypt's Nile Delta—A Cautionary Tale." *GSA Today* 14, no. 1: 4–10.

Trampier, J. R. 2014. *Landscape Archaeology of the Western Nile Delta*. Atlanta: Lockwood Press.

Wilson, P. 2007. "The Nile Delta." In T. A. Wilkinson, ed. *The Egyptian World*. London: Routledge, pp. 15–28.

M

Maat

To the ancient Egyptians, *Maat* was a natural force present in the created universe that was embodied in the form of a goddess. Her name is an abstract noun derived from the verb *maa*, meaning "to guide" or "to direct" (Allen 2000, 115); *Maat* then was the embodiment of ideas of order, truth, balance, the way things should be, and that which is good. Individuals endeavored to live their lives in accordance with *Maat* so as to achieve eternity in the afterlife, and every ritual action of the king in state temples was performed so as to maintain *Maat* and ensure the continuity of life on earth.

Maat was believed to have come into existence at the moment of creation, at sunrise, and she was thus closely linked with the sun god. The earliest references to *Maat* in the written record, primarily in the form of name elements, date to the Second and Third Dynasties and can be understood to correspond with the growing cult of Ra. *Maat*'s presence at the first moment of creation and relationship to the cosmic order also appears in the spells of the Pyramid Texts and Coffin Texts. Coffin Text Spell 80, for example, includes the speech of the creator god Atum. Here, *Maat* is identified with the goddess Tefnut, who was part of the first divine pair created by Atum:

> Then Atum said: Tefnut is my living daughter,
> she is together with her bother Shu.
> "Life" is his name,
> "Maat" is her name. (Assmann 2001, 178)

Prior to creation, the universe was understood to have been a vast, dark, and watery expanse. As the creator brought order into the world, the nothingness of precreation was associated with chaos (*isfet*). Isfet was the opposite of *Maat*, and while its existence could never be fully eradicated, it was considered necessary for the two forces to remain in balance, one never overwhelming the other. The performance and maintenance of *Maat* was one of the primary roles of the king. In his role as high priest in the cult of every god or goddess, the king was shown in temple reliefs constructing new religious monuments and performing the daily offering rituals. All offerings presented to the temple gods could be understood as *Maat*. This connection is made clear in passages from the Coffin Texts that state that the gods "live on *Maat*" and in offering ritual scenes where the object presented before the god was identified in the accompanying text as *Maat* (Hornung 1982, 214; Teeter 1997, 82). An image of the goddess herself could even appear as the offering being given to the god or goddess by the king, as a way for the king to lend legitimacy to

A bronze seated figure of *Maat*. She can be shown as a female with a tall ostrich feather on her head, or just shown as the feather, which is the hieroglyphic symbol for the ancient Egyptian word "truth" or "justice." The most important responsibility of the king of Egypt was the upholding of *Maat*. (Werner Forman/Universal Images Group/Getty Images)

his own actions, and therefore his reign.

In art, *Maat* was usually depicted anthropomorphically as a woman with a tall ostrich feather secured atop her head by a band or ribbon. As with other goddesses, she could be depicted with wings attached to her outstretched arms in a protective pose toward the image or cartouche of the king. In scenes illustrating the presentation of *Maat* by the king, she was shown as a simplified figure, crouched or seated with drawn-up knees and primarily identifiable by her feather emblem. This pose appeared in both two-dimensional and three-dimensional art; small figures of the seated goddess were fashioned out of materials such as bronze and faience, and in these three-dimensional images, it becomes clear that the goddess's body was fully wrapped in a cloak or shroud.

In the funerary literature tradition of the Book of the Dead, *Maat* played a pivotal role in the judgment of the dead. In one of the most important Book of the Dead texts (Spell 125), the deceased would enter the Hall of Two Maats and recite a speech known as the "Negative Confession" before a divine tribunal to attest to having lived a life in accordance with *Maat* and be admitted into the realm of the blessed dead. The text of Spell 125 was accompanied by a vignette that depicted the moment of judgment: the heart of the deceased, which was believed to contain an individual's personality and memories, was weighed on a scale against *Maat*. Upon the scales, *Maat* was depicted in her seated form or simply as the ostrich feather. A negative judgment would result in the heart of the deceased being consumed by the Devourer, depriving the person of an afterlife. While this episode is first codified in the New Kingdom Book of the Dead manuscripts, the concept of a divine judgment based on *Maat* was already present in the Pyramid Texts, where it was applied to the deceased king.

Thoth, the ibis-headed god of writing, was also depicted in the Book of the Dead Weighing of the Heart vignettes, as he attended the judgment to record the results and help guide the deceased into the afterlife. In his cult at Hermopolis,

Thoth was regarded as the chief judge among the gods, who upheld or protected *Maat*. The two divinities further complemented each other in their associations with the sun (*Maat*) and the moon (Thoth). Egyptian artisans and temple workshops interpreted this relationship between the two gods in the creation of composite group statues, which may have been used for votive offerings, and amulets, which were likely interred with their owners. In these objects, the ibis of Thoth was represented as the dominant figure, while *Maat* was shown on a smaller scale, either as a seated woman or as her feather emblem. The tip of Thoth's beak extends toward or touches the top of the feather, thus creating a balanced artwork that symbolized the importance of cosmic order and wisdom in Egyptian religious thought.

Emily Russo MacIntosh

See also: Book of the Dead; Coffin Texts; Cult Ritual, Temple; Ra; Thoth

Further Reading

Allen, James P. 2000. *Middle Egyptian: An Introduction to the Language and Culture of the Hieroglyphs*. New York: Cambridge University Press.

Assmann, Jan. 2001. *The Search for God in Ancient Egypt*. Translated by David Lorton. Ithaca, NY: Cornell University Press.

Hornung, Erik. 1982. *Conceptions of God in Ancient Egypt: The One and the Many*. Translated by John Baines. Ithaca, NY: Cornell University Press.

Kahl, Jochem. 2007. *"Ra Is My Lord": Searching for the Rise of the Sun God at the Dawn of Egyptian History*. Wiesbaden: Harrassowitz.

Taylor, John H., ed. 2010. *Journey through the Afterlife: Ancient Egyptian Book of the Dead*. Cambridge, MA: Harvard University Press.

Teeter, Emily. 1997. *The Presentation of Maat: Ritual and Legitimacy in Ancient Egypt*. Chicago: Oriental Institute of the University of Chicago.

Magic

The ancient Egyptian term *heka*, plural *hekau*, is generally translated in English with the word "magic," but *heka* also represents a god with that name. The anthropomorphic god Heka, generally holding a snake-shaped staff, plays a fundamental role in creation. Heka personifies the creative power necessary for the formation of the cosmos, and for this reason, he is often depicted at the side of the main gods of creation, Atum-Ra and Osiris. In the solar boat, he is part of the divine following of the sun god, participating in the daily journey in the netherworld. In one papyrus of the Book of the Dead, Papyrus Greenfield, Heka appears near the throne of Osiris, the king of the dead.

The personification of *magic* is part of the way the ancient Egyptians dealt with the principles and phenomena that they considered important in their social and religious lives and culture, such as *Maat*, "Justice," or *Sia*, "Perception." These kinds of minor deities were not worshipped in temples on earth, but their function was greatly recognized in daily and funerary religious practices. In the case of Heka, his popularity was very well attested in the Ptolemaic-Roman Period (332 BCE–495 CE), when a statue of the god was kept in the temple of Esna.

Because "Magic" was a god and part of creation, the idea of negative magic, or "black magic," was not an ancient Egyptian belief. In magic spells employed for the protection and well-being of the dead in the netherworld, the deceased wishes "to become Heka" (Coffin Texts, Spell 261) or to keep "magic" in his or her belly; magic can be eaten or drunk so that the belly becomes a container of its power, and one can "live on magic." The one "great of magic," *wer hekau*, was a common epithet for deities and a symbol of the uraeus, the divine royal cobra.

Other terms in ancient Egyptian that relate to the concept of magic power and acts are also known: *ra*, for instance, related to spoken magic, as found in spells for daily as well as funerary use, and the term *pekheret*, "remedy," indicates those magico-medical prescriptions where medical and magical religious knowledge merged together. The main function of magic in ancient Egypt was defensive; as stated in the "Instructions for King Merikara" from the Tenth Dynasty, around 2000 BCE, humankind needed Heka to "ward off the blow of events."

Defensive magic materialized through a variety of forms, texts, and artifacts. Amulets, statuettes, papyri, and other magic objects were widely used by the ancient Egyptians, from the elite to the lower social strata of the population, to ward off all kind of dangers, from supernatural evil beings to human enemies, nightmares, illnesses, and the plague. In the funerary realm, defensive magic was extremely necessary for the survival of the deceased in the regions of the netherworld, which were populated by malevolent beings and demonic animals, such as snakes, crocodiles, and noxious insects. The funerary spells copied on the walls of the pyramid's burial chamber, the Pyramid Texts, and on coffins and papyrus, the Coffin Texts and the ancient Egyptian Book of the Dead, all included spells of defensive magic. Similar texts for protection from all kind of dangers were copied down on papyrus strips rolled up and worn on the neck. These are the "Oracular Amuletic Decrees," which were believed to be divine oracles transmitted to the temple priests and were probably sold by the latter to parents of newborns. In the opening of these "decrees," it was said that the god would keep safe the owner "from every male spirit, every female spirit," and the list of dangers continued with what looks like an exorcistic list of events to avoid and evil beings to expel from everyday life. Similar lists of human and supernatural enemies and of unlucky events are also found in magical papyri for everyday use, which were especially en vogue during the Ramesside Period (1295–1069 BCE); a few of them, found in the workmen's village of Deir el Medina, are characterized by being very small, so they could have been used as amulets hung on the neck.

Defensive magic could also function through objects decorated with more images than texts and were used in daily life as well as in tombs, as part of the funerary equipment of the deceased in the afterlife. This, for instance, is the case of the amuletic ivory wands known by the name "apotropaia" that were especially produced during the Middle Kingdom (2055–1650 BCE). They were employed as a tool of protection around the beds of women giving birth or probably against nightmarish demons during sleep. The wands are decorated with rows of supernatural beings and apotropaic gods, such as the dwarf god Bes and his female counterpart Beset; some of them bear the inscriptions that say, "protection by night and protection by day" or "protection around her everyday." Bes and other

A protective, or apotropaic, wand made out of hippopotamus ivory, dating to the Middle Kingdom. They were used in daily life and also put into tombs. These wands seemed to have been used mainly in birth rituals and for babies, and so were put into the tombs for protecting rebirth in the afterlife. (Theodore M. Davis Collection, Bequest of Theodore M. Davis, 1915/The Metropolitan Museum of Art)

protective beings are called *sau ashaw*, "the many protectors." The hieroglyph for *sa*, "protection," represented a magic amulet in itself; it was used as attribute for deities and supernatural beings, and it recalls the need for magical protection in the mythological accounts of birth, death, and the maintenance of creation and kingship, where the main deities Ra, Osiris, and Horus play a central role.

When defensive magic was not used soon enough or did not achieve its aim of warding off and preventing danger, the ancient Egyptians could use a different kind of spell and objects that we could interpret as representative of "curative magic." In this category belong healing statues, such as "Horus on the crocodiles" or the "Horus cippi" stelae, which were believed to possess healing powers for curing poisonous bites of snakes and scorpions, wounds, and diseases. In the Horus cippi, the myth of Horus hiding in the marshes from his brother Seth and protected by his mother and the great magician, Isis, is evoked, similar to what can be seen in many spells on papyri. The child god is depicted on the stelae trampling on crocodiles and holding snakes, scorpions, oryxes, and lions in his hands. Another minor god, "Shed the Savior," whose iconography was very similar to that of Horus the Child, had the same healing function on amuletic objects and stelae.

The Horus cippi were especially in use during the Late Period (664–332 BCE), and the most popular specimen of this category of magical objects is the Metternich Stela, dating to the Thirtieth Dynasty (380–343 BCE). This stela is especially important for understanding how curative magic was conceived, as it contains, beside the depiction of a series of protective divine figures, many spells against poison stings and snake bites along with an account on how Horus, while being ill in the marshes, was healed by Isis and Thoth.

Finally, we have evidence in the later sources from Ptolemaic and Roman Egypt (332 BCE–395 CE) of what is generally known as "love magic," which aims at binding (both physically and spiritually) the victim to the charm perpetuator through a series of practices involving spoken spells, potions, and amulets. Love

Magical Bricks

Magical bricks are mentioned in the Book of the Dead, Spell 151. These are mudbricks, each with a different object on it, and each was to be placed in the hidden niche in one of the cardinal directions: brick with reed stick on the south, brick with wooden mummy figure on the north, brick with faience djed pillar on the west, and brick with mud Anubis figure on the east. On each brick was a recitation stating what it protected from, beginning with "This spell is to be spoken over. . . ." These bricks were placed in both royal and nonroyal tombs and were used from the New Kingdom (1550 BCE) to the Late Period (664 BCE). All four of these bricks were found undisturbed in the tomb of Tutankhamun.

Lisa K. Sabbahy

magic can be considered a subcategory of what we could call "transformative magic," and it includes various spells employed by the deceased in the netherworld to be able to change status and form and acquire divine powers. The "spells of transformation" of the Book of the Dead mention the wish to transform into or "take the forms of" a god; a bird, such as a falcon or a sparrow; or a divine symbol of rebirth, such as a lotus flower.

The important role that magic played in ancient Egypt during the long span of the pharaonic history is also attested in the frequent mention of magicians in literary texts. Priests, doctors, literate men, and occasionally wise women, as well as other figures of professional ritualists performing in the temple or the private sphere, could cover the function of magician when needed, showing that this role, and all that it represented, was seen as fundamental for the well-being of humankind in this as well as the next world.

Rita Lucarelli

See also: Afterlife; Book of the Dead; Childbirth; Coffin Texts; Horus; Pyramid Texts

Further Reading

Borghouts, J. F. 1978. *Ancient Egyptian Magical Texts: Translated.* Nisaba 9. Leiden: E. J. Brill.

Dieleman, Jacco. 2015. "The Materiality of Textual Amulets in Ancient Egypt." In Dietrich Boschung and Jan Bremmer, eds. *The Materiality of Magic.* Paderborn: Wilhelm Fink, pp. 23–58.

Edwards, I. E. S. 1960. *Hieratic Papyri in the British Museum. Fourth Series. Oracular Amuletic Decrees of the Late New Kingdom: Edited, Together with Supplementary Texts in Other Collections.* 2 vols. London: Trustees of the British Museum.

Leitz, Christian 1999. *Magical and Medical Papyri of the New Kingdom.* Hieratic Papyri in the British Museum 7. London: British Museum Press.

Nyord, Rune. 2009. *Breathing Flesh: Conceptions of the Body in the Ancient Egyptian Coffin Texts.* Chicago: University of Chicago Press.

Pinch, Geraldine. 1994. *Magic in Ancient Egypt.* London: British Museum Publications.

Price, Campbell. 2016. "On the Function of 'Healing' Statues." In Campbell Price, Roger Forshaw, Andrew Chamberlain, and Paul T. Nicholson, eds. *Mummies, Magic and Medicine in Ancient Egypt: Multidisciplinary Essays for Rosalie David.* Manchester: Manchester University Press, pp. 169–182.

Raven, Maarten. 2012. *Egyptian Magic: The Quest for Thoth's Book of Secrets*. Cairo: American University in Cairo Press.

Ritner, Robert K. 1993. *The Mechanics of Ancient Egyptian Magical Practice*. Studies in Ancient Oriental Civilization 54. Chicago: University of Chicago Press.

Marriage and Divorce

Ideally, it would appear that the ancient Egyptians expected to have a monogamous and lifelong marriage that produced children. The unit of a husband and wife with children seems to have been an expectation of ancient Egyptian society. Life spans were not long, 25–30 years, and maternal mortality was high. This meant that people married young, and many men must have lost their wives in childbirth and probably remarried. A study based on ancient Egyptian texts and representations concluded that "affection and love were an integral part of the ideals of marriage in ancient Egypt" (Gee 2008, 102).

The situation was different in royal families, however, as the king married a number of women, probably to ensure that he had a son, and one who would live into adulthood, to take the throne after him. There were times in pharaonic history when the king married his sister or half-sister. This seems to have been the case in both the Middle Kingdom (2055–1650 BCE) and early New Kingdom (roughly 1550–1400 BCE). Such a marriage would concentrate power and access to the throne to a smaller group of people, but it also tied into the king's position of being divine. The king was Horus, son of the god Osiris and his sister-wife, Isis, and so following this divine pattern, the king could marry his own sister as well. There is no evidence outside of the royal family, however, for incestuous marriages, although later in Ptolemaic and Roman times (30 BCE–395 CE) brother-sister marriage is known.

How marriages were arranged and carried out in ancient Egypt is not clearly understood. There is very little written evidence about marriage, and it is all from the Late Period (664–332 BCE) or Ptolemaic or Roman Periods and may not reflect earlier pharaonic practice or tradition. Marriage does not seem to have been an institution that needed to be sanctioned by religion or the state. It did not seem to need a ceremony or any particular official witnessing it. There is some slight evidence of an oath, but there is more evidence for contracts involving communal property. It appears marriage was a matter of the woman publicly moving in with the man, with the understanding that it was long-term, and their children would inherit their property. The ancient Egyptian word for *marriage* was a phrase that translates as "establish a house," something that the man was expected to do, and "enter into a household," which generally applied to the woman. There is some, although not completely clear, written evidence from the New Kingdom (1550–1069 BCE) village of Deir el-Medina that suggests gifts were either given or received by the man or the woman's parents at the time of the marriage.

In the New Kingdom, some pharaohs married sisters and daughters of foreign rulers as part of a strategy to ensure ongoing peaceful relations. In particular, foreign marriages are well documented from the reign of King Amenhotep III in the later Eighteenth Dynasty (1390–1352 BCE). A princess from the Near Eastern empire of Mitanni arrived for Amenhotep III, accompanied by 371 ladies in waiting and an enormous list of gifts. A second Mitannian royal bride arrived 26 years later, again with hundreds of attendants and gifts broken into four long lists of 250 groups of items; one item alone was "four beautiful horses that run swiftly" (Kozloff 2012, 29). The king of Egypt never sent any of his daughters to foreign kings in return, however.

Divorce seems to have been much the same as marriage, but in reverse, in the sense that it involved the woman moving out of the man's house. But there are court documents about divorce, as it involved the division of communal property. The phrases used for *divorce* were "throw out," which was something done by the man, or "go away," which was what the woman did. Written evidence, again from the village of Deir el-Medina, shows that it was almost always the man who requested a divorce, not the woman. The reasons, when they are stated, are similar to nowadays, such as the man wanting to marry someone else, constant fighting, and adultery. As adoption seems to have been quite simple, not being able to have children did not seem to have been a reason to divorce.

There is evidence of the man who divorces his wife speaking an oath involving the property to be given her, which seems to have been one-third of their communal property. If the woman was being divorced for adultery, she lost that third but kept any of the property that she brought into the marriage. In the Late Period and also the Ptolemaic Period, contracts are preserved that were signed at the time of the marriage, guaranteeing the wife property and a payment if her husband were to divorce her. There are also other documents that supply the woman with proof of being divorced so that she was free to marry again.

Lisa K. Sabbahy

See also: Deir el-Medina; Families; Foreign Relations and Treaties; Law; Women

Further Reading

Eyre, C. J. 1984. "Crime and Adultery in Ancient Egypt." *Journal of Egyptian Archaeology* 70: 92–105.

Gee, John. 2008 "Love and Marriage in the Ancient World: An Historical Corrective." *Journal of the Society for the Study of Egyptian Antiquities* 35: 83–103.

Kozloff, Arielle. 2012. *Amenhotep III: Egypt's Radiant Pharaoh.* New York and Cambridge: Cambridge University Press.

Meier, Samuel. 2002. "Diplomacy and International Marriages." In Raymond Cohen and Raymond Westbrook, eds. *Amarna Diplomacy: The Beginnings of International Relations.* Baltimore and London: Johns Hopkins University Press, pp. 165–173.

Robins, Gay. 1993. *Women in Ancient Egypt.* London: British Museum Press.

Rowlandson, Jane, and Ryosuke Takahashi. 2009. "Brother-Sister Marriage and Inheritance Strategies in Greco-Roman Egypt." *Journal of Roman Studies* 99: 104–139.

Smith, H. S. 1998. "Marriage and the Family in Ancient Egypt, I. Marriage and Family Law." In M. J. Geller and Herwig Maehler, eds. *Legal Documents of the Hellenistic World.* London: Warburg Institute, University of London, pp. 46–57.

Toivari-Viitala, Jana. 2001. *Women at Deir el-Medina.* Leiden: Nederlands Instituut Voor Het Nabije Oosten.

Mathematics

Our knowledge of ancient Egypt mathematics is based on a small number of sources that offer an insight into a complex system that is sometimes similar and sometimes significantly different from our modern mathematics. Understanding these differences can be the key to a better comprehension of the ancient system.

THE SOURCES

The ancient Egyptian civilization lasted for over 30 centuries, and mathematics was widely used in administrative, architectural, and agricultural contexts. And yet the vagaries of preservation and discovery allowed the retrieval of only about a dozen ancient Egyptian mathematical texts, all dating to the same period, the Middle Kingdom, roughly 2055–1650 BCE. The longest and best preserved is the Rhind Mathematical Papyrus, which starts with this sentence: "Accurate reckoning for enquiring into things, and the knowledge of all things, mysteries . . . all secrets" (Clagett 1999, 122). The other extant mathematical sources are the Moscow Mathematical Papyrus, the Lahun Mathematical Fragments, the Berlin Papyrus, two wooden tablets, and the Mathematical Leather Roll. Other textual sources from administrative and architectural contexts, such as the Reisner Papyri, contain precious information on how mathematics was used and thus reflect the ancient mathematical knowledge, even if they were not specifically written about mathematics.

The scarcity of primary sources and the uneven information that they contain represent a significant challenge and pose several questions on the evolution of the ancient Egyptian mathematical system, on its mechanisms, and on its influence on later cultures. As we shall see below, some problems of interpretation can be solved by adopting the ancient Egyptian point of view: counting like the ancient Egyptians did, following their procedures, and, in general, seeing things from their mathematical perspective.

NUMBERS, FRACTIONS, AND OPERATIONS

In modern mathematical terms, "the number system in ancient Egypt can be described as a decimal system without positional (place-value) notation" (Imhausen 2016, 18). In other words, the ancient Egyptians counted on base 10, as we do today, but differently from us. They did not have the equivalent of "0" (zero); they used one symbol for the unit, which was repeated up to nine times to indicate the numbers from 1 to 9, then one symbol for 10, one for 100, one for 1,000, and so on, up to 1,000,000, which worked on the same principle. Numbers would be therefore expressed by sequences of symbols, each repeated as many times as necessary to indicate their quantity.

Today, we use a decimal marker, either a point or a comma, to separate the fractional from the integer portion of a number. The ancient Egyptians instead used "parts" of units, such as one-third, one-sixth, one-fifteenth, and so on; today, we describe this system as based on "unit fractions," which we express as 1/3, 1/6, or 1/15, and so on (Riemer 2014, 14). The only exception was the much considered fraction 2/3.

Any fractional quantity would be expressed by a sequence of unit fractions in decreasing order of magnitude: 3/5, for instance, would never be expressed as 1/5 + 1/5 + 1/5, but rather as 1/2 + 1/10; 5/13 (that is, the number 5 divided into 13 parts) would be expressed as 1/4 + 1/13 + 1/26 + 1/52 (from the recto of the Rhind Mathematical Papyrus), and so on. The extant mathematical texts provide abundant information on how multiplication and division were performed by progressively doubling or halving numbers, whereas the techniques used to perform addition and subtraction is never explicitly stated. The four operations were indicated by specific expressions: the clear "to lay on" for addition; the rather obvious "to reduce" for subtraction; and the colorful "to bow the head with . . . times . . ." for multiplication and division, which could also be described as "to make . . . to find . . ." and "to call . . . before . . .," respectively (Imhausen 2016, 85).

UNITS OF MEASUREMENT

The basic unit of length was the cubit, that is, the forearm; it was divided into six palms, each in turn divided into four fingers. In official contexts, the royal cubit was used instead: this was seven palms long, corresponding to just over 52 centimeters. Areas were measured by means of squares or stripes corresponding to 10 × 10, 100 × 100, 1 × 100, or 10 × 100 cubits, and volumes by means of cubes 1 × 1 × 1 cubits and "slices" of a cubic cubit corresponding to 1 cubit × 1 cubit × 1 palm and to 1 cubit × 1 cubit × 1 finger. The capacity of grain containers was measured by means of two main units of measurement, a smaller one called *heqat* (corresponding to ca 4.8 liters) and a larger one called *khar*. The weight of metals and stone was measured in *deben*, originally corresponding to just over 13 grams. Over time, the necessity to establish fixed relations among themselves as well as with foreign units of measurements led to significant modifications to both the value of some units and to their subdivisions. This necessity became more stringent in the Ptolemaic Period because of a marked increase in the Mediterranean trade.

It is important to bear in mind that, in some cases, measurements were based on completely different concepts in comparison with our modern mathematical system. To express the slope of a surface, for instance, the ancient Egyptians used the concept of *seqed*, that is, the horizontal displacement of the sloping surface from the vertical, measured in palms and fingers, at the height of one cubit. In other words, they dealt with right-angled triangles in which one cathetus always corresponded to one cubit, and the other to the horizontal displacement of the sloping face.

THE MATHEMATICAL TRAINING

All the extant mathematical sources from ancient Egypt are school textbooks, and they consist of procedures and tables. Procedure texts are examples of assignments that scribes could encounter during their working practice, including the various steps to solve the problems as well as the final results. They include administrative and architectural problems: distribution of ratios, calculation of the volume of granaries, or of the base, height and slope of a pyramid. As many of them entailed complex calculations involving integers and fractions, tables of results were available to the scribes for consultation.

The Rhind Mathematical Papyrus, for instance, contains both types of texts: a series of sample procedures as well as a table listing the results of the number 2 divided by the odd numbers from 3 to 101. In other words, this table contains the results of the doubling of most of the odd "unit fractions" that a scribe would have the chance to come across, a useful tool to perform multiplication and division.

Even if it is generally possible to express a result in more than one sequence of "unit fractions," the tables list only one result for each entry. Several attempts have been made to determine the rules that regulated the final choice, with dubious results. In general, all we can say is that the preference was given to short sequences and to small numerators, which are rather obvious criteria to keep the calculations as simple as possible.

PROBLEMS OF INTERPRETATION

The ancient Egyptian mathematical texts were discovered at the end of the 19th century, in a period in which rigor and proof were perceived as fundamental assets of mathematics. This led to a negative perception of ancient Egyptian mathematics, caught in the more general and recurring trend to make a distinction between "vulgar" (mainly commercial) and "higher" (more abstract) mathematics (Stedall 2012, 28–29). Moreover, the tendency to express ancient mathematical concepts and problems in modern mathematical language without paying the due attention sometimes led to misunderstandings and errors of interpretation.

In recent years, a more respectful approach to ancient mathematical texts allowed a better comprehension of these sources; most of the problems arise from our expectations and are fueled by some apparent similarities between the ancient and the modern mathematical systems. A typical example is represented by the calculation of the area of the circle. Blinded by the modern method, consisting of squaring the radius and multiply it by pi, some scholars mistakenly describe the ancient Egyptian method as having used the approximate value of 3.16 to perform the same calculation. Actually, the Egyptians calculated the area of a circle by squaring 8/9 of the diameter, which corresponds to a completely different process that has nothing to do with the concept of pi (Stedall 2012, 35). The precision that we expect today from this calculation for our own aims does not find any correspondence in the ancient Egyptian sources, where the area of a circle was one of the steps required to calculate of the volume of a cylindrical granary (e.g., Rhind Mathematical Papyrus, problem 41); the aim for which the ancient Egyptian school texts were written was fully satisfied.

Seemingly, even if using modern degrees is an efficient and immediate way to describe among ourselves the slope of the ancient Egyptian pyramids, it is only when we use the ancient *seqed* that we can identify the actual geometrical tools used by the ancient builders and reconstruct their evolution. To better understand ancient Egyptian mathematics, freeing our mind from preconceptions is a fundamental step to get as close as possible to the ancient mind-set.

Corinna Rossi

See also: Education; Scribes and Scribal Equipment

Further Reading

Clagett, M. 1999. *Ancient Egyptian Science: A Source Book*. Vol. 3, *Ancient Egyptian Mathematics*. Memoirs of the American Philosophical Society 232. Philadelphia: American Philosophical Society.

Imhausen, A. 2016. *Mathematics in Ancient Egypt: A Contextual History*. Princeton, NJ: Princeton University Press.

Reimer, D. 2014. *Count Like an Egyptian. A Hands-On Introduction to Ancient Mathematics*. Princeton, NJ: Princeton University Press.

Ritter, J. 2000. "Egyptian Mathematics." In H. Selin and U. D'Ambrosio, eds. *Mathematics across Cultures: The History of Non-Western Mathematics*. Dordrecht: Kluwer Academic Publishing, pp. 115–136.

Rossi, C. 2004. *Architecture and Mathematics in Ancient Egypt*. Cambridge: Cambridge University Press.

Stedall, J. 2012. *The History of Mathematics: A Very Short Introduction*. Oxford: Oxford University Press.

Medicine and Doctors

The ancient Egyptians had a medical profession that is documented through medical papyri, wall reliefs with accompanying texts, names and titles of doctors, and surgical instruments. Mummified remains are an exceptional source of knowledge about what diseases the ancient Egyptians suffered from and provide evidence of medical practices. Contrary to modern medicine, which is based on scientific evidence, ancient Egyptian medicine was mainly empirical, that is, knowledge obtained by observation and experimentation. The main objective was to treat the symptoms rather than the cause of the disease. The medical profession was highly stratified since the Old Kingdom (2686–2160 BCE), and the medical doctors (*swnw*) had different ranks, titles, and specialties. Among the ranks of medical doctors, the Egyptians included chief of doctors, the eldest of doctors, and inspector of doctors. Other ranks or titles referred to royal connections, such as doctor of the palace, doctor to the king, or inspector of palace doctors. There are also titles for three specialties in terms of parts of the body, so these must have caused the most common problems. In terms of a modern equivalent, they were dentist, gastroenterologist, and ophthalmologist.

The earliest mention of doctors dates to the Third Dynasty of the Old Kingdom (2686–2160 BCE). Imhotep was high priest of Heliopolis, chief lector priest, and the architect responsible for the construction of the Step Pyramid complex of King Djoser (2667–2648 BCE). Scholars also believe he was the original author of the Edwin Smith Papyrus, which deals with treating wounds. Imhotep was invoked in later times for help in sickness and infertility and was equated by the Greeks with their own god of medicine, Asclepius. A man named Hesy-re, whose tomb was found on north side of the Step Pyramid of Djoser in Sakkara, held the title chief of dentists and doctors.

The "House of Life," or *Per-Ankh* in Egyptian, was located in a cult temple and functioned as a library for the keeping of papyri, undoubtedly including medical papyri as well. It is not clear, however, as some scholars have claimed that the *Per-Ankh* functioned as a "medical school."

The Egyptian doctor had many divine patrons, and some priests functioned as doctors. Sakhmet, goddess of war and plague, was also thought to be able to protect and cure, and the title *swnw* was often associated with the title priest of Sakhmet. Selket was the goddess of scorpions, but he could also be called upon to provide protection from scorpions. Priests of Selket were called on for help with bites from snakes and scorpions, which must have been common in the ancient Egyptian Nile River environment. When there was no practical way to treat a medical problem, magic was used, so doctors, priests, and magicians all took part in the treatment of illness.

There must have been other medically related professions, such as midwives, who assisted with childbirth; wet nurses, who took care of infants; and possibly people who were the equivalent of modern pharmacists. Although no specific word for *pharmacist* has been found, in the medical papyri, it is written "you shall prepare for him," as if the medical doctor, or *swnw*, prepared the medicine, but other prescriptions indicate "then you shall cause one to prepare for him" (Nunn 1996, 132), as if another person would be called upon to do it.

According to Clement of Alexandria, a Greek priest who lived during the second century BCE, the ancient Egyptian priests had 42 sacred books of human knowledge, and the last six were about medicine. These books had the following content: structure of the human body, diseases, doctors' instruments, remedies, eyes and diseases of eyes, and diseases of women (Nunn 1996, 24). Although none of these texts have survived, the knowledge from them could have been passed on during the Greco-Roman Period.

Twelve different medical papyri are known from ancient Egypt, the most important of which are Papyrus Ebers, Papyrus Edwin Smith, and Papyrus Kahun. They are all written in hieratic script, the cursive form of hieroglyphs; nine date to the New Kingdom (1550–1069 BCE) and the other three to Ptolemaic-Roman times (332 BCE–395 CE). The longest of them, and most extensive Egyptian medical text, is the Ebers Papyrus, which is said to have been found in a tomb on the West Bank of Thebes. The papyrus itself dates to the ninth regnal year of King Amenhotep I (1525–1504 BCE).

The Ebers Papyrus is a collection of remedies for internal diseases, but it is not organized in any particular way. The papyrus includes pharmaceutical preparations for headache, cough, bites, wounds, burns, swellings, and problems with the stomach, eyes, teeth, ears, throat, finger, and toes. Each remedy has a dosage for each component in the preparation or prescription. There are two particularly interesting parts in the papyrus. It contains the first attempt to theoretically explain the disease, *wekhedu*, which could arise in any part of the body. The Egyptians never say what *wekhedu* is, but it seems that it is associated with the

Modern drawing based on a scene from the tomb of Ipuy in the cemetery of Deir el-Medina on the West Bank of Thebes. A workman has gotten something in his eye, and the local village "doctor" is removing it. (DeAgostini/Getty Images)

bowels and could travel to anywhere in the body causing illness. The papyrus, also for the first time, gives a description and explanation of the circulatory system and the way that the pulse should be taken.

Medical prescriptions include products of mineral, plant, and animal origin. Honey is the most common item in all the prescriptions. An extensive number of plants are included in the treatments, such as acacia, grapes, wine, beer, figs, pomegranates, dates, onions, castor oil, and lotus. Unfortunately, many Egyptian words still remain unknown, and not all the ingredients can be identified. Animal ingredients can be fat; blood; the liver of an animal, such as an ox; milk of human or cow; or excrement of a crocodile, Among the mineral products described are natron, alum, malachite, and ochre.

The Papyrus Edwin Smith dates to the early New Kingdom, around 1550 BCE, but it is thought to have been originally composed by the architect Imhotep, the builder of the Step Pyramid. The papyrus was purchased, and it is not known where it was found. It contains analysis and treatments of 48 different types of wounds, starting with the head and moving down. Unfortunately, the papyrus breaks off at chest level and is not complete. The papyrus describes the examination of the physical problem by the doctor, then a diagnosis is made, and, finally, the treatment is spelled out. In a few cases, it is simply recommended that the patient be kept as is, and it is clear from the way it is put that there is nothing to be done. This can be seen in Case 8 of the papyrus, which seems to be about a severe skull fracture (Breasted 1930, 201–216).

The Papyrus Kahun, dated to the 29th regnal year of King Amenemhat III (1831–1786 BCE), was found by Flinders Petrie at the site of Kahun, now generally referred to as Lahun, in 1889. It deals with gynecology and veterinary illnesses. The gynecological part of the papyrus describes how to identify a pregnancy, ingredients for contraceptives, and treatments for various female illnesses. The veterinary part of the papyrus includes treatment for birds, dogs, and cattle.

In these papyri, and the others known, it seems clear that the ancient Egyptians had no real knowledge of the internal organs or the internal workings of the human body. But they could deal with things they could see, such as a bleeding cut, something swollen, or a fractured bone. Human remains from ancient Egypt have supplied many examples of a properly healed fracture. However, the cause of anything internal could not be understood or treated. There does not seem to be any evidence of surgery, other than procedures to the body's surface, such as lancing an infection or an amputation, although only a few examples of amputation have been found. It is often claimed in popular works that the ancient Egyptians performed brain surgery, but there is no evidence for this at all.

Maria Rosa Guasch-Jané

See also: Childbirth; Dental Heath; Disease; Magic

Further Reading

Allen, J. P. 2005. *The Art of Medicine in Ancient Egypt*. New Haven, CT: Yale University Press.

Breasted, James Henry. 1930. *The Edwin Smith Surgical Papyrus*. Chicago: University of Chicago Press.

Bryan, C. P. 1930. *Ancient Egyptian Medicine: The Papyrus Ebers*. London: Ares Publishers.

Forshaw, Robert. 2016. "Trauma Care, Surgery and Remedies in Ancient Egypt: A Reassessment." In Campbell Price, Roger Forshaw, Andrew Chamberlain, and Paul Nicholson, eds. *Mummies, Magic and Medicine in Ancient Egypt: Multidisciplinary Essay for Rosalie David*. Manchester: Manchester University Press, pp. 124–141.

Nunn, J. F. 1996. *Ancient Egyptian Medicine*. London: British Museum Press.

Reeves, C. 2001. *Egyptian Medicine*. Buckinghamshire, UK: Shire Publications.

Strouhal, E. 1996. "For Every Malady, a Cure." In E. Strouhal, ed. *Life of the Ancient Egyptians*. Cairo: American University in Cairo Press, pp. 243–251.

Megiddo, Battle of (ca. 1457 BCE)

The Battle of Megiddo was a military conflict during the 23rd year of Thutmose III's (1479–1425 BCE) reign between the Egyptian army and a coalition of Syro-Palestinian armies under the leadership of the ruler of Kadesh, who may have been allied with the Hurrian state of Mitanni. The battle is commemorated in the Annals of Thutmose III on the walls of the Temple of Amun at Karnak, in modern-day Luxor, as 1 of at least 14 campaigns in Syro-Palestine conducted during his reign. Brief descriptions of the Battle of Megiddo are also preserved on a stele at

Gebel Barkal, in northern Sudan, established by Thutmose III in his 47th regnal year, and a stele at Armant, in Upper Egypt, from his 49th regnal year. These texts constitute the earliest detailed battle narrative in history. The battle at the city of Megiddo, now Tell el-Mutesellim, in northern Israel, took place during Thutmose III's first northern campaign, which was conducted for the purpose of quelling a rebellion by a number of city-states rallied under the rulers of Megiddo and Kadesh. The events of the campaign were recorded on a leather scroll by a chief military scribe and were later placed in the archives at Karnak Temple. Years later, excerpts were taken from this war diary for preservation as a monumental inscription at the temple.

At the outset of the 23rd year of his reign, only the first year of his sole kingship after the death of his coregent Hatshepsut (1473–1458 BCE), Thutmose III conducted his first northern campaign for the purpose of overthrowing his enemies in the north and extending Egypt's borders. Thutmose III was camped at Yehem, in modern-day Israel, having left Egypt with his army the previous month. While at Yehem, he summoned his war council to discuss news of the ruler of Kadesh, who was likewise encamped with his army at the fortified city of Megiddo, along with armies he had gathered from other Syro-Palestinian regions, including Naharin, Khor, and Qode. The king's advisers informed him of three roads from Yehem to Megiddo: a southern route through the town of Tanaach, a northern route to the north of Djefti, and a direct route through the town of Aruna, but one that traversed a mountain pass so narrow that the troops would have to walk single file through it, with one horse behind the other. They advised the king to choose either the southern or northern approach to Megiddo and avoid the Aruna route because they feared an ambush in the confined mountain pass. The king, unafraid of the narrow path, declared that he would proceed through Aruna with any man who would follow him and that he himself would lead the vanguard. After stopping for a night in Aruna, the king and the vanguard of the army emerged from the mountain pass at the valley of Qina at noon the following day without encountering any enemy soldiers; the enemy had expected them to arrive by way of the safer northern or southern routes. Thutmose III commanded his army to halt in the valley for the night to allow for the remainder of his troops to traverse the mountain pass and join them. At seven in the evening, they pitched camp near the brook of Qina, distributing rations and posting sentries while the troops prepared for battle the following day.

On the morning of the battle, Thutmose III deployed one wing of his army to the south of the Qina brook and one wing to the northwest of the city, and he led the central attack. The rulers of Kadesh and Megiddo, who are unnamed but identified as "the vile enemy" in the text, retreated with their soldiers, repulsed by the very image of Thutmose III's might. As the enemy soldiers retreated into the city, members of the Egyptian army stopped to plunder their weapons, gear, and chariots, which allowed Megiddo's inhabitants to seal the gates of the city. The text describes how many of the foreign soldiers who fled before the Egyptian army had to be hauled over the walls of the city to enter, including the ruler of the city itself. Unfortunately, the sizes of neither army are provided in the annals, but according to the Victory Stele from Gebel Barkal, there were 330 foreign rulers gathered at Megiddo to fight on behalf of the ruler of Kadesh, each with an army.

Thutmose III

Thutmose III was a king during the Eighteenth Dynasty (1539–1292 BCE) who inherited the throne as an infant or young child after his father, Thutmose II (1492–1479 BCE), died as a young adult. Because of his young age, his stepmother and aunt, Hatshepsut (his own mother, Isis, came from a nonroyal family), was appointed to serve as his regent until he came of age for sole rule. Around the seventh year of his reign, Hatshepsut adopted a titulary and began to style herself as an Egyptian king, even changing her image to that of a man's during his ninth regnal year. After Hatshepsut's death in the 22nd year of their coregency, Thutmose III conducted his first northern campaign, culminating in the Battle of Megiddo, the largest and most important military event of his reign. He is known for his aggressive foreign policies both in Syro-Palestine and Nubia, emulating those of his father and grandfather, Thutmose I. After reigning for an impressive 54 years, he was buried in a tomb in the Valley of the Kings (KV 34) that is famous for its wall scenes of the *Amduat*, a book of the underworld.

Taylor Bryanne Woodcock

The Egyptian army was forced to remain encamped outside the city, besieging it. The soldiers were ordered to dig a trench surrounding the city and to construct a wall around the ditch using wood from Megiddo's fruit tree groves to prevent anyone from escaping the city during the siege.

After a seven-month siege, the foreign rulers surrendered to Thutmose III with tributes of grain and wine; lapis lazuli and precious metals; enormous herds of horses, cattle, goats, and sheep; and nearly a thousand chariots. The king commanded that they swear an oath of allegiance to him that they would never again rebel against him. After accepting their oaths, he allowed them to return to their homes riding on donkeys, as he had taken all of their horses. The Egyptian army returned to Egypt laden with the spoils of war, including over 2,500 prisoners, some of whom had surrendered during the siege and some of whom were the children of the rulers he had defeated. Thutmose III's victory at Megiddo illustrated to other regional powers, including the Hittites, that Egypt's tactical and military superiority extended far beyond Egypt's borders, and it secured Megiddo as one of Egypt's vassal states for centuries.

Taylor Bryanne Woodcock

See also: Army; Chariot; Weapons and Armor

Further Reading

Cline, Eric H., and David B. O'Connor. 2006. *Thutmose III: A New Biography*. Ann Arbor: University of Michigan Press.

Faulkner, Raymond O. 1942. "The Battle of Megiddo." *Journal of Egyptian Archaeology* 28: 2–15.

Nelson, Harold H. 1913. *The Battle of Megiddo*. Chicago: University of Chicago Press.

Redford, Donald B. 2003. *The Wars in Syria and Palestine of Thutmose III*. Leiden: Brill.

Shea, William H. 1979. "The Conquests of Sharuhen and Megiddo Reconsidered." *Israel Exploration Journal* 29, no. 1: 1–5.

Primary Document—Account of the Battle of Megiddo

In this excerpt, King Thutmose III (r. 1479–1425 BCE) leads the attack on the Palestinian city of Megiddo.

> His Majesty set out upon a chariot of fine gold, equipped with his insignia of combat, like Horus, strong of arm, Lord of action, and like Theban Montu, his father Amun strengthening his two arms. The southern horn of His Majesty's army was south of the mountain brook at Qina, while the northern horn was north-west of Megiddo, and His Majesty was in the middle of them, Amun protecting his body in the melee, and the strength of Seth pervading his limbs. Then, His Majesty was powerful indeed in front of his army, and when they saw His Majesty being powerful, they fled headlong to Megiddo with faces of fear. They abandoned their horses and their chariots of gold and silver. They were dragged into this town by being hoisted by their clothing, for the people had closed this town on them. They let down clothes in order to hoist them up into this town. Now, if only His Majesty's army did not set their hearts to capturing the things of these enemies, or they would capture Megiddo in an instant! While the vile enemy of Kadesh and the vile enemy of this town were dragged scrambling to enter into their town, the fear of His Majesty enters their limbs, and their arms are weak. Then the power of His uraeus was on them. Then their horses and their chariots of gold and silver were captured, being easy prey. Their troops laid down in prostration, like fish in the curve of a net.
>
> Source: Translated by Taylor Bryanne Woodcock from Sethe, Kurt. 1907. *Urkunden der 18. Dynastie, Neuntes und Zehntes Heft. Urkunden des Ägyptischen Altertums IV.* Leipzig: J. C. Hinrichs'sche Buchhandlung, pp. 6557–6659, lines 85–88.

Meidum

The ancient site of Meidum is on the west side of the Nile, a little more than 60 miles south of Cairo. Flinders Petrie first explored the site in 1891, and he worked there again in 1909. The site is dominated by the pyramid, called "Sneferu Endures," built by King Sneferu at the beginning of the Fourth Dynasty. Early studies suggested the pyramid belonged to his father, King Huni, but that has since been disproved. There are several large mudbrick mastabas north of the pyramid, which seem to have belonged to members of the king's family. One mastaba, that of the king's son Rahotep, contained the famous and beautiful statues of him and his wife, Nofret, which are now in the Cairo Museum. Another, the mastaba of the king's son Nefermaat and his wife, Atet, was where the famous painted scene of the "Meidum Geese" was found. Both of these masterpieces are in the Egyptian Museum in Cairo.

The Meidum pyramid is the earliest known true pyramid, although now its appearance has been greatly changed in ancient and more modern times by the quarrying of stone from the pyramid, which also produced the mound of rubble around the base of the pyramid. An earlier theory had suggested the pyramid had collapsed, perhaps in an earthquake. The pyramid was first built as a tall seven-stepped pyramid. Then an eighth step was added. At the end of construction, the steps were filled in and cased, producing a smooth-sided true pyramid.

The pyramid of Meidum, built by King Sneferu of the early Fourth Dynasty, was the first true pyramid, not step pyramid, built in ancient Egypt. It was badly damaged later by the removal of the limestone outer casing. (DeAgostini/Getty Images)

On the east side of the pyramid is a small chapel with an offering table flanked by two round-topped stelae, for the king's name, but they were left blank. An open causeway leads east from the chapel to a valley temple, which is unexcavated and now under modern fields. The entrance into the pyramid was on the north side, where a corridor leads down to the burial chamber. There is a small southern pyramid or tomb on the southwest side of the pyramid.

From workmen's graffiti, it is clear that Sneferu stopped work at Meidum in his regnal year 15, when he moved to Dahshur, first building the Bent Pyramid, which had to be abandoned because of cracking, and then building his North Pyramid, where he was ultimately buried. At the same time he finished and cased his North Pyramid, his workmen also cased and completed the pyramid at Meidum. While both the Meidum Pyramid and the Bent Pyramid had small chapels with round-topped stelae set up on their east sides, the North Pyramid had a mortuary temple because that pyramid was where the king was actually buried.

Lisa K. Sabbahy

See also: Dahshur; Pyramids

Further Reading

Hapur, Yvonne. 1986. "The Identity and Positions of Relief Fragments in Museums and Private Collections: The Reliefs of R'-htp and Nfrt from Meydum." *Journal of Egyptian Archaeology* 72: 23–40.

Lehner, Mark. 1997. *The Complete Pyramids*. London: Thames and Hudson.

Petrie, W. M. F. 1892. *Medum*. London: David Nutt.

Reader, Colin. 2015. "The Meidum Pyramid." *Journal of Egyptian Archaeology* 51: 203–224.

Memphis

Memphis, the city that, according to the myths and classical legends, was founded by the first king of Egypt, around 3000 BCE, is recognized as the dynastic capital of all of pharaonic Egypt. The name Memphis is the way the Greeks wrote the ancient Egyptian word *Mn-nfr*, the name of the pyramid town of King Pepi I of the Sixth Dynasty, which was a large suburb by Greek times (2321–2287 BCE). But this name also designates the first nome, or province, of Lower Egypt as well. However, the oldest name of this city was *Inb-Hjd*, the "White Wall."

Strategically situated between the north, Lower Egypt, and the south, Upper Egypt, Memphis became both the capital and the official residence of the Old Kingdom pharaohs (2686–2160 BCE). But its importance in the history of pharaonic Egypt continued, even after losing some of the status as capital to other cities during the Middle Kingdom (2055–1650 BCE) and the New Kingdom (1550–1069 BCE), owing to religious and cultural reasons. In pharaonic cultural memory, Memphis would forever preserve the attribute of being the ancient city of tradition, where the most relevant royal rituals would take place, such as the coronation ritual and the Sed festival, the ritual renovation of royal power every 30 years.

Aside from that, substantial economic activity concentrated in the area of Memphis because its geographic location allowed control of the delta as well as of the commercial routes from the different directions of the Levant, the Red Sea, and the Sahara. This intense commercial activity was complemented by the enormous economic dynamism that took place around its most important temple, the temple of the god Ptah, and the Memphite royal necropolis that extended all the way from the pyramid of Abu Roasch, in the north, to the pyramid of Meidum, to the south.

The city became one of the most significant religious centers of the land, raising the tutelary god of Memphis, Ptah, to one of the principal gods of creation in ancient Egyptian mythology. Ptah, the patron deity of artists and artisans and god of wisdom and knowledge, formed one of the most important divine triads with Sakhmet, his wife, and Nefertem, his son. The most common representation of this god reveals a standing man wrapped as a mummy with a dark cap on his head, with the straight-bottomed beard of the king tied on his chin. He wears a broad collar and holds in his hands the scepters of *was*, a symbol of prosperity; *djed*, a symbol of stability; and *ankh*, a symbol of life.

The animal manifestation of Ptah—"the living image" of Ptah—was the Apis bull, the most popular of the Egyptian deified animals, which is depicted with a solar disk and *uraeus* between his horns. This animal was black with a white belly and hooves and had a triangular spot on its head and another in the form of a crescent or a vulture on its back. When the Apis bull died, it was embalmed and buried in a great ceremony at the catacombs of Memphis, known as the Serapeum. The cult of the Apis is attested since the beginning of the formation of the Egyptian state to the Roman Period.

Memphis also consecrated itself as one of the more relevant centers of culture and intellectual activities in pharaonic Egypt. All these reasons transformed the city into the biggest population center in all of ancient Egyptian history.

Origin of the Name "Egypt"

By the time of the New Kingdom (1550–1069 BCE), an enormous temple complex for Ptah lay south of the king's palace at Memphis. It is said to have been as large as, or larger than, the Karnak Temple complex in Luxor. The name of the temple was *Hw(t)-ka-Ptah*, or the "Temple of the Soul of the God Ptah."

The Hw-ka-Ptah (a final *t* was not pronounced in later pharaonic times) was obviously a very large and important part of the city. Beginning in 332 BCE, when Alexander the Great took Egypt from the Persian Empire, large numbers of Greeks came to Egypt not only as tourists but also to settle and live there as well. The name that the Egyptians used for Ptah's temple became the name the Greeks used for the city itself, and with a Greek pronunciation, Hw-ka-Ptah became Aigyptus and, much later in English, Egypt. It is thought that the Arabic shortening of the name *Aigyptus* to *Gypt* is the origin of the word *Copt*.

Lisa K. Sabbahy

But how did such an important city practically vanish? Today, ancient Memphis seems confined to the modern city of Mit-Rahina, where some monument ruins of the ancient capital are preserved in situ. Classical authors such as Herodotus, Strabo, and Diodorus of Sicily described a place that, in its last phase, seemed to coincide with the modern site of the ruins of Mit-Rahina. But even when they talk about the importance and extension of this city, they never refer to it as the capital. The same happens in the references cataloged in Arab medieval literature and in accounts of travelers like William of Tyre, Benjamin of Tudela, and Joos van Ghistele. Since that point on, no news of the ancient city seems to exist. It would only be spoken again in 1585, due to the reports of the traveler François de Pavie. This occurrence would transform Memphis—and its possible location—into a relevant theme for academic debate. However, the city's first detailed maps only appeared during the second half of the 18th century, after Napoleon's expedition. Curiously, Denon, one of the scholars who went with Napoleon on this expedition, when referring to Memphis in his writings, notes that the northern and southern frontiers of the ancient city were delimited by two pyramid complexes: Giza, on the north, and Sakkara, on the south. This idea, of the connection of the city with the two pyramid complexes, echoes other travelers and scholars. Despite this, it was the members of Napoleon's scientific expedition who would link the ancient Memphis to the ruin site of Mit-Rahina. One of the explanations for this association is directly connected with the density of archaeological remains found there.

Despite this, the academic debate regarding the effective extension of the city carried on. Petrie, who directed six excavation seasons in the area in 1909 to 1913, calculated at the time that the city of Memphis would have extended about eight miles from north to south and four miles from east to west, including the suburban areas and gardens (Jeffreys 1985, 6–7). His map, still based on the one that Karl Lepsius presented after an excavation in 1843, in Kôm Rabi'a became, for years, the base for further investigation. A new map was only produced during the end of the 1950s by Rudolf Anthes, who, between 1955 and 1956, performed a new excavation in Memphis (Jeffreys 1985, 16). Meanwhile, Jeffreys, who since 1985 has directed the Project "Survey of Memphis," stated that, in its most important period, "Memphis was a great metropolis that occupied, at least six miles from north to south" (Jeffreys 2000, 24).

How can we explain that a city that remained the capital for so long left so little behind? Several factors seem to have contributed to the city's demise. Memphis was near the Nile River, and the alterations of its course, that have moved progressively toward the east over the centuries, has caused a natural erosion of the older remains of the site. On the other hand, "the rate of sediment accumulation in the valley floor of the Memphite region is estimated at one metre per millennia. . . . This would place a second millennia BCE settlement several metres below the modern ground surface" (Love 2003, 77). Another explanation for the remains of this ancient city disappearing is the activity of the *sebakh* diggers who have been stealing "the compost" of the ancient city of Memphis to be used as fertilizer for agricultural purposes. And lastly, one cannot forget that during the Middle Ages, the Memphite monuments were systematically dismantled or destroyed; their stones were used to build some of the churches and mosques of Cairo. The proximity to the new capital determined the excessive destruction of the ancient metropolis. Therefore, today, what one sees of the primitive capital is very little, for the city is under the desert sands or buried below modern constructions.

Maria Helena Trindade Lopes

See also: Cities and Villages; Nile River; Ptah; Sed Festival

Further Reading

Jeffreys, D. 1985. *The Survey of Memphis.* Vol. 1. London: Egypt Exploration Society.

Jeffreys, D. 2000. "Investigating Ancient Memphis, Pharaonic Egypt's Northern Capital." *Archaeology International* 3: 24–27.

Jeffreys, D. 2008. "Archaeological Implications of the Moving of the Nile." *Egyptian Archaeology* 32: 6–7.

Jeffreys, D., and L. Giddy. 1991. "Looking for Memphis." *EA* 1: 5–8.

Kemp, B. 1976. "A Note on Stratigraphy at Memphis." *Journal of the American Research Centre in Egypt* 13: 27.

Love, S. 2003. "Questioning the Location of the Old Kingdom Capital of Memphis, Egypt." *Papers from the Institute of Archaeology* 14: 70–84.

Love, S. 2006. "Stones, Ancestors, and Pyramids: Investigating the Pre-Pyramid Landscape of Memphis." In M. Barta, ed. *The Old Kingdom Art and Archaeology—Proceedings of the Conference Held in Prague, May 31–June 4, 2004.* Prague: Publishing House of the Academy of Sciences of the Czech Republic, pp. 209–218.

Snape, S. 2014. *The Complete Cities of Ancient Egypt.* London: Thames and Hudson.

Mining

Egypt is particularly rich in mineral resources. The deserts on either side of the Nile valley are geologically complex, with a wide range of deposits and formation processes that have resulted in a great variety of minerals. These resources were exploited by the Egyptians from the earliest times, through mining, quarrying, and collection from alluvial deposits. Some of the most extensively mined materials were gold and copper, but numerous metals, gemstones, and salts were also sought.

Because of Egypt's geology, many mines were located deep within the desert. Minerals were mined from both the Eastern and Western Deserts as well as the Sinai Peninsula. Controlling the distant sources of these materials probably played a large role in the expansion of Egyptian political influence into the desert territories. Because of the harsh conditions in the desert, expeditions to the mining regions were seasonal and required considerable logistical support. For this reason, they lent themselves to military-style excursions. A considerable corpus of stone-cut inscriptions left in the desert by members of these expeditions paints a picture of state-organized, official missions, sometimes involving thousands of people, led by military personnel. There is evidence that some of the laborers were conscripted or coerced, possibly colonized populations or prisoners of war.

Mining sites may be recognized archaeologically by the workings themselves, but also by heaps of slag, smelting furnaces, washing tables, crucibles, ingot molds, grinding querns, and by dwellings and administrative buildings. Often, mining areas were active for several centuries as their deposits were slowly worked to exhaustion. The routes between mining sites and the Nile valley bear numerous inscriptions and graffiti left by miners and administrators, which provide information about the dates, objectives, and composition of the mining expeditions. The Turin Papyrus map, often referred to as one of the oldest maps in the world, shows a route through the Wadi Hammamat to a gold-mining camp at Bir Umm Fawakhir. The Wadi Hammamat is a desert valley long used as the most direct route from the Nile valley into the mining regions of the Eastern Desert and across the desert to the Red Sea coast. The map on the Turin Papyrus, which dates to about 1150 BCE, shows an established settlement at the gold mine, complete with a temple, a monument to the king, a well, and a reservoir.

Having a reliable source of water near such a camp was vital, and the search for water in the arid deserts was itself a kind of prospecting. Several inscriptions record the discovery of natural water sources or the successful opening of wells that could support a workforce at a mining camp. Failing such a stroke of luck, a water supply had to be carried in from the nearest source.

Although the Egyptians utilized many minerals very early on, it is likely that they were at first collected from erosional and alluvial deposits on the surface, rather than being methodically extracted from the earth. The first materials mined in Egypt were probably copper and its colorful ores. Copper objects appear as early as the Badarian Period, although they do not become frequent until the late Predynastic. These are likely to be of "native" copper, which occurred naturally in metallic form. The earliest evidence for the mining and smelting of copper ores dates to the Early Dynastic period (3000–2686 BCE).

Throughout Egyptian history, copper ores were smelted at the site of extraction. The raw ores were heated on a charcoal fire and fanned either by a bellows or simply by the wind. This rudimentary method was sufficient to separate the copper, which was later sorted from the charcoal and slag by hand. It could then be melted into ingots for transportation. Ingot molds have been found at some quarry sites, indicating that all of the processing of the raw ore was done at the source.

The most worked deposits of copper are located in the Sinai Peninsula, but the metal is found throughout the entire Eastern Desert. Many sources of copper are also sources of malachite and turquoise, blue-green minerals. Turquoise has been prized for jewelry throughout Egyptian history, and rich green malachite was crushed for cosmetics beginning very early. It is possible that prospecting for these gems alerted the Egyptians to the related copper sources. Both malachite and turquoise are especially connected with the goddess Hathor, who became a primary deity of mining activity and the desert regions in general. Shrines to Hathor, where miners dedicated votive offerings to the goddess, were common at mining camps. Mining inscriptions record official gifts of offering tables, linen, and live cattle and fowl, which were transported with the expedition to be offered at Hathor's desert temples.

The logistical effort required to transport live cattle into the desert gives an indication of the high level of organization of mining expeditions. Starting in the Old Kingdom (2686–2160 BCE), expeditions were undertaken in the king's name and involved numerous specialized personnel, including architects, "artisans of the palace," treasurers, scribes, and even judges. This level of state involvement in mining suggests that its profits went directly to the state treasury, making mining an important economic activity for the kings of ancient Egypt. The acquisition of precious stones and metals was a major factor driving Egyptian political and territorial expansion. This imperialist activity intensified in the Middle and New Kingdoms, especially as the Egyptians pushed south into the gold-rich regions of Lower Nubia.

Gold was used in Egypt very early. It could be found in relatively pure form in alluvial placer deposits throughout the country, enabling its collection from the surface without complicated infrastructure. As demand for the metal grew, however, prospection resulted in the discovery and exploitation of underground gold seams. The extraction of gold from the surrounding rock was a labor-intensive process. Gold-bearing stone was broken up inside the mine with stone or copper tools and carried out in baskets. Then the stone was heated to make it brittle. Afterward, it was crushed with hammers and in hand mills. The resulting dust was washed across cloth or fleece to separate the particles by density, and the gold was removed by hand.

Middle Kingdom superintendents record in their inscriptions that they "forced the Nubian chiefs to wash the gold" (Breasted 1906, 274). The implication of coercion reflects the aggressive official posture of Egypt toward Nubia during the Middle Kingdom (2055–1650 BCE). Archaeological evidence shows that Egyptians and Nubians were living alongside one another at mining camps in Nubia, where round Nubian huts and material culture intermingle with Egyptian styles. Both Egyptian and Nubian laborers were participating in the backbreaking work of mining. Nevertheless, the social dynamics between Nubian miners, Egyptian miners, and Egyptian mine administrators must have been nuanced and variable.

In addition to copper and gold, other metals were mined in Egypt, although not in nearly the same quantities. Lead, occurring in several places along the Red Sea coast, was utilized beginning in the Predynastic Period, beginning around 5000 BCE. Metallic iron occurs in Egypt, but it was not frequently worked until very late in ancient Egyptian history. There is some debate as to whether silver was imported or mined within Egypt. Much Egyptian gold is naturally alloyed with silver, creating a metal called *electrum* that was highly prized for its pale color.

Egypt's wide variety of gemstones was also exploited in ancient times. Turquoise, found in the Sinai Peninsula, was mined beginning at least as early as the First Dynasty (3000–2890 BCE). In addition to turquoise, carnelian was used extensively in jewelry in all periods. Sources of carnelian, as well as garnet, were exploited in the Western Desert near Aswan. In the Middle Kingdom and during the Roman Period, the amethyst deposits of the Eastern Desert were thoroughly mined, particularly at the site of Wadi el Hudi. The Romans mined for emeralds, which are also found in the Eastern Desert. Other stones that were sought as gems for beads, scarabs, amulets, and inlays include agate, calcite, feldspar, hematite, jasper, peridot, and sard. Many of these gems naturally occurred near or in the same deposits as copper or gold or with building stones like granite that were the focus of major quarrying operations. As a result, even if they were not the objects of targeted mining expeditions, they were collected and transported back to the Nile valley as an auxiliary product.

Additionally, various types of salts constituted a major mined resource. Table salt, or sodium chloride, is found in many places in the Egyptian desert and was widely used for culinary and other applications. Natron, a vital ingredient in the mummification process, was mined from a source in the northwestern desert. Finally, deposits of alum, used in tanning leather and dyeing cloth, were intensively worked in the oases of the Western Desert during the Roman Period.

Laurel Darcy Hackley

See also: Deserts; Gold; Jewelry; Nubia; Quarrying; Silver

Further Reading

Baines, J., and J. Malek. 2000. *Cultural Atlas of Ancient Egypt.* New York: Checkmark Books.

Breasted, J. 1906. *Ancient Records of Egypt: Historical Documents from the Earliest Times to the Persian Conquest.* Chicago: University of Chicago Press.

Diodorus, Siculus, and J. Skelton. 1968. *The Bibliotheca Historica of Diodorus Siculus.* London: Oxford University Press.

Harrell, J., and V. Brown. 1992. "The Oldest Surviving Topographical Map from Ancient Egypt (Turin Papyri 1879, 1899 and 1969)." *Journal of the American Research Center in Egypt* 29: 81–105.

Klemm, R., and D. Klemm. 2013. *Gold and Gold Mining in Ancient Egypt and Nubia: Geoarchaeology of the Ancient Gold Mining Sites in the Egyptian and Sudanese Eastern Deserts.* Heidelberg: Springer.

Lucas, A., and J. Harris. 1962. *Ancient Egyptian Materials and Industries.* Chatham, UK: W. & K. Mackay & Co Ltd.

Nicholson, P., and I. Shaw. 2000. *Ancient Egyptian Materials and Technology.* Cambridge: Cambridge University Press.

Mortuary Temples. *See* Temples, Mortuary

Mummies, Royal

Mummification, in its broadest sense of the wrapping of the body, with or without associated chemical treatment, goes back to late Predynastic times, around 3200 BCE, with the earliest examples found at Hierakonpolis clearly of high-status personages. However, complete mummies of kings are not known until the New Kingdom (1550–1069 BCE). Nevertheless, fragmentary remains, or potential remains, of royal mummies can be identified as far back as the First Dynasty (3000–2890 BCE). The earliest is part of a bracelet-wearing linen-wrapped arm, found in the tomb of King Djer at Abydos in 1901, where a human skull had been found shortly before. The relatively small size of these remains has led to the suggestion that they might have belonged to Djer's wife, rather than the king himself.

In the 1930s, a number of pieces of a mummified body, most notably a left foot, were found in the burial chamber of Djoser (2667–2648 BCE) at Sakkara dating to the Third Dynasty. They display a technique consistent with the Old Kingdom and were found in a location unlikely to have been used for later intrusive burials, but radiocarbon dates are much later than expected, presenting problems in assessment. Mummy fragments were also found within Sneferu's (2613–2589 BCE) Fourth Dynasty Red Pyramid at Dahshur in 1950, including pieces of the skull. A conflict between archaeological and radiocarbon is also found regarding parts of a desiccated human body found in the Fourth Dynasty Third Pyramid of Menkaura at Giza in 1837.

Of secure date are the fragments of the mummy of the Fifth Dynasty king Neferefre (2448–2445 BCE), found in his burial chamber at Abusir in 1997–1998, including part of the skull, the left shoulder, and the left hand. Remains of the mummy of Isesi, also of the Fifth Dynasty, were found amid the broken remains of the king's sarcophagus at Sakkara in 1947. The pyramid of Isesi's successor, Unas (2375–2354 BCE), preserved a left arm and hand, together with pieces of a skull, while that of the Sixth Dynasty founder Teti (2345–2323 BCE) held a shoulder and an arm. A hand was all that survived of the mummy of Pepy I (2321–2287 BCE). A complete mummy was found in the pyramid of the next king, Nemtyemsaf I, but in view of its style of mummification, it may be a later intrusive burial. All these latter remains were found in 1880.

Moving on to the Eleventh Dynasty, some pieces of the skull and some other bones were found in the burial chamber of Mentuhotep II's (2055–2004 BCE) temple tomb at Deir el-Bahari in 1909. From the Twelfth Dynasty, some leg bones were recovered from Senusret II's (1877–1870 BCE) pyramid at Lahun in 1924. Finally, from the Middle Kingdom, the damaged skeleton of the Thirteenth Dynasty (1773–1650 BCE) king Hor was found in his tomb at Dahshur in 1894.

In contrast to the fragmentary remains surviving from earlier times, the majority of kings' mummies of the New Kingdom have survived by virtue of having been removed from their own tombs to hiding places during the Twentieth and Twenty-First Dynasties (1186–945 BCE). Seqenenra Taa, the penultimate king of the Seventeenth Dynasty (1580–1550 BCE), was also saved the same way, being one of a large number of bodies reburied in tomb number TT320, near Deir el-Bahari, early in the Twenty-Second Dynasty and found in 1871. The body is poorly preserved, and the head is covered with horrific combat wounds.

The body of his successor, Kamose, was found intact in a reburial at Dra Abu'l-Naga in 1857, but the body collapsed when exposed. On the other hand, his successor, Ahmose I, the founder of the Eighteenth Dynasty in 1550 BCE, was found in Theban Tomb 320, as was the next king, Amenhotep I; the mummy has never been unwrapped. X-rays show that it was the earliest royal mummy of the New Kingdom to have its arms crossed at the breast. The mummy of Thutmose I is unknown, despite a mummy identified as such in the Cairo Museum. The mummy of Thutmose II (1492–1479 BCE) was, however, found in Theban Tomb 320, as was the mummy of Thutmose III (1479–1425 BCE).

It has been suggested that the female king Hatshepsut (1473–1458 BCE) is represented by a mummy that was found in Valley of the Kings, Tomb KV60, on the basis of an apparent match of a tooth found in a box bearing her name to roots in situ in the jaw of the mummy as revealed by CT scanning. However, there remain doubts both as to the validity of the match and consequent conclusions.

The body of Amenhotep II (1427–1400) was found in his own tomb, Valley of the Kings KV35, in 1898, where the mummy had been restored after robbery during the Twentieth or Twenty-First Dynasty. Originally left in the tomb, it was removed to Cairo in 1932. Amenhotep II had later been joined in KV35 by other

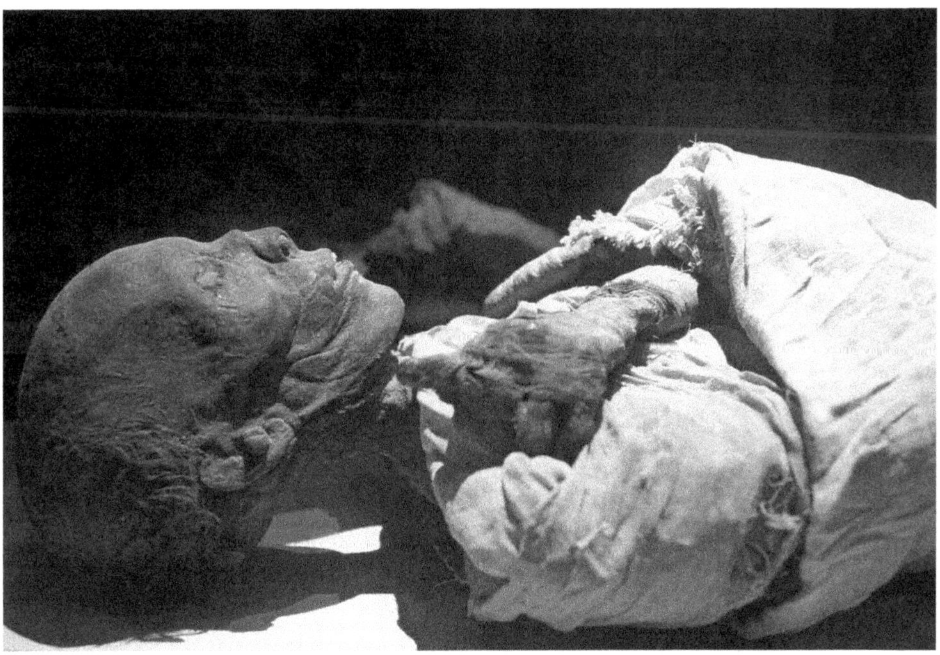

This is the mummy of King Thutmose II, the son of Thutmose I of the Eighteenth Dynasty. Thutmose II was the husband of his half sister, Queen Hatshepsut, and they had one daughter, Neferure. (Patrick Landmann/Getty Images)

royal mummies removed there for safety, including those of Thutmose IV (1400–1390 BCE) and Amenhotep III (1390–1352 BCE).

A mummy, now reduced to a skeleton by damp conditions, found in Tomb KV55 in 1907, certainly belongs to either Akhenaten or Smenkhkare, but there is as yet no unanimity over which king it belongs to. The female king Neferneferu-aten, probably originally Akhenaten's wife Nefertiti, may be represented by the 'Younger Woman' found in KV35 and identified on genetic grounds as the mother of Tutankhamun. Tutankhamun's (1336–1327 BCE) mummy was found intact in his own tomb, KV62, in 1922.

Nothing is known of the mummy of Ay, nor of Horemheb, unless some of the bones found in his tomb, KV57, are his. The coffin of Ramses I was found in TT320, but his mummy has never been positively identified. A body acquired in the 1860s for the Niagara Falls Museum has been proposed as his and was transferred to the Luxor Museum in 2004; however, the identification is by no means secure.

On the other hand, the body of Seti I (1294–1279 BCE), the second king of the Nineteenth Dynasty, was found in Theban Tomb 320, as was that of Ramses II (1279–1213 BCE). Merenptah's (1213–1203 BCE) mummy was found in KV35, as was one identified as Seti II, although the mummy's identity has been questioned. Siptah's (1194–1188 BCE) mummy was also found in KV35.

The mummy of Sethnakhte is unknown, but Ramses III (1184–1153) was found in Theban Tomb 320. A CT scan has shown that he died from a slashed throat; the king is known to have been the object of a conspiracy. His successors, Ramses IV, V and VI, were all found in KV35, the latter very badly damaged by tomb robbers. The last known king's mummy of the New Kingdom is that of Ramses IX (1126–1108), found in Theban Tomb 320.

After the New Kingdom, only a handful of royal mummies survive. The mummy of the Twenty-First Dynasty (1069–945 BCE) Panedjem I was found in Theban Tomb 320, while his son Pasebkhanut I was found intact in his tomb NRT-III at Tanis in 1940. Unfortunately, the wrappings and flesh had been totally destroyed by the damp conditions in the tomb. This was also true of all the other kings' mummies found in the tomb, Amenemopet, Siamun, and Pasebkhanut II, whose mummies were completely destroyed, and Shoshenq IIa of the Twenty-Second Dynasty (945–715 BCE).

The skull and part of the arm of a local king of Thebes during the Twenty-Second Dynasty, Horsieset I, was found in his tomb at Medinet Habu in 1932, while a skull and a few bones were recovered from the Twenty-Fifth Dynasty king Shabitka's (702–690 BCE) pyramid at El-Kurru in the Sudan in 1916. The final remains potentially identifiable with those of a king of ancient Egypt are some bones found in the sarcophagus of Naefarud I of the Twenty-Ninth Dynasty (399–380 BCE) at Mendes in 1887.

Aidan Dodson

See also: Abydos; Hierakonpolis; Mummification; Tanis; Valley of the Kings

Further Reading

Derry, D. E. 1935. "Report on the Human Remains from the Granite Sarcophagus Chamber in the Pyramid of Zoser." *ASAE* 35: 28–30.

Derry, D. E. 1940/41. "An Examination of the Bones of King Psusennes I." *Annales du Service des Antiquités d'Égypte* 40: 969–970.

Filer, J. 2002. "Anatomy of a Mummy." *Archaeology* 55, no. 2: 26–29.

Harris, J. E., and K. R. Weeks. 1973. *X-Raying the Pharaohs*. London: Macdonald.

Harrison, R. G. 1966. "An Anatomical Examination of the Pharaonic Remains Purported to Be Akhenaten." *Journal of Egyptian Archaeology* 52: 95–119.

Hawass, Z., Y. Z. Gad, S. Ismail, R. Khairat, D. Fathalla, N. Hasan, A. Ahmed, H. Elleithy, M. Ball, F. Gaballah, S. Wasef, M. Fateen, H. Amer, P. Gostner, A. Selim, A. Zink, and C. M. Pusch, 2010. "Ancestry and Pathology in King Tutankhamun's Family." *Journal of the American Medical Association* 303, no. 7: 638–647.

Hawass, Z., and S. N. Saleem. 2016. *Scanning the Pharaohs: CT Imaging of the New Kingdom Royal Mummies*. Cairo: American University in Cairo Press.

Jones, Jana 2002. "Towards Mummification: New Evidence for Early Developments." *Egyptian Archaeology* 21: 5–7.

Leek, F. F. 1972. *The Human Remains from the Tomb of Tut'ankhamūn*. Oxford: Griffith Institute.

Strouhal, E. 2006. "Identification of King Raneferef According to Human Remains Found in the Burial Chamber of the Unfinished Pyramid." In M. Verner, ed. *Abusir IX: The Pyramid Complex of Raneferef: The Archaeology*. Prague: Czech Institute of Egyptology, Charles University, pp. 513–518.

Mummification

Mummification of various types was practiced for over 3,000 years of Egyptian history, only ceasing to be the norm when Coptic Christianity took hold in Egypt. To some extent, the origin for the idea of preserving the body must have been closely allied to the belief in an afterlife. The concept that the soul needed a body to reanimate if it were to survive eternally and enjoy all the benefits of the afterlife—which was very similar to an ideal "real" life—was apparently established at the dawn of Egyptian civilization.

Mummification was not static: its technology developed and varied considerably over time, fashions changed, religious beliefs evolved, and there were differences between both regions and workshops as well as variations based on economic considerations. Presumably, the client, in conjunction with the embalmers, chose the method of mummification based on individual taste, budget, and the technologies and materials available at the time. Success rates among mummification methods varied in terms of ability to preserve the body; thus, many mummies have turned to dust, leaving behind skeletons wrapped up in thick layers of bandages.

Our understanding of mummification technology is derived from a variety of sources. These include examinations of the mummies themselves, analyses of mummification materials, a handful of Late and Greco-Roman papyri dealing with different aspects of mummification, embalmers' bills, embalming caches, chemical analyses of embalming agents, classical texts, and experimental mummification. Used in conjunction, these elucidate the practical aspects of producing mummies as well as some of the religious beliefs and acts necessary for their production.

Initial impressions are gleaned from autopsies and examinations of the mummies themselves; the earliest scholars actually unwrapped mummies, while more recent ones have remained content to observe without destruction More recently, this has been augmented by radiographic imaging that is becoming increasingly refined, as seen by computer tomography (CT) scans that permit visual access to desiccated soft tissues as well as the amulets, jewels, other inclusions, and wrappings. Chemical analyses, such as gas chromatography and mass spectrometry, provide insights into the embalming agents used to preserve the body, and historic studies are aided by ongoing aDNA studies that might establish the identities of royal mummies and their familial relationships.

The main objective of mummification was the preservation and wrapping of the body to create an eternal image that could be animated by the *ka* and *ba*, aspects of the spirit and soul, and it was ultimately necessary to effect the transformation of the deceased into an *akh*, a transfigured spirit. The chief steps involved evisceration, sometimes excerebration, followed by desiccation using natron, anointing with oils and resins, and wrapping, often with amulets interspersed in the bandages, before the body was covered by a mask or coffin bearing the name and face of the deceased. The traditional length of time for mummification was 70 days, 40 for desiccation and 30 for the wrapping and its accompanying rituals. This duration was equated with the length of time that the constellation Sirius vanished from the sky, only to reappear, or be "resurrected," at the start of the Egyptian's New Year and the inundation.

As mummification technology changed diachronically, geographically, and across socioeconomic levels, so did the materials used in embalming, although at least some items remained fairly constant: natron and resin. Natron is a mixture of sodium bicarbonate, sodium carbonate, sodium sulfate, and sodium chloride that occurs naturally in Egypt, most commonly in the Wadi Natrun located northwest of Cairo. Natron played a key role in mummification, as it both desiccates and defats, leaving the skin, ligaments, tendons, and bones intact. Although common salt could have occasionally been used in economical burials, natron remained the preferred desiccant. In its most refined state, natron is white, so it was an ideal purification material.

Resins of different types, including frankincense, myrrh, and gum Arabic, were used to seal the interior and exterior of the body to avoid bacterial growth and also to help hold bandages in place. Resins were also applied to the skin, and this lent the body a faintly golden hue when first applied, thus stressing the transformation of the deceased from a human to a divine with flesh of gold.

After desiccation, the body was wrapped. This involved not only wrapping the body in linen bandages, interspersed with amulets, but also reciting a series of prayers over it, thus creating both a physical and magical cocoon that would protect it. After mummification was complete, the bodily and embalming detritus from the procedure was buried in relatively close proximity to the body, as these materials that had touched the body were regarded as sacred.

The word *mummy* is not the ancient Egyptian term for the preserved body of the deceased, which is *sah*, but rather originates in the Arab name for these bodies, *mumia*, or ones bearing *mum*, a form of pitch or bitumen. This sobriquet was applied to ancient Egyptian preserved bodies because many of them had a blackened appearance, as they were covered in a thick, black, somewhat tarry material that the Arabs took to be bitumen or pitch.

The majority of bodies from the Predynastic Period (5300–3000 BCE) were either naturally desiccated due to desert sand or reduced to skeletons. Indeed, it has been posited by many scholars that the accidental uncovering by wind or animals of the naturally preserved bodies led to a desire to conserve the body. Early efforts in the field of artificial preservation occurred during the Naqada II period at Hierakonpolis and Adaima. Corpses were laden with linen bandages, and extra padding over the heads and bodies made the deceased appear more fleshed out. The few intact mummies recovered dating to the Early Dynastic Period (3000–2686 BCE) were wrapped in linen and placed in rectangular clay or wooden coffins, beds, or stone sarcophagi in a flexed position. The viscera remained intact, and it is possible that natron was used for desiccation, although, as no examples have been tested to date, this is not a certainty.

More formal mummification started in the Old Kingdom (2686–2160 BCE) with evisceration from the left side, with the use of natron and resins becoming more common. The left side was favored in ancient Egypt because it was the side of the heart, the seat of the soul and the life force. The evisceration process was not used for all Old Kingdom mummies. The oldest proof of an eviscerated body comes from the Fourth Dynasty, in the form of Queen Hetephere's chest, which contained some of her visceral packages. Excerebration was known but infrequently practiced. Mummy wrappings in the Old Kingdom were unlike those of earlier and later mummies in that the last layers were modeled, creating a linen-clad likeness of the corpse. Facial features were painted on to further emphasize the likeness. The mummy might also be dressed with jewelry and clothing, thus creating a portrait statue of the deceased. Some bodies were covered with a final layer of plaster sculpted to resemble the deceased and then painted; in some cases, only the head was treated in this way, perhaps so that the deceased could be recognized in the hereafter.

Another technique for evisceration seems to have been introduced in the Middle Kingdom. Cedar or juniper oil was inserted into the deceased via the anus, the opening was covered with linen, and the body was desiccated by placing it in natron, a mineral salt. The corpse was then taken out of the natron, and the linen covering was removed; the now liquid viscera were emptied by applying pressure to the deceased's stomach. Arms were generally placed at the side. The completely wrapped and cocooned body was positioned on its side within the coffin.

The majority of elite and royal mummies studied date from the New Kingdom. Evisceration through the side is common, initially with a vertical cut, and then, around the reign of Thutmose III, via a diagonal incision, parallel to the iliac crest, although variations occur. The brain is more frequently removed via the nostril-ethmoid bone route, although it is by no means the norm. Desiccation continued to be achieved by inserting packets of natron into the body and burying the body in powdered natron. Toward the latter part of the New Kingdom, cosmetic enhancement of mummies starts, with false eyes of onion bulbs introduced into the orbits, painted brows, and, in the case of Ramses II (1279–1213 BCE), nose stuffing so that it retains its shape. Variations in arm positions proliferate, both in royal and elite contexts, although for less elite burials, men's arms covered their genitalia and women's arms lay at their sides. Linen wrappings continued to be used, frequently in a spiral around the body and each limb and extremity. Some innovations take the form of shrouds bearing painted decoration or texts from the Book of the Dead, which seem to start being a feature during the reign of Hatshepsut and Thutmose III (1473–1425 BCE).

Many innovations were introduced in the Twenty-First Dynasty, with the emphasis on making the deceased look as if she or he were merely lying down or asleep. The mummified viscera were put back into the body, the body was stuffed to make it look lifelike, stone and glass eyes were added, and bodies were bathed in ochre washes, yellow for women and red for men. Details of eyebrows and lips were enhanced with makeup, and great attention was paid to the coiffure. Bodies were well wrapped, and images of Osiris were painted on shrouds, with accompanying texts, ensuring that the deceased was well protected in his or her journey to the afterlife.

By the mid–Twenty-Second Dynasty, attention given to making the body look alive decreased, possibly due to the economic and political difficulties of the era or to changing religious ideas. However, the tendency to pack the torso with linen and resins was a feature for the elite mummies of this time. During the ensuing years, evisceration was not consistently carried out or was not complete. Insufficient drying time resulted in the disintegrating of the flesh; bodies were liberally covered with a generous use of resins and oils, all of which contributed to the deterioration of the body. Viscera, when removed, were returned wrapped up and placed between the legs. While embalmers continued using resins mixed with oil and beeswax to coat the mummy, bitumen was also occasionally used, turning the bodies very black. The Saite Period saw a return of canopic jars as a standard part of the funerary equipment, with the viscera being deposited there.

Mummies of the Ptolemaic-Roman Period (332 BCE–395 BCE) vary dramatically, and it is not clear whether this disparity is a reflection of socioeconomic status, embalming house "styles," or religious variation. It seems that this era saw an overall increase in mummification, as the remains of men, women, and children from this era are numerous. While elite Ptolemaic mummies have relatively well-preserved bodies, as time progressed, less care was taken. Evisceration, particularly in the Roman era, became less common. Viscera, when removed, were often placed by the legs. There is a marked increase in the use of resinous substances as well, often making bodies very heavy. The resins no doubt were meant to create a shell around a poorly preserved body so it would hold its shape, and it also had magical, medical, and religious connotations. Many of the mummies are black as a result. It is possible that at the time of application they were more golden, to evoke the flesh of the gods, and have darkened over time. Alternatively, and more possibly, the resinous mixture was dark to start, suggestive of the color of Osiris and the black regenerative soil of the floodplain. In some Roman mummies, faces, nails, and other body parts were gilded, emphasizing the transformation of the deceased into a divine being. Hand positions also change; in the Ptolemaic era, there are many more individuals with their arms crossed over the chest with the hands on their shoulders, reminiscent of the god Osiris and perhaps underlining the transformation of the deceased into an Osiris. Roman bodies, on the other hand, tend to have the arms by their sides.

The bandaging of mummies, particularly in the late Ptolemaic and early Roman Periods, became a greater focus than the preservation of the body. Wrappings are extremely elaborate, often with multiples of seven bandages being used. Sometimes instructions on the type and placement of the bandages are inscribed on them. Shrouds, particularly painted ones, become more common, particularly with red, a powerful color associated with the sun. Very typical of the third century BCE to the third century CE are different colored bandages woven into lozenges or coffers, often marked by a gold boss or a smear of gilt in the center, that envelop the body, with painted panels or plaster masks covering the face.

Salima Ikram

See also: Afterlife; Animals; Animals, Sacred and Mummies; Mummies, Royal; Osiris

Further Reading

D'Auria, Sue, Peter Lacovara, and Catharine Roehrig. 1988. *Mummies & Magic: The Funerary Arts of Ancient Egypt*. Boston: Museum of Fine Arts.

Harris, James, and Kent Weeks. 1973. *X-Raying the Pharaohs*. New York: Charles Scribner's Sons.

Hawass, Zahi, Yehia Z. Gad, and Somaia Ismail. 2010. "Ancestry and Pathology in King Tutankhamun's Family." *Journal of the American Medical Association* 303: 638–647.

Ikram, Salima, and Aidan Dodson. 1998. *The Mummy in Ancient Egypt: Equipping the Dead for Eternity*. London: Thames and Hudson.

Jones, Jana. 2002. "Towards Mummification: New Evidence for Early Developments." *Egyptian Archaeology* 21: 5–7.

Riggs, Christina. 2014. *Unwrapping Ancient Egypt*. London: Bloomsbury.

Music and Musical Instruments

There is an exceptional amount of visual and physical evidence of the role of music in ancient Egypt and the instruments that were played. Tomb scenes of work in the field often include a musician with an instrument like a flute, keeping up the rhythm of the work

Funeral banquets of the New Kingdom (1550–1069 BCE) include a harper, and often the accompanying inscription has the words of a special harper's song, encouraging those on earth to have a good time because it will not last; everyone ends up in the cemetery. It is interesting that the harpist is often shown blind, and it is possible that being a harpist was a profession that a blind person could go into. In other banquet scenes, there was often a group of three female musicians, with a harp, a lute, and double oboe. There is a well-known scene in the Old Kingdom (2686–2160 BCE) Sakkara tomb of Mereruka; he is relaxing on his bed at home while his wife plays the harp for him. Religious rituals had their own instruments, clappers, and a shaking instrument, like the sistrum. Drums and trumpets can be seen in some military scenes, but their use was probably more to control and direct the soldiers than to play music.

On the other hand, there is no written music known from ancient Egypt and no evidence for musical notation. Musical knowledge must have been passed from

Scene of two female musicians in the tomb of the vizier Rekhmire on the West Bank of Thebes, dating to the earlier Eighteenth Dynasty. One woman is playing the harp, the most common ancient Egyptian musical instrument, and the other woman plays the lute, an instrument that came into Egypt from the Near East during this dynasty. (Corel)

teacher to student, but there is no evidence of training or practicing. Nothing is known of the life of a musician or of a musician's position in society. Music clearly played an important role in the life of the ancient Egyptians, but there is still more to be learned.

The musical instruments played by the ancient Egyptians can be broken into three main groups: (1) an instrument like a drum with a stretched membrane that vibrates; (2) an instrument like a flute, in which air is the vibrating method; and (3) an instrument like a harp, in which a stretched string vibrates. Other noise-making objects that were commonly used in ancient Egypt but were not really musical instruments were different types of clappers and shakers, almost all tied to religious or cult rituals or festivals.

The most common instruments of the Old Kingdom were the arched harp and a tube instrument like an end-blown flute, referred to as a *nay*, as this is the Arabic word for the exact same instrument that is still played in Upper Egypt today. They are commonly shown in private tomb scenes beginning in the Fourth Dynasty

(2613–2494 BCE). The musicians are almost always male. Female musicians become more common in the Middle Kingdom (2055–650 BCE), and in the New Kingdom, female groups of musicians are typical in banquet scenes. There were also clappers, flat wooden pieces carved in the shape of forearms with hands. These are most commonly associated with dancers and rituals or festivals tied to the goddess Hathor. Sometimes the wrist part of the clapper is decorated with the head of Hathor. These dance groups, called *khener*, performed for the goddess Hathor and are well-known from the Old and Middle Kingdoms. The goddess Hathor is tied to music and so is her son Ihy, who is always shown as a child holding a sistrum.

By the time of the New Kingdom, many more instruments are known, having come in from Syro-Palestine and areas of the Mediterranean with the formation of Egypt's empire in the Near East. There are also many painted tombs from the New Kingdom at Thebes that supply visual evidence of musical instruments and intact private tombs from Thebes, as well, that have preserved the actual instruments.

The most common harp is now boat-shaped and is sometimes played standing, as it is as tall as the harpist. Other stringed instruments are the lute, which came from Mesopotamia, and the lyre, which also came from the East. The very first representation of a lyre in Egypt was in the Twelfth Dynasty (1985–1773 BCE) Middle Kingdom tomb at Beni Hassan, Tomb 3, which showed Bedouins coming in from the Eastern Desert to trade black eye paint; one man seems to be playing the lyre as they arrive. The double oboe also comes to Egypt from Mesopotamia. It consists of two tubes, with finger holes on the front, joined at the top and going down in an inverted T-shape. It has been suggested that the musician played the notes on one tube, while the other tube acted as a drone.

Two particularly interesting instruments are the two trumpets that were found in the Tomb of King Tutankhamun (1336–1327 BCE) in the Valley of the Kings. A gilded copper or bronze one was found in a box in the antechamber, while a silver one was in the southeast corner of the burial chamber wrapped in reeds. Inside each trumpet was a wooden core that fit exactly into the entire instrument. The bell-shaped ends of the trumpets were decorated with figures of the deities Ra, Amun, and Ptah, and both have the name of the king on them. The silver trumpet was played in 1939 in the Cairo Museum and broadcast to the world on BBC radio. It shattered, possibly because of the modern mouthpiece inserted, but was able to be repaired. In 1941, the copper one was blown.

Lisa K. Sabbahy

See also: Beni Hasan; Dance; Silver; Tomb of Tutankhamun

Further Reading

Manniche, Lise. 1976. *Musical Instruments from the Tomb of Tutankhamun*. Oxford: Griffith Institute.

Manniche, Lise. 1991. *Music and Musicians in Ancient Egypt*. London: British Museum Press.

Onstine, Suzanne. 2016. "Women's Participation in the Religious Hierarchy of Ancient Egypt." In S. Budin and J. Turfa, eds. *Women in Antiquity: Real Women across the Ancient World*. London and New York: Routledge, pp. 218–228.

Myth

The Greek term *mythos* originally simply meant a "story," written or told. In most Egyptological studies, the term *myth* refers to a sacred narrative, a story about gods; human actors are rare in surviving Egyptian materials. A definition that harmonizes well with the surviving evidence from Egypt and beyond sees myth as a narrative tool seeking an explanation of human existence and social reality in symbolic terms.

Most Egyptian myths can be divided into two broad groups: cosmic and royal. These groups intersect, however, because kingship was conceived as modeled on the rule of the solar creator in the sky, while the organization of the pantheon, in turn, reflected terrestrial political structures. What is more, in the Egyptian worldview, similarities in function or form can render deities and other actors interchangeable or lead to their being fused. A good example is child gods, such as youthful forms of Horus (e.g., Harpokrates), the lunar deities Ihy and Khonsu, or the young sun god Harakhte or Nefertem. The iconography of all these can interchange, and in myth, they may adopt one another's parents and functions. Such overlaps can lead to fusions or syncretism of deities, and the new divine form may then supplant the traditional deities in mythical settings. The king, as the representative of Horus on earth, easily slots into this system.

Some texts equate two or more deities explicitly. In Coffin Text 331, when the goddess Hathor proclaims, "I am Wadjet," she refers to her own function as the Solar Eye of the morning, which is commonly manifested in the uraeus goddess, the cobra that spits fire against the sun god's enemies. In such cases, the second deity, Wadjet, essentially functions as a classifier, expressing a particular set of characteristics or role. This also finds expression in the metaphorical use of deities, as when, in a Demotic wisdom book, all women are said to represent the "work" of either Mut or Hathor. Here Mut serves as a metaphor for the benevolent, maternal woman and Hathor for the more volatile and dangerous female, who can also be embodied in the leonine Sakhmet or Tefnut. All these goddesses share much of their iconography and are often syncretistically fused.

On the opposite end of the mythical spectrum, a deity may have many functions, of which only a selection is evoked in any one context. Their mythical personality may therefore seem inconsistent, appearing with diverging characteristics. Hathor, with her many aspects, is the prototype of all women, which means that she can be a mother, daughter, and wife. Some mythical groupings hence represent her as the child and spouse of the sun god or of Horus, while in other combinations, she is their mother—illustrating the flexibility of myth. When mythical narratives were written down, such flexibility became restricted to some extent, but it remained characteristic of Egyptian myth.

SOLAR MYTHS

The dominant cosmic myths concerning the progression of the sun across the sky emphasize birth or the cyclical reappearance of the solar creator out of the chaotic primeval ocean, which is equated with night. The constant unfailing quality of this event was seen as a token of cosmic order, *Maat*, and eternal cyclically renewed life. This process and speculation on what happened to the sun when it disappeared from view in the evening could be expressed by means of various mythical images and actors. During the diurnal cycle, the morning sun, often shown as the dung beetle Khepri, pushed the solar disk up into the sky, or it was born as a solar child (commonly Harakhte) by the sky goddess Nut, frequently shown seated within the sun disk, on the fender of the solar barque, or atop a budding lotus flower as Nefertem.

The mature sun god Ra appears as a hawk. He travels across the sky in a barque, with a retinue of helpers that may include Seth, who in the Osiris myth is a nemesis of Osiris and Horus. Seth wards off evil embodied in the snake demon Apophis, who is intent on halting the solar journey and interrupting the cosmic cycle. In his evening form, the sun god Atum normally appears as a ram-headed anthropomorphic figure, often explicitly shown as aged and seated within a solar disk. Sunset conceptions include the sky goddess Nut swallowing the sun or its being received on the horns of the cow goddess Hathor in the western mountain of Thebes, from where it embarks on a journey through the underworld, the Duat.

The sun god's return to the eastern horizon is the particular focus of the Netherworld Books, which describe the solar process through the divisions and

The god Seth in the prow of the solar boat, protecting the sun god, Ra, from the evil serpent Apophis. The depiction is from a Third Intermediate Period Book of the Dead. (Werner Forman/Universal Images Group/Getty Images)

landscapes of the Duat. Helping deities and demons propel the solar barque through this realm. The blessed dead are temporarily revived as the barque passes by, a conception modeled on the image of the ruler of the netherworld, Osiris, who is often shown as illuminated by the sun god. This luminous event is also understood as the merging of the sun god with Osiris in the middle of the night, with the latter understood as the sun's nighttime equivalent. The resulting form, Ra-Osiris, is a powerful guarantor of cyclical rejuvenation. The judgment of the dead seems to also be associated with the middle of the night.

Further hawk-headed, and thus celestial, deities display solar aspects and are fused in iconography and myth. Notable is Horus the Behdite, who is especially associated with Edfu, in Upper Egypt. The Ptolemaic Period (332–30 BCE) temple of Edfu bears one of the most complete mythical accounts of a story elsewhere known as the *Contendings of Horus and Seth*, with Horus vanquishing his and his father's enemy, Seth, in the form of a hippopotamus. This myth was performed in an annual festival and provides important evidence for cultic drama. While its core derives from the Osirian cycle, large parts bear cosmic meanings, potentially describing how the sun god returns northward after the winter solstice. Several mythical accounts make it clear that the sun god is old and weak at the end of the day or year, creating an opportunity for rebellion.

In *The Book of the Heavenly Cow*, an uprising is explicit. Mankind has plotted against Ra, and the demoralized sun god calls on his disk and Eye goddess, leonine Hathor-Sakhmet, to punish humankind. Once unleashed, she cannot be easily stopped, so the land is inundated with red ochre–colored beer, which the goddess mistakes for blood and drinks, rendering her inebriated and happy. Thus, humankind is saved.

The leonine Eye goddess, as Hathor-Tefnut, also features in another cosmic myth that accounts for an absent solar Eye—commonly interpreted as an explanation for the winter solstice. The solar Eye is said to be "distant," having departed from the god to dwell in Nubia or the Fayum oasis. In the *Myth of the Solar Eye* or *The Distant Goddess*, the Eye needs to be coaxed back to Egypt and becomes enraged when she finds herself supplanted; she must then be appeased with beer, offerings, and music in the course of important annual festivals.

LUNAR MYTHS

The moon god Thoth is the deputy or vizier of the sun god at night. As the nighttime counterpart of the sun god, Osiris can also appear as the moon. One possible explanation for the anger of the solar Eye in the *Myth of the Distant Goddess* may be that it is directed at a lunar Eye; it is Thoth, with the Eye goddess's brother Shu, who retrieves her from Nubia. The moon's waxing and waning through the month lent itself to a mythical account of a stolen cosmic Eye that must be restored, and another mythical explanation hence refers to it as the Eye of Horus, which was stolen from Horus by Seth when the two fought, according to an episode of the *Contendings of Horus and Seth*. As the Eye started out "far" from its owner and was later brought back, the "Eye of Horus" became a common term for anything desired and brought, especially cultic offerings.

STELLAR MYTHS

Some major gods were identified with stars or constellations from early on. Osiris is identified with the constellation Orion from the Pyramid Texts onward, and his sister-wife, Isis, with Sothis-Sirius, while their nemesis Seth can appear as the Big Dipper. Later astronomical compositions identify various forms of Horus with planets and associate Seth with Mercury. Some scholars propose that episodes of the *Contendings of Horus and Seth* describe the behavior of Venus and Mercury as interchanging morning and evening Stars. Astronomical texts and images present additional mythical narratives, mostly explaining specific astral phenomena. Nut gives birth to and swallows the stars daily, just as she does the sun.

SOURCES

Evidence for myth can be found in many contexts and sources, of which only a tiny fraction has survived, and many myths were surely present in the oral sphere before written or pictorial formats emerged. In the absence of fully narrative mythical accounts, scholars often speak of mythemes, sections of myths. Royal or priestly titles as well as personal names may reveal functions or mythical aspects of deities. The earliest known title of kings, the Horus name, demonstrates that god's royal function during state formation. Later priestly titles and epithets of the God's Wives of Amun include "God's Hand" and "God's Daughter," referring to episodes of solar myths. The names of some deities may themselves reveal mythical conceptions. An example is Onuris, "He who brings the Distant One," whose name relates to the myth of the solar Eye that was removed from the sun god and returned in the *Myth of the Distant Goddess*. The earliest extensive texts about gods and myths stem from the funerary *Pyramid Texts*, which provide abundant information about names, functions, and groupings of gods, albeit not in coherent narrative form. The later Book of the Dead adds pictorial illustrations to many of the conceptions presented. Hymns, which praise the manifold powers of a god or goddess, paint a detailed picture of a deity's aspects and functions, including their myths.

Theological and cult-geographical materials inscribed on some temples explain particular forms and festivals of deities and provide more information on myths. Also, rituals, partly yielding from the same contexts and partly from ritual papyri, may ascribe mythical roles and characteristics to cultic performers and cite mythical episodes to make the ritual more effective. The same is true for magical and medical texts, which usually focus on a mythical precedent—the patient is to share in the good fate of his mythical counterpart—normally Horus, who was protected by Isis, or the victorious sun god overcoming the attack of the snake demon Apophis. Some myths, such as the *Story of Isis and Re*, are to date only attested in such contexts.

The iconography of deities often enhances our understanding of myths, as Egyptian gods are usually represented bearing a functionally or mythically relevant icon on, or as, their heads. Some icons represent full mythemes, as with the

Hathor cow stepping out of the Western Mountain at Thebes to receive the setting sun. In a few cases, whole myths are represented in sequences of images, as in the *Netherworld Books* or the *Myth of the Divine Birth.* Some architectural forms represent material realizations of myths. The forms of tombs embody mythical conceptions of the afterlife, with pyramidal superstructures evoking solar rebirth from the primeval mound and New Kingdom (1550–1069 BCE) royal tombs' descending corridors representing the sun's descent into the Theban mountain and progression through the night. The design of temples incorporates such features as a primeval mound, a "horizon" represented by the pylon, and a sacred lake, which was particularly important in temples of solar Eye goddesses and may have represented the red flood associated with the *Destruction of Mankind.*

Structures could be reinterpreted as mythical locations, as with the tomb of the First Dynasty (3000–2890 BCE) king Djer, which was considered to be the tomb of Osiris no later than the Middle Kingdom, beginning in 2055 BCE. During festivals, different parts of such mythical landscapes were connected in ritual processions, with statues of gods interacting in keeping with mythical stories. An example is the annual celebration of the "Mysteries of Osiris" at Abydos, which reenacted the god's death and resurrection.

In sum, Egyptian myth was a means of conceptualizing and describing the world, and at the same time, it served to explain and control it. Hence, myths could be used for such variegated purposes as explaining cosmic phenomena, legitimizing a particular political situation or change, or plainly providing the metaphors to express a social situation or need. Its inherent flexibility ensured its survival, in various recreations and adaptations, over many millennia and beyond Egypt proper, as evident, for example, in the dissemination of the Isis cult throughout the Greco-Roman world. Its meanings and structures must thus have been relevant in non-culture-specific ways.

Katja Goebs

See also: Funerary Books, Royal; Hathor; Horus; Kingship Myths; Myths, Creation; Osiris; Ra

Further Reading

Baines, J. 1991. "Egyptian Myth and Discourse: Myth, Gods, and the Early Written and Iconographic Record." *Journal of Near Eastern Studies* 50: 81–105.

Frankfort, H., et al. 1946. *The Intellectual Adventure of Ancient Man: An Essay on Speculative Thought in the Ancient Near East.* Chicago and London: University of Chicago Press.

Goebs, K. 2002. "A Functional Approach to Egyptian Myth and Mythemes." *Journal of Ancient Near Eastern Religions* 2: 27–59.

Goebs, K. 2013. "Egyptian Mythos as Logos: Attempt at a Redefinition of 'Mythical Thinking.'" In E. Frood and A. McDonald, eds. *Decorum and Experience: Essays in Ancient Culture for John Baines.* Oxford: Griffith Institute, pp. 127–134.

Hornung, E. 1996. *Conceptions of God in Ancient Egypt: The One and the Many.* Translated by J. Baines. Ithaca, NY: Cornell University Press.

Pinch, G. 2002. *Egyptian Mythology.* Oxford: Oxford University Press.

Myths, Creation

Ancient Egyptian creation is conceived of in terms of the generation of form and matter out of "undifferentiatedness," which is identified with disorder and chaos. The creative act hence also orders the disordered components of precreation, which are—most explicitly in the traditions associated with Hermopolis—conceived as four elements, which become eight with their female counterparts and so make up an Ogdoad. Their ordering implies the introduction of *Maat,* or cosmic order, into the world and serves as a mythical prototype for overcoming the ubiquitous threats to this order. Creation is accomplished when the creator god Atum ("He who is not" and also "He who completes") emerges, without being born, from the undifferentiated primeval ocean, Nun. The creator uses his mental and physical powers to fashion the world out of himself by differentiating his "oneness" into separate and gendered elements, thus "making One into Many." Religious centers around Egypt developed their own versions of this creation account.

HELIOPOLIS

Heliopolis, the Old Kingdom (2686–2160 BCE) theological center, is associated with the oldest version of Egyptian creation. It is the location of the primeval mound upon which the self-created, as yet undifferentiated, Atum transforms himself into the created world; in this role, he may also appear as Tatenen, a personification of the "rising land," or the cosmic child god Nefertem, the lotus flower, as or from which the solar creator appeared on the mound. By self-impregnation—usually through masturbation and swallowing his own semen—he engenders the male Shu, the god of light and air, and the female Tefnut, who may represent humidity but in later periods is one of the solar Eye goddesses and forms of the sun god's disk. They come forth from his mouth, being spat or coughed out. This first generation of created gods conceives the second, the sky goddess Nut and the earth god Geb, through sexual intercourse. Nut arches above Geb during the day, supported by her father, Shu. At night, Geb and Nut conceive the sun god and the many stars anew. They are born between her thighs in the morning and evening, respectively; travel along her belly; and are swallowed again at the other end of the daily cycle.

The most prominent children of Nut are those of the Osiris cycle—Osiris, Isis, Seth, and Nephthys—representing the institution of kingship and the state as well as aspects of the eternal cycle of royal birth, accession, death, and succession. The mythical cycle ends with the accession of Horus, son of Osiris and Isis, who is embodied in the reigning king. Together with their ancestors, these deities constitute the Heliopolitan Ennead, the Group of Nine Gods, and the basis of the state pantheon. As the sun god is born again every day, and in his evening form is also called Atum, every sunrise represents a repetition of the moment of creation, in Egyptian terms "the first time." Since the Heliopolitan Ennead thus includes deities both of the solar cycle and of the Osirian family, those mythical complexes were seen as a single unit already in the Pyramid Texts. Perhaps to prove a local temple's preeminence over Heliopolis at times when the latter was no longer the predominant religious center, new versions of this myth were developed.

HERMOPOLIS

Hermopolis in Middle Egypt was the cult center of the lunar god Thoth. Its creation account focuses on the eight cited aspects of precreation, the Ogdoad, comprising four male and four female primeval deities in frog and snake form, respectively. These most commonly comprise Unlimitedness (*Heh* and *Hehet*), Undifferentiatedness of the watery abyss (*Nun* and *Naunet*), Darkness (*Kek* and *Keket*), and Hiddenness (*Amun* and *Amunet*). These deities produce an egg bearing the creator, who was likely Thoth in origin, but in known texts is always the solar (Ra-)Atum. After this point, creation follows the Heliopolitan model. Although parts of the myth appear from the Pyramid Texts onward, most attestations are late.

MEMPHIS

The creation account of Memphis focuses on the faculties of creative thought, *Sia*, and utterance, *Hu*, of the chief local deity, the god of craftsmen, Ptah, who in this way devises the processes first attested at Heliopolis. In this way, he appears as preeminent to the Heliopolitan creator. A full account of the Memphite Creation is attested only from the Twenty-Fifth Dynasty (747–656 BCE), and it may have been devised at that time or potentially in the Ramesside Period (1295–1069 BCE), when Memphis gained in importance.

ESNA

At Esna, Hu and Sia are attributed to a local creator deity, the female equivalent of the primeval ocean, Mehetweret or Neith, who is conceptualized as the celestial cow, Ihet. In a well-preserved Roman Period (30 BCE–495 CE) text, Neith/Ihet creates the world by making seven utterances that lead to the sun's birth out of the Nun and to the creation of the world and of humanity—with man evolving from the tears of the sun god's eye and the gods from the saliva of his lips.

THEBES

In Thebes, the Heliopolitan creation was elaborated by attributing stages of the creative act to the local deity Amun-Ra. The fullest known account dates to the Ptolemaic-Roman Period (332 BCE–495 CE), when it was inscribed in the temple of Khonsu, Amun's offspring with his consort Mut. Amun, the "Hidden One," begot himself in secret and came forth from an egg atop a primeval mound. In this version, he appears in the form of the snake Kematef, "He who completes his time," who first creates the Theban Ogdoad, and then the world and all other living beings from himself.

FAYUM

In the Fayum, a different episode is prefixed to the account. The Ptolemaic-Roman Period *Book of the Fayum* presents the local Lake Moëris as the primeval ocean from which creation emerged and which is at the same time embodied in a primeval creator, Nun. Nun presides over an Ogdoad of deities, identical with those of Hermopolis, and creates Amun; the rest of creation proceeds from there.

ELEPHANTINE

In Elephantine, a later episode within the creative process is the focus. The ram god Khnum forms humanity and their kas, as well as the gods, on his potter's wheel. Khnum evolved into a creator of all in later periods.

Egyptian creation accounts were thus developed and enhanced according to local, geographical, historical, and political requirements until a range of equally valid versions existed side by side. In this way, they poignantly illustrate the flexibility and adaptability of Egyptian myth.

Katja Goebs

See also: Kingship Myths; Memphis; Myth; Osiris; Ptah; Ra

Further Reading

Allen, J. P. 1988. *Genesis in Egypt: The Philosophy of Ancient Egyptian Creation Accounts*. Yale Egyptological Studies 2. New Haven, CT: Yale University Press.

Hornung, E. 1996. *Conceptions of God in Ancient Egypt: The One and the Many*. Translated by J. Baines. Ithaca, NY: Cornell University Press.

Lesko, L. 1991. "Cosmogonies and Cosmology." In B. Shafer, ed. *Religion in Ancient Egypt: Gods, Myths, and Personal Practice*. London: Routledge, pp. 88–122.

Pinch, G. 2002. *Egyptian Mythology*. Oxford: Oxford University Press.

N

Names. *See* Personal Names

Nile River

The Nile flows the entire length of Egypt, after originating much farther south in Africa. It starts out as two rivers, the Blue Nile and the White Nile, which merge together near Khartoum, in the Sudan. The water of the Blue Nile comes from Lake Tana, in Ethiopia. Early in the summer, monsoons in the Indian Ocean dump rain on the Ethiopian highlands. The rain runs down the highlands, taking soil with it, and flows into Lake Tana, which then fills the Blue Nile with water and silt. The Blue Nile carries 84 percent of the water that comes to Egypt in the annual inundation, while the White Nile, which flows all year from Lake Victoria, brings a steady stream of water but only makes up 14 percent of the Egyptian Nile's water (Brewer and Teeter 2007, 24).

The floodwaters are noticed in southern Egypt in the later part of July. The water spills over the natural silt levees along the river and fills up the land on both sides of the river, between the river and the desert plateaus. In Upper Egypt, the arable land is limited to narrow strips along the sides of the river, while the delta, or Lower Egypt, is wide and flat. In ancient times, there were five branches of the Nile in the delta that led to the Mediterranean Sea. The water not only irrigated the land but covered it with silt from both the White Nile and Blue Nile, which created a perfect fertilizer. The height of the inundation was very important, not only for the crop yield the following spring, but village houses and other structures would be damaged if the water was too high. A typical flood would put four to five feet of water over the fields. The water would be on the fields for up to two months before it soaked down into the soft clay beds below or drained away downstream.

Other than irrigation, fertilization, and a source of water, the Nile was also important to the ancient Egyptians for transportation. The Nile connected the whole country, and in the minds of the Egyptians, travel meant boats. Going downstream was with the current, but to go upstream, boats used a sail and tacked back and forth across the river, blown by the prevailing northeast winds. Travel, of course, was always fastest during the inundation, when the water was deepest. In the late spring and early summer before the inundation, the Nile's riverbed could be virtually empty of water.

The southern border of ancient Egypt was at the First Cataract, the last and northernmost of the six granite formations that broke up the Nile River. The Sixth

Nilometer

A nilometer is a way to watch how the water of the Nile is rising during inundation. It was a straight flight of stairs cut down into the ground, or sometimes cylindrical, like a large well, with the stairs going around the walls. Every year, the height of the water and the date were marked on the wall. The large state temples in Upper Egypt, such as Dendera and Edfu, had nilometers, as did the islands of Philae and Elephantine.

Lisa K. Sabbahy

Cataract is just north of modern Khartoum, in the Sudan. The cataracts made travel by boat treacherous in places, and the ancient Egyptians had to take boats out of the river and carry them around the cataracts or cut canals through the granite for the boats.

Lisa K. Sabbahy

See also: Agriculture; Lower Egypt; Ships and Shipping; Upper Egypt

Further Reading

Brewer, Douglas, and Emily Teeter. 2007. *Egypt and the Egyptians*. 2nd ed. Cambridge: Cambridge University Press.

Sampsett, Bonnie. 2003. *A Traveler's Guide to the Geology of Egypt*. Cairo: American University in Cairo Press.

Primary Document—Thutmose III Returns from a Campaign

In this text, King Thutmose III (1479–1425 BCE) is returning from a military campaign in the Sudan, and his boat cannot get through the canal cut in the cataract.

> Regnal year fifty, first month of summer, day twenty-two under the Majesty of the King of Upper and Lower Egypt, Menkheperra, given life. His Majesty ordered to dig this canal after he found it blocked with stones. No boat traveled upon it. He traveled upon it, his heart happy. He had slaughtered his enemies. Name of this canal: "The Canal is Well Opened. Menkheperra Lives Forever." The Canal will be cleaned every year by the fishermen of Elephantine.
>
> Source: Translated by Lisa K. Sabbahy from hieroglyphic text. Sethe, Kurt. 1961. *Urkunden der 18. Dynastie*. Berlin: Academie Verlag, 814, lines 10–815, line 2.

Nomes and Provincial Administration

Egypt had a complex bureaucracy operating at the national, regional, and local levels. Information for provincial administration is found throughout pharaonic history; however, the extant textual, archaeological, and art historical records of the Old and Middle Kingdoms, a period from 2686 to 1650 BCE, particularly in Middle and Upper Egypt, are the most abundant. Some sites are better understood than others due to the nature of the textual and archaeological records, and it remains a question as to the degree to which a single system operated in each province and the extent of regional differences over time.

SOURCES

Textual records, including royal and private monuments; documentary sources, such as administrative papyri and ostraca; and archaeological remains, including those of settlements, objects, and pottery, provide evidence for provincial administrative officials, their duties, and the system in which they worked. Private monuments, including tombs and funerary stelae, are inscribed with administrative titles and autobiographical information, which can be used to reconstruct the timeline and affairs of officials' careers. Archaeologically, seal impressions, small pieces of mud that preserve the impression of a scarab or stamp seal, have proven critical for understanding administrative activities in settlements and fortresses. Through collating the institutions, titles, and designs of seals; their back types; and their archaeological contexts, scholars can trace the daily activities of different officials and identify networks of interaction between different institutions at the local, provincial, and national levels.

DEFINING THE PROVINCES

The ancient Egyptian word for a "province" was *sepat*. Today, the term "nome," the Greek *nomos*, is used. There were 42 nomes—22 in Upper Egypt, from Elephantine to Meidum, and 20 in Lower Egypt, Memphis, and the delta. The nomes are conventionally numbered from south to north, following the Nile; for example, Elephantine is the first nome of Upper Egypt. Each nome also had a unique standard that would serve as its emblem and a primary administrative center, which could, in some cases, such as with Elephantine, be identified as the nome itself. Other nomes are named by their symbol, such as the Oryx nome, or the 16th nome of Upper Egypt.

Smaller divisions of the Nile valley are attested as early as the Early Dynastic Period (3000–2686 BCE), although evidence for a coherent administrative system is not encountered until the Old Kingdom (2686–2160 BCE). The system was likely not imposed as a single administrative act, but rather developed around key population and religious centers and expanded along with the state. Irrigation and agriculture may have played a role in establishing early boundaries. These boundaries were relatively stable, but they were not static and changed over time, as did the primary city in some nomes.

It has been proposed by Engel that an organized provincial system may date as early as King Den of the First Dynasty (3000–2890 BCE). Seal impressions, labels attached to burial goods, and pot-marks and inscriptions on vessels in royal and elite tombs of the Early Dynastic Period bear symbols that can be associated with specific locations, including those that later constituted nomes. Inscriptional evidence this early is limited and provides no clear information of how different locations operated or the precise nature of their relationship to and interaction with the state. Inked pottery inscriptions from the Step Pyramid complex of King Djoser (2667–2648 BCE) identify administrators of the Oryx nome, indicating the existence of provincial officials by the time of the Third Dynasty.

During the reign of either King Huni (2637–2613 BCE) or King Sneferu (2613–2589 BCE) of the early Fourth Dynasty, seven small accretion-technique step pyramids were erected at key provincial centers, stretching from Elephantine to Seila, in the Fayum. These pyramids were not burials, but rather markers of royal authority outside the capital and, perhaps, foci for the celebration of the royal cult. Their placement may have been in association with royal domains or estates, giving evidence for royal investment and interest in the provinces. Clear evidence for the organization of the provinces and their officials into a larger system becomes more abundant during the course of the Old Kingdom. Administrative titles are frequently encountered in private inscriptions from the Fourth Dynasty on. Fragments of relief from the depictions of the seasons in the sun temple of King Niuserra of the Fifth Dynasty (2445–2421 BCE) depict a procession of personified locations, including nomes, presenting offerings.

STRUCTURE AND INSTITUTIONS

The vizier was the administrative head of the country, above administrators of Upper and Lower Egypt, who, in turn, oversaw the provinces. During the late Middle Kingdom (2055–1650 BCE), the Upper Egyptian nomes were organized together and administered as "the District of the Head of the South" under the office of vizier. The official in charge of a nome is called the "nomarch." The specific Egyptian title used for this position changed over time and, in some periods, varied geographically. The primary title during the Old and early Middle Kingdom was the "Great Chief" (*hery-tep aa*) of the nome, first attested in the Sixth Dynasty. The title ceased being used during the late Twelfth Dynasty, and the position of mayor (*haty-a*) of the primary city in a province took on the responsibilities of the office.

The position of nomarch, although a royal appointment, was frequently held by a single family, with the position passing between male family members. Family genealogies of officials can be reconstructed through their funerary monuments. The office was inheritable, but it could also be sold. The Second Intermediate Period Juridical Stela in the Cairo Museum (JE 52453) relates the inheritance and sale of the office of *haty-a* of the town of el-Kab between two family members. The office of the vizier was involved in the transaction, and the stela commemorating it was erected in temple of Amun at Karnak. These local families amassed considerable power and resources over time. In Upper Egypt, two Old Kingdom mayors of Elephantine and Edfu, Heqaib and Isi, were later deified, with local cults lasting into the Second Intermediate Period (1650–1550 BCE). Powerful local families could present a threat to national unity and the state, particularly during times of weak royal authority. The decentralized nature of the First Intermediate Period (2160–2055 BCE) resulted in increased local autonomy and wealth in the provinces, challenging the state and serving as bases for competing political dynasties.

Nevertheless, the concentration of power within local elite families was a necessity for stability and control of areas and resources outside the capital zone. The state navigated its relationship with the provinces in different ways, including intermarriage between women of the royal house and elite families. Provincial officials often speak to their royal appointment in their funerary texts and the pleasure of the king in their carrying out of duties, but the state also removed officials. The Coptos Decree of Nubkheperra Intef of the Seventeenth Dynasty (1580–1550 BCE), in the Cairo Museum (JE 30770), records an inspection conducted by national officials and royal intervention, stripping a corrupt local official, Teti, and his heirs, of his office in the local temple of Min and its associated benefits.

The mayors of the late Middle Kingdom were also in charge of local religious institutions, bearing the additional title of "Overseer of Priests" or "Overseer of the Temple." In addition to its religious importance, the local temples had associated production facilities supplying temple offerings that were, in turn, used to pay its staff. The mayoral residence and local temple were key administrative and economic nodes, interacting with one another and other administrative units, such as production and storage facilities, agricultural land, and human resources. Although not a provincial capital, the town of Wah-Sut in Abydos, associated with the mortuary complex of King Senusret III (1870–1831 BCE), exemplifies this integrated network of local, regional, and national administrative units. Through the seal impressions found at different areas of the site, in association with the archaeological remains and textual sources, archaeologists have modeled the operations of the mayoral residence, temple, production and storage areas, and houses of other local elite officials, including their interactions with other institutions in Abydos and the state.

The nomarchs also had obligations relating to the management of state resources. Taxes were assessed and collected on agriculture and livestock. The Eighteenth Dynasty tomb of Rekhmire (TT 100) shows a procession of local and regional officials bringing taxes of cattle, agricultural products, and other goods. The text called the *Duties of the Vizier*, also in Rekhmire's tomb, narrates the relationship between the provinces and the state vis-à-vis the office of vizier. The date of the text and the administrative system it describes, whether belonging to the Middle Kingdom or New Kingdom, or a combination thereof, remain debated; however, it presents an Egyptian view of the nature of this relationship.

Provinces were also responsible for supplying labor for royal works, including construction projects and expeditions, that is, "corvée labor." Nomarchs were charged with raising the labor, and individual Egyptians were responsible for participating. These workforces were meticulously documented. A list of fugitives who absconded from service are identified by their regional affiliations in the Thirteenth Dynasty "fugitive list" on Papyrus Brooklyn 35.1446. Specific nomes served as important bases for access to mining and trade routes to the Eastern and Western Deserts and Red Sea. Local leaders in these areas were often involved, including goods acquisition and raising the expeditionary force. Rock inscriptions and graffiti in mining and quarrying areas evidence the officials on the expeditions and the parts of the Nile valley from whence they came.

Kathryn E. Bandy

See also: Administration; Labor; Officials; Seals and Sealing; Vizier

Further Reading

Engel, Eva-Maria. 2013. "The Organisation of a Nascent State: Egypt until the Beginning of the 4th Dynasty." In Juan Carlos Moreno García, ed. *Ancient Egyptian Administration*. Leiden: Brill, pp. 19–40.

Grajetzki, Wolfram. 2009. *Court Officials of the Egyptian Middle Kingdom*. London: Duckworth.

Marouard, Gregory, and Hratch Papazian. 2012. "The Edfu Pyramid Project: Recent Investigations at the Last Provincial Step Pyramid." *Oriental Institute News and Notes* 213: 3–9.

Moreno García, Juan Carlos. 2013. "The Territorial Administration of Egypt in the 3rd Millennium." In Juan Carlos Moreno García, ed. *Ancient Egyptian Administration*. Leiden: Brill, pp. 85–152.

Quirke, Stephen. 2004. *Titles and Bureaux of Egypt, 1850–1700 BC*. London: Golden House Publications.

van den Boorn, G. P. F. 1998. *The Duties of the Vizier: Civil Administration in the Early New Kingdom*. Studies in Egyptology. London: Kegan Paul.

Wegner, Josef. 2012. "Institutions and Officials at South Abydos: An Overview of the Sigillographic Evidence." *Cahiers de Recherches de l'Institut de Papyrologie et d'Égyptologie de Lille: Société Urbaines en Égypte et au Soudan* 22: 77–108.

Willems, Harco. 2013. "Nomarchs and Local Potentates: The Provincial Administration in the Middle Kingdom." In Juan Carlos Moreno García, ed. *Ancient Egyptian Administration*. Leiden: Brill, pp. 341–392.

Nubia

Nubia is the name used in modern scholarship for northern Sudan, usually divided into Lower (or northern) Nubia and Upper (or southern) Nubia. The name *Nubia* was first used in the Roman period (30 BCE–641 CE) for the region south of Egypt, beginning at the First Cataract of the Nile and ending just south of the Dongola Reach. During the prehistoric period, this region was home to Nubian cultures now called the A-Group and C-Group. Contemporary to the Egyptian Old Kingdom, Nubia was the location of several indigenous chiefdoms known by the Egyptians as Wawat, Irtjet, Satju, Yam, and Medja. Egyptian involvement in Lower Nubia during the Middle Kingdom (1980–1760 BCE) was characterized by the creation of a militarized buffer zone through the construction of a string of massive mudbrick forts. During the New Kingdom Period (1539–1292 BCE) of colonial expansion, the Egyptians regionally divided the whole of Nubia for administrative purposes into Wawat (Lower Nubia) and Kush (Upper Nubia), over which the king's son of Kush presided.

The A-Group (3700–2800 BCE), so termed by American archaeologist George Reisner in 1907 after his identification of several previously unknown prehistoric cultures in Lower Nubia, was a complex seminomadic society. Scholars divide the A-Group culture into three chronological phases: Early, Classic, and Terminal. A-Group settlements and cemeteries are restricted to Lower Nubia, the northernmost site being located at El Kubania, 10 kilometers north of Aswan, and the southernmost site located just south of the Second Cataract. A-Group cemeteries, most notably at Qustul, Dakka, and Sayala, illustrate a stratified society of wealthy, middle, and lower classes. Tomb sizes varied greatly and contained varying numbers and types of prestige objects, such as "eggshell ware," items of personal adornment, mirrors, and copper axes. A-Group burials were usually oval pits less than a meter deep in which individuals were buried on their sides in a contracted position, sometimes on reed mats. While the A-Group peoples certainly had a trade relationship with Predynastic Egypt as evidenced by Egyptian objects in A-Group burials, the A-Group did not constitute an offshoot of Egyptian culture as previously thought. The final phase, Terminal A-Group, came to an abrupt end shortly after the Egyptian unification of Upper and Lower Egypt, and evidence of Lower Nubian cultures until the C-Group several centuries later is absent from the archaeological record. The existence of Reisner's B-Group burials as a unique cultural development that was intended to fill this chronological gap has since been recognized as impoverished or plundered A-Group burials.

The C-Group (2300–1600 BCE), similarly named as the result of Reisner's initial excavations, emerged as a distinct pastoral society in Lower Nubia as Egyptian control of the region lessened toward the end of the Old Kingdom (2543–2120 BCE). Scholars divide the C-Group culture into five chronological phases: Ia, Ib, IIa, IIb, and III, corresponding to the Sixth Dynasty (2305–2118 BCE) through the Second Intermediate Period (1759–1539 BCE) in Egypt. C-Group peoples inhabited the area between the First and Second Cataracts of the Nile and reoccupied many A-Group sites. Cemeteries make up the majority of known C-Group sites, located on both banks of the Nile. The importance of livestock, primarily goats, sheep, and cattle, is demonstrated by the presence of animal burials within the tombs and the animal skulls, sometimes painted, that were placed around the tombs. C-Group burials consisted of stone rings within which the contracted body of the deceased was laid and covered with gravel. The presence of Egyptian objects in C-Group burials was the result of continued interaction with Egypt during the Old Kingdom and First Intermediate Period. C-Group cemeteries continued to be used until the end of the Second Intermediate Period, when the C-Group culture disappeared from the archaeological record. This disappearance is usually interpreted as the result of "Egyptianization" through prolonged contact with generations of Egyptians stationed at the forts.

During the Middle Kingdom, Senusret I (1920–1875 BCE) began the construction of eight forts between the Second and Third Cataracts to solidify Egypt's control of Lower Nubia. This first wave of Egyptian expansion consisted of "plains type" forts built along the banks of the Nile (now called Buhen, Aniba, Kuban, Serra, and Ikkur), which were composed of meters-thick mudbrick ramparts with round or square towers and access to the Nile by a gateway. The interiors of the forts contained mudbrick buildings around narrow streets that were used for barracks, workspaces, and granaries.

The second wave of Egyptian expansion into Lower Nubia occurred when Senusret III (1837–1819 BCE) extended Egyptian control by beginning construction of new forts (now called Mirgissa, Shalfak, Semna, Kumma, and Uronarti)

King's Son of Kush

Despite Egypt's many campaigns to Nubia during the Old Kingdom, and its militarized presence during the Middle Kingdom, it was not until the beginning of the New Kingdom that an administrative position was created to manage Wawat (Lower Nubia) and Kush (Upper Nubia) as colonized regions of Egypt. The invention of a new position, first known as the "king's son and overseer of foreign countries" during the reign of Amenhotep I (1514–1494 BCE), then remodeled as the "king's son of Kush" under Thutmose I (1493–1483 BCE), expressed Egypt's desired colonial relationship with Nubia by appointing an Egyptian official who acted as viceroy over the region at the behest of the Egyptian king. Although not a literal relative of the king, the "king's son of Kush" maintained a close relationship with the king because of the political and economic importance of his position. Two deputies served him, one appointed over Wawat and one over Kush, and they were permanently stationed in Nubia. The king's son himself lived in Egypt, but he traveled south annually to oversee the administration of these southern regions, which included the formal collection of an annual tax of cattle, servants, soldiers, and luxury goods from each region. He also oversaw a regional army under the direction of the "commander of the archers of Kush" that, when necessary, reinforced the Egyptian king's imperial control over Kush by subduing Nubian revolts.

Taylor Bryanne Woodcock

on the bluffs at different points along the Second Cataract. These Middle Kingdom forts were designed to serve as garrisons for battalions of Egyptian soldiers sent on a regular basis from Egypt who provided security for Egyptian expeditions, monitored Nubian travelers, and patrolled the deserts, as described by their Egyptian names, including "Warding off the Bow-people" and "Repelling the *Medjay*." The "Semna Dispatches," a series of fragmented papyri composed by Egyptian administrators at the Fort of Semna, details some of the activities the Egyptian soldiers were expected to monitor and report to Egypt, including small groups of *Nehesyu* (Nubians) who visited the forts to conduct trade with the Egyptians. The location of the Kuban and Ikkur forts at the entrance to Wadi Allaqi, one of the important locations of Egyptians gold mines, gives an indication of their role in securing and protecting Egyptian access to Nubia's rich mineral resources. The forts also functioned as military and economic hubs for launching and supplying campaigns conducted by Egyptian kings against Kush in the south.

During the Second Intermediate Period, when Egypt lacked centralized power, the Egyptians relinquished control of these forts. Parts of some forts, such as Askut and Buhen, continued to be inhabited by descendants of the Egyptian Middle Kingdom population whose allegiance had shifted to the king of Kush in the south, as well as by people from the southern Kerma culture, who established a cemetery at Mirgissa.

During the New Kingdom, Egyptian modus operandi shifted from militaristic control in Nubia to colonial control, characterized by temple towns that were inhabited by Egyptian officials who often intermarried with local Nubians and shared settlements, cemeteries, and religious practices. During the reign of Thutmose III (1479–1425 BCE), Egyptian influence reached its southernmost point in

Upper Nubia when he established an Egyptian outpost at the Fourth Cataract. The Middle Kingdom forts themselves underwent a revival during the New Kingdom. Many were refortified and reoccupied by Egyptian personnel, and new settlements, cemeteries, and temples were established in connection with them. Occupation of the forts and temple towns by Egyptian soldiers and officials representing Egyptian interests in the region ended with the Twentieth Dynasty (1190–1077 BCE). These Lower Nubian sites, including those belonging to the A-Group and C-Group as well as all of the Middle Kingdom forts, except for Shalfak and Uronarti, were lost when they were submerged beneath Lake Nasser after the construction of the Aswan High Dam in 1964.

Taylor Bryanne Woodcock

See also: Abu Simbel; Forts and Fortifications

Further Reading

Adams, William. 1977. *Nubia: Corridor to Africa*. London: Allen Lane.

Edwards, David N. 2004. *The Nubian Past: An Archaeology of the Sudan*. London: Routledge.

Fisher, Marjorie M., Peter Lacovara, Salima Ikram, and Sue D'Auria, eds. 2012. *Ancient Nubia: African Kingdoms on the Nile*. Cairo: American University in Cairo Press.

O'Connor, David B. 1993. *Ancient Nubia: Egypt's Rival in Africa*. Philadelphia: University of Pennsylvania.

Shinnie, Peter. L. 1996. *Ancient Nubia*. London: Kegan Paul.

Primary Document—Senusret III's Conquest of Nubia

The granite cataracts on the Nile were a hindrance to river travel. This stela of the Twelfth Dynasty king Senusret III, the great conqueror of Nubia and builder of the forts in the Second Cataract, comes from his southernmost fort at Semna.

> Regnal year 16, third month of winter, the making of the boundary of His Majesty south to Heh.
>
> I have made my boundary south of my father's. I have made in excess of what has been handed over to me. I am a king who speaks and who acts. . . . Now, as for any of my sons who will maintain the boundary made by My Majesty, he is my son who is born to My Majesty. A son is pleasing, protective of his father, who maintains the boundary of who has begotten him. Now, as to who shall lose it, shall not fight for it, he is not my son, he is not born to me.

Source: Translated by Lisa K. Sabbahy from *Aegyptische Inschriften aus der Königlichen Museen zu Berlin*. 1913. Vol. I. Leipzig: J. C. Hinrichs, pp. 257–258, lines 2–5 and 17–20.

O

Obelisk

An obelisk is a tall pillar with a pointed or pyramidion top. For the most part, obelisks are made out of granite because a very hard stone is needed. An obelisk, like a pyramid, is a solar symbol, as it is related to the *benben,* the primeval mound on which the sun god appeared and created the world. Obelisks were set up in front of temples and also could be put in front of tombs. Generally, obelisks are put up in pairs, although single obelisks are not unknown. King Thutmose III (1479–1425 BCE) set up a single obelisk at the eastern end of Karnak Temple. The obelisk was moved to Rome in ancient times and now stands in the Piazza San Giovanni. The word *obelisk* comes from a Greek word; the ancient Egyptian name for one was *tekhen.*

The earliest known royal obelisk is that of the Sixth Dynasty king Teti I (2345–2323 BCE) at Heliopolis, although only the upper half is preserved. Some scholars include the earlier large, squat pyramidions known from the Fifth Dynasty Sun Temples at Abu Ghurab as obelisks, but they were much wider and also, at least based on the one of King Niuserra (2445–2421 BCE), the best preserved; it had a staircase inside so that the king, or high priest, could go up and view the sun. Beginning in the Fifth Dynasty, some private tombs at Giza and Sakkara had a pair of small, limestone obelisks out in front, with the name and titles of the tomb owner carved on the front side.

The oldest obelisk still standing at Heliopolis, and the only obelisk still preserved from the Middle Kingdom (2055–1650 BCE), is that of Senusret I, the second king of the Twelfth Dynasty. It was once part of a pair of obelisks set at the entrance into the Temple of Ra. The obelisk is 66 feet tall and weighs 120 tons (Quirke 2001, 136).

Many more obelisks were erected in the New Kingdom. Thutmose III placed a pair at Heliopolis, but they were later taken to Alexandria and set in front of the Temple of Julius Caesar. In more modern times, one of "Cleopatra's Needles" was taken to London and the other to New York City. Queen Hatshepsut (1473–1458 BCE) set up a pair of obelisks behind her father's Fourth Pylon at Karnak Temple. One still stands, at 98 feet tall (Quirke 2001, 138), and parts of the other can still be seen near the Sacred Lake. The inscription on the base of Hatshepsut's standing obelisk states that it took seven months to quarry them.

Still lying in the granite quarry at Aswan is another of Hatshepsut's obelisks, which unfortunately cracked and was left in place. It offers excellent evidence for how obelisks were quarried. The rock around the obelisk was pounded away

The remaining obelisk of a pair of granite obelisks that were set up at Karnak Temple by Hatshepsut, when she ruled as king. They were placed behind the Fourth Pylon, or gateway, built by her father, King Thutmose I. (Noelia Morán/Dreamstime.com)

by workers with balls of diorite, a harder stone than granite. Had this obelisk not cracked, it then would have been separated from the stone below it by wedges.

One of the scenes in the lowermost southern terrace of Hatshepsut's mortuary temple at Deir el-Bahari shows an enormous barge carrying the two obelisks being pulled by 15 small boats with rowers. The obelisks are laying end to end down the middle of the barge, still fastened to the sledges that were used to drag them. What scholars are not sure about, however, is how the ancient Egyptians stood these obelisks up, but they certainly used "building ramps, levers and ropes" (Arnold 2009, 166).

Lisa K. Sabbahy

See also: Abu Ghurab; Heliopolis; Ra; Ships and Shipping; Temples, State

Further Reading

Arnold, Dieter. 1991. *Building in Egypt: Pharaonic Stone Masonry.* Oxford: Oxford University Press.

Arnold, Dieter. 2009. *The Monuments of Egypt: An A–Z Companion to Ancient Egyptian Architecture.* Cairo: American University in Cairo Press.

Habachi, Labib. 1984. *The Obelisks of Egypt: Skyscrapers of the Past.* Cairo: American University in Cairo Press.

Naville, Edouard. 1908. *The Temple of Deir el-Bahari.* Part 6. London: Egypt Exploration Fund.

Quirke, Stephen. 2001. *The Cult of Ra: Sun Worship in Ancient Egypt.* London: Thames and Hudson.

Primary Document—Text from Obelisk of Hatshepsut

This text is from the base of one still standing obelisk of Queen Hatshepsut (1473–1458 BCE) at Karnak Temple. In the text, the queen is stressing her love and loyalty to her divine father, Amun.

She made as her monument for her father, Amun, Lord of the Thrones of the Two Lands, Foremost of Ipet Sut, making for him of two great obelisks of hard granite of the southern region, their upper part of electrum, of the best of all the foreign lands. They are seen on the two sides of the river. Their sun rays flood the Two Lands when the sun disk shines in their midst, like he appears in the horizon of heaven.

Source: Translated by Lisa K. Sabbahy from Sethe, Kurt. 1961. *Urkunden der 18. Dynastie*. Vol. 2. Berlin: Akademie Verlag, p. 362, lines 10–16.

Primary Document—Text from Stela at Mortuary Temple of Amenhotep III

This is the beginning of a description of the mortuary temple of King Amenhotep III (1390–1352) on a stela set up at that mortuary temple on the West Bank of the Nile at Thebes.

He made his monument for his father, Amun, Lord of the Thrones of the Two lands, making for him an august temple on the west side of Thebes, a monument for ever and ever, of beautiful, light sandstone. All worked with gold. The floor made pure with silver, all its doors with fine gold. Its width is very great, it is embellished forever.

Source: Translated by Lisa K. Sabbahy from Helck, Wolfgang. 1984. *Urkunden der 18. Dynastie. Text der Hefte 20–21*. Berlin: Academie Verlag, p. 1648, lines 6–12.

Primary Document—Text from Obelisk of Senusret

King Senusret (1956–1911 BCE), of the Middle Kingdom, erected two obelisks at the temple of the sun god Ra at Heliopolis. One obelisk of the pair still stands, and the following inscription is cut on each of the four sides. Three of the five names of the king's titulary use the phrase "repeating-of-births," which in English is perhaps best translated as a "renaissance."

Horus, long live the Repeating-of-Births, King of Upper and Lower Egypt, Kheperkara, Two Ladies, long Live the Repeating-of-Births. Son of Ra, Senusret, beloved of the souls of Heliopolis, given life forever. Horus of Gold, long live the Repeating-of-Births. The good god Kheperkara, First Occasion of the Heb-Sed. He made [it] to be given life forever.

Source: Translated by Lisa K. Sabbahy from the obelisk at the archaeological site of Heliopolis.

Offerings, Votive

Different terms are used as correlates or substitutes for the word *votive*: offerings, gifts, and dedications, among others. Each has a nuanced meaning, but in their most basic sense, in the context of ancient cult, these words refer to an item given to a deity to establish a connection between a person and the divine. A votive can be a personal item repurposed as an offering, such as some cloth or jewelry, or it could be made specifically for dedication. Though many votive objects are small or modest, they attest to the vivid and pervasive presence of the gods in the minds of Egyptians and their central role in daily life. In Egypt, where access to the gods was carefully controlled, particularly in temples where the gods were thought to live, votives gave some people the opportunity to bridge that space. On the large scale, investigations into donor identity and trends in votive type speak to dramatic shifts and adaptations in cult practice.

Ancient Egypt had a rich tradition of votive use from its earliest history, and votive objects abound in the archaeological record. Repurposed items can be difficult to identify as cult objects, while most perishables, such as food and flora, degrade and disappear, even in Egypt's dry climate. Nevertheless, large amounts of durable votives survive, particularly those made of stone, clay, metal, and faience. Rigorous study of small-scale votives has been limited, in part because past scholars have been drawn to larger finds, and also because the lack of context for many small finds hindered our understanding of their use. However, increasingly detailed archeological records from new excavations and archival reviews of older fieldwork have led to a recent surge in analysis and contextualization.

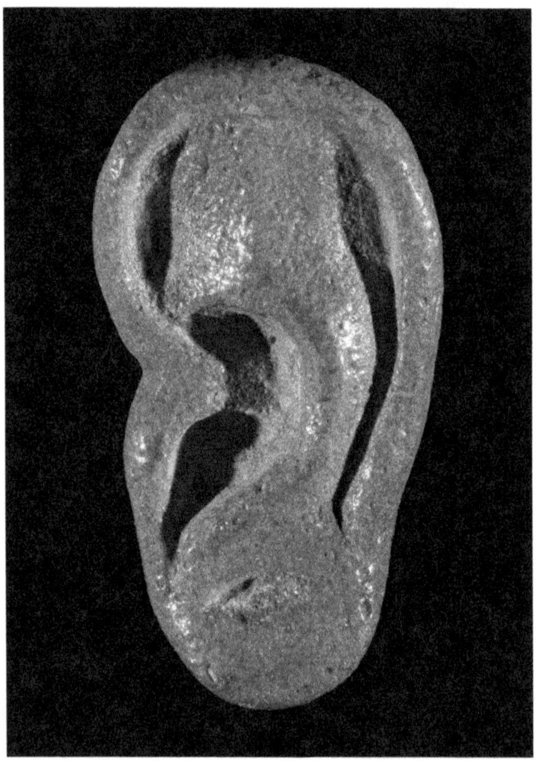

A pottery ear that was left at a small shrine as an offering to a god or goddess. An ear was left so that it would help the deity hear the prayer or request for help by the person who left the offering. Votive ears were very common as offerings in ancient Egypt and could also be made out of faience. (Christian Larrieu/Bridgeman Images)

Votives from the Early Dynastic Period (3000–2686 BCE) and the Old Kingdom (2686–2160 BCE) include items such as miniature vessels, amulets, and anthropomorphic and zoomorphic figures. One of the earliest votive offerings from Egypt is also among the most famous: the Narmer Palette was discovered in a temple at Hierakonpolis, ancient Nekhen, one of the most important sites in Upper Egypt during the Predynastic and Early Dynastic periods (5300–2686 BCE). This cosmetic palette is a ceremonial item inscribed with early Egyptian hieroglyphs, and it shows one of the first representations of Egyptian kingship; some of the images also imply the existence of a unified Upper and Lower Egypt.

Gaps, however, loom in the votive record, as a result of shifts in practice and variable preservation, temporally and geographically. In the Middle Kingdom (2055–1650 BCE), fewer votives are recorded, especially in temple settings. Instead, a greater wealth of evidence comes from the New Kingdom (1550–1069 BCE), particularly in the form of dedications to the goddess Hathor, such as those discovered at Deir el-Bahri. These included items that related to her cult or were seen as pleasing to the goddess, such as sistra, beads, and jewelry. Figurines of nude women, as well as phalli, emphasized her procreative and regenerative aspects.

The frequency and intensity of dedication reached its peak in the first millennium BCE, gradually increasing in the Third Intermediate Period (1069–664 BCE) and flourishing in the Late and Ptolemaic Periods (664–30 BCE). At temples, greater emphasis was placed on costlier items in metal and often comprised depictions of deities, including anthropomorphic, zoomorphic, and hybrid figures. A wide variety of animals were also systematically farmed and slaughtered to produce animal mummies that numbered in the millions; extensive catacombs were laboriously excavated to house them, best exemplified by those at the Sacred Animal Necropolis at North Sakkara.

Votive practices in temples gradually declined in the Roman Period (30 BCE–595 CE) as the Egyptian temple network atrophied. Domestic practice remained active, as we can see at Naukratis, where terracotta figures were used into the third century CE, but even in the domestic sphere, the variety and number decreased after the first century BCE. Most votives from the second and third millennia BCE were individually crafted, though faience was produced in molds early on. Serial production for metal and terracotta statuettes began comparatively later, in the latter part of the first millennium BCE.

The majority of votives were dedicated at temples. Usually they are discovered in secondary contexts called *caches*—burials of votives or other cult equipment after they have been taken off display. Votives were also used in domestic cult and were placed outside of tombs as a part of funerary cult. Domestic cult items could be housed in small shrines in the home or community and were commonly made of modest materials, such as clay or faience. Many domestic votives draw on temple motifs and knowledge, but they give greater weight to deities such as Bes, Tawaret, and nude goddesses, which have connotations of prosperity, rebirth, and fecundity. Some deities, such as child gods or Isis-Hathor, may inhabit multiple spheres of influence (temple, domestic, funerary), but they differ in material or style, depending on the context. After use, some domestic offerings were placed in deposits, while others were discarded in midden heaps or scattered loosely in town debris.

The burial and preservation of particular votives speaks to the vitality and power of such items. In ancient Egypt, statuary, amulets, cult equipment, and animal mummies were not lifeless simulacra. Instead, they were considered living, active participants in cult rites or spells. At least some underwent the ritual of the Opening of the Mouth, which animated the statues to allow them to breathe, eat, and see. Performers of ritual acts desired and utilized the power that these figures embodied, but that same force was also considered potent and dangerous. Burying such items helped to harness or tame that ritual power. Sometimes offerings also appear to have been deliberately broken—both those preserved in temples and discarded in towns. Breakage patterns also hint at an active role for some offerings in rituals; for instance, certain spells call for amulets or small statuettes to be broken or thrown into flames.

Because votive offerings had their own vitality, the material used to craft one was often chosen for its perceived latent power. Precious metals and rare, expensive woods were used for some of the most elaborate votive offerings. Their cost and artisanship undoubtedly added to their prestige. However, these materials also had appeal beyond their cost. The skin of the gods, for instance, was likened to gold and their bones to silver, imbuing both materials with divine significance. Cheaper materials also had magical connotations. Faience, an inexpensive silicate material, was valued for its shine and jewel-like appearance; its most common hue, a bright blue-green, had associations with life and rebirth. Various stones were selected for their color or strength, such as the deep blue of lapis lazuli. As a result, the value of a votive did not always have a direct correlation with its cost, and cheaper, ritually significant materials were desired by the wealthy and poor alike.

The identity of donors, and their motivations, can be difficult to assess, even in periods when votives were plentiful. Some offerings, such as large-scale temple statues, present a biography, including titles, in the hopes that the donor be included in the temple cult and share in the offerings presented to the temple's deity in perpetuity. Less august and smaller dedications often have brief formulaic inscriptions that may not include titles. Few detail the occasion or reasoning behind the offering. Domestic votives rarely have inscriptions of any kind. Thus, the status, occupation, wealth, gender, and motivations of many donors are open for question.

Sandra S. Heinz

See also: Animals, Sacred and Mummies; Hathor; Magic; Opening of the Mouth; Religion, Personal

Further Reading

Barrett, Caitlín. 2015. "Terracotta Figurines and the Archaeology of Ritual: Domestic Cult in Greco-Roman Egypt." In Stéphanie Huysecom-Haxhi and Arthur Muller, eds. *Figurines grecques en context: Présence muette dans le sanctuaries, la tombe et la maison.* Villeneuve d'Ascq: Presses Universitaires du Septentrion, pp. 401–419.

Hill, Marsha, ed. 2007. *Gifts for the Gods: Images from Ancient Egyptian Temples.* New Haven, CT: Yale University Press.

Ikram, Salima, ed. 2005. *Divine Creatures: Animal Mummies in Ancient Egypt.* Cairo: American University in Cairo Press.

Kemp, Barry. 2006. *Ancient Egypt: Anatomy of a Civilization.* 2nd ed. New York: Routledge.

Nicholson, Paul, Salima Ikram, and S. Mills. 2015. "The Catacombs of Anubis at North Saqqara." *Antiquity* 89, no. 345: 645–661.

Pinch, Geraldine. 1993. *Votive Offerings to Hathor.* Oxford: Griffith Institute.

Raven, Maarten. 1988. "Magic and Symbolic Aspects of Certain Materials in Ancient Egypt." *Varia Aegyptiaca* 4: 237–242.

Stevens, Anna. 2006. *Private Religion at Amarna: The Material Evidence.* Oxford: Archaeopress.

Teeter, Emily. 2011. *Religion and Ritual in Ancient Egypt*. Cambridge: Cambridge University Press.

Thomas, Ross. 2013–2015. "Ptolemaic and Roman Figures, Models and Coffin-Fittings in Terracotta." In Alexandra Villing, Marianne Bergeron, Giorgos Bourogiannis, Alan Johnston, François Leclère, Aurélia Masson, and Ross Thomas, eds. *Naukratis: Greeks in Egypt*. https://www.britishmuseum.org/pdf/Thomas_Ptolemaic_figures.pdf.

Officials

The king sat at the top of an administrative pyramid. He was mainly responsible for the judiciary and his priestly duties, but he was ably assisted by a veritable army of competent officials who ran the government, from the palace affairs to the main treasury and granary, the labor force and the army, and other provincial affairs.

Although, in theory, the king was responsible for all facets of running the country, in practice, he had to delegate many of these duties. The king would hold a formal session in the palace's audience chamber (a ceremony referred to as a "royal sitting"), listen to his courtiers' reports, and give them his orders. A high official of the palace describes his responsibilities during such a function as "ushering in the dignitaries and causing the king's nobles to go to their proper places," all the while "generating the palace's regulations and making every man know his duties" (Sethe 1909, 966–967). These high officials, who formed the very upper echelons of society, were very conscious of their status within their own close circles. As one of the pieces of instructional or wisdom literature points out, "A woman is asked about her husband, but a man is asked about his occupation" (Quack 1994, 303).

Close to the king were the administrators of the royal household. Chief of these was the "Great Overseer of the House," or high steward, who took care of everyday business at the palace and administered the king's properties. The chief queen also had her own steward, who looked after her chambers and her business concerns. At the court, the king's immediate entourage included a herald, who acted as the king's mouthpiece within the palace and throughout the country and also reported events to the king; an "Overseer of the Audience Chamber," or chamberlain, who seems to have been in charge of court protocol; the "Overseer of the Scribes of the Royal Documents," the king's personal scribe, who also oversaw the maintenance of the royal archives; an "Overseer of the Royal Private Apartments" (these are sometimes imprecisely rendered as "harem," although the term belongs to another culture), who was the general manager of the palace's living quarters; and cupbearers, fan bearers, and other officials deemed important—and safe—enough to be near the person of the king.

Other titles that indicated a position at the court were more honorific than indicative of positions that warranted remuneration. Some of the most important among these were the members of the elite (*iry-pat*) and "Foremost of Action" (*haty-a*), which are often translated as "Hereditary Noble" and "Prince," respectively. These renderings may have been true for the very early periods of Egyptian history, but they eventually simply become indicators of very high rank and membership in the nobility.

Among the high officials of the realm, the busiest was probably the *Tjaty,* or, as commonly rendered today, the "vizier" (a term that derives from an Arabic word). He was essentially the second in the chain of command after the king. His dizzying array of responsibilities included the direction of the judiciary; the national collection of taxes; the relationship between the palace and the provincial governments; the management of arable land, especially after the annual flooding; the selection of various officials; and others. To accomplish all this must have required a large body of assistants; therefore, the vizier had his own steward, herald, and chief scribe, who was himself the director of many other scribes.

Next in importance was the chief treasurer. A translation of the titles that the ancients used for this include the "King's Seal-Bearer" and the "Overseer of the House of Silver," as by the Ramesside Period (1295–1069 BCE), the word *silver* was the word used to denote our notion of *money.* He was responsible for the storehouses that held precious metals, such as silver and gold; semiprecious stones, such as lapis-lazuli, turquoise, and amethyst; rare imported woods, such as ebony and cedar; and ivory, which was also imported.

Another eminent official was the "Overseer of All Royal Works," who administered the building projects for which ancient Egypt is so famous. In the Old Kingdom (2686–2160 BCE), these would have included not only temples but also the famous pyramids. Later, after pyramids had ceased being built, the major building projects were the temples to the gods and deceased kings and the royal tombs. Other important government officers were the "Overseer of the Fields" and the "Overseer of the Granaries," who were responsible for the crops from planting to harvest and their subsequent storage, respectively. Also connected to food production was the "Overseer of the Cattle," who was in charge of an annual accounting of all the animals owned by the crown throughout the land.

The army was another department that came under the palace's jurisdiction. Before the New Kingdom, the personnel for military campaigns mostly consisted of units levied by royal request throughout the country. By the New Kingdom, following the so-called wars of liberation of the Second Intermediate Period (1650–1550 BCE), the crown decided to have a standing army to maintain its territorial holdings in Western Asia. This force was placed under the direction of the "Great Overseer of the Army," who had responsibility over the infantry, chariotry, and, somewhat later, navy. Naturally this commanding officer had many subordinates. These included a regular overseer of the army, a deputy of the army, a royal messenger, and numerous scribes.

It is important to note that a significant part of all these departments and ministries—both at the court and throughout the country—was a large bureaucracy maintained by a multitude of scribes. They meticulously kept track of every move within their jurisdiction, and the surviving records provide a window into ancient Egyptian administration.

Life at the court brought its own expectations and regulations. These officials lived and worked in a rigidly structured society, where their position depended on not only their service to the crown but also the king's goodwill. Thus, a high official claims that he had "access to his lord in private and then stayed silent about what he had seen" (Helck 1955, 1430), while others bragged that they could "stride freely toward the steps of the throne" (Sethe 1909, 1183) or "enter (the throne room) bearing good news and come out praised (for it)" (Sethe 1909, 961).

Little is known about the actual duties of most of these high officials. What remains of their work consists of standardized representations on tomb chapel walls and simple attestations of the titles they bore. There are some hints, however, of the everyday life of these officials and the time pressure under which they performed for their superiors. A representation of work done in a mayor's estate during the early Eighteenth Dynasty (1550 BCE) clearly shows this demand in the numerous hieroglyphic captions that urge workers on, such as one where a field hand prods a fellow laborer, "Hurry up with the work so that we can go home at a proper time!" This pressure is reflected by the mayor himself, who claims that he was "not negligent of what had been assessed to him," that is, his dues to the crown (Tylor and Griffith 1894, pl. 3). Officials in ancient Egypt may have been at the top of the social ladder, but their privileges came with significant responsibilities.

Ronald J. Leprohon

See also: Nomes and Provincial Administration

Further Reading

Grajetzki, Wolfram. 2009. *Court Officials of the Egyptian Middle Kingdom*. London: Duckworth.

Helck, W. 1955. *Urkunden der 18. Dynastie*. Berlin: Akademie Verlag.

Leprohon, R. J. 1995. "Royal Ideology and State Administration in Pharaonic Egypt." In Jack M. Sasson, ed. *Civilizations of the Ancient Near East*. Vol. 1. New York: Charles Scribner's Sons, pp. 273–287.

Moreno Garciá, Juan Carlos. 2013. *Ancient Egyptian Administration*. Leiden: Brill.

Quack, J. F. 1994. *Die Lehren des Ani*. Göttingen: Vandenhoeck & Ruprecht.

Sethe, K. 1909. *Urkunden der 18. Dynastie*. Leipzig: J. C. Hinrich'sche Buchhandlung.

Strudwick, Nigel. 1985. *The Administration of Egypt in the Old Kingdom*. London: Rutledge and Kegan Paul.

Tylor, J. J., and F. Ll. Griffith. 1894. *The Tomb of Paheri at El Kab*. London: Egypt Exploration Fund.

Opening of the Mouth

The "Opening of the Mouth" is the name scholars have given to an extremely important funerary ritual made up of quite a number of actions, perhaps the most important of which was the symbolic opening of the mouth of the deceased so that they could speak and eat again in the afterlife. Although this ritual seems to have begun in the Old Kingdom (2686–2160 BCE), it is best known and illustrated in the New Kingdom (1550–1069 BCE), and so this discussion will focus on that time period. The most complete depiction of the Opening of the Mouth ritual is shown in the Theban tomb (number 100) of the vizier Rekhmire of the Eighteenth Dynasty (1550–1295 BCE), which has 51 separate scenes. Typically, in the New Kingdom, a stela or an illustration in the Book of the Dead shows one important

The funeral ritual of the Opening of the Mouth is shown in this illustration from a New Kingdom Book of the Dead, belonging to a scribe called Hunefer. Various ritual objects were used to touch different parts of the mummy so that the deceased could come alive and function in the afterlife. (CM Dixon/Heritage Images/Getty Images)

scene from this ritual, the actual opening of the mouth, which is carried out with an adze, a carpenter's tool, tipped with meteoritic iron being put up to the face of the mummy so that its mouth could talk, its eyes could see, and its ears could hear.

The point of this ritual is an "activation" or "animation" of the deceased so that they could live again and function in the afterlife. It could be carried out on the statue of the deceased or the mummy, or both, as both the statue and mummy were thought of as bodies for the *ka*, or soul of the deceased. A newer interpretation of the ritual ties it in with actions that are carried out on a newborn right after birth, such as clearing the mouth and cutting the umbilical cord. This interpretation is based on the type of instruments that are used in certain parts of the ritual.

The funeral procession would leave the embalming house and take the mummy of the deceased on a sled to the tomb. In front of the tomb's entrance, a priest, possibly wearing a mask of the jackal god Anubis, stood the mummy up in its coffin, which faced the south, so that the light of the sun god Ra was upon it. At least two priests were present, a lector priest who would do the recitations and a *sem* priest, wearing a leopard skin, who acted as Horus, the son of Osiris, and therefore symbolically served in that role for the deceased. After the most important part of the ritual, the opening of the mouth, a series of different implements would be held up to different parts of the body to animate them as well.

Another part of the ritual involved the cutting off of the foreleg of a small calf and its immediate offering to the deceased as a way of transferring life to it. Sometimes this included a second animal sacrifice, and a heart was offered up to the deceased as well. In the tomb of Rekhmire, on the south wall, this part of the text reads, "the foreleg is cut off for your *ka* (or soul) and the heart for your mummy" (Davis 1943, pl. 86, line 6). On the north wall, in one of the ritual scenes, the sem priest and his helper offer a leg and heart to a statue of Rekhmire (Davis 1943, pl. 106, top left). After all the parts of this ritual to resurrect the deceased had been carried out, the deceased was purified and then given food offerings. After that, the coffin was placed in the tomb, and the tomb was closed and sealed. In a contemporary Theban tomb, that of Sennefri, chancellor of Thutmose III, Tomb 99, "stylized adzes and wooden ox-legs" were found, although it was not clear whether they were "the actual objects used in the ritual" or were put into the burial "to ensure the effective continuation of the ritual" (Bohleke and Strudwick 2017, 115).

In the same way that the Opening of the Mouth Ritual at the funeral animated the deceased for life in the hereafter, this ritual was also carried out in temples so that the temple "and all its individual parts and furnishings became alive and active" (Blackman and Fairman 1946, 90). The Opening of the Mouth was carried out at the temple in the festival of the New Year, which would have been sometime in late July to early August, when the inundation came and the Sothis star made its heliacal rising and was seen once again, beginning the ancient Egyptian New Year.

Lisa K. Sabbahy

See also: Afterlife; Book of the Dead; Cult Ritual, Temple; Mummification; Priests

Further Reading

Assmann, Jan. 2001. *Death and Salvation in Ancient Egypt*. Ithaca, NY: Cornell University Press.

Blackman, A. M., and H. W. Fairman. 1946. "The Consecration of an Egyptian Temple According to the Use of Edfu." *Journal of Egyptian Archaeology* 32: 75–91.

Bohleke, Birant, and Nigel Strudwick. 2017. "A Label for Opening of the Mouth Implements from the Burial of Sennefri (TT99) and Remarks on the Ritual." *Études et Travaux* 30: 105–123.

Cruz-Uribe, Eugene. 1999. "Opening of the Mouth as Temple Ritual." In E. Teeter and J. Larson, eds. *Gold of Praise: Studies on Ancient Egypt in Honor of Edward F. Wente*. Chicago: Oriental Institute of the University of Chicago, pp. 69–73.

Davies, Norman de Garis. 1943. *The Tomb of Rekh-Mi-Re at Thebes*. Vols. 1 & 2. New York: Metropolitan Museum of Art.

Forshaw, Roger. 2014. *The Role of the Lector in Ancient Egyptian Society*. Archaeopress Egyptology Series 5. Oxford: Archaeopress, chapter 8, pp. 107–114.

Roth, Anne. 1993. "Fingers, Stars and the 'Opening of the Mouth': Nature and Function of the *ntrwj*-Blades." *Journal of Egyptian Archaeology* 79: 57–79.

Taylor, John, ed. 2010. *Journey through the Afterlife: Ancient Egyptian Book of the Dead*. Cambridge, MA: Harvard University Press.

Teeter, Emily. 2011. *Religion and Ritual in Ancient Egypt*. Cambridge: Cambridge University Press.

Opet Festival

Along with the Valley, New Year's, and Min festivals, the annual Opet was one of the most important feasts in the ancient Egyptian calendar. It celebrated the inundation and the resulting renewal of all that is, including nature and the environment, the king and kingship, and even of the god Amun, the king of the gods himself.

The second month of *Akhet* (the season of the inundation), *Paophi*, when the Opet feast was celebrated, owes its name to this most important of Theban festivals. A relatively new celebration, especially when compared to the Wagy and Khoiak, which are attested since the Old Kingdom (2686–2160 BCE), the Opet appears in the archaeological record only from the reign of Hatshepsut (1473–1458 BCE) in the Eighteenth Dynasty of the New Kingdom.

The Opet festival was so named after Luxor Temple, which was called *Ipet-resyt*, "the southern sanctuary" in Egyptian, and its most salient feature was the transportation of the image of Amun from Karnak, the main temple of this god, to Luxor Temple and then back. Both temples are located in ancient Thebes (modern Luxor), on the east bank of the Nile, but unlike most other temples, where an east-west axis is the norm, Karnak has an additional north-south processional way, while Luxor Temple is oriented north-south. This may have been the case since its inception due to its connection with the Opet festival and, hence, Karnak. That the earliest confirmed remains of this temple also date to the reign of Hatshepsut supports this notion, but the possibility of an earlier date for the temple and Opet festival should not be excluded.

Mirroring the fastest method of travel in ancient Egypt, as well as how the sun god Ra was believed to undertake his daily journey in the sky, gods' images, when transported, were placed in portable barks that could be carried by groups of priests. How the bark was then conveyed from Karnak to Luxor Temple changed over time. According to sources from the reigns of Hatshepsut and Thutmose III (1479–1425 BCE), primarily on the walls of the former's Red Chapel in Karnak and temple in Deir el-Bahari, Amun's image was carried to Luxor Temple by priests along a land route linking the two temples, and then returned to Karnak via the Nile with his ship, *Amun-Userhat*. The scenes depicting the Opet festival on the walls of the colonnade in Luxor Temple, primarily carved during the reigns of Tutankhamun (1336–1327 BCE) and Ay (1327–1323 BCE), show the river route being used for both legs of the journey. It is not impossible for the land route to have still been occasionally used for the journey to Luxor Temple, as evidenced by the restoration work undertaken by Nectanebo I (380–362 BCE) of the Thirtieth Dynasty on the route linking Karnak and Luxor Temples. Ultimately, it is unknown when either route was used or why, but Lanny Bell offers some possibilities (Bell 1997, 162). Another change that occurred in the reign of Tutankhamun, or possibly from that of Amenhotep III (1390–1352 BCE), is that, in addition to the bark of Amun, those of the other two members of the Theban Triad, Mut, his wife, and the moon god Khonsu, their son, were also transported to Luxor Temple, along with a fourth bark that contained the image of the king.

Formerly, it was commonly believed that the Opet festival celebrated the *hieros gamos*, "divine (or sacred) marriage," of Amun with Mut, which would have resulted in the (re)birth of the king and confirmed his legitimacy (Wolf 1931, 72–74). This argument at least partially rested on the inaccurate translation of *Ipet-resyt* as "the southern harem." Lanny Bell (Bell 1985) has since proposed a different but not necessarily mutually exclusive (Bell 1985, 263) interpretation.

In accordance with the ancient Egyptians' cyclical conception of nature, all of creation, including gods and the environment, aged and withered over the course of the calendrical year and required renewal. The Opet festival was celebrated during *Akhet*, when all of life and the created world was regenerated by means of the inundation, in a reenactment of the moment of creation. Aside from being the primary venue for the Opet festival, Luxor Temple served as the house of its own version of Amun, Amenemopet, the same god in his role of creator, whose sanctuary at the southern end of the temple was believed to have been built on the primeval mound whence he had once proceeded to bring all that exists into being. The king, by visiting him in Luxor Temple during the crucial time of the inundation—and thus creation—and tapping into his creative powers, effected Amun-Ra of Karnak's regeneration, along with that of the entirety of creation (Bell 1997, 157, 174–176). Amenemopet was also a form of the royal *ka* (Bell 1985, 259; Bell 1997, 174–176), and therein lies the importance of the Opet festival to the king.

The concept of the royal *ka* is central to understanding the rituals that took place in Luxor Temple after the statues were transported there. Like the *ka* of the average Egyptian, the royal *ka* was not forever bound to a single individual but to their lineage, which, in the king's case, is the totality of his predecessors. It was thus that the ancient Egyptians came to terms with their kings' divinity and humanity: while individual rulers died, the office of kingship was eternal, and the royal *ka*, the divine element of a king's personhood, simply moved from the previous incumbent to his successor (Bell 1997, 131–132, 137–144; see also Bell 1985, 256–259). Among the primary aims of the Opet festival was the renewal the royal *ka* in the propitious season of *Akhet.* Beyond simple renewal, the Opet festival resulted in the complete, albeit ultimately transient, merging of the king with the royal *ka*, such that one became indistinguishable from the other. For a brief period, the king became fully divine.

This was achieved after the king and Amun-Ra of Karnak had arrived in Luxor Temple. There, the god would have proceeded to crown the king, who would have knelt before him with his back turned to the god. Aside from being a repetition of the first time that the king was crowned, and thus a reconfirmation of his kingship and legitimacy, this would have been understood as the transmission of the royal *ka* from Amun-Ra to his son, as certain scenes clearly indicate (Bell 1997, 173, figs. 48, 50, and 54). Afterward, the king proceeded into the bark sanctuary, which served as the resting place of the bark of Amun. There, the king presented him with offerings, and, in the quid pro quo relationship between gods and humanity characteristic of many ancient religions, he would have in turn been rewarded. The boon that would have conferred upon him for each offering made was based on wordplay (Bell 1985, 281; Bell 1997, 173–174). The king would have then knelt before his father, Amun-Ra, this time facing him, and the god would have crowned him a second time, this time once and for all. His powers were thus transferred to the now divinized ruler, who had become one his with royal *ka*, and his kingship was reconfirmed (Bell 1985, 281–283; Bell 1997, 174).

The Opet festival could therefore be used to legitimize various rulers: Horemheb, who was not royal, celebrated what could be termed his coronation ceremony on this occasion (Gardiner 1953, 13–31). In this light, it should not be surprising that the oldest attestation of the Opet festival and Luxor Temple itself is from the reign of the female king Hatshepsut. Even if they existed before her reign, she is the one who seems to have developed the festival and ideology behind the royal *ka*: her exceptional circumstances required her to stress her possession of—or rather possession by—the royal *ka* and descent from Amun himself (Bell 1985, 290–291). Intimately connected with this is her series of divine birth and coronation scenes in her temple at Deir el-Bahari, in which she states that Amun was her actual father and that he had ordained that she be king. The intimate connection between the king's divine parentage, the Opet festival, and Luxor Temple is further reinforced by the presence of Amenhotep III's own divine birth scenes in the core of the temple.

Arto Belekdanian

See also: Sed Festival

Further Reading

Acetta, Kelley. 2013. "Access to the Divine in New Kingdom Egypt: Royal and Public Participation in the Opet Festival." In C. Graves, et al., eds. *Current Research in Egyptology 2012*. Oxford: Oxbow Books, pp. 1–21.

Bell, Lanny. 1985. "Luxor Temple and the Cult of the Royal *Ka*." *Journal of Near Eastern Studies* 44: 251–294.

Bell, Lanny. 1997. "The New Kingdom 'Divine' Temple: The Example of Luxor." In Byron E. Shafer, ed. *Temples of Ancient Egypt*. Ithaca, NY: Cornell University Press, pp. 127–184.

Gardiner, Alan. 1953. "The Coronation of King Haremhab." *Journal of Egyptian Archaeology* 39: 13–31.

Oracles

Oracles are best known from the New Kingdom (1550–1069 BCE), when they were used to show divine approval for actions or decisions, such as the god Amun seeking out the young Thutmose III in Karnak Temple, signaling that he was to be the next king after the death of his father. Hatshepsut also used the oracle of Amun to justify the expedition she sent to Punt. Later, in Ramesside times, the nonroyal use of the oracle of the deified king Amenhotep I and his mother, Ahmose-Nefertary, was used to settle all types of disputes in the village of Deir el-Medina, many of them based on property ownership. It would seem that the local court, or *kenbet*, had "roughly equivalent areas of jurisdiction and power" (McDowell 1990, 114). Priests would come out from the village chapel on festival days carrying the image of Amenhotep I on a kind of litter with poles on their shoulders.

Depending on what was being decided, the movement of the priests carrying the image gave the answer. If a "yes" or "no" were needed, the image would be carried forward for "yes," or would return backward, signaling "no." Sometimes ostraca, small pieces of limestone used to write on, were buried on the side of the path the priests walked on, with an ostracon stating "yes" buried on one side and another saying "no" buried on the other, and the image would dip one way or another. If the oracle was asked to find a person who was guilty of stealing, or something similar, the image would be carried through the village until it stopped at the house of the guilty person.

In the Third Intermediate Period, when the king ruled the north and the High Priests of Amun the south, the god Amun ruled Egypt through oracles. At Karnak, these "state" oracles would be given in the courtyard between the Ninth and Tenth Pylons. Also at this time, text scholars call "oracular amuletic decrees" appear, offering oracular statements protecting nonroyal individuals, usually with the statement that the oracle "keeps them safe." When one of the Theban gods, Amun, Mut, or Khonsu, promised to protect the health of someone, often a child, the text was rolled up and worn around the neck, sometimes inside a small cylinder container made out of wood or even gold.

Lisa K. Sabbahy

See also: Amun; Deir el-Medina; Karnak

Further Reading

Bierbrier, Morris. 1984. *The Tomb-Builders of the Pharaohs*. New York: Charles Scribner's Sons.

Cline, Eric, and David O'Connor, eds. 2006. *Thutmose III: A New Biography*. Ann Arbor: University of Michigan Press.

Lucarelli, Rita. 2009. "Popular Beliefs in Demons in the Libyan Period: The Evidence of the Oracular Amuletic Decrees." In G. Broekman, R. Demarée, and O. Kaper, eds. *The Libyan Period in Egypt: Historical and Cultural Studies into the 21st–24th Dynasties*. Leuven: Peeters, pp. 231–240.

McDowell, A. G. 1990. *Jurisdiction in the Workman's Community of Deir el-Medina*. Leiden: Nederlands Instituut voor het Nabije Oosten.

McDowell, A. G. 1999. *Village Life in Ancient Egypt: Laundry Lists and Love Songs*. Oxford: Oxford University Press.

Quirke, Stephen. 2015. *Exploring Religion in Ancient Egypt*. Chichester, UK: Wiley Blackwell.

Orality. See Literacy and Orality

Osiris

Few ancient Egyptian gods could rival the popularity of Osiris, who, aside from being one of the major "state" gods, such as Amun, Ra, and Ptah, was also widely worshipped outside of the royal family and the priesthood. As a god that died but achieved a successful transition to the afterlife, he delivered the hope for a similar outcome to all. He was a god of death, resurrection, fertility, agriculture, and the inundation.

Despite the availability of an abundance of sources on this deity, Osiris's origins remain obscure, as does the etymology of his name. It seems that he was originally not as popular as other gods with whom he later came to be associated, such as Horus and Seth, who are attested from the Early Dynastic Period and perhaps even earlier. His oldest textual attestation, in which he already appears as a

The god Osiris, painted in the Nineteenth Dynasty tomb of Sennedjem at Deir el-Medina, on the West Bank of Thebes. Osiris holds the crook and flail as he is the king of the underworld, and his skin is shown dark—either black or dark green—to symbolize fertility, life, and growth. (Roger Wood/Corbis/VCG via Getty Images)

deity of extreme importance and with a complex web of associations, is in the Pyramid Texts of Unas (2375–2345 BCE) of the Fifth Dynasty. The Pyramid Texts are the collection of spells, or rather "utterances," that were carved on pyramids' interior walls, the primary goal of which was to bring about the deceased king's resurrection and ascension to the sky. The oldest pictorial evidence of Osiris, on the other hand, dates to the preceding reign, that of Djedkara Isesi (2414–2375 BCE), in the form of a fragment of a wall relief. Here, however, he is not depicted in his usual form of an anthropomorphic, mummiform, deity wearing the Upper Egyptian White Crown, or alternatively the *atef*, holding the crook and the flail. Rather, his free left arm suggests that he was depicted as an anthropomorphic deity. The head, which has not survived, may have been that of a jackal, as with other funerary deities, such as Anubis or, alternatively, Khentiamentiu, whose identity became subsumed under his own by the Fifth Dynasty (2494–2345 BCE) and his name a title of his.

Corn Mummy

Corn mummies represented the god Osiris and were made by priests in the last month of the season of inundation. They mixed river water, river silt, and barley seeds, and then they pressed this mixture into the two halves of a gold mold in the shape of a mummy. These molds were about 18 inches long. The two halves were then set into a rectangular tank and watered until there were sprouts covering the two halves. Then the two halves were taken out of the mold, pressed together, and bound with linen, forming a mummy. It was dried in the sun and then put into a special sycamore coffin. The corn mummy from the year before was taken out of the coffin and buried in a cemetery just for this purpose. By the end of the Late Period (343 BCE), there were corn mummy cemeteries all over Egypt.

Lisa K. Sabbahy

Khentiamentiu means "the Foremost of the Westerners," "the West" referring to the land of the dead, where the sun sets, or "dies." He is attested from the First Dynasty (3000–2890 BCE) and had "lord of Abydos" as his title, where his temple was located. Osiris, too, bore this title, but he was more often referred to as the "lord of This," the province that included this city. This, in combination with his association with the White Crown, suggests a southern origin for this god. Countering this notion, however, is Osiris's title of "the lord" or "foremost of Djedu" (Greek Busiris, modern Abusir), located in Lower Egypt, that is attested just as early. Furthermore, this city's own local deity, Andjety, who also came to be absorbed by Osiris, was depicted with the crook and flail, iconography that he lent Osiris.

The crook and the flail, as royal regalia, associate Osiris with the king. Indeed, he was believed to have actually ruled Egypt in its mythical past, and in the First Dynasty necropolis of Umm el Qa'ab in Abydos, the tomb of Djer (no confirmed dates available) came to be regarded as that of Osiris. He was incorporated into Heliopolitan theology and included in the Ennead, or group of nine gods, wherein the sun god Ra, or Atum, was seen as the primordial creator deity who once directly ruled over Egypt. He was eventually followed by his grandson Geb, the god of the earth, who in turn transferred his authority to Osiris, who thus became king, with his sister Isis as his wife. He was later killed, apparently by drowning, at the hands of his jealous brother Seth, the god of confusion.

According to the Greek version of the myth, as told by Plutarch in *De Iside et Osiride*, Seth tricked Osiris into getting into a coffin that he then sealed and threw in the Nile. Isis eventually found this coffin, but this was discovered by Seth who then dismembered the body. She managed to gather the pieces, which were put together by Anubis to form the first mummy, and Isis resurrected her deceased husband for long enough to conceive a son, Horus, the rightful heir to the throne. Many depictions of this momentous event exist, including a sarcophagus built for Osiris himself, possibly by Khendjer of the Thirteenth Dynasty (1773 to after 1650 BCE; no confirmed dates available for Khendjer), installed in his supposed tomb in Umm el Qa'ab. Upon reaching adulthood, Horus challenged Seth and reclaimed the throne, while Osiris went from being Egypt's ruler to the king of the underworld, and order was restored.

This mythic cycle held immense appeal. On the one hand, it set the precedent for filial royal succession, with every king, like Osiris, going from being the king of the living to "the Foremost of the Westerners," as his son, embodying Horus, sat on the throne of Egypt. This was not mere analogy, for every deceased king actually became Osiris, and this was the powerful message that this mythic cycle had for the population at large: his death, and subsequent mummification and rebirth in the next life, with the aid of family and funerary rituals, gave hope for salvation and set a precedent that everyone could emulate. Thus, in funerary literature, like kings, the deceased came to be identified as "the Osiris [so-and-so]." This, however, could only be achieved if the deceased had a led a righteous life. Spell 125 of the Book of the Dead, another funerary text aimed at aiding the deceased in his transition to the afterlife, shows Osiris in one of his most important roles as the judge presiding over the weighing of the deceased's heart against the feather of *Maat*, "justice, order." A heavy heart meant a sinful life, which entailed a barring from the afterlife, while the opposite meant the successful transition to a peaceful afterlife.

The death and resurrection of Osiris were essential to the identity of this god of agriculture and vegetation, who was also associated with the earth itself. Just as Osiris had to die to be reborn, so the land could only be regenerated through the inundation, that is, drowning, which thus allowed for new crops to grow. For this reason, Osiris was often depicted either with green or black skin, the former due to his connection with vegetation and the latter to the color of the silt deposited by the annual flood, which also gave the whole country its name to the ancient Egyptians, *Kemet*, "the black (land)."

Osiris beds were placed in tombs. These consisted of a hollow frame in the shape of the mummiform Osiris that was filled with earth in which seeds were sown. These would have then grown after the tomb was sealed, actualizing the resurrection of Osiris and, hence, that of the deceased. Osiris was early on identified with Orion (*Sah* in Egyptian), a constellation that rose above the horizon just before Sirius (Sothis), identified with Isis, the rising of which (ideally) heralded the coming of the flood and marked the beginning of the new calendrical year and first season of the year, the inundation, and thus the beginning of another agricultural cycle. Osiris beds were used in Osirian religious festivals to indicate the successful renewal of nature as well.

Djed Pillar

The hieroglyphic word *djed* means "enduring" or "stable." The djed pillar is thought to be the backbone of the god Osiris. It appears as a symbol, particularly at Abydos, the cult center of the god Osiris. The most well-known depiction of a djed pillar is in the hall of Osiris in the Seti I (1294–1279 BCE) temple at Abydos, which shows the king pulling the pillar and setting it upright. The raising up of the djed pillar was an annual ritual carried out by the king beginning in the New Kingdom (1550–1069 BCE).

Lisa K. Sabbahy

The Khoiak festival celebrated the renewal of nature, as seen in the regrowth of vegetation after the flood, and therefore began in the last days of this season, over the course of which Osiris would have died. The celebrations reached a climax on the last day, when a pillar in the form of the *djed* hieroglyph meaning "stability," a symbol of Osiris, was erected in a ritual called the "raising of the *djed* pillar," thus symbolizing his resurrection. Uncoincidentally, the following day was the first month of the second season, the season of the inundation, in which crops grew after the receding of the floodwaters, confirming to all that Osiris had been successfully revivified.

Another celebration, the festival of Osiris, took place in Abydos. An official named Ikhernofret, who served Senusret III (1870–1831 BCE), recorded his participation in this festival. It began with the procession of Wepwawet, "the Opener of Ways," a funerary jackal deity, apparently here regarded as Osiris in his lifetime, in which he symbolically defeated his enemies. This was followed by the death of Osiris, mourning, and the transportation of his image from his temple to the "tomb of Osiris" in a place called Peker, presumably the tomb of Djer, after which he was brought back to his temple, resurrected.

Arto Belekdanian

See also: Horus; Isis; Seth

Further Reading

O'Connor, David. 2009. *Abydos: Egypt's First Pharaohs and the Cult of Osiris.* London: Thames & Hudson.

Quirke, Stephen. 1992. "Power on Earth: Osiris and Horus." In Stephen Quirke, ed. *Ancient Egyptian Religion.* London: British Museum Press.

Silverman, David P. 1991. "Divinity and Deities in Ancient Egypt." In Byron E. Shafer, ed. *Religion in Ancient Egypt: Gods, Myths, and Personal Practice.* London: Routledge, pp. 7–87.

Smith, Mark. 2017. *Following Osiris: Perspectives on the Osirian Afterlife from Four Millenia.* Oxford: Oxford University Press.

P

Palaces

In ancient Egypt, the palace was the home of the king and his family, but it was also a place of audience, ceremony, and administration. Palaces were used for a variety of state activities, including the reception of foreign envoys and gifts, judgments and legal hearings, reward ceremonies, royal announcements, debates, and the appointment of high officials. Royal palaces were built throughout Egyptian history; however, because the Egyptians constructed them from perishable materials, such as mudbrick and wood, in locations close to the Nile where settlements still stand today, few palaces have survived into modern times in a good state of preservation or are inaccessible to archaeologists. Nonetheless, some palaces have been excavated, with the best preserved ones dating to the New Kingdom (1550–1069 BCE) at Memphis, Tell el-Amarna, and Malqata. Others are known from textual sources alone.

The most grandiose residences were built in royal cities, including Memphis, Thebes, Pi-Ramses, and Tell el-Amarna. In such locations, palaces of various sizes and functions existed—ones that were primarily residential, administrative, or ceremonial (using the categories of Egyptologists), as well as harem palaces—and could be used by successive kings; the palace of King Thutmose I at Memphis, for example, was still in use under King Tutankhamun, 160 years later. However, many kings preferred to build their own palaces around the country; indeed, textual evidence points to a palace quarter existing at Memphis, where successive kings built their palaces beside one another along the riverfront.

During their frequent travels around Egypt, kings stayed either in temporary camps, set up in advance of their arrival, or in one of the royal rest houses dotted around the country, called "mooring places of pharaoh" by Egyptians. An example of such an abbreviated palace existed at Giza under Tutankhamun, while a small palace at Giza, also of the Eighteenth Dynasty (1550–1295 BCE), stood in front of the Valley Temple of King Khafra. Such abbreviated palaces might have inspired the design of the small, predominantly mudbrick palaces that stood beside the first court of royal mortuary temples in the New Kingdom. These mortuary temple palaces were probably not used in life, but rather were meant for the spirit of the dead king. Examples have been uncovered at the mortuary temples of Seti I, Ramses II, Merenptah, and Ramses III, with an earlier version evident in the Eighteenth Dynasty mortuary temple of Aye and Horemheb.

Although various Egyptian words for "palace" are referenced in textual sources, the most frequently found terms are *per-aa*, "great house," the palace complex's main residential building, and *per-nesu*, "king's house," the administrative sector of the palace, where offices for staff and storage areas were located. Often, palaces mentioned in textual sources are not known archaeologically. Major palaces of Middle Kingdom date (2055–1650 BCE), for example, are described in literary tales, such as the palace of Amenemhat I at Itja-tawy in the *Teachings of Amenemhat* and the palace of Senusret I in the *Tale of Sinuhe*, but neither have been discovered during excavations. During the New Kingdom, an important palace stood beside the Temple of Amun at Karnak, but, again, no trace of its existence has been found to date.

OVERVIEW OF PALACE ARCHITECTURE AND DECORATION

Though no two palaces were exactly alike, they did share commonalities; there was an entrance area, followed by a columned hall at the center, and then the royal throne room and private quarters at the back of the building. The same layout was followed in temples, which were regarded as houses of the gods. This general palace layout can be seen in scenes from private tombs, particularly those at Tell el-Amarna, in which entrance rooms can be seen giving way to a larger columned hall at the center of the palace, followed by private chambers, including the royal bedroom, at the rear.

Like Egypt's temples, Egyptian palaces display symbolism through their architecture. At Merenptah's (1213–1203 BCE) palace in Memphis, its entrance gateway associated the building with the horizon and the rising sun, powerful symbols of rebirth and order. The floor level rose as it passed from the entrance toward the throne dais at back of the building, simulating the mound of creation—the first land to emerge from the waters at the beginning of time according to Egyptian mythology. The king's throne was located where a god's shrine is found in temples. The palace's columns, with their plant motifs, represented the marshes at creation, and scenes of the king smiting enemies on the columns and bound foreigners on the throne dais showed the pharaoh's supremacy over the people of the world and served as magical protection from disorder.

Palaces were often decorated with scenes of nature. The best examples have been found in the palaces built by Akhenaten at Tell el-Amarna, and those of Amenhotep III at Malqata, all dated to the Eighteenth Dynasty. In the Great Palace at Amarna, in room E, the floor was painted to represent two rectangular pools of water filled with fish. Along the edge of each pool, artists painted marshes with ducks and calves, while at the edge of the room, the paintings represented offering stands and bouquets. Passing between the two pools was a pathway decorated with images of bound Nubian and Asiatics enemies. In the bedroom of Amenhotep III in his palace at Malqata, the ceiling was decorated with images of the goddess Nekhbet as a vulture and the walls with the protective deity Bes as well as symbols of life and *tyt* knots associated with the goddess Isis.

The focal point of any royal palace was the throne room where audiences were held. Access to the throne room was highly restricted, and passage from one sector of the palace to another was monitored. Before entering the palace for a royal audience, any courtier attempting to gain access was stopped by guards. And it was not only security that concerned these sentries; courtiers also had to display the requisite level of purity before they could stand before the king. According to a Twelfth Dynasty story known as the *Tale of the Shipwrecked Sailor*, courtiers were required to wash their hands, while the Twenty-Fifth Dynasty Victory Stele of King Piye (747–716 BCE) says that those entering the palace were forbidden from eating fish. Based on the account of an Eighteenth Dynasty official named Ineni, once inside the palace, the courtiers were made to stand, were counted, and then were placed in two rows. Only then were they allowed to leave the waiting area known as the "place of silence" to enter the throne room for the audience. Throughout the process, they had to remain silent. Outside the throne room, the king could appear before larger crowds—for example, when rewarding soldiers and courtiers—from the palace's "Window of Appearance"; such a window can still be seen overlooking the first courtyard of the mortuary temple of Ramses III (1184–1153 BCE) at Medinet Habu.

MAJOR ARCHAEOLOGICAL REMAINS OF PALACES

From early in Egyptian history, the niched and paneled outer walls of the palace enclosure, hung with colorful reed matting, became a symbol of power; walls featuring this form of "palace facade" decoration, as it is referred to by scholars, have been discovered at Hierakonpolis and Abydos, both dated to the reign of King Khasekhemwy of the Second Dynasty (2890–2686 BCE), and it can often be seen decorating Old Kingdom elite sarcophagi. Few palace remains are known from the Middle Kingdom (2055–1650 BCE), though a palace-like structure, probably home to a local mayor, was excavated at Bubastis. Palace remains of Second Intermediate Period date (1650–1550 BCE) have been uncovered at Tell el-Daba, also known as Avaris, in the delta; among these was a palace of the Hyksos king Khayan, which features Near Eastern architectural influences. A palace of similar date, seemingly built under King Seqenenre Tao II at Deir el-Ballas, in southern Egypt, was probably associated with campaigns against the Hyksos.

After Tell el-Daba's phase as capital of the Hyksos, a palace precinct was constructed there under Tuthmosis III (1479–1425 BCE). Surprisingly, two of the palaces (F and G) from this time were once decorated with Minoan wall paintings, including scenes of griffins, hunting, a bull leaping, and maze patterns. Also from the reign of Tuthmosis III, archaeologists have uncovered a harem palace—a residence for female royal family members and their staff—at Gurob in the Faiyum Oasis; this continued in use into the late Ramesside Period. A series of palaces were also constructed under Amenhotep III at Malkata, on the west bank of the Nile at Thebes, for the king's Sed festival ceremonies—rituals performed after a king had reigned for 30 years and then roughly every few years afterward. These palaces formed part of a much larger complex, including housing for courtiers, a temple to Amun, and administrative offices.

Four palaces have been identified at the city of Tell el-Amarna, all built during the reign of Akhenaten. Of these, the North Riverside Palace was probably Akhenaten's main residence in the city; the North Palace was home to Princess Meritaten, the king's eldest daughter; the Great Palace was a large complex, encompassing state apartments, probably with a Window of Appearance, housing for the royal family and their staff, and a banqueting hall; and the King's House, connected to the Great Palace by a bridge, featured apartments, storage areas, and seemingly a Window of Appearance.

The Nineteenth Dynasty palace of Merenptah at Memphis primarily served a ceremonial function. The royal apartments were abbreviated but adequate for the king to spend his time while preparing for his appearance in the throne room or at its Window of Appearance. Built during the Twentieth Dynasty, the western and eastern high gates at the temple of Medinet Habu may have been used as royal apartments; reliefs in the eastern high gate show the king relaxing with his daughters while playing the board game senet. These gates were probably part of a larger residential quarter in the outer temple area. Palace remains from after the New Kingdom are not well evidenced, with the best preserved example being the palace of King Apries (589–570 BCE) at Memphis from the Twenty-Sixth Dynasty.

Garry John Shaw

See also: Bubastis; Harem; Literature, Fiction; Memphis; Sed Festival; Tell el-Amarna; Tell el-Dab'a; Temples, Mortuary

Further Reading

Amarna Project. "North City." http://www.amarnaproject.com/pages/amarna_the_place/north_city/index.shtml.

Bietak, M. 2017. "Introduction to Palaces in Egypt: What They Tell Us about the Ruler, Administration and Culture." In M. Bietak and S. Prell, eds. *Palaces in Ancient Egypt and the Ancient Near East.* Vol. 1, *Egypt, Contributions to the Archaeology of Egypt, Nubia and the Levant IV.* Vienna: Austrian Academy of Sciences Press, pp. 23–38.

Kemp, B. J. 1977. "The Palace of Apries at Memphis." *Mitteilungen des Deutschen Archäologischen Instituts, Abteilung Kairo* 33: 101–108.

Lacovara, P. 1997. *The New Kingdom Royal City.* London: Keegan Paul International.

Menshawy, S. el. 2003. "The Protocol of the Ancient Egyptian Royal Palace." In Z. Hawass, ed. *Egyptology at the Dawn of the Twenty-First Century: Proceedings of the Eighth International Congress of Egyptologists.* Cairo: American University in Cairo Press, pp. 400–406.

O'Connor, D. B. 1991. "Mirror of the Cosmos: The Palace of Merenptah." In E. Bleiberg and R. Freed, eds. *Fragments of a Shattered Visage: The Proceedings of the International Symposium on Ramses the Great.* Memphis: Memphis State University, pp. 167–198.

O'Connor, D. B. 1995. "Beloved of Maat, the Horizon of Re: The Royal Palace in New Kingdom Egypt." In D. O'Connor and D. P. Silverman, eds. *Ancient Egyptian Kingship.* Leiden: E. J. Brill, pp. 263–300.

Shaw, G. J. 2012. *The Pharaoh: Life at Court and on Campaign.* London and New York: Thames and Hudson.

Weatherhead, F. 1992. "Painted Pavements in the Great Palace at Amarna." *Journal of Egyptian Archaeology* 78: 179–194.

Personal Names

In Ancient Egypt, the name *ren* was an essential dimension of both the divine and the human being, as important as the body; the *ka*, the "double"; and the *ba*, the "akh" and the "shadow." The name manifested the being, expressed its identity, and was a fundamental survival element. So, when a mother, after the birth, named her child, this corresponded to an act of creation, such as that of the god Ptah, who created by his speech. She was also guaranteeing that, through this name, his or her own survival would be ensured. One would survive through the permanence of their name among the living.

That a name represents you and is part of you presents risks. In a society that believed that the name spoke the being or manifested the essence of the individual, knowing the name could be dangerous if its owner became vulnerable to magical attack. It was believed by those who carried out the destruction of royal cartouches that eliminating the presence of a name in a cartouche eliminated the existence of its owner. The destruction or loss of any part or aspect of you, such as the name, erases you not only from memory but from existence. "To prevent namelessness in the hereafter, the Egyptians tried to make their names endure for all eternity" (Hornung 1992, 178).

Episodes happened in ancient Egyptian history when the name of an individual was obliterated from inscriptions or the name of a king removed from monuments. The most well-known cases happened in the New Kingdom (1550–1069 BCE), with Hatshepsut, the queen who ruled as pharaoh, and with Amenhotep IV, the pharaoh who introduced the cult of the Aten in Egypt and changed his name to Akhenaton (1352–1336 BCE). In this regard, it is interesting to note that in the trial documents of the harem conspiracy that killed King Ramses III, the men who led the conspiracy are given false names, such as "Ra hates him," "Ra will blind him," and "Evil in Thebes," so that not only are their actual names obliterated, but they are given names that condemn them (Peden 1994, 210).

In ancient Egyptian mythology, there are stories of the secret names of gods and the tricks that other gods play to try and find out their names, such as in the myth *The Secret Name of Ra* (Jacq 1985, 49–52). Isis, the goddess of magic, par excellence, in ancient Egypt, tries, in every way possible, to find the secret name of the sun god with no success. Ra does not yield to the tricks of the goddess and does not reveal his secret name, ensuring his freedom and independence from the goddess of magic.

At the end of the Old Kingdom (2686–2160 BCE), the custom began of expanding the identity of an individual via the use of two or three names: a bigger name, rarely used, usually formed over a divine (theophoric) or royal one (basilophoric) and designated by the expression "great name," and two smaller names, the "good name" (*rn nfr*), the familiar and daily used name, and the "small name" (*rn nds*), usually an abbreviation or a hypocoristic form of the bigger name. These different names can be found, but not always.

Ancient Egyptian names can be divided into groups. One of the largest is the names that were formed from the name of gods, called *theophoric names*. These names may be based on the name of a local god or the god or goddess most revered by a certain family. There are also names using the names of kings, or *basilophoric names*. It may be the king reigning when the child was born, or the king most beloved and remembered by the family. Then there were names that in their formulation did not contain either of these elements. Examples of some the categories of Egyptian names are the following:

1. Names that evoke the protection of a deity: "Isis said: she shall live"; "That Amun save him"; "He is in the hands of Amun."
2. Names that evoke the coincidence of the birth on the same day as a religious festival: "Hathor is in festival"; "Amun is in the sacred barque"; "Mut is in the valley."
3. Names that evoke a birth during a specific reign: "The son of Ahmoses"; "Ramses is the son of Ptah"; "Ramses, the beloved of Amun, is wealthy in years."
4. Names that are related to the survival of lineage: "My brother is with me"; "She shall be my heiress"; "My brother is born."
5. Names related to a physical trait or personality: "The blind"; "The sweet."
6. Names suggesting an ethnic origin: "The Syrian"; "The nomad."
7. Names that are simply objects or animals: "The cat"; "The apple"; "Lapis-lazuli."

In general, ancient Egyptian names are complete grammatical sentences. They break into two large groups: those that are rather formal, and those that are considered "birth names," that is, something said when the baby was born.

Maria Helena Trindade Lopes

See also: Afterlife; Childbirth; Harem

Further Reading

Baines, J. 1991. "Society, Morality, and Religious Practice." In E. B. Shafer, ed. *Religion in Ancient Egypt: Gods, Myths, and Personal Practice.* London: Cornell University Press, pp. 123–200.

Hlouchová, M. P. 2016. "Old Kingdom Sun Cult on the Basis of Theophoric Anthroponyms." *Prague Egyptological Studies* XVII: 67–78.

Hornung, Erik. 1992. *Idea into Image: Essays on Ancient Egyptian Thought.* New York: Timkin Publishers.

Jacq, C. 1985. *Egyptian Magic.* Warminster, UK: Aris and Phillips.

Lopes, M. H. T. 1998. "Les Noms Propres au Nouvel Empire." In C. J. Eyre, ed. *Proceedings of the Seventh International Congress of Egyptologists.* Leuven: Uitgeverij Peeters, pp. 703–711.

Murray, Margaret Alice. 1908. *Index of Names and Titles of the Old Kingdom.* London: Quaritch.

Ranke, H. 1935, 1952, 1977. *Ägyptischen Personennamen.* Bd. I, II, III. Glückstadt: J. J. Augustin.

Teeter, E. 1986. "Observations on the Presentation of the Ramesside Prenomen." *VA* 2: 175–184.

Vinson, S. 2009. "The Names 'Naneferkaptah,' 'Ihweret,' and 'Tabubue' in the 'First Tale of Setne Khaemwas.'" *Journal of Near Eastern Studies* 68, no. 4 (October): 283–304.

Personal Religion. *See* Religion, Personal

Philae Island

Philae Island, called Philae in Greek after the Egyptian *Pa-iw-rek*, was located at the First Cataract of the Nile about seven kilometers south of modern Aswan, which was the ancient border between Egypt and Nubia. Buildings were added on the island from the Egyptian Late Period (664–332 BCE) to Christian times, where approximately 20 surviving structures, dating primarily to the Ptolemaic and Roman periods (304 BCE–394 CE), surround the main temple. This temple is dedicated to the goddess Isis and her triad, including Osiris and Horus. Still-standing buildings in the complex include a kiosk located on the south edge of the island, an open-air court bordered by colonnades on the east and west sides that contains temples to Arensnuphis and Imhotep, a chapel to Mandulis, and a small temple of uncertain use. These structures front a pylon with an attached gate, which is before an inner open-air court, bordered by a colonnade on the east side. The west side of the court is bordered by a birth house. An inner pylon forms the north, or rear edge, of this court and marks the entrance to Isis's temple proper.

This temple is surrounded by a girdle wall, which originally extended from the outer pylon, and separates the temple from the space surrounding it. The wall includes a gate that originally led out west to the island of Biga. Directly northwest

The island of Philae just south of the First Cataract was the location of the cult temple of Isis, wife of Osiris and mother of Horus. The entire temple complex was moved from its original island to save it from the rising waters of Lake Nasser. (Ekaterina Polyashova/Dreamstime.com)

of the Isis temple is the small temple of Harendotes. A temple to the Roman imperial cult sits north of the main temple, and a temple to Hathor and the kiosk of Trajan are located to the east. The complex was documented, removed, and reconstructed on Agilkia Island between 1972–1980 through the UNESCO campaign to save Nubian antiquities from flooding after the installation of the Aswan High Dam.

Religious veneration on Philae Island may have begun in Dynasty 25 (770–656 BCE) in the reign of Taharqo (690–664 BCE). However, Gerhard Haeny (1985, 202) called a kiosk built in the name of the Twenty-Sixth Dynasty king Psammetichus II (595–589 BCE) the "earliest structure which definitely belongs to Philae." Building at least from the Twenty-Sixth Dynasty is further supported, as Philae was linked through the cult of Osiris to the neighboring island of Biga, which was the location of Abaton, one of the god's mythical burial places. The first fully surviving structure on Philae dates to the reign of Dynasty 30 king Nectanebo I (380–363 BCE), who built a kiosk that was later relocated to the southern edge of the island by Ptolemy II (285–246 BCE).

Philae was a major regional cult center for Nubian and Egyptian populations, and the classical author Strabo (17.1.49) described it as "a common settlement of Ethiopians (Nubians) and Egyptians." Philae was the nexus of the Nubian-Egyptian border, and deities from both pantheons were venerated at the site, especially the Philean triad, Isis, Osiris, and Horus (in three forms); deities of the First Cataract region, Khnum-Ra, Satet, and Anuket; and Nubian deities Arensnuphis and Mandulis. Other deities at Philae include Hathor, Thoth, Sakhmet, Amun-Ra, Mut, Nekhbet, Wadjet, Bes, and the deified architect Imhotep. Under Augustus, the construction of an imperial cult temple on the island added the Roman emperor to this host.

Isis was a primary focus of regional cultic identity at the border and a chief deity in both Nubian and Egyptian pantheons. Her worship focused on her role as sister/wife and rejuvenator of Osiris and mother and protectress of Horus. Isis, Osiris, and Horus were widely worshipped in Egypt and Nubia, while Philae remained Isis's most important cult site for both populations. Numerous rites and festivals, such as the national festival of Khoiak and the local Festival of Entry, honored Isis in her role as sister/wife and rejuvenator of Osiris. The Khoiak festival, named for the month in which it occurred (November–December), marked the end of the inundation and reenacted the funeral of Osiris. The festival culminated in a boat procession in which the cult statue of Isis left Philae Island and sailed to Biga Island on day 22 of the month of Khoiak.

Pilgrims from far abroad in Nubia and Egypt recorded their cultic participation at Philae, especially during processional festivals such as Khoiak and the Festival of Entry, with graffiti detailing their ritual support for the goddess carved into the temple walls. Other graffiti in the region indicate there was a tradition of carving texts into the temples in demotic Egyptian, Meroitic, and Greek. The island was the site of a bourgeoning transcultural ritual landscape centered on pilgrimage to the temple of Isis. Alongside Egyptians and Nubians living in the region, members of the Roman military were stationed in the area and frequented the temple precincts. Furthermore, people came from all over the Mediterranean world, as by the first century CE, Isis was a pan-Mediterranean goddess with many sites of worship, including the famous temple at Pompeii. Philae Island was known as Isis's most important temple throughout the Mediterranean, and ancient tourist itineraries to Egypt culminated at the famous island.

Erin A. Peters

See also: Horus; Isis; Nubia; Osiris; Ptolemaic Egypt; Temples, State

Further Reading

Ancient Egyptian Architecture Online Project (AEGARON). http://drupaldev.aegaron.ucla.edu.

Arnold, Dieter. 1999. *Temples of the Last Pharaohs*. New York: Oxford University Press.

Dijkstra, J. H. F. 2008. *Philae and the End of Ancient Egyptian Religion: A Regional Study of Religious Transformation (298–642 CE)*. Leuven: Peeters.

Haeny, G. 1985. "A Short Architectural History of Philae." *Bulletin de l'Institut français d'archéologie orientale* 85: 197–233.

Lyons, Henry George. 1896. *A Report on the Island and Temples of Philae*. London: Waterlow.

Lyons, Henry George. 1908. *A Report on the Temples of Philae*. Cairo: National Printing Department.

Rutherford, Ian. 1998. "Island of the Extremity: Space, Language, and Power in the Pilgrimage Traditions of Philae." In D. Frankfurter, ed. *Pilgrimage and Holy Space in Late Antique Egypt*. Leiden: Brill, pp. 229–256.

Török, Laszlo. 2009. *Between Two Worlds: The Frontier Region between Ancient Nubia and Egypt, 3700 BC–AD 500*. Leiden: Brill.

Vassilika, Eleni. 1989. *Ptolemaic Philae*. Leuven: Peeters.

Police

There is not clear evidence in most of pharaonic history for the title of an official who would be the equivalent of a modern "policeman." The best evidence, however, comes from the New Kingdom (1550–1069 BCE). Tomb 9 at Tell el-Amarna, ancient name Akhet-Aten, belongs to a man named Mahu who carries the title "overseer of Medjau of Akhet-Aten." A Medjay, (plural: Medjau) was a nomadic Nubian from the hill country of the Eastern Desert. These men had been hired as mercenaries by the Egyptians during the Second Intermediate Period, and they had gained the reputation as being warlike and tough. *Medjay* became synonymous with the word for *policeman*, whether or not that person was a Nubian, and so Mahu was in charge of the policemen of Tell el-Amarna. Excavation in the center of the city at Tell el-Amarna found a structure on the eastern edge of that part of city that has been called the "Police Barracks"; it includes stalls and what appears to be a large well in the center (See Kemp 1986, 94, fig. 6.2).

Scenes in Mahu's tomb show him involved with his responsibility for the security of the city. In a scene on the southwest wall, Mahu, in his chariot with his driver, is shown ordering the capture of three criminals and taking them to the vizier. On the northeast wall is perhaps a more important scene for Mahu's status, as he is shown, with all the policemen lined up behind him, greeting and adoring the king and queen as they drive out of the Aten Temple in their chariot.

In another New Kingdom settlement, the village of Deir el-Medina, which housed the workmen who cut the royal tombs in the Valley of the Kings, the titles "Medjau of the Tomb" and "Overseers of the Medjau of the Tomb" are known. These men were not considered part of the village population of Deir el-Medina, but they provided security for it and also played a role in the administration of certain aspects of the village. Even the mayor of the West Bank of Thebes carried the title of "Overseer of the Medjau of the Tomb." In the reign of Ramses IV, when the work crew of the village had expanded to 120 men, it was noted that there were 60 Medjau. In various written documents, about two dozen personal names for these Medjau have been recorded. They are all common ancient Egyptian names, so there is no reason to assume they were other than Egyptian.

In the Tomb Robbery Papyri, reporting on the investigation into the robbing of royal tombs on the West Bank of Thebes in the late Twentieth Dynasty (1186–1069 BCE), Medjau are mentioned as accompanying the men inspecting the damage at the tombs and also as testifying against the thieves in some cases, but the role they play is not that prominent.

Lisa K. Sabbahy

See also: Officials

Further Reading

Černy, Jaroslav. 1973. *A Community of Workmen at Thebes in the Ramesside Period.* Cairo: Institute Français D'Archéologie Orientale du Caire.

Davies, N. D. G. 1906. *The Rock Tombs of El-Amarna, IV.* London: Egypt Exploration Fund.

Kemp, Barry. 1986. *Amarna Reports III.* London: Egypt Exploration Society.

McDowell, A. G. 1990. *Jurisdiction in the Workmen's Community of Deir el-Medina.* Leiden: Nederlands Instituut Voor het Nabbije Oosten.

Pottery

Ancient Egyptian pottery is a key tool used by Egyptologists to understand life over the 3,000 years of Egyptian history, as it is virtually indestructible and ubiquitous on archaeological sites. Ceramics were used in daily life as well as for funeral, religious, and ritual purposes. As such, they allow vivid reconstructions of human behavior.

MANUFACTURE

Ceramics are created through the combination of ingredients, clay, temper, and water, which make up the *fabric* of the vessel. In ancient Egypt, two different clay sources were exploited: Nile silt clay and marl clay. Nile silt layers were deposited along the Nile riverbed from the Upper Pleistocene down to the present day. This made it readily accessible to all living in the Nile valley. Nile silt clay has a very similar chemical composition along the entire length of the Nile, making it difficult to pinpoint where exactly a Nile silt pot was manufactured based purely on its fabric. Clay from these deposits are high in iron and silica, and it fires pale beige to brown in an oxidized environment or black in a deoxidized environment.

Marl clay is calcareous and was sourced from the wadis and mountains of Egypt, with sources known along the desert fringes at Ballas in the Qena region, north of Luxor, and at Amarna. Marl clay fires to a white or cream color in an oxidizing environment, although when cut in section, it can show orange, pink, and green shades. If fired above 1,000 degrees, it can "self-slip" to a deep green. It is much harder than Nile silt fabric. These two fabrics were also combined to form mixed fabrics, which can be difficult to identify. Both Nile silt and Marl clay can be further subdivided into fabric groups based on their temper inclusions, hardness, and pore density. Although these are the two basic fabrics exploited in the Nile valley, kaolinite clays were also in use in the Western Desert oases from the First Intermediate Period (2160–2055 BCE) and were used to manufacture specific gourd forms that were exported to the Nile valley. In the Roman Period, another kaolinite source at Aswan was exploited.

Ceramicists on excavations in Egypt typically begin their work by establishing a site-specific fabric typology, which has proved difficult to correlate between sites in the past. This led to the establishment of the Vienna System, a framework intended to be used as a starting point for the broad classifications of pottery fabrics beyond such site-specific typologies. This hoped to enable a broader comparison of fabrics used and manufactured across the Nile valley.

Nile silt fabrics are classified into Nile silt A–E. Nile silts A–C were differentiated by differing size and quantity of their sand and straw tempers, whereas Nile D is distinguished by the presence of limestone temper. Nile E appears to be restricted to the eastern delta and is characterized by its soft, sandy quality. Marl fabrics are classified into Marls A–F. These are differentiated by their firing colors and by the quantity and size of their limestone inclusions. Typically, these fabrics are restricted to different time periods and used to manufacture particular vessels; for example, cooking pots are commonly manufactured in a Nile C, whereas amphorae in the New Kingdom (1550–1069 BCE) are frequently produced in the north in Marl D.

FIRING AND PRODUCTION

Once clay had been acquired, the primary processing stage prepared it for manufacture. Clay would have arrived at a potter's workshop dried, so it would require crushing and mixing with water. Some clay was levigated—the process by which fine clay particles are sieved from coarse particles and other inclusions. The Tomb of Kenamun (Theban Tomb 93) shows a potting scene that has been theorized to include a levigation pool. Other scholars disagree and suggest it shows the mixing of clay, which was typically trampled by potters. Finally, the clay was wedged, or stamped, and kneaded by the potters on the floor to compact it and remove air bubbles, something demonstrated in Tomb 15 of Bakt III at Beni Hasan. At this stage, various tempers could be added, depending on the vessel's ultimate purpose. Straw, sand, small stones, and grog were most commonly added to Nile silt vessels. Straw was valued for cooking pots, as it burned away during firing, leaving voids in the vessel walls. This allowed for a pot's expansion during cooking. Calcium carbonate pieces were sometimes added to marl silt vessels, although these can also be natural inclusions in the clay. The prepared clay was now ready to be worked.

There are several potential methods to shaping pottery. In the Predynastic Period (5300–3000 BCE), pots were made by hand using one of four methods: (1) pinching by hand; (2) shaping over a mold or core, commonly used for bread molds; (3) the paddle and anvil method (the use of tools to compact the vessel walls); or (4) coil building, where rings of clay were smoothed together to form a pot. The simple potter's wheel, which was turned by hand, was developed in the Fifth Dynasty (2494–2345 BCE); the majority of vessels were then manufactured using the wheel, enabling the production of regular forms. These vessels bear clear "rilling marks" along their surfaces, which distinguish them from handmade vessels.

Pots could be painted, pre- or postfiring, with a brush, a finger, or a compass. The most commonly used colors were black and red, although white, yellow, and blue are known. Other vessels were given a slip, a thin coat prefiring, or a wash, a thin coat added postfiring. Pots could also be burnished or polished, where the vessel was left to go leather hard before a stone or soft fabric was used to rub the exterior until it shone. Other decoration includes incised, impressed, or stamped patterns or applied decoration.

Firing could be done in a kiln or an open bonfire. Pottery hardens when fired at temperatures above 600 degrees Celsius. Nile silt clay is typically fired between 700 and 800 degrees Celsius, whereas marl is fired at the higher temperature of 800 to 1,000 degrees Celsius. Early kilns were found in Predynastic buildings at Hierakonpolis, and across Egypt, sites such as temples often had personal kilns, although it is likely that many kilns within the wider community were multipurpose.

FORMS

A ceramic typology is a method of displaying ceramics according to shared traits at a given site or time period. Flinders Petrie was the first Egyptologist to attempt to systematically sort and arrange pottery into types and to chart vessel evolution for dating purposes. Today, a ceramicist's first job is to create a site-specific typology that identifies the forms used at a particular site.

Egyptian vessels can be divided into restricted and unrestricted vessel forms. Restricted forms are vessels with a small mouth-to-body ratio index and include storage jars, bottles, and pilgrim flasks. Unrestricted vessels have a wide mouth-to-body ratio index and include bowls, plates, and cooking pots. The form of such vessels can reveal their function. Large unrestricted vessels like bowls are ideal for eating but impractical for storage, whereas restricted jars with a small opening, such as bottles, prevent luxury contents from evaporating. Round-based cups are unable to stand on a surface unaided and were perhaps intended for passing around in a feasting context. Many vessels were likely for ritual or symbolic use rather than for use in daily life. The placement of miniature vessels in graves or foundation deposits (ritual burials of ceremonial objects under buildings) was likely intended to represent the real vessel. Others were filled with symbolic contents; at Sakkara, beer jars containing mud or ash were found.

Pottery is probably the most common object known from ancient Egypt. Potsherds are everywhere at ancient Egyptian archaeological sites. This complete vessel dates from the Predynastic Naqada II Period, roughly 3500 BCE–3200 BCE. It is made of marl clay and painted with decorations showing a boat with oars, and animal and human figures. (The Metropolitan Museum of Art/Rogers Fund, 1920)

Sculpted vessels also occur. Animal pots occur in the Predynastic Period and later in the Second Intermediate Period in the delta (1650–1550 BCE). Female figurine vases were only produced between the reigns of Tuthmosis III and Amenhotep III (1479–1352 BCE) and are theorized to have been special containers for breast milk that were produced in a single workshop over a short period of time. Pottery was relatively standardized across Egypt, but during the Intermediate periods, regions often exhibited stronger individualism.

CHRONOLOGY OF HIGHLIGHTS

Predynastic. Pottery first appears in the Nile valley in the sixth millennium BCE, and it was handmade throughout the Predynastic Period. Vessels could be polished red or black or decorated with white painted lines (C-ware). Marl clay was first exploited from Naqada II, about 3500–3200 BCE, and was used to make D-ware storage jars, or "decorated ware." These were painted in a dark brown, with images showing animals and boats. Others were painted to imitate stone vessels.

Old Kingdom. The potter's wheel was developed in the Fifth Dynasty, with the earliest depiction of pottery manufacture in the Tomb of Tiy at Sakkara. Beer jars and "flower pots" were standard additions to tombs at this time and are thought to represent the "bread and beer" offerings referred to in offering scenes, as they represented daily food and drink. It has been suggested that they were of a standard volume to use as payment for workers in pyramid towns. Fine ware was also in circulation, such as Meidum bowls used for milk.

Middle Kingdom. Miniature vessels were a common addition to tombs at this stage and are thought to have acted as symbols representing the full-size vessels. Other interesting forms include fish bowls, oval dishes bearing an incised fish, which were used in feasts. At the end of the Middle Kingdom, about 1650 BCE, Tell el-Yayudiyeh ware appears among the Hyksos inhabitants of the Nile Delta.

New Kingdom. The New Kingdom saw a golden age in Egyptian wealth and subsequent material culture. Large amounts of foreign pottery were imported from Mycenae, Crete, Cyprus, and the Levant and deposited in elite graves and palace sites. Wine jars attest to a viticulture industry in the delta as well as abroad. This period is also known for blue painted pottery, which appears throughout the Eighteenth (1550–1295 BCE) and Nineteenth (1295–1186 BCE) Dynasties. Vessels were painted prefiring with floral garlands and geometric patterns in a mix of cobalt aluminate spinel, sourced from the Western Desert oases. Polychrome pottery was also blue, but it was painted on with a copper-based pigment postfiring. After the New Kingdom, Egyptian pottery underwent significant changes in production and style that are still poorly understood. There was strong influence from Mycenae and, later, Rome.

FOREIGN INFLUENCE

Non-Egyptian vessels are known in Egyptian contexts from the Predynastic Period and attest to the state's relationships with other peoples across the Eastern Mediterranean and ancient Near East. Items such as stirrup jars from Mycenae or amphorae from the Levant were desired for their contents, but Egyptian potters also imitated many of these imported forms. Items such as Cypriote base-ring jars, pilgrim flasks from the Levant, and Canaanite amphorae were all experimented with in Egypt, although only a select few remained in the permanent Egyptian repertoire.

Loretta Kilroe

See also: Beer; Foundation Deposits; Predynastic Period; Wine

Further Reading

Arnold, D., and J. Bourriau, eds. *An Introduction to Ancient Egyptian Pottery.* Mainz: Zabern.

Bourriau, J. 1981. *Um El-Ga'ab: Pottery from the Nile Valley before the Arab Conquest.* Cambridge: Cambridge University Press.

Bourriau, J., P. Nicholson, and P. Rose. "Pottery." In P. Nicholson and I. Shaw, eds. *Ancient Egyptian Materials and Technology.* Cambridge: Cambridge University Press, pp. 121–147.

Bourriau, J., and H.-A. Nordström. 1993. "Ceramic Technology: Clays and Fabrics." In D. Arnold and J. Bourriau, eds. *An Introduction to Ancient Egyptian Pottery.* Mainz: Zabern, pp. 149–190.

Doherty, S. 2015. *The Origins and Use of the Potter's Wheel in Ancient Egypt*. Oxford: Archaeopress.

Maxzynska, A. 2016. "Pottery as a Source for Studying Cultural Changes: The Problem of the Lower Egyptian-Naqadian Transition." In B. Bader, C. Knoblauch, and E. Köhler, eds. *Vienna 2—Ancient Egyptian Ceramics in the 21st Century*. Peeters: Leuven, pp. 387–402.

Nicholson, I. 1993. "The Firing of Pottery." In D. Arnold and J. Bourriau, eds. *An Introduction to Ancient Egyptian Pottery*. Mainz: Zabern, pp. 149–190.

Warden, L. 2014. *Pottery and Economy in Old Kingdom Egypt*. Boston: Brill.

Wodzinska, A. 2009. *A Manual of Egyptian Pottery*. Boston: Ancient Egyptian Research Associates.

Predynastic Period (ca. 5300–3000 BCE)

The Predynastic Period dates roughly from 5300–3000 BCE and is regarded as the formative period for Egyptian civilization, when many features attested in pharaonic times were emerging and developing. According to Manetho, who wrote a history of Egypt in the early third century BCE, Egypt was originally ruled by dynasties of gods, followed by demigods, and then the First Dynasty (3000–2890 BCE), which emerged from the city of This in the nome of Abydos in Upper Egypt. The chronology of Predynastic Egypt was first established by William Matthew Flinders Petrie by using the method of sequence dating of pottery from cemeteries, a relative dating method that allows assemblages to be arranged in a rough serial order. This system has since been reviewed by more modern scholars, but its main achievements are unchanged.

Three archaeological cultures were established by Petrie, Amratian, Gerzean, and Semainean, which are now regarded as three chronological phases of the Naqada culture, named Naqada I, Naqada II, and Naqada III, respectively. Research of later scholars after Petrie brought to light other cultures, such as the Badari culture, which developed in Middle Egypt and spread to the south. It was the immediate predecessor of the Naqada I culture. The indigenous Lower Egyptian culture, also known as Maadi-Buto culture, emerged in the Nile Delta more or less simultaneously to Naqada I in the south. The Naqada II culture spread from central Upper Egypt into the delta and gradually replaced the local material culture, although some local traditions merged with the southern ones, in the Naqada III period.

Because the Nile covered the valley with a thin layer of alluvium during the annual inundation and changed its course over time, the Predynastic settlements in the alluvial plain are practically unknown, in contrast to the cemeteries along the desert fringe. In some cases, such as at the sites of el-Kab, Armant, and Karnak, Predynastic cultural layers were found below pharaonic settlements, proving that the alluvial plain was settled from the beginning of the Predynastic Period. Archaeological field surveys have shown that the border area of the annually flooded valley and the desert was inhabited, and general conclusions on the settlement patterns could be drawn by analysis of such areas. The first inhabitants were nomadic or seminomadic populations that had shifted to a sedentary way of life. In the early Predynastic Period, the settlements and cemeteries were rather equally distributed. In the middle of the period, they moved in the direction of the alluvial plain, and prominent centers began to join together, forming large low-density settlements. In time, these centers became smaller but more densely populated, and their structure exhibited functional, hierarchical, and spatial divisions of society. The centers where this type of process was most dynamic became capitals of early states, sometimes called proto-states or proto-kingdoms.

Remains of houses were discovered at some sites. Wattle and daub was the most common technique of constructing walls, and the floor was sometimes covered with mud. Storage pits as well as hearths were placed in and outside the dwellings. Houses discovered at the site of Badari were round in plan, with the lower parts of the walls sometimes made of stones and mud and the upper parts of reeds and wood. The "Burnt House" at Hierakonpolis presents wattle-and-daub construction made on a rectangular plan. It consisted of one room with a workspace surrounded by a fence outside of the house. Houses discovered at Ma'adi had wattle-and-daub superstructures, but some of them had also semisubterranean constructions with stonewalls, related to the construction of dwellings in southern Palestine. An administrative and production complex was discovered at Tell el-Farkha in the delta. In the oldest strata, structures were made of perishable materials, but the later Naqada II center was made of unfired mudbricks. Depictions of sanctuaries known from Predynastic and Early Dynastic Periods convey forms of sacral structures made of wood and reeds.

Very characteristic for Predynastic Egypt is the production of stone palettes, which were used to grind pigments for body decorations. During Naqada I, palettes were of simple geometric shapes like rhomboids, but during Naqada II, elaborate shapes gained popularity, for example, fish, birds, and gazelles. In Naqada III, geometric forms came back. At the end of the Predynastic Period, the most sophisticated palettes had depictions showing hunting, military, and symbolic scenes. The best-known example is the Narmer Palette.

Mace-heads were another characteristic type of artifact. The original function of the stone mace-head was that of a weapon, and it was simply a stone with a hole drilled through its center fixed onto a wooden staff. Such artifacts became more elaborate in time and developed to be status symbols as well. The best known, the Scorpion and Narmer maceheads, known by the names of the Dynasty 0 kings they belonged to, are too big to be carried or used during any fight. Their richly decorated surfaces were used to convey ideological scenes. Flint production was also characteristic of the Predynastic Period. The pieces produced can be divided into utilitarian tools, such as scrapers, knives, or arrows, and luxury items that exhibit a high level of sophistication, such as cherts in the shape of animals and knives made for ritual functions.

Nile clay was used for pottery production, which after firing was red and brown in color. The most characteristic for Badari and Naqada I–II culture are the so-called black-topped wares. The name originated from a pot with a red body and black rim. This effect was achieved by the special way of firing the pots. During Naqada II, marl clay from *wadis*, or valleys, became utilized in pottery production. The properties of marl are different than those of the Nile clay, for example, after firing, marl has a brighter surface than Nile clay. This new property led to a change in decoration. Some of the Naqada I Nile clay pots were decorated with the use of white paint on the red background of the vessels, creating what is called white cross-lined ware, but since the Naqada II, dark red or brown paint was used to make depictions on the bright background, creating "decorated ware." The decorations of the white cross-lined pots show mainly animals and hunting scenes, but Naqada II decorated wares are characterized by scenes of boats surrounded by elements of landscape, flora, and fauna. The following Naqada III pottery was no longer so richly decorated, and potmarks and incised patterns were made.

Art of the Predynastic Period also includes the decorated tomb at Hierakonpolis (Tomb 100), the first known tomb in Egypt with a painted wall. The tomb consists of two rather small, connected spaces built with mudbrick down in a pit dug for the tomb. The walls were covered with mud plaster, and one of them was painted. The depictions are similar to those on pottery, showing boats, hunting and trapping animals, and warriors fighting. The decoration on the Gebelein linen is similar in style and shows rulers during ceremonies. These depictions, and others on luxury objects like knife handles and the palettes and mace-heads discussed above, emphasize power and control over both humans and animals. Rock art of the Predynastic Period is also characterized by similar depictions of boats, animals, and hunting.

Tombs are the basic source of evidence for the Predynastic Period because most of the known archaeological sites in Upper Egypt are cemeteries. In contrast, a larger number of settlements are known from Lower Egypt. The earliest tombs were simple round pit burials, which in many cases contained pottery vessels, flints, and personal ornaments. They gradually evolved into more complex structures. Beginning in Naqada II, the division between wealthy tombs of the elite, rectangular in plan and with mudbrick walls and sometimes several chambers, and poorly equipped burials became apparent. In some cemeteries, for example, at Hierakonpolis, Naqada and Abydos, parts of the cemeteries were restricted for only elite burials. The rulers of Hierakonpolis had elaborate superstructures made in wattle-and-daub technique and decorated in colorful patterns and scenes. These structures, such as Tomb 16, were surrounded by burials of exotic wild animals. In some instances, early forms of mummification have been recognized at the cemeteries of Hierakonpolis and the Upper Egyptian site of Adaima. Cemetery U, in Abydos, was the cemetery of the rulers from This. Tomb Uj, with 12 chambers, was the largest found. Although plundered, it still contained luxury items and imported wine jars. Cemetery B, just to the south, contained the tombs of the kings of Dynasty 0.

The most important centers of Upper Egypt for the Predynastic Period were Hierakonpolis, Gebelein, Naqada, and This, and they were competing for hegemony. By the time of Naqada II, Upper Egyptian culture was expanding to the north, and a new elite cemetery emerged at Tarkhan. Contemporary developments in the delta are poorly known, but important centers were Buto and Tell el-Farkha. Together with Tell el-Iswid, they exhibit the acculturation process of Lower

Egyptian and Upper Egyptian cultures. By Naqada III, Egypt was united by the rulers of Dynasty 0.

Wojciech Ejsmond

See also: Abydos; Hierakonpolis; Pottery; State Formation

Further Reading

Mczyska, A. 2013. *Lower Egyptian Communities and Their Interactions with Southern Levant in the 4th Millennium BC*. Studies in African Archaeology 12. Pozna: Pozna Archaeological Museum.

Midant-Reynes, B. 2000. *The Prehistory of Egypt: From the First Egyptians to the First Pharaohs*. Translated by Ian Shaw. Oxford: Wiley-Blackwell.

Teeter, E., ed. 2011. *Before the Pyramids: The Origins of Egyptian Civilization*. Oriental Institute Museum Publications 33. Chicago: Oriental Institute of the University of Chicago.

Wengrow, D. 2006. *The Archaeology of Early Egypt: Social Transformations in North-East Africa, c.10,000 to 2,650 BC*. Cambridge World Archaeology. Cambridge: Cambridge University Press.

Priestesses

Women served as priestess, or *hemet-netjer*, in ancient Egypt beginning in the Old Kingdom (2686–2160 BCE), but with only a few exceptions, they were all either a priestess of the goddess Hathor or the goddess Neith. Neith was an important goddess from the delta at the very beginnings of the ancient Egyptian state and was tied to war and hunting. Hathor was the cow goddess and the daughter of Ra and wife of Horus, and, as such, she was closely tied to the king as well as women in general. Based on the evidence of inscriptions from the Old Kingdom and the following First Intermediate Period (2160–2055 BC), there were at least 470 known priestesses of Hathor that were mostly concentrated in Memphis and northern Upper Egypt.

Men who were priests were not only divided into different categories of priesthood, for example, a *wab* priest or a lector priest, but in some cases, like at the sun temples at Abusir, there is evidence of phyles, or groups of priests, and how they rotated in and out of the temple duties. There is no evidence like this for female priests. There may have been differences because there is no evidence that females went to school, as only young boys did. Most scholars assume that the Hathor priestesses were from the upper echelons of Egyptian society, and so they may have been trained to read and write at home. There is no evidence for a female lector priest, who would be the one to read and recite at rituals.

These priestess positions disappear altogether by the later Middle Kingdom, around 1870 BCE. In the New Kingdom (1550–1069 BCE), women have a new religious position, that of *shamayt*, or "chantress." For the most part, the evidence for women with this title is in Thebes, and the women are wives of important officials. The symbols of their position are the sistrum and the menat, the two objects symbolizing Hathor that are always held by her priestesses. The sistrum and menat became symbols of a woman who held a cultic position, and in Thebes that meant

Menat

The menat, along with the sistrum, were symbols of the goddess Hathor and were held by women who served her cult. The menat was a heavy necklace or collar, with a mass of small beads attached to a single strand of beads going to a counterpoise, which would balance the weight of the beads. The nicest counterpoise would be made out of bronze. The necklace could be worn or held. The small beads were rattled and gave off a similar sound to the sistrum.

Lisa K. Sabbahy

the cult of the god Amun. The title shamayt is first known in the reign of Queen Hatshepsut; it makes sense that women would play a greater role while she was king. The title was also very common under the early Ramesside kings, when there was a religious backlash to the Amarna Period, as well as in the Twenty-First Dynasty, when the High Priests of Amun began to rule from Thebes. The title is known down to Ptolemaic times.

Lisa K. Sabbahy

See also: Amun; Hathor; Music and Musical Instruments; Priests

Further Reading

Gillam, Robyn. 1995. "Priestesses of Hathor: Their Function, Decline and Disappearance." *Journal of the American Research Center in Egypt* 32: 211–237.

Graves-Brown, Carolyn. 2010. *Dancing for Hathor: Women in Ancient Egypt.* London: Continuum.

Onstine, S. L. 2005. *The Role of the Chantress (šm'yt) in Ancient Egypt.* Oxford: Archaeopress.

Robins, Gay. 1993. *Women in Ancient Egypt.* London: British Museum Press.

Priests

The word for "temple" in ancient Egyptian was *per*, "house," or *hoot*, "mansion." This concept of the temple as a divine residence also explains the nature of the temple's priesthood. As the temple was the god's house, so the priests were the god's household staff. In fact, the ancient Egyptian name for the highest rank of priest, the *hem-netjer*, literally means "servant of the god"; although it is often translated as "prophet," "priest" is a better translation.

The most important priest of a cult was the first high priest, and the second, third, and fourth high priests followed him. The first prophet of an important state cult, such as that of the god Amun of Karnak Temple in the New Kingdom (1550–1069 BCE), was an extremely powerful official. He did not have to minister to the spiritual needs of a congregation, but he had to manage the temple and its holdings, which could be considerable. By the later New Kingdom, for example, the cult of Amun of Karnak and its priesthood were the most powerful economic institution in the country.

We do not have any real understanding of how a priest was trained, but they certainly all went to school and began as scribes so that they were literate. The autobiographical inscription of Bakenkhons, who was High Priest of Amun during part of the reign of Ramses II (1279–1213 BCE), gives us a glimpse into his career. Bakenkhons had two block statues that were found at Karnak Temple. The details of his autobiography are written on the statue that is now in the Egyptian Museum in Munich. Bakenkhons attended 4 years of school, which would have been spent reading and writing, and then trained in the horse stables of King Seti I, the father of Ramses, for 11 years. He then was a wab priest of Amun for four years, followed by being a god's father of Amun for 12 years. After that, he was the third high priest for 15 years, and the second high priest for 12 years. Then, Bakenkhons attained the office of High Priest of Amun, and remained so for the next 27 years (Frood 2007, 41). Very few ancient Egyptians would have lived this long, however, so the life of Bakenkhons cannot be seen as typical.

A few more bits of information can be found in the inscription on the second statue of Bakenkhons, now in the Egyptian Museum in Cairo. He says that he was "the son of the second priest of Amun at Karnak" and that he was "taught to be a wab-priest in the domain of Amun . . . under the guidance of his father" (Frood 2007, 43). Scholars know that by the Ramesside Period (1295–1069 BCE) jobs in ancient Egypt were hereditary; here is proof. This inscription also shows that he was trained "on the job," following in his father's footsteps.

The ordinary classes of priests, the wab priests, were officials and noblemen who spent three months of every year living and serving in the temple, broken up between months of living their usual life at home. *Wab* means "pure," and these priests had to remain ritually pure so that they could handle cult implements and carry the sacred boat of the god when it went forth from the temple. As the ancient Egyptians traveled everywhere in boats, on the river and canals, they envisioned that the gods also traveled by boat, even when carried on land. When a divine image went out of its temple in procession, it was placed inside a shrine in the middle of a small boat on carrying poles. On land, this boat was carried on the shoulders of the priests, and for longer journeys, it was placed on a larger divine boat on the river.

Older officials in the temple, above the wabs, were the god's fathers, who seemed to be in charge of supplies for the daily offerings and taking care of and documenting cult objects and temple property. The high priests were the ones who carried out the ritual in the temple for the care and feeding of the deity. They had high enough status to actually go into the chapel and could be present at the opening of the shrine containing the divine image.

Other priests could function in temple situations as well as in funerals, such as the lector priest, who specialized in recitation and recited the spells needed to aid the deceased in entering into the afterlife. The lector priest always wore a white sash diagonally across his chest. The sem priest, who can be recognized by his leopard skin, carried out the Opening of the Mouth ritual at the funeral to enliven the deceased so that they could live again in the underworld. Lector priests also recited temple rituals and could be found taking part in royal rituals as well, such

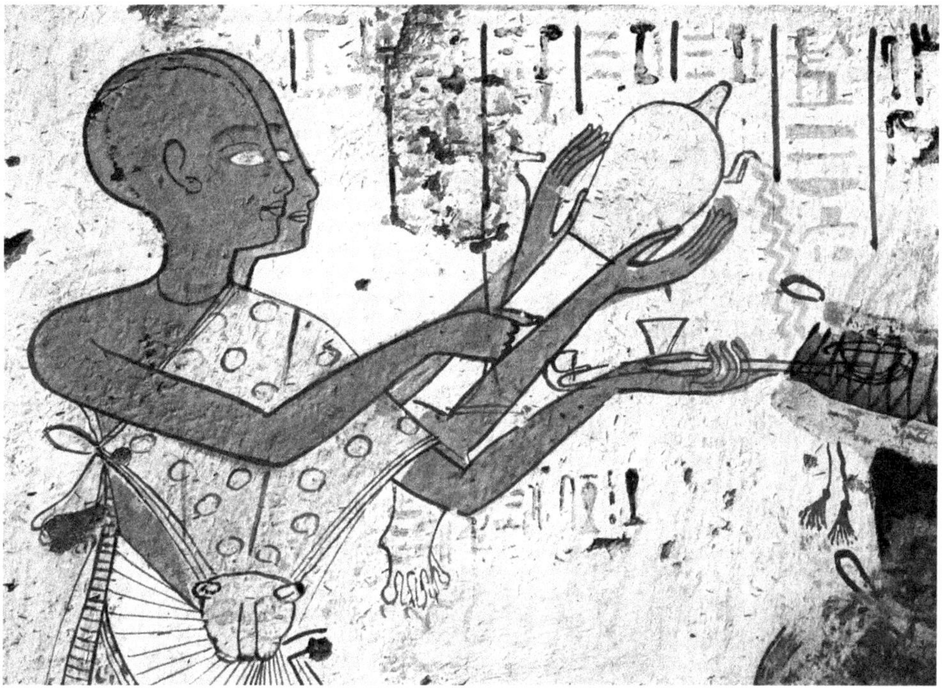

These two ancient Egyptian priests, shown in an Eighteenth Dynasty tomb on the West Bank of Thebes, are dressed in leopard skins and are libating and censing at the funeral of the tomb owner, Userhet. (Universal History Archive/UIG via Getty Images)

as the Sed festival. *Ka*-priests may well have been the most common ancient Egyptian priests, as they were the ones who brought the daily offerings to the tomb to feed the *ka* of the deceased. They would have signed a contract to receive produce from the estate of the deceased, and after offering it, they received it as their salary.

Purity was very important for the ancient Egyptian priest. Purity consisted of being physically clean by washing, sometimes three or four times, which also included rinsing the mouth with natron. Sometimes priests are seen with shaven heads, which could also be a way of being clean.

Lisa K. Sabbahy

See also: Amun; Barque, Sacred; Karnak; Scribes and Scribal Equipment

Further Reading

Forshaw, Roger. 2014. *The Role of the Lector in Ancient Egyptian Society.* Archaeopress Egyptology 5. Oxford: Archaeopress.

Frood, Elizabeth. 2007. *Biographical Texts from Ramessid Egypt.* Atlanta: Society of Biblical Literature.

Sauneron, Serge. 1960. *The Priests of Ancient Egypt.* London: Evergreen Books.

Shafer, Byron. 1997. "Temples, Priests, and Rituals: An Overview." In B. Shafer, ed. *Temples of Ancient Egypt.* Ithaca, NY: Cornell University Press, pp. 1–30.

Teeter, Emily. 2011. *Religion and Ritual in Ancient Egypt.* Cambridge: Cambridge University Press.

Provincial Administration. *See* Nomes and Provincial Administration

Ptah

The god Ptah was one of the most important deities in ancient Egypt, along with Ra, Osiris, and Amun. The earliest evidence for Ptah is on a First Dynasty (3000–2890 BCE) stone vessel found at the site of Tarkan. The figure of the god standing and holding scepters in his hands is clear, and up above, his name is written in hieroglyphs. Ptah is almost always shown standing, in human form, in a kind of shrine. He seems wrapped, almost like a mummy, and stands on a base, as if he is a statue. In his hands, he holds the *was*-scepter, the *ankh*, and the *djed* pillar. He wears a skull cap on his head that leaves his ears free; the cap is usually blue. Ptah's complexion is dark, usually green or black, like that of Osiris, indicating he is tied to life, resurrection, and fertility. He wears a short, straight beard, like the king, not the curled-up beard that gods wear.

The god Ptah was the god of Memphis, the capital of ancient Egypt and also the location of the royal residence for a majority of Egyptian history. Ptah was a creator god and also the patron deity of craftsmen of all types. This is a depiction of Ptah in the tomb of Queen Nefertary in the Valley of the Queens. (Art Directors & TRIP/Alamy Stock Photo)

The main cult place of Ptah was Memphis. Ptah may well have been a local god at Memphis at the time of state unification in Egypt, when the First Dynasty located the capital and royal residence there, but he became a state god. Part of the Ptah Temple, the western court with columns, dating to the reign of Ramses II, still stands at the site, now modern Mit Rahina. Ptah at Memphis was always called "Ptah, south of his wall," which has never been entirely understood. As Ptah was closely tied to the king, the name could have something to do with the fact that the Temple of Ptah was directly south of the king's palace. It has also been suggested that the word "wall" actually refers to the high white wall of limestone at Tura, clearly still visible today, from which Memphis lay slightly south.

Because of his cap, which is like one that craftsmen, especially

Shabaka Stone (EA 498)

The Shabaka Stone is a rectangular piece of conglomerate or basalt, about 26 by 53 inches, that was carved in the Twenty-Fifth Dynasty (ca. 780–656 BCE) under the Kushite king Shabaka with what is known as the Memphite Theology, the creation mythology of the god Ptah of Memphis. The stone was later used as part of a grinding mill, and so the 60 lines of text on the block are very badly damaged. The block was found at Memphis and acquired by the British Museum in 1805. In the text on the block, Shabaka says in the inscription that he found the original text very damaged, so maybe it was on papyrus and he had it copied. It is now thought that the original probably dates to the Ramesside Period.

Lisa K. Sabbahy

those working in metals, wore in the Old Kingdom (2686–2180 BCE), and the fact that Ptah resembles a statue, Ptah seems to have been tied to craftsmen. This is confirmed by the title of the high priest of the Memphis temple, "greatest of the directors of the arts." In the New Kingdom (1550–1069 BCE), the workmen at the village of Deir el-Medina, who cut and decorated the tombs of the kings in the Valley of the Kings, worshipped Ptah at a rocky outcrop southwest of the village. Villagers set up stelae there to both Ptah and Meretseger, the snake goddess of the village. One workman named Neferabu called upon Ptah, the "Lord of Truth," thanking him for a recovery from illness.

There are also stelae from the mortuary temple of Amenhotep III on the West Bank of Thebes dedicated to Ptah of the "Hearing Ear." One of the stela just has ears carved on it to help the god hear the prayer of the person offering it. The stelae seem to all come from the area of the entrance into the north side of peristyle court of the temple, so a chapel for Ptah must have been in that area. The temple was destroyed in an earthquake in the Nineteenth Dynasty (1295–1186 BCE), and it seems the cult of Ptah moved to the mortuary temple of Ramses III (1184–1153 BCE) at Medinet Habu when that temple was built.

By the time of the New Kingdom, Sakhmet, the lioness goddess of war and plague, had become the spouse of Ptah, and their nuclear family was complete with the addition of Nefertem, the god of the blue lotus, who is first associated with Sakhmet in Coffin Texts of the Middle Kingdom (2055–1650 BCE). Ptah is also a creator god, as put forth in the Memphite Theology, a text that might not have been written until the New Kingdom. Ptah created by thinking in his heart and speaking, and the word became the created thing. This theological text is known from the Shabaka Stone.

The *ba* of Ptah was thought to be manifested in the sacred bull named Hapi, or Apis, in its Greek form. The Apis lived in the southwest section of the Ptah Temple with its mother and was embalmed and buried in the Serapeum at Sakkara when it died. The earliest known Apis bull buried there belongs to the reign of Amenhotep III, and the latest burials are from the Ptolemaic Period (332–30 BCE).

Lisa K. Sabbahy

See also: Deir el-Medina; Memphis; Myths, Creation

Further Reading

Bierbrier, Morris. 1984. *The Tomb-Builders of the Pharaohs*. New York: Scribner's Sons.

Love, Serena. 2006. "Stones, Ancestors and Pyramids: Investigating the Pre-Pyramid Landscape of Memphis." In M. Barta, ed. *The Old Kingdom Art and Archaeology*. Prague: Publishing House of the Academy of Sciences of the Czech Republic, pp. 209–220.

Pinch, Geraldine. 2004. *Egyptian Myth: A Very Short Introduction*. Oxford: Oxford University Press.

Shafer, Bryon. 1991. *Religion in Ancient Egypt: Gods, Myths, and Personal Practice*. Ithaca, NY: Cornell University Press.

Stadelmann, Rainer. 2015. "Ptah Who Listens to Prayers in the Mortuary Temple of Amenhotep III at Thebes." *Bulletin of the Egyptological Seminar* 19: 613–617.

Verner, Miroslav. 2013. *Temple of the World: Sanctuaries, Cults, and Mysteries of Ancient Egypt*. Cairo: American University in Cairo Press.

Ptolemaic Egypt (305–30 BCE)

When Alexander the Great entered Egypt in 332 BCE, he marched to the ancient Egyptian capital city of Memphis, where tradition has it that he was crowned pharaoh. He also made offerings to the Egyptian gods, particularly the Apis bull of the god Ptah of Memphis. Then Alexander headed to the coast to choose the site of his future city, Alexandria. After pointing out the boundaries of the city and the location of all the main buildings to his architect, Alexander headed west to consult the oracle of the god Amun, or Zeus-Amun, as the Greeks knew him, at Siwa oasis. It is not known what Alexander asked the oracle, or what answer he received, but ancient sources say that the oracle either confirmed his divine descent from Zeus-Amun or his future rule over the entire world.

Alexander the Great left Egypt to continue his campaign in the East, dying in Babylon in 323 BCE. During the trip to return his body to Macedonia for burial, Ptolemy, one of Alexander's generals, instead took his body back to Memphis, where it remained until Ptolemy II took it to Alexandria and placed it in a tomb in the center of the ancient town. Called the Soma, Alexander's tomb was located where the two main streets of Alexandria crossed. This area became the royal cemetery used by the Ptolemies. Alexander the Great was at first succeeded by his half brother, Philip Arrideaus, and then by his son, Alexander IV, who was killed as a young boy. At this point, Alexander's empire breaks apart, and beginning in 305 BCE, his general Ptolemy rules in Egypt as King Ptolemy I Soter.

The city of Alexandria was completed under the first three Ptolemies; the time of Ptolemy III Euergetes was the highpoint of the city's splendor. Although little of the original city is left today, numerous ancient sources describe its wonders. The city was roughly rectangular in shape and divided in five districts, each named after a letter of the Greek alphabet. The districts were inhabited by Greeks, Egyptians, and Jews, the largest group being Greeks, as Alexandria was first and foremost a Greek city.

The city's location was picked because of its natural harbor. The Greeks divided the harbor in two by an artificial barrier, the Heptastadion, which connected the mainland to the island of Pharos just offshore. The great, or royal, harbor was on the east, and a smaller harbor, called *Eunostos*, "Good Return," was on the west. The lighthouse of Pharos was originally about 400 feet high and built in three sections. The bottom part was square in shape, the middle octagonal, and the upper part cylindrical. The lighthouse was completed in 279 BCE.

The Ptolemaic royal palace was on the mainland opposite the lighthouse, and its complex included the Mouseion, the library of Alexandria. It was the largest library of the ancient world and contained around 500,000 papyrus rolls. A large part of the library may have been destroyed in a battle between Julius Caesar and Pompey in 48 BCE. In any case, the library was completely destroyed in 269 CE when the entire palace complex was burned down.

A smaller library was located in the Serapeum, the temple complex sacred to the god Serapis, a deity created by the Ptolemies to fuse Egyptian and Greek beliefs. Serapis took the form of the Apis bull, a manifestation of the god Ptah of Memphis and the god Osiris. The gold and ivory cult statue of Serapis, said to have been carved by the Greek sculptor Bryaxis, was brought to the Serapeum from Asia Minor. Serapis resembles the Greek god Zeus, but he has heavy forelocks and wears a wheat basket, symbolic of fertility, on his head. The Serapeum was located on a low acropolis in the southwest part of Alexandria. Although nothing remains of the temple, foundation deposits dated to Ptolemy III (246–221 BCE) were found. The Serapeum was destroyed by Christians in 391 CE and the cult statue dragged through the streets.

Another significant building of ancient Alexandria was the Temple of Caesar, built by Cleopatra VII but finished by Augustus, who used it for his own cult. In front of the temple stood two obelisks that had originally been placed at the Temple of Heliopolis by Thutmose III (1479–1425 BCE). These two obelisks are referred to as Cleopatra's Needles; one is now in London and the other in New York City.

The kingdom of the Ptolemies consisted of Egypt, Cyprus, and Cyrenaica, and it was one of three powerful kingdoms, along with Macedonia, in Greece, and the Seleucids, in Syria and Mesopotamia. There was constant rivalry, at least between the Ptolemies and the Seleucids, and they fought six Syrian wars from the reign of Ptolemy II 285–246 BCE) to that of Ptolemy VI (180–145 BCE). The Ptolemies needed a strong economy to finance their army and navy and a stable situation in Egypt to be able to turn their attention to external conflicts. New Greek cities were established in the Fayum, and land reclamation was carried out there, vastly increasing its agricultural output.

Although the Ptolemies were Greek, they took up the role of ruling as pharaohs; marrying their sisters, as the Egyptian kings had often done; and building temples to curry favor and support from the priesthoods. Unfortunately, by the reign of Ptolemy IV, things began to decline because of family infighting, rebellion in Upper Egypt against the oppressive administration, outbreaks of mob rule in Alexandria, and economic problems. A serious problem was also the growing power of Rome. First Macedonia and then the Seleucids fell to Rome; by 58 BCE, they had annexed Cyprus. Ptolemy XII (80–51 BCE) was heavily in debt to Rome. His daughter, Cleopatra VII, who ruled from 51 BCE until her death in 30 BCE, did her best to retain and rule her independent Egyptian kingdom, but there was no stopping Octavian, who took Egypt in 30 BCE, making it part of the Roman Empire.

Lisa K. Sabbahy

See also: Obelisk; Philae Island; Roman Egypt; Temples, Ptolemaic-Roman

Further Reading

Chauveau, Michel. 1997. *Egypt in the Age of Cleopatra.* Ithaca, NY: Cornell University Press.

Thompson, Dorothy. 2005. "The Ptolemies and Egypt." In A. Erskine, ed. *A Companion to the Hellenistic World.* Oxford: Blackwell, pp. 105–120.

Walker, Susan, and Peter Higgs, eds. 2001. *Cleopatra of Egypt: From History to Myth.* Princeton, NJ: Princeton University Press.

Wojciechowska, Agnieszka. 2016. *From Amytaeus to Ptolemy: Egypt in the Fourth Century B.C.* Wiesbaden: Harrassowitz.

Punishment. *See* Crime and Punishment

Punt

Punt was an eastern polity on the Horn of Africa with which the Egyptians had a trade relationship from the Old Kingdom (2543–2120 BCE) until the end of the New Kingdom (1539–1292 BCE). For over a thousand years, Punt was the source of numerous luxury goods imported to Egypt, including obsidian, ebony, ivory, leopard skins, ostrich eggs and feathers, gold, electrum, plant aromatics such as myrrh, and exotic animals. Punt continued to appear in topographical lists during the Ptolemaic Period (331–30 BCE), although by that time it had been centuries since an expedition went to the distant land. Throughout Egyptian history, Punt experienced a privileged position among Egypt's diverse neighboring peoples; it was never subjugated or colonized by the Egyptians, nor given negative or subjugating epithets in monumental inscriptions, as other foreign peoples who posed a threat to Egypt's imperialist policies were. Likely because of Punt's association with myrrh and incense, both sacred and essential items for temple rituals, Punt was often called "God's land," and because of its location on the eastern horizon, it was called "the land of the horizon-dwellers."

Punt (or Pwenet) appears in Egyptian records for the first time during the Old Kingdom, when it was listed on the Palermo Stone as the source of large quantities of myrrh, electrum, malachite, and unguent brought to Egypt during the last year of Sahura's (2428–2416 BCE) reign. Scenes from his pyramid causeway at Abusir illustrate that myrrh trees were brought from Punt and planted in Egypt, a practice that remained in use until the Twentieth Dynasty (1190–1077 BCE). Expeditions were dispatched to Punt by Egyptian kings to barter with the Puntites, called *Puntiu* by the Egyptians, for luxury goods with two destinations, Punt and Bia-Punt, often translated as "Mine of Punt." These expeditions could have

Decorated block from the Temple of Queen Hatshepsut at Deir el-Bahari on the West Bank of Thebes. It depicts the king and queen of the land of Punt greeting the expedition arriving from Egypt. (Pictures from History/Bridgeman Images)

been conducted over land, by traveling south along the Nile valley, or water, via the Red Sea. The Sixth Dynasty (2305–2118 BCE) autobiography of Harkhuf records that he brought a dwarf back from Yam for King Pepi II, similar to a dwarf once brought from Punt for King Isesi (2365–2322 BCE).

An Eleventh Dynasty (2080–1940 BCE) inscription in Wadi Hammamat (a dry riverbed through the Eastern Desert) describes how a chief steward named Henenu led an expedition to Punt on behalf of King Mentuhotep III (1958–1947 BCE). Henenu's expedition crew of 3,000 men plus donkeys traveled through the wadi from Koptos (modern-day Qift) to the harbor site, a distance of nearly 100 miles, and dug over a dozen wells along the route for his and future expeditions. The crew carried with them supplies for the voyage, goods to barter with in Punt, and the timber for the ship that would be built and launched on the coast. In the 1970s, the discovery of Mersa Gawasis, an ancient harbor on the Red Sea coast called *Saww* in antiquity, provided archaeological verification of these and numerous other inscriptions and for the famous Deir el-Bahari relief scenes from the reign of Hatshepsut (1479–1458 BCE). A Twelfth Dynasty (BCE) inscription of Antefoker, vizier during the reign of Senusret I (1920–1875 BCE), at Mersa Gawasis describes an expedition crew of 3,700 who followed the same route, bringing with them the dismantled ships that had first been constructed in Koptos and were reassembled at the harbor.

Almost nothing about Puntite society and culture was preserved through Egyptian sources, and their indigenous language and autonym (a self-reflexive ethnonym) will likely remain unknown to us. The heads of Puntite communities were called "chiefs" or "great ones" in Egyptian texts, a title that the Egyptians used for foreign rulers of some other ethnic groups as well. The Puntite chiefs are mentioned in several texts as willing providers of Puntite exotica so desired by the Egyptians, but their social roles remain undefined beyond the fact that there were several Puntite chiefs at once, perhaps an indication of several cultural territories in close proximity or a chiefdom society. A scene of a Puntite chief named Parahu and his wife, Atiya, who is depicted in a very un-Egyptian heavyset fashion, is preserved at Deir el-Bahari. Both Parahu and his wife are adorned with beaded necklaces; Atiya also wears bracelets and anklets, while Parahu carries a dagger in his belt. Parahu, along with other Puntite men in the scenes, wears a beard in contrast to the Egyptian men, a Puntite attribute also noted in the scene's captions. The scenes include several depictions of conical Puntite huts of thatched construction sitting on stilts high off the ground. These huts were apparently multilevel, the top level accessed with a ladder, shown illustrated several times, and the bottom level being enclosed and functional, although the Egyptian scenes show no doorways. The Puntites also appear in many New Kingdom Theban tomb scenes, such as TT 39, belonging to Puymere, and TT 100, belonging to Rekhmire, where they are shown in procession bringing exotica to Egyptian officials. In Egyptian scenes, the Puntites are painted with varying shades of red and brown skin. These scenes indicate that not only did the Egyptians travel to Punt but they received Puntite traders as well.

The problem of Punt's exact location remains unresolved. Traditionally, Punt was believed to stretch across both sides of the Red Sea and include parts of Somalia and the Arabian Peninsula. Efforts to identify Punt's geographic location have primarily concentrated around its representation in Egyptian scenes and texts; Egyptian texts describe Punt as being located to the south and east of Egypt and accessible via the Red Sea. The Defenneh stele, dating to the Twenty-Sixth Dynasty (664–525 BCE), mentions "rainfall upon the mountain of Punt," an unfortunately vague reference that has nevertheless been an important one that scholars have used to associate Punt with tropical rains in the Horn of Africa. The most informative artistic renderings of Punt are the relief scenes on the second terrace of Deir el-Bahari, Hatshepsut's memorial temple in modern-day Luxor, that depict the expedition she dispatched to Punt during her reign. These scenes contain images of distinctly African flora and fauna—giraffes, hamadryas baboons, doum palms, and a rhinoceros—which disproves an Arabian or more eastern location. The detailed aquatic life depicted in the seafaring portions of these scenes corroborate a Red Sea or Indian Ocean voyage and make a Mediterranean locale impossible.

Most scholars now agree that Punt was most likely located in southeastern Sudan, northeastern Ethiopia, or the Eritrean coast. As archaeologist Rodolfo Fattovich has proposed, future solutions to Punt's illusive location will most likely be supplied through archaeological explorations in the Horn of Africa rather than from further examination of the Egyptian sources.

Taylor Bryanne Woodcock

See also: Nubia

Further Reading

Bard, Kathryn A., and Rodolfo Fattovich. 2013. "The Land of Punt and Recent Archaeological and Textual Evidence from the Pharaonic Harbour at Mersa/Wadi Gawasis, Egypt." In Stephen Chrisomalis and André Costopoulos, eds. *Human Expeditions: Inspired by Bruce Trigger*. Toronto: University of Toronto Press, pp. 3–11.

Danelius, Eva, and Heinz Steinitz. 1967. "The Fishes and Other Aquatic Animals on the Punt-Reliefs at Deir El-Baḥri." *Journal of Egyptian Archaeology* 53: 15–24.

Fattovich, Rodolfo. 1996. "Punt: The Archaeological Perspective." *Beiträge Zur Sudanforschung* 6: 15–29.

Harvey, Stephen P. 2003. "Interpreting Punt: Geographic, Cultural, and Artistic Landscapes." In David O'Connor and Stephen Quirke, eds. *Mysterious Lands*. London: UCL Press, pp. 81–91.

Kitchen, Kenneth. 1993. "The Land of Punt." In Thurstan Shaw, ed. *The Archaeology of Africa: Food, Metals, and Towns*. Abingdon, UK: Routledge, pp. 587–608.

Kitchen, Kenneth. 2004. "The Elusive Land of Punt Revisited." In Paul Lunde and Alexandra Porter, eds. *Trade and Travel in the Red Sea Region*. Oxford: Archaeopress, pp. 25–31.

Meeks, Dimitri. 2003. "Locating Punt: Geographic, Cultural and Artistic Landscapes." In David O'Connor and Stephen Quirke, eds. *Mysterious Lands*. London: UCL Press, pp. 53–80.

Phillips, Jacke. 1996. "A Note on Puntite Housing." *Journal of Egyptian Archaeology* 82: 206–207.

Pyramid Construction

The ancient Egyptians had all the natural resources they needed to accomplish building a large pyramid. The site of the pyramid was picked for nearby quarries that would supply the stone blocks for the core of the pyramid. Only the casing blocks would come from across the river at Tura. If that was done during the inundation, the boats could get very close to the quarry at Tura and also bring the blocks as close as possible to the pyramid. Some parts of the pyramid interior were done in granite that comes from the quarries at Aswan at the First Cataract. These blocks could also be moved more quickly during the inundation. Also, during the inundation, all the peasants were freed from work in the fields, so if extra hands were needed, a huge workforce was available. From what we know, a large pyramid of the Fourth Dynasty (2613–2494 BCE), like that at Northern Dahshur or the Great Pyramid at Giza, took 20–23 years to complete, so it was considered a long-term project.

To build a pyramid, huge amounts of rope needed to be made, and wood had to be gathered and made into sledges and levers. Bronze chisels and saws were needed and large wooden hammers. Food and drink also had to be available daily for all the workers and structures like barracks where they could live.

Cubit

A cubit, or *meh* in ancient Egyptian, was 20.6 inches and was based on the measure of a man's forearm. In fact, the hieroglyphic for *cubit* was a forearm. Cubits were used for measuring for building, measuring land, and measuring the height of the Nile's annual inundation. A number of cubit rods have been found in ancient Egyptian tombs, and it is assumed that the tomb owner must have needed it in his work. Cubit rods are made out of wood or stone and have markings on them dividing the cubit into seven "palms," and each palm into "four digits."

Lisa K. Sabbahy

The base of the pyramid had to be laid out and was oriented to true north, which could have been done by observing circumpolar or northern stars. The sides had to be straight and the exact same length, which might have been difficult, as the measuring cords could stretch. It is amazing that the Great Pyramid only has a difference of "7.9 inches between the longest and the shortest sides" (Edwards 1961, 256). The base also had to be level, although it is not entirely clear how that was done. Then the blocks could begin to be brought in to cover the base with horizontal courses of stone. "Hauling tracks" had to be made so that there was a hard surface to drag the sledges with blocks that weighed on an average two tons apiece. After an experiment in building an actual small pyramid, Lehner has suggested that 20 men could have hauled one of these blocks from the Khufu quarry at Giza to the base of the pyramid and return with their empty sled once every hour (Lehner 2017, 415), He also worked out with his crew that 12 men could quarry eight stone blocks a day (Lehner 2017, 419). The ancient Egyptians could have had hundreds working in the quarries and dragging blocks simultaneously.

As the pyramid began to go up, ramps were most certainly used, either straight ramps that got longer as they went up or one ramp that wrapped around the pyramid. The problem with straight ramps is that the ramp could become impossibly long in keeping it at a low enough angle to be able to drag the heavy blocks up. There may well have been a mixture of both kinds of ramps. There is some evidence that the Fifth Dynasty (2494–2345 BCE) pyramids at Abusir may have had interior ramps going into the middle of the pyramid and that this ramp may have helped construct the corridor into the pyramid (Arnold 2009, 186). Evidence of ramps can still be seen at some pyramid sites. They were made of limestone chips, river mud, and gypsum, and, at some sites, like Lisht, there were mudbrick retaining walls on the sides of the ramps. If ramps went up onto the body of the pyramid, they would have been removed as the casing blocks were put on, starting from top to bottom. Casing blocks were almost always limestone from Tura, although sometimes the very bottom courses of the pyramid were cased in red granite from Aswan. One block that would be very difficult to put into place is the pyramidion, the very last pointed block that topped the pyramid. It may very well have been taken up as the pyramid rose so that it was basically already in position at the end, as it would have been difficult to have many workers up at the top to position it.

Middle Kingdom (2055–1650 BCE) pyramids differ somewhat from Old Kingdom (2686–2160 BCE) pyramids. By the reign of Senusret II, the pyramids were constructed out of mudbricks, sometimes with stone cross walls, and then cased in white limestone. These pyramids have lost their casing, for example, the Hawara Pyramid of Amenemhat III as well as his "Black" pyramid at Dahshur, and the mudbrick does not hold up well.

Lisa K. Sabbahy

See also: Astronomy; Giza; Quarrying; Pyramids; Sledge

Further Reading

Arnold, Dieter. 1991. *Building in Egypt: Pharaonic Stone Masonry*. Oxford: Oxford University Press.

Arnold, Dieter. 2009. *The Monuments of Egypt: An A–Z Companion to Ancient Egyptian Architecture*. Cairo: American University in Cairo Press.

Edwards, I. E. S. 1961. *The Pyramids of Egypt*. Harmondsworth: Penguin Books.

Lehner, Mark. 1997. *The Complete Pyramids*. London: Thames and Hudson.

Lehner, Mark, and Zahi Hawass. 2017. *Giza and the Pyramids*. Cairo: American University in Cairo Press.

Verner, Miroslav. 2001. *The Pyramids*. New York: Grove Press.

Pyramid Texts

The Pyramid Texts (PT) represent the oldest, and one of the largest, collections of religious texts surviving from ancient Egypt. They owe their modern designation to the fact that they were inscribed on the walls of the subterranean structures pertaining to a number of Old Kingdom (2686–2125 BCE) royal pyramids at Sakkara, near modern Cairo, normally in the sarcophagus and antechambers as well as in some corridors. They first appear in the pyramid of the last ruler of the Fifth Dynasty, Unas(ca. 2350 BCE), and then in the monuments of the kings of the Sixth Dynasty. From the reign of Pepi I (ca. 2300 BCE), the corpus was also used in the pyramids of some queens. Here it is notable that originally only particularly important royal mothers had access to the texts, while later on, a number of king's wives benefited from them. As royal funerary texts, the PT survived into the Eighth Dynasty, where they are attested in the pyramid of King Aba, and even into the First Intermediate Period, being used for the Herakleopolitan king Wahkhara Khety (ca. 2050 BCE). They are not attested in royal funerary contexts in the ensuing Middle Kingdom. A total of 16 text pyramids are today attested, of which 6 are pyramids of a king.

After the breakdown of the Old Kingdom, the Pyramid Texts underwent a process of development that led to their being accessible to high-ranking officials outside of the royal family proper in the First Intermediate Period and Middle Kingdom, adorning their coffins and at times other burial equipment or tomb walls. There they appear either as unaltered copies of the original texts (list of sources in Allen 2006, ix–xi) or as somewhat edited versions incorporating new or local religious ideas. The materials of the latter enlarged corpus is today known as the Coffin Texts. Parts of the Pyramid Texts were still, if more sporadically, used in the tombs of some New Kingdom and Late Period officials, and even on some later royal sarcophagi.

LANGUAGE, FORMAT, AND ORIGIN

The Pyramid Texts are written in Old Egyptian, the earliest fully attested stage of the ancient Egyptian language and script, which was used in the Old Kingdom (2686–2160 BCE) but survived also into the Middle Kingdom Coffin Texts. Recent scholarship generally agrees that at least part of the materials found in the Pyramid Texts first existed in the oral sphere of transmission and to a limited extent also in a number of other written modes/contexts before they were monumentalized as carved hieroglyphic texts on the walls of royal pyramids. Specifically, the origin of a considerable portion is today believed to lie in the performance of funerary rituals, which eventually came to be written down and sections of which were then chosen to accompany the deceased kings into the afterlife to ensure their eternal existence. Their magical efficacy is underlined by the mostly green coloring of the hieroglyphs—an important color symbolizing regeneration—and by the deliberate and frequent mutilation of hieroglyphs representing living beings, such as birds or snakes, which were clearly believed to be rendered incapacitated in this way and thus could not pose a danger to the deceased. The oral background of the corpus is, among other things, evinced by the annotation "To recite" (*djed medu* in Egyptian) preceding every utterance or "spell" in the pyramid of Unas (2375–2345 BCE). This, in conjunction with dividing lines at the end of each unit, has allowed scholars to distinguish 227 different spells in that pyramid; by the time of his successor Teti (2345–2323 BCE), every line of text was headed in this way, and the corpus gradually increased from then on. In the pyramid of Pepi II (2278–2184 BCE), the repertoire comprised over 700 spells, with new compositions still coming to light to this day; presently, the known number of texts is around 900.

HISTORY OF SCHOLARSHIP

The Pyramid Texts were discovered by Gaston Maspero in 1880, who also published the first edition and a French translation of the texts found in the pyramid of Unas in 1894. By 1899, the Pyramid Texts known at that time were included among the textual materials drawn on for the compilation and publication of the first Egyptian dictionary edited by Erman and Grapow between 1926 and 1931, *Wörterbuch der Aegyptischen Sprache*, and were evaluated and eventually published and translated into German by Kurt Sethe between 1908 and 1922. English translations of the texts, first by Samuel Mercer and then by Raymond Faulkner, appeared in 1952 and 1969, respectively. As of 1925, Pyramid Texts of queens as well as the fragmentary remnants of the texts of King Aba of the Eighth Dynasty, around 2181 BCE, became known, and these were included in Faulkner's translations. In 1963, the *Mission archéologique française de Sâqqara* (MAFS) was founded and has since published many new text fragments; in the tradition of

Excerpt from a Pyramid Text

Below is a translated portion of Pyramid text 419:

The doors have been opened onto those whose places are hidden. . . . Remove your earth, shake off your dust, raise yourself, that you may travel in company with the Akh-spirits, for your wings are those of a falcon, your gleam is that of a star. . . . You are a great one with intact wereret-crown! May you provide yourself with your limbs of ore, (that) you (may) ferry across the sky . . . and make your abode . . . among the Imperishable Stars, who follow Osiris.

Source: Translated by Katja Goebs. PT 419 §§747a–749e.

Maspero, these texts are presented by pyramid, while a new edition of all known texts in the tradition of Sethe was recently published in digital format by James Allen in 2013.

As stated, scholars have long asserted the Pyramid Texts' origin in funerary rituals, which has entailed a long-standing debate on the sequence in which they should be read. As no two pyramids contain the same selection of texts, it is difficult to reconstruct a coherent funerary ritual sequence either from the outer rooms inward toward the sarcophagus chamber or the other way around. Egyptologists have also studied the Pyramid Texts as evidence for the oldest attested Egyptian religious beliefs. Specifically, they have debated issues such as the Egyptian conception of a "soul" as presented in these texts, the evidence for mythical stories contained in them, their reflecting the Egyptians' observation of specific astronomical phenomena, and what can be gleaned of their beliefs surrounding the topography of the celestial realm. A further important field of study concerns their exact relationship with the Coffin Texts and later corpora of Egyptian religious writings, and thus the evolution of Egyptian religious thought as a whole. A good example is the role of Osiris in the Pyramid Texts, which some scholars postulate is a later addition to their mythical materials.

THEMES AND FUNCTION

The primary purpose of fixing the Pyramid Texts on the walls of funerary monuments was clearly to ensure the continued afterlife of the deceased king or queen. Such a signification is in line with the proposed ritual background from which at least part of the spells may have been drawn, the format in which they were executed and distributed on the tomb walls, and the many references to religious and mythical themes and actors found in them. In fact, the Pyramid Texts provide us with the earliest account of Egyptian afterlife beliefs, describing and illuminating such fundamental issues as the transfiguration (*sakhu* in Egyptian) of the deceased after death, the celestial realm he wishes to reach and the paths leading to and through it, and the divine inhabitants of the sky and their forms and modes of existence and movement there. Yet, they also grant us a glimpse of more mundane aspects of Egyptian life, such as types of food; specific festival days and their required offerings; varieties of clothing, boats, or cattle; or aspects of the administration of the state, for example, where particular administrative titles are used to refer to the divine actors encountered by the deceased or where processes in the transmission of royal power are described.

The religious significance of the Pyramid Texts is underscored by a stonemason's construction mark that was found in the pyramid of Queen Ankhesenpepi II. Written in ink on blocks behind those walls of the funerary chamber that would have borne her Pyramid Texts, the gloss "Divine" or "Sacred Book" (*medjat netjer* in Egyptian) was jotted down. It is likely, therefore, that this was the ancient title of the corpus.

In a nutshell, inscription of the Pyramid Texts in funerary monuments ensured the eternal afterlife of the deceased by aiding him in his transfiguration into an inhabitant of the celestial realm. By identifying or otherwise associating the person with the gods of the sky, which appeared there in what was perceived as a succession of cosmic rulers, among other things, the deceased was integrated into the never-ending cycle of interchanging day and night (Goebs 2008). As such, he would partake in the celestial inhabitants' divine, immortal physique and their prerogatives of eternal food and other provisions as well as travel along the same celestial paths. These royal prerogatives became accessible to a broader section of society with the Middle Kingdom Coffin Texts.

Katja Goebs

See also: Coffin Texts; Myth; Pyramids; Sakkara

Further Reading

Allen, James P. 1989. "The Cosmology of the Pyramid Texts." In W. K. Simpson, ed. *Religion and Philosophy in Ancient Egypt*. Yale Egyptological Studies 3. New Haven, CT: Department of Near Eastern Languages and Civilizations, Yale University, pp. 1–28.

Allen, James P. 2005. *The Ancient Egyptian Pyramid Texts*. Edited by T. J. Lewis. Writings from the Ancient World. Atlanta: Society of Biblical Literature.

Allen, James P. 2006. *The Egyptian Coffin Texts*. Vol. 8, *Middle Kingdom Copies of Pyramid Texts*. Oriental Institute Publications. Chicago: Oriental Institute.

Allen, James P. 2013. *A New Concordance of the Pyramid Texts*. http://ancientworldonline.blogspot.ca/2013/07/a-new-concordance-of-pyramid-texts.html.

Berger-El Naggar, Catherine, et al. 2001. *Les textes de la pyramide de Pépy Ier*. 2 vols. Mission Archéologique Française de Saqqâra; Mémoires de l'Institut Français d'Archéologie Orientale 118. Cairo: Institut Français d'Archéologie Orientale.

Faulkner, Raymond O. 1969. *The Ancient Egyptian Pyramid Texts Translated into English*. 2 vols. Oxford: Clarendon Press.

Goebs, Katja. 2008. *Crowns in Egyptian Funerary Literature: Royalty, Rebirth, and Destruction*. Griffith Institute Monographs. Oxford: Griffith Institute.

Hays, Harold M. 2012. *The Organization of the Pyramid Texts: Typology and Disposition*. Probleme der Ägyptologie. Leiden: Brill.

Hornung, Erik. 1999. *The Ancient Egyptian Books of the Afterlife*. Translated by David Lorton. Ithaca, NY: Cornell University Press.

Pyramids

The very earliest kings of ancient Egypt, those of the first two dynasties, (3000–2686 BCE) were buried at the site of Abydos, in Upper Egypt, except for two to three kings of the Second Dynasty who were buried at Sakkara. These first tombs at Abydos were basically a burial chamber dug in the ground and covered by a mound of earth that was contained within a square structure called a *mastaba*. Then, separate from this, a large rectangular mudbrick enclosure was built to provide space for kingly rituals and celebrations to be carried on for eternity. The best preserved of these large enclosures is that of King Khasekemwy of the Second Dynasty, which is more than 120 by 60 meters in size and had walls that were more than 10 meters high. The tombs also expanded, becoming multichambered, and had an entrance with a staircase. What stayed the same at Abydos, however, was that the burial was in a mastaba out in the desert at an area known as Umm el-Ga'ab, and kingly rituals were carried out in the enclosures, which were built near the Temple of Osiris at the edge of cultivation. This meant that every royal burial complex was made up of two separate parts. The royal Second Dynasty tomb evidence at Sakkara is all substructures, with chambers and corridors underground; scholars have no evidence for what kind of superstructure was above the ground.

The kings of the Third Dynasty, who were buried at Sakkara, continued this form of burial tradition, but they put the two parts built at Abydos in one complex together, with the mastaba set inside the large enclosure. The first and most famous of these is the Step Pyramid Complex of King Djoser (2667–2648 BCE), which for the first time was built of stone instead of mudbrick. The bulk of the pyramid is limestone, and granite is used in the burial chamber. Djoser's tomb started as a mastaba, but then a series of additions were made to the sides and top that changed his mound into a structure of five steps. It is not known why the king's architect, Imhotep, decided to add steps onto his mastaba. Perhaps, it was simply to make the tomb higher and more monumental. A step pyramid resembles a giant staircase, and a slightly later Pyramid Text spell states that a staircase should be made for the king so that he may ascend to heaven on it.

The enclosure of the Step Pyramid was rectangular and oriented north to south. The entrance was on its north side, through the mortuary temple on the north. This aligned the corridor from the burial chamber to the North Star, which the Egyptians called the "Imperishable One," allowing the king's soul to go up, join the stars, and also become imperishable. At the south end of the enclosure is the "South Tomb." Its purpose is not entirely understood, but it may have been a tomb for king's soul or perhaps a tomb symbolic of Abydos, the place where the earliest kings were buried in southern Egypt. In any case, pyramids after this time have a tomb to the south.

The importance of the mound in association with a burial goes back to the creation of the world in ancient Egyptian mythology. In the beginning, there was nothing but dark sky and a dark, watery abyss known as Nun. Then a small mound of earth rose out of Nun, just like the land of Egypt rising out of the yearly flood, and the sun god, sometimes said to be in the form of a great gray heron, alighted on this mound and created life. This primeval mound, called the *benben*, was the place of birth, and that included rebirth in the afterlife. The *benben* was depicted by the ancient Egyptians with a round top, but eventually it became triangular, so that the tip of a pyramid and the top of an obelisk were solar symbols; they were *benben*s.

A little more than a hundred years after the reign of King Djoser, King Sneferu of the Fourth Dynasty (2613–2589 BCE) built the first true pyramid, a pyramid with smooth, slanting sides. This pyramid is at the site of Meidum, near the entrance into the Fayum. The pyramid does not look terribly impressive now, as the outer casing blocks and even many of the blocks from the actual structure of the pyramid have been quarried away. In Sneferu's time, however, the pyramid would have been cased with gleaming white blocks of Tura limestone, polished until they formed an absolutely smooth surface down the four sides of the pyramid. Another Pyramid Text spell says that the king could ascend to heaven on the "hardened rays of the sun"; certainly, the glistening sides of a true pyramid might have appeared like hardened sunrays.

Scholars do not completely understand the switch from a step pyramid to a true pyramid, but they assume that it had religious connotations. The relationship of the king to the sun god takes on new importance at this time. The kings of the Fourth Dynasty adopted a new title, the "Son of Ra," which was written above the cartouche containing their birth name. Ra was the sun god, and so this title expresses the close relationship between the god and the king. Fourth Dynasty pyramid complexes changed the direction of their orientation to match the movement of the sun. A true pyramid complex is not surrounded by a rectangular structure oriented south to north but is a series of structures oriented from east to west:

Great Pyramid

The Great Pyramid, built by King Khufu (2589–2566 BCE) of the Fourth Dynasty, is the largest of the three pyramids built at Giza, and it is the largest ancient pyramid ever built. It is 449.5 feet high and covers an area of 13.1 acres (Lehner and Hawass 2017, 143). It is estimated that 2.3 million blocks of stone were used to build the pyramid, which was constructed of local limestone quarried right near the pyramid, and then cased with finer limestone from the Tura quarries across the river. Almost all the casing is gone now, but some casing blocks can still be seen at the very bottom of the pyramid.

The burial chamber of the king was put up in the body of the pyramid and is reached by an ascending corridor, the last part of which is known as the Grand Gallery, the ceiling of which is slightly more than 26 feet high (Lehner and Hawass 2017, 152). The large granite sarcophagus that held the king's coffin is still in place in the burial chamber. Graffiti found on the blocks of the relieving chambers above the burial chamber mention year 19 of King Khufu, so it had taken that long to build the pyramid to that point. Out in front of the east side of the pyramid are three queen's pyramids, and slightly farther to the east is a cemetery of mastaba tombs for Khufu's sons and daughters.

Lisa K. Sabbahy

Reference

Lehner, Mark, and Zahi Hawass. 2017. *Giza and the Pyramids*. Cairo: American University in Cairo Press.

The Bent Pyramid of King Sneferu is named for its "bent" appearance. The rock bed upon which it was built was unstable, causing the pyramid to sink and crack during construction. The builders may have reduced the steepness of the angle toward the top to take weight off the structure. (Jorge Lascar)

the valley temple and then a long roofed causeway leading up to the mortuary temple against the east face of the pyramid. These structures follow the path of the sun so that the king's mummy entering the valley temple and being taken up through the causeway to the mortuary temple to be buried in the pyramid followed the setting, or "death," of the sun in the west. The king's pyramid was then a *benben*, a mound from which he could be reborn. The pyramid complex of King Khafra is the best preserved and most complete from the Fourth Dynasty.

Other structures are also found in a true pyramid complex. There is almost always a small south pyramid, as discussed above; small pyramids for the king's female family members; and pits with boats for the king's afterlife travels. Sneferu left the Meidum pyramid unfinished (he had it cased later) and built two further pyramids at Dahshur, the first, the so-called Bent Pyramid, which had to be abandoned because of cracking as the weak rock bed below settled, and then the Northern Pyramid, begun in year 29 of his reign, in which he was buried.

This pyramid is only slightly smaller in size than the Great Pyramid at Giza built by his son, Khufu. The pyramid complex of Khufu's son Khafra at Giza is the best preserved of all the true pyramid complexes, with the valley and mortuary temples still remaining. The Great Sphinx of Giza was also probably sculpted in the reign of Khafra.

The pyramids of the Fifth and Sixth Dynasties were much smaller in size than those of the Fourth Dynasty, but their mortuary temple plans became more complex and were extensively decorated: basalt floor, limestone walls covered with painted relief scenes, granite columns taking the form of palm trees, and inscriptions inset with copper. The best-preserved example of a pyramid complex from the Fifth Dynasty is that of King Sahura (2487–2475 BCE) at Abusir. At the end of the Fifth Dynasty, the first Pyramid Texts are found in the pyramid of King Unas (2375–2345 BCE) at Sakkara. Pyramid Texts then become standard in Sixth Dynasty pyramids for both kings and queens.

The kings of the Middle Kingdom (2055–1650 BCE) continued to build true pyramids, although a number of changes began to take place in the complex. The first Middle Kingdom pyramids were those of King Amenemhat I (1985–1956 BCE) and his son, Senusret I (1956–1911 BCE), who built their pyramids at Lisht, near their new royal residence, known as Itja-tawy, located north of Meidum. Amenemhat I's pyramid complex is not well-preserved, and parts were built from reused Old Kingdom blocks. Senusret I's complex shows the standard plan of an Old Kingdom pyramid complex from the Sixth Dynasty. The pyramids that follow show architectural changes. For example, the Lahun pyramid of Senusret II (1877–1870 BCE) had a valley temple, but there are no traces of a causeway and little in the way of evidence for a mortuary temple. The pyramid itself, although built on a core of solid limestone, was completed with mudbrick and then cased with limestone. The limestone casing has all been quarried away, so the pyramids look very sad and weathered today.

The Dahshur pyramid of Senusret III was surrounded by a rectangular niched enclosure, reminiscent of the walls of the Step Pyramid Complex. It is also unusual because along with the small pyramids for queens and daughters, typical of pyramids of the Old Kingdom, the actual burial chamber for his main queen was cut under the structure of the pyramid itself. The so-called Black Pyramid of Amenemhat III (1831–1786 BCE) at Dahshur was also brick-built and covered with limestone casing. With the casing gone, the brick structure is badly weathered and damaged. There was evidence of a causeway and valley temple at the pyramid, but no evidence of a mortuary temple has been found. The Hawara pyramid, a second pyramid belonging to Amenemhat III (1831–1786 BCE), in the Fayum, was oriented north to south. In front of the pyramid was a mortuary temple so large and complex and with so many chapels that Ptolemaic-Roman tourists later called it the "Labyrinth," but there is no known evidence of a causeway or valley temple.

One last change seen in the Middle Kingdom was that the entrance corridor into the pyramid, which had always been on the north side since the time of King's Djoser's Step Pyramid, began to be put on another side of the pyramid, or be hidden. For example, at Lahun, the entrance of the pyramid of Senusret II was a shaft cut down into the bedrock outside of the south side of the pyramid. After going down more than 50 feet, the shaft then went horizontally under the pyramid in the direction of the burial chamber. In the Hawara pyramid of Amenemhat III, the entrance into the pyramid was in the body of the pyramid, but on the southwest side. Once inside, the corridor to the burial chamber was no longer in a straight line, but constructed with turns and false walls to confuse tomb robbers. One corridor was actually just a "blind passage" that went straight north and then ended.

These changes in the plan of the corridors and chambers of the royal pyramid must not have been successful in protecting royal burials, because at the beginning of the New Kingdom (1550 BCE), the tombs of pharaohs were not built but cut into rock, hidden in the Valley of the Kings, an isolated wadi, or valley, on the West Bank of Thebes in Upper Egypt that was easily guarded. While the pyramids had been magnificent monuments by which the kings ascended up to heaven, they were very visible and had all been robbed and desecrated.

Lisa K. Sabbahy

See also: Abusir; Abydos; Dahshur; Giza; Hawara; Lahun; Pyramid Construction; Pyramid Texts; Sakkara

Further Reading

Arnold, Dieter. 1988. *The Pyramid of Senwosret I*. New York: Metropolitan Museum of Art.

Arnold, Dieter. 2002. *The Pyramid Complex of Senwosret III at Dahshur: Architectural Studies*. New York: Metropolitan Museum of Art.

Arnold, Dieter. 2015. *The Pyramid Complex of Amenemhet I at Lisht: The Architecture*. New Haven, CT: Yale University Press.

Edwards, I. E. S. 1993. *The Pyramids of Egypt*. Rev. ed. London: Penguin Books.

Lehner, Mark. 1997. *The Complete Pyramids*. London: Thames and Hudson.

Lehner, Mark, and Zahi Hawass. 2017. *Giza and the Pyramids*. Cairo: American University in Cairo Press.

Verner, Miroslav. 2002. *The Pyramids: The Mystery, Culture and Science of Egypt's Great Monuments*. London: Grove Press.

Verner, Miroslav. 2017. *Abusir: The Necropolis of the Sons of the Sun*. Cairo: American University in Cairo Press.

Q

Quarrying

The majority of preserved remains from ancient Egypt are of stone. The ancient Egyptians used stone for sculpture, reliefs, architectural elements, jewelry, and as domestic utilitarian tools. The sources of stone came mainly from the Nile valley and Eastern Desert, while the Western Desert hosted a few mines as well. For the most part, ancient quarries in Egypt remain relatively unexcavated and isolated in the desert, providing archaeologists with the unique opportunity to study how ancient mining communities functioned and worked together. More recent research by geologists and Egyptologists has increased our understanding of the ancient methods of procuring stone and ancient mining communities.

A wide variety of stones were used throughout Egyptian history for different purposes. Both limestone and sandstone were used for architectural elements and sculpture starting in the Early Dynastic Period (3000–2686 BCE). Limestone was mined throughout the Nile valley, while sandstone mines were located in the Nile valley south of Esna. Granite was used for architectural elements, such as columns, thresholds, and lintels, as early on as the First Dynasty (3000–2890 BCE). The principal source of granite for the ancient Egyptians was at the First Cataract in Aswan, where several mines were located, including the islands of Sehel and Elephantine, as well as the quarry on the East Bank known today as the Unfinished Obelisk Quarry.

Some stones were mined for use as ornamental stones due to their dramatic colors, patterns, and ability for high polishing after they were worked. From the site of Gebel el-Asr (Khafra's Quarry) in the Western Desert, both anorthosite gneiss and gabbro gneiss were mined and used for fine sculpture and stone vessels, most intensively from the late Predynastic up to the Sixth Dynasty. Under the bright desert sunlight, both stones from this mine produce a "striking blue glow," which might explain their appeal for royal statuary during the Fourth to Sixth Dynasties (2345–2181 BCE). Basalt was mined in the Fayoum region, at Widan el-Faras. This material was popular in the Early Dynastic and Old Kingdom periods for stone vessels and pavements in pyramid complexes, likely due to its dark blue color, which possibly represented the primeval waters from which the mound of creation had risen.

Another stone is metagraywacke, a hard stone that is green-gray in color and has a high polish when finished. The ancient name for this stone type was *bekhen*, and it was mined in the Wadi Hammamat area of the Eastern Desert. Metagraywacke was used throughout the Pharaonic era and into the Roman Period (30 BCE–495 CE) for statuary and sarcophagi. Another well-known ornamental stone is Egyptian alabaster, sometimes named calcite-alabaster and, erroneously, as travertine. This stone's translucent character was appealing for the ancient Egyptians, and it was principally mined in the area of Middle Egypt, from the Early Dynastic through the Ptolemaic era. Egyptian alabaster was used for everything, from small vessels to sarcophagi, temple pavements, and even monumental statuary.

During the Roman occupation of Egypt, new mines were opened and exploited for stones with new technologies, particularly iron tools. This included the mine at Mons Claudianus, where gray granodiorite was quarried for use back in Rome for building columns. The mine is located along the Red Sea, and freshly mined stone was transported over 150 kilometers through the desert until it reached the Nile valley near Qena, where it was then transported up the Nile River to the Mediterranean Sea. Another stone heavily extracted by the Romans was andesite-dacite porphyry, also known as "imperial porphyry." This hard purple stone was used exclusively by the imperial court in the Roman and Byzantine Periods for statuary, basins, and internal wall veneer. There is evidence of this stone being worked as small bowls during the Pharaonic era, but these were likely made from smaller boulders that were collected on the desert's surface. During the Ptolemaic (332 BCE–30 BCE) era, some exploitation of this stone took place at Gebel Dokhan, near the Red Sea. However, by the reign of the emperor Tiberius, full-scale mining of the stone started in the Mons Porphyrites area of the Eastern Desert.

Gemstones were also mined for use in jewelry and for making protective amulets, seals, and inlays for furniture and coffins. One theory suggests that the mining of gemstones was necessary for some pharaonic rulers to bribe their high officials and to secure their positions of power. A well-known gemstone used in ancient Egypt was lapis lazuli, which was imported from as far away as Afghanistan during the Pharaonic era. Some gems, such as carnelian and jasper, naturally occur on the surface of the desert plateau and were likely collected by hand rather than being mined. However, other gems were mined and extracted by the Egyptians. Common gemstones that were mined by the ancient Egyptians include malachite, garnet, mica, and turquoise. Various quartz stones were also mined from the Eastern Desert, such as amethyst and rock crystal from Wadi el-Hudi or Gebel el-Asr. During the Roman Period, emerald mining in the Eastern Desert increased and was conducted in the area between Myos Hormos and Berenike. It is believed that most of the gemstones listed above came from Egyptian sources, although there have only been a few mines located so far in Egypt where these gemstones were quarried.

During the Pharaonic era, mining of hard stone was principally done with pounders made from dolerite or sometimes granite, silicified sandstone, or anorthosite gneiss. These pounders were employed to either knock off small chunks of bedrock to carve out trenches and undercuts around large blocks of stone. Test shafts, or "proofing holes," were sometimes carved around large blocks of stone, such as the Unfinished Obelisk in Aswan, to test the stability of the rock before large groups of workmen began carving the stone away. When possible, the ancient Egyptian quarrymen would use fire setting to weaken and crack the surface and then use pounders to carve a trench. Fire setting is the process of building low, mudbrick walls that run parallel to each other that are then filled with fuel to burn. Once the fire has burned for some time, water is thrown onto the fire to cool and "shock" the stone below, causing cracks and fissures to form along the mud-brick line. Quarrymen then come in with stone pounders to hack away the weakened stone along the trench. Sometimes, though not often, wooden or stone levers were utilized to remove large blocks along these cut trenches. From the archaeological evidence, it appears that some preliminary polishing of the stone was done in the quarry before its removal. Final polishing of the granite, whether at the quarry or the construction site, was done by means of quartz powder mixed with water, which created a type of paste that was rubbed across the surface of the stone to smooth and polish it.

Starting in the Ptolemaic Period, and continuing into the Roman era, iron-wedge technology was used for extracting hard stones from the bedrock. The Ptolemaic and Roman quarrymen would carve a series of small and shallow rectangular holes along a rock surface, which they then hammered iron chisels back and forth into until the rock split. This technique is called the "pointillé technique," and it allowed for exact, controlled lines of separation, creating a more efficient way of mining hard stones.

Pharaonic mining of soft stone, such as limestone or sandstone, was done by means of chisels and wooden mallets. Trenches were carved around the potential block, and, once complete, an undercut was done by means of hammer and chisel to extract the block from its position. Once removed from the mine, the quarrymen would dress the stone and clean its surface before it was transported back to the Nile valley. The chisels were made from either copper or bronze, which had to be sharpened often throughout the extraction process. By the Ptolemaic and Roman Periods, iron chisels were introduced into the soft stone mining process.

Various methods were used for transporting the cut stone blocks from the mine back to the Nile valley. Iconographic evidence during the Pharaonic Period illustrates teams of workmen using wooden sledges to transport large blocks of stone. For quarries that were located farther away from the Nile, stones were loaded onto wooden sledges, which were then pulled by animals or groups of men across wooden beams. Several mines still have paved roads associated with them made from local materials; however, the preserved roads do not show evidence of track marks, raising questions of how exactly these blocks may have been transported via the paved roads. During the Ptolemaic and Roman Periods, it was more common for large stone blocks to be transported by wagons pulled by draft animals via an extensive network of roads. Harbors and canals were also used to transport blocks of stone to the Nile, as is evident at the Unfinished Obelisk Quarry in Aswan. Large blocks of granite were dragged onto barges in dry docks at the quarry, where they waited for the coming inundation. Once the Nile flood took place, the canal and quarry harbor would fill with water, and the transport of the large stone blocks could continue to its final destination via the Nile.

Ancient inscriptions describe thousands of workmen being employed to work as part of the state-sponsored mining expeditions, with numbers ranging from just over 1,000 up to 19,000 (Sadek 1980, 17 and 103; Bloxam 2007, 23). However, the archaeological evidence that remains at ancient quarries does not necessarily support the testaments of the inscriptions. The associated settlements of stone quarries range from low stone walls, no taller than 1.5 meters, to single-level stone circles, used to support either windbreaks or temporary shelters. At the quarries of Widan el-Faras or Gebel el-Asr, archaeologists estimate that the known settlements could only support teams of 20–25 men (Bloxam 2007, 25–26). However, closer readings of the quarry inscriptions show that only a small number of men were named as "stoneworkers" or "quarrymen," suggesting that smaller groups of skilled workmen, perhaps with close kinship relations, were employed to work at the stone mines. A large number of men used for the mining workforce were perhaps conscripts during the annual Nile flood, where a huge portion of the population was free from work for three months.

An autopsy of the mummy of Nakht at the Royal Ontario Museum in Canada revealed that the deceased had traces of granite dust in his lungs. Researchers suggest that the young man possibly worked at a stone workshop or quarry for some time, which explains why he inhaled so much dust. If this were a correct hypothesis, Nakht's mummy would be the only physical remains of an ancient miner known to Egyptologists.

The largely exaggerated numbers in the mining campaign inscriptions could indicate a complex network of hierarchy for the procurement of stone throughout the Nile valley. For the quarries located closer to the Nubian border in the south, such as the amethyst mines at Wadi el-Hudi, both textual and archaeological evidence suggests that Nubians were employed to work alongside the Egyptian miners. Depending on the local terrain, the mining settlements could range from fortified hilltop settlements, such as the settlement at Wadi Magharab or Site Five at Wadi el-Hudi, or they could be rectangular fortifications on the wadi floors, especially at mining sites between the First and Fourth Cataracts during the expansion and colonization of Nubia in the Middle Kingdom.

Nicholas R. Brown

See also: Jewelry; Mining; Obelisk; Pyramids

Further Reading

Bloxam, E. G. 2007. "Who Were the Pharaoh's Quarrymen?" *Archaeology International* 2005/2006: 23–27.

Harrell, J. A. 2002. "Pharaonic Stone Quarries in the Egyptian Deserts." In R. Friedman, ed. *Egypt and Nubia: Gifts of the Desert.* London: British Museum Press, pp. 232–243.

Harrell, J. A., and P. Storemyr. 2009. "Ancient Egyptian Quarries—an Illustrated Overview." In N. Abu-Jager, E. G. Bloxam, P. Degryse, and T. Heldal, eds. *Quarryscapes: Ancient Stone Quarry Landscapes in the Eastern Mediterranean.* Trondheim, Norway: Geological Survey of Survey of Norway, Special Publication 12, pp. 7–50.

Hawass, Z. 2009. "The Unfinished Obelisk Quarry at Aswan." In S. Ikram and A. Dodson, eds. *Beyond the Horizon: Studies in Egyptian Art, Archaeology, and History in Honour of B. J. Kemp.* Cairo: Supreme Council of Antiquities, pp. 143–164.

Klemm, D., and R. Klemm. 2001. "The Building Stones of Ancient Egypt—a Gift of Its Geology." *African Earth Sciences* 33: 631–642.

Liszka, K. 2015. "Gems in the Desert: Recent Work at Wadi el-Hudi." *Egyptian Archaeology* 46: 37–40.

Reyman, T., M. R. Zimmerman, and P. K. Lewin. 1977. "Histopathologic Investigation." *Canadian Medial Association Journal* 117: 470–472.

Sadek, A. 1980. *The Amethyst Mining Inscriptions of Wadi el-Hudi: Part I: Texts*. Warminster, UK: Aris and Phillips, Ltd.

Shaw, I. 1994. "Pharaonic Quarrying and Mining: Settlement and Procurement in Egypt's Marginal Regions." *Antiquity* 68, no. 258: 108–119.

Shaw, I. 2002. "Life on the Edge: Gemstones, Politics and Stress in the Deserts of Egypt and Nubia." In R. Friedman, ed. *Egypt and Nubia: Gifts of the Desert*. London: British Museum Press, pp. 244–251.

Queens

The ancient Egyptian queen held the title *hemet-nesu*, which means "Wife of the King." Unlike other people, the ancient Egyptian king could have more than one wife, and by the time of the late Middle Kingdom, roughly around 1700 BCE, there is evidence of the title "King's Great Wife," which indicated the principal and most important of the queens. It was the oldest son of the King's Great Wife who was considered to be the king's successor to the throne. The queen was considered to be the medium by which royal power transferred from father to son; a king's mother passed on to him the legitimate right to rule. A good example of King's Great Wife was Queen Nefertari, the wife of King Ramses II (1279–1213 BCE), who is prominently depicted alongside her husband throughout her lifetime. She appears with Ramses II in his regnal year 1 and is shown on all his important monuments, the last time being year 24 at Abu Simbel, by which time scholars think she must have died.

Image of Nefertari, wife of Ramses II of the Nineteenth Dynasty, in her tomb in the Valley of the Queens on the West Bank of Thebes. Her most important title, "Great Wife of the King," is written in the vertical line of inscription above her hands. (Barry Iverson/The LIFE Images Collection/Getty Images)

What is interesting is that if a royal son was very young when his father died, he was crowned king, but his mother actually ruled for him until he was older. There seems to be evidence for this situation as early as in the First Dynasty, and there is clear evidence later, in the Sixth Dynasty, when the mother of King Pepy II (2278–2184 BCE) ruled for him when he took the throne at the age of six. There are also a few cases when a queen actually became

Hatshepsut

Hatshepsut was the daughter of King Thutmose I (r. ca. 1504–1493 BCE) and the wife of her half brother Thutmose II (r. 1493–1479 BCE). Thutmose II died after a reign of only a few years. As far as we know, he and Hatshepsut only had one child, a daughter, Nefer-ure, although Thutmose II had a son, Thutmose, still only an infant, from another wife, named Isis. This son became King Thutmose III, and Hatshepsut, instead of his mother, Isis, served as regent for him. Then sometime between two and seven years later, Hatshepsut took a throne name, Ma'at-ka-Re, and proclaimed herself king in a coregency with Thutmose III. Coregencies were fairly common in ancient Egypt, but they usually consisted of an elderly king naming his son and heir ruler with him so that succession to the throne was already decided when he died. In Hatshepsut's situation, she named herself coregent with a very young boy.

There is some evidence that at the beginning of her kingship, Hatshepsut was depicted with a mixture of the attributes of queen and king, but then there was a change, and she was depicted as male, with a male physique and clothing, although it was known that Hatshepsut was a woman. Hatshepsut and Thutmose III ruled together for 22 years, until Hatshepsut died of natural causes. After her death, Thutmose ruled for another 32 years. In year 42 of his reign, his son, Amenhotep II, became king with him in a coregency. It was at this time that Hatshepsut's monuments were defaced, apparently to promote the legitimacy of the family line of Thutmose III and strengthen the kingship of Amenhotep II.

Lisa K. Sabbahy

king, such as Sobek-neferu at the end of the Twelfth Dynasty and Tausret at the end of the Nineteenth. The most famous of the queens who ruled was Hatshepsut (1478–1458 BCE), who was the daughter of Thutmose I and the wife and queen of Thutmose II, who was her half brother. Marriage between royal siblings was commonplace in ancient Egypt. Not only did this reflect the pattern of brother-sister marriage found in the myths about Egyptian deities, for example, Osiris and his wife, Isis, are siblings, but it also limited who could claim the throne by family relationship.

The king of Egypt was considered to be divine, as he was the incarnation on earth of the falcon god, Horus, son of Osiris. The queen had no comparable divine position, but she could consort with divinity. This position changes somewhat in the New Kingdom (1552–1069 BCE), when certain queens, such as Queen Tiye, wife of Amenhotep III, and Queen Nefertari, wife of Ramses III, are deified as the goddess Hathor, Tiye in her temple at Sedeinga in Nubia and Nefertari in the small temple at Abu Simbel.

In each of the Kingdoms, Old, Middle, and New, the queen had other titles and epithets accompanying her main title, "Wife of the King." In the Old Kingdom, the titles "the One who sees Horus and Seth," "Great of Affection," and "Great of Praise" were the three most commonly added titles. By the time of the Middle Kingdom, there were two simple and basic patterns to the queen's titulary: "Hereditary Noblewoman and Wife of the King," and "Wife of the King and She who is Joined to the White Crown." Additional titles of a more political nature appeared in the Middle Kingdom as well, such as "Mistress of Women" and "Mistress of the Two Lands."

In the beginning, there does not seem to have been any special regalia worn or held by the queen. In the Old Kingdom, the king's mother wore a vulture headdress, symbolizing her position as mother (the ancient Egyptian words for *mother* and *vulture* were the same, so this is a kind of play on words), but the queen had nothing special marking her position. By the time of the Middle Kingdom, both the queen and the princess wear the *uraeus*, the rearing cobra that adorned and protected the forehead of the king. These Middle Kingdom royal women could also wear a modius, a kind of platform, with double plumes. In the reign of Amenemhat III (1831–1786 BCE), his daughter, Princess Neferu-Ptah, put her name in a cartouche, and by the early New Kingdom, queens regularly used the cartouche. Also at the beginning of the New Kingdom, the queen held a flywhisk that resembled both the flail held by the king and the hieroglyphic sign *mes*, which means, "to give birth." By the reign of Amenhotep III (1390–1352), in the later Eighteenth Dynasty, the ancient Egyptian queen could wear a sun disk, double plume, cow's horns, and a single or double uraeus. This headgear was standard for queens from then on.

Queens of the Old and Middle Kingdoms were buried in small pyramids within the enclosure of the pyramid complex of their husbands. In the New Kingdom, the queens' burials were all in Thebes on the West Bank of the river. By the time of the Nineteenth Dynasty, queens were buried in the Valley of the Queens. The most beautiful and famous tomb there is the tomb of Nefertari, Chief Wife of Ramses II.

Lisa K. Sabbahy

See also: Abu Simbel; Valley of the Queens; Women

Further Reading

Arnold, D. 1996. *The Royal Women of Amarna*. New York: Metropolitan Museum of Art.

Cooney, Kara. 2014. *The Woman Who Would Be King: Hatshepsut's Rise to Power in Ancient Egypt*. New York: Crown.

Troy, L. 1986. *Patterns of Queenship in Ancient Egypt: Myth and History*. Uppsala: Boreas 14.

Ziegler, C. 2008. *Queens of Egypt from Hetepheres to Cleopatra*. Monaco: Grimaldi Forum.

Primary Document—Hatshepsut Becomes Regent for Thutmose III

In this text, King Thutmose II (1492–1479 BCE) of the of the Eighteenth Dynasty has just died; his only son, Thutmose III, probably still a young baby, has become king; and his stepmother, Hatshepsut, is serving as regent for him and governing the land in his name.

> (He) went forth to heaven, joining the gods. His son stood in his place as king of the Two Lands. He ruled on the throne of the one who had begotten him. His sister, the God's Wife, Hatshepsut arranged the affairs of the land. The Two Lands were under her governance. Work was done for her.

Source: Translated by Lisa K. Sabbahy from Sethe, Kurt. 1961. *Urkunden der 18. Dynastie*. Vol. 1. Berlin: Akademie Verlag, 59, lines 14–17 and 60, lines 1–3.

R

Ra

Ra was the ancient Egyptian sun god and one of the creator gods. This deity took a multitude of forms that varied depending on his location and function. Most frequently, Ra was identified as the midday sun, traveling by boat high in the sky above. His influence permeated all strata of Egyptian society and culture, as his continual visible presence in the sky reinforced his preeminence in the ancient Egyptian pantheon of gods. Throughout Egyptian history, despite the rise and fall in prominence of other deities, Ra's influence in the sky, on the earth, and in the underworld remained intact.

The sun god Ra-Horakhty is presented an offering by the deceased on this wooden stela of the Third Intermediate Period from Thebes. In the register above, the solar disk is shown in the sacred boat of the sun god, in which he travels through the sky. (Rogers Fund, 1928/The Metropolitan Museum of Art)

In art, Ra is identifiable as the solar disk, shown frequently encircled by a protective cobra and sometimes depicted with outstretched wings. Ra was also depicted as a falcon with a sun disk crowning his head or portrayed with a human body and the head of a falcon. As the sun, Ra had varying forms that represented the sun at differing times of day. As the morning sun, Ra was represented with a scarab head, and as the evening sun, he was represented with the head of a ram. At noon, he was portrayed as a falcon-headed deity.

Moreover, in later periods of Egyptian history, Ra was frequently merged with other ancient Egyptian gods to become other forms of the sun. For example, Ra-Horakhty was a combination of Ra and Horus that represented the morning sun, while Atum-Ra was a combination of Ra and Atum that represented the evening sun. In these forms, Ra can be depicted in his anthropomorphic form as a man with the head of a falcon. Perhaps the most prominent synchronized form of Ra was his combination with the god Amun during the New Kingdom, whose cult at Thebes remained popular for the rest of pharaonic history and beyond. Nevertheless, Ra continued to maintain his own separate identity and cult along with these varying manifestations.

Although referenced in kings' names as early as Raneb from the Second Dynasty (2890–2686 BCE), the earliest cult of Ra began in the Fourth Dynasty (2613–2648 BCE), during which time the title "Son of Ra" was added to the king's titulary, and kings began to incorporate "Ra" into their own names. Examples from the Fifth Dynasty (2494–2345 BCE) include kings Sahura, Neferirkara, Shepseskara, Nyuserra, and Djedkara. The prominence of the solar cult during the Old Kingdom was manifested physically as sun temples, which featured obelisks and solar courts, with interior decoration that focused on nature as the gift of the sun. It is believed that the earliest of these temples was erected at Heliopolis, where ancient Egyptians believed life first began. It was also the primary cult center of Ra as a creator god.

The Heliopolitan cosmogony describes Ra's status as a creator god. According to this creation myth, it was Ra who emerged first from the primeval waters of Nun, sparking the beginning of the known world. Then, he created from himself the first gods, Shu and Tefnut, as air and moisture. These two gods bore Geb and Nut, the earth and sky, who in turn bore Osiris, Isis, Seth, and Nephthys. Together, these nine gods form the Ennead.

Although primarily associated with the sky, mythology notes that Ra once ruled on the earth as king. This myth was recorded as a narrative account referred to as the *Book of the Heavenly Cow* that described humanity's rebellion against the gods. Hathor, as the fiery eye of Ra, is dispatched to punish the humans who conspired against Ra. She is only stopped after becoming drunk on beer disguised as blood. Despite Hathor's successful quelling of the humans, Ra withdraws from earth to dwell in the sky. He leaves his son, Shu, to rule in his absence, thus establishing the institution of hereditary kingship.

Additionally, Ra's journey across the sky influenced the ancient Egyptian concept of time, dividing the day into 12 hours, during which Ra was visible in the sky, and 12 hours of night, during which Ra traversed the Netherworld. His reappearance over the horizon each morning signified the constant renewal of the cosmos and the created world.

During the Old Kingdom, it was the hope of the deceased king to join the sun god on his solar barque as he journeyed across the sky. This desire was established in the Pyramid Texts from the Old Kingdom, a series of spells inscribed on the burial chambers of kings from the Fifth and Sixth Dynasties. Here, Ra is described in a multitude of forms, as mentioned above, as he emerges from the eastern horizon and sets in the western horizon. During the Middle Kingdom (2055–1650 BCE), the deceased became one with Osiris, a counterpart to Ra in the Netherworld. Nevertheless, Ra's importance continued as a protector of the Osiris and the deceased in the afterlife. Ra's protective function is immortalized in his scarab form, with scarab amulets becoming popular apotropaic forms.

During the New Kingdom, funerary literature focused on the sun god's nocturnal journey through the Netherworld. Scholars term the compositions illustrating Ra's chthonic (underworld) journey *Netherworld Books*, while his nocturnal journey across the heavens are called *Books of Sky*. Initially, these compositions were inscribed on royal tomb walls and other burial equipment, and later written on papyri, and inscribed on sarcophagi as they became accessible to the larger population in the Ptolemaic Period (322 BCE–30 CE). This genre of compositions included extensive figural illustrations of the sun god and his companions as they traversed the Netherworld between sunset and sunrise. During the 12 hours of the night, Ra provides for the blessed dead and punishes the damned. He merges with the corpse of Osiris, which rejuvenates Ra and allows him to battle his enemy par excellence, Apophis. The dualistic relationship between Ra and Osiris is highlighted in each of the Netherworld Books and allows Ra to be reborn in the eastern horizon each morning.

Another composition of note is titled the *Litany of Ra*. This recitation further describes and praises Ra as he descends into the Netherworld, renewing the blessed dead and punishing the damned. In this and all other funerary compositions that emphasize Ra, the deceased sought to identify themselves with each manifestation of Ra, to highlight the connection between himself and the creator god.

Amber Lue Ward

See also: Amun; Aten; Hathor; Horus; Isis; Osiris; Ptah; Seth

Further Reading

Assmann, Jan. 1995. *Egyptian Solar Religion in the New Kingdom: Re, Amun and the Crisis of Polytheism*. Translated by A. Alcock. London: Kegan Paul International.

Hornung, Erik. 1999. *The Ancient Egyptian Books of the Afterlife*. Translated from the German by David Lorton. Ithaca, NY: Cornell University Press.

Kahl, Jochem. 2007. *"Ra Is My Lord": Searching for the Rise of the Sun God at the Dawn of Egyptian History*. Menes 1. Wiesbaden: Harrassowitz.

Quirke, Stephen. 1992. *Ancient Egyptian Religion*. London: British Museum Press.

Quirke, Stephen. 2001. *The Cult of Ra: Sun-Worship in Ancient Egypt*. London: Thames & Hudson.

Wells, R. A. 1994. "Re and the Calendars." In Anthony J. Spalinger, ed. *Revolutions in Time: Studies in Ancient Egyptian Calendrics*. San Antonio: Van Siclen Books, pp. 1–37.

Religion, Personal

Personal religion in ancient Egypt is one of the most difficult areas of Egyptology to study. One of the main challenges is the fact that most of the information we have about ancient Egypt comes from two main contexts: funerary and royal. These contexts are very valuable in terms of information on funerary beliefs and state religion, but they are unfortunately not as informative for those who wish to understand how the average ancient Egyptian person perceived and interacted with the divine.

Private religion can be defined as "religious action in an everyday context." (Baines 1987, 79) The ancient Egyptians believed that there was a hierarchy of existence: Gods, kings, the "blessed dead," and humankind. Their personal religion centered on the relationship between humankind and the gods or the deceased. According to ancient Egyptian thought, the world is full of dangers that have to be averted. The sources of these dangers include nature, gods and demons, and the blessed dead. These very same sources of danger could also be sources of aid and protection against affliction. For this reason, the private religion of the ancient Egyptians was mainly concerned with appeasing the gods and the blessed dead and having the latter intercede on their behalf with the gods. This divination was mainly through oracles and consultation with seers. Our knowledge of this form of religion is limited by the fact that most of the surviving information dates to the New Kingdom (1550–1069 BCE) and later. However, some data motions toward private religious practice much earlier in ancient Egyptian history. The reason why evidence is lacking from earlier periods is because pre–New Kingdom, there were regulations in place that banned all depictions of religion in civilian settings.

APPEASEMENT, GRATITUDE, AND INTERCESSION

The private religion of the ancient Egyptians is reconstructed through the objects dedicated by them to the gods, requesting good health and safety, as an expression of gratitude for reversing an affliction inflicted by them upon people who have displeased them, or requesting the intercession of a divine power with divinities higher up in the hierarchy of divinity. Ancient Egyptians dedicate sacred objects, such as private stelae, to the gods and divine dead alike. The stelae are put up in religious buildings by their dedicators, who present the offerings with the aim of appeasing the divine powers, giving thanks for the good in their lives, and begging forgiveness for their sins.

Ancestor worship was a very important part of private religion in ancient Egypt. The most important sources of information on this type of religion include letters to the dead, stelae dedicated to ancestors, and possibly what are known as anthropoid, or ancestor, busts. Some letters to the deceased still survive, dating back as far as the late Old Kingdom period (2686–2181 BCE). The letters, discovered in tombs, were typically inscribed upon bowls that once contained edible offerings to the deceased. Ancient Egyptians believed that the owner of the tomb would consume the food offering, read the letter on the bowl, and respond. Other letters, often addresses to the *akhu*, or the spirits of the dead, were written on linen and papyrus. The idea behind *akh*, plural *akhu*, has drawn the attention of numerous scholars over the years. All have struggled to pin down an exact definition and a full explanation of how *akh* was formally achieved. In his work, R. J. Demarée offers the following definition:

> The notion of *akh* as a designation refers to the special status of several categories of gods, including those who can exercise malign influence, and especially to the blessed state of deceased human beings who have been "admitted" among the company of the gods. . . The term *akh* by itself can be applied to gods as well as to

> deceased human beings. . . .The ability to act whether favorably or malignantly, is expressed by the adjective *iqr*, excellent. The *akh iqr* is an "able spirit" insofar as he has the power to help his supporters and to act against his antagonists. (Demarée 1983, 276–277)

Most of the information on private religion in ancient Egypt derives from ancient Egyptian settlements, most notably Deir el-Medina. Deir el-Medina is the village that housed the workmen who built the tombs in the royal necropolis. When the settlement was excavated, numerous items dedicated to the gods, deified ancestors, and deceased spirits (*akhu*) were found on site. Houses in the workmen's village contained what are known as the *akh iqr n Ra* stelae, loosely translated as the "Effective Spirit of Ra" stelae. An *akh iqer n Ra* is believed to be a human who, once dead, is given an elevated position, complete with special powers that enable him or her to protect Ra from harm, as she or he accompanies the sun on his daily sojourn. Anthropoid busts were also found in Deir el-Medina homes. These sculptures are mostly of stone and occasionally of wood and other materials. It is believed that they may have represented recently deceased ancestors and that the busts served as a medium of sorts between the living and the *akhu*.

The first room of the typical Deir el-Medina home contained a large, two-foot-high brick platform in one corner, measuring about five by two and a half feet in size. The platform had several steps leading up to it and included an attached brick structure that extended up toward the ceiling. The outside of this structure was often decorated with pictures of household deities, including Bes, the god devoted to childbirth. Scholars originally took these decorations to mean that the brick structure was a birthing bed, one which linked ancestors with future generations. However, contemporary scholars now prefer to see this structure as an altar, making the first room of the house a personal chapel.

The presence of statues depicting deceased royal figures provided evidence of ancestor worship in Deir el-Medina, particularly in the workmen's village. Amenhotep I (1525–1504 BCE) and his mother, Ahmose-Nefertary, who are regarded as the patron gods of the village, are the most prominent. They frequently appeared in tombs and on stelae as deities worshipped by the villagers. It is possible that Amenhotep I was the king who founded this settlement of workers on the West Bank, and so he was worshipped for this reason.

Various human beings were deified throughout ancient Egyptian history, breaking the barrier between humans and the gods. A few famous examples of such figures being Imhotep, Amenhotep son of Hapu, and kings Sneferu, Nebhepetre Mentuhotep, Amenhotep I, Ahmose-Nefertary, Amenhotep III, and Ramses II. Some kings were even deified while still alive, such as Amenhotep III and Ramses II of the New Kingdom (1550–1069 BCE). They were, however, not regarded as equal to the gods, but they seem to have acted, along with nonroyal ancestors, as intermediaries to them.

DIVINATION

Divination was a form of future prediction practiced in ancient Egypt. One method of divination involved a public procession that carried the statue of a god, referred to as an *oracle*, through the streets. The procession made several stops, during which people presented their questions and requests to the god. How the statue of the god responded to these questions is unclear, but it seems that it was through some sort of gesture. Documents from Deir el-Medina reveal that oracles were used as a means for resolving disputes, in conjunction with the court, or *kenbet*. When an ancient Egyptian court delivered an unsatisfactory verdict, the case was often presented to the oracle of the god for the final decision. At Deir el-Medina, oracle processions were usually performed during the festival days of Amenhotep I, when his image would have been carried out of his chapel and through the village.

Seers were women who were believed to be able to see into the future or know the unknown. The ancient Egyptians referred to such a woman as *ta rekhet*, or "the wise woman." Seers are best documented in the village of Deir el-Medina. The gods were thought to manifest themselves to the "wise woman," thus revealing to her matters that were unknown to regular people. This divine manifestation is known as the *bau*, plural of *ba*, of the gods, and it could also be manifested through dreams. There are letters known from Deir el-Medina telling people to go to the wise woman to see about the death of a particular person as well as other health problems, such as something affecting the eyes.

MAGIC, MEDICINE, AND RELIGION

In ancient Egypt, magic, medicine, and religion are often undistinguishable. The ancient Egyptian word for "magic" is *heka*, which James Allen translates as "the ability to make things happen by indirect means" (Allen 2010, 160). This sort of ancient magic was the force that created the universe and gave power to the gods. When utilized by humans, *heka* fought against disease and negative events and cured preexisting sickness. Rarely, it was used to inflict bodily harm. Scholars have concluded that ancient Egyptians likely saw religion, magic, and medicine as inextricably linked. All three elements worked codependently to fight against evil forces and help Egyptians to attain optimal health and happiness.

Yasmin El Shazly

See also: Deification; Deir el-Medina; Magic; Offerings, Votive

Further Reading

Allen, J. 2010. *Middle Egyptian: An Introduction to the Language and Culture of Hieroglyphs*. Cambridge: Cambridge University Press.

Baines, J. 1987. "Personal Religion and Piety." *Journal of Egyptian Archaeology* 73: 79–98.

Borghouts, J. F. 1982. "Divine Intervention in Ancient Egypt and Its Manifestation." In R. J. Demarée and Jac. J. Janssen, eds. *Gleanings from Deir el Medineh*. Leiden: Nederlands Instituut voor het Nabije Oosten, pp. 1–70.

Borghouts, J. F. 1994. "Magical Practices among the Villagers." In L. Lesko, ed. *Pharaoh's Workers*. Ithaca, NY: Cornell University Press, pp. 119–130.

Demarée, R. J. 1983. *The Ax Iqr n Ra-Stelae: On Ancestor Worship in Ancient Egypt*. Leiden: Nederlands Instituut voor het Nabije Oosten.

Gunn, B. 1916. "The Religion of the Poor in Ancient Egypt." *Journal of Egyptian Archaeology* 3: 81–94.

Kemp, Barry. 1995. "How Religious Were the Ancient Egyptians." *Cambridge Archaeological Journal* 5, no. 1: 25–54.

Stevens, Anna. 2006. *Private Religion at Amarna: The Material Evidence.* Oxford: Archaeopress.

Weiss, Lara. 2009. "Personal Religious Practice: House Altars at Deir El-Medina." *Journal of Egyptian Archaeology* 95: 198–208.

Roman Egypt (30 BCE–395 CE)

After losing the decisive naval battle at Actium in 31 BCE, Cleopatra VII (51–30 BCE) and Marc Antony retreated to Alexandria. Following their suicides and the death of Caesarion, Cleopatra's son and last of the Ptolemies, Octavian (30 BCE–14 CE) annexed Egypt as a Roman province in 30 BCE. In a short visit to the new province, the future emperor Augustus installed a prefect as the highest administrator and his representative. The post was a high honor, and many Romans advanced their political and military careers by serving as prefect in Egypt. The Roman conquest was a watershed for Octavian and put him in the position to become the first emperor and accept the title Augustus from the Senate in 27 BCE.

Egypt was Rome's most wealthy eastern province, in part because its grain was the largest single source supplying Rome and the rest of the Mediterranean. Alexandria was also the second-largest city next to Rome, and until annexation, it was the cosmopolitan capital of the Hellenistic world. Further, essential trade routes ran throughout the country and made the Nile valley location paramount. Egypt was also important because of its cultural and ideological power—the land of the pharaohs was understood as an ancient seat of knowledge, particularly regarding agricultural development. For these reasons, and following similar precedent from other provincial conquests, Augustus and the Roman administration built on local pharaonic and Ptolemaic precedents and introduced new Roman social, fiscal, and legal structures to transition Egypt into a province of the Roman Empire. One of the key ways Augustus, and all emperors until the division of the Roman Empire in 395 CE, built on local precedents was taking on the role of Egyptian pharaoh in Egypt's religious-political system while also acting as emperor.

While building on local systems, Augustus and future emperors also put forth measures that secured Egypt's transition to a province similar to other provinces, like Galatia, Asia, or Bithynia. For instance, there was a transitional period in which some military intervention from Rome was combined with colonial settlement. Direct rule was imposed through the establishment of an agent of the emperor, in Egypt's case, the prefect (*praefectus Aegypti*). Roman legions were deployed to key locations; the historic southern border between Egypt and Nubia at Syene, modern Aswan, was the stronghold of the Roman army in Upper Egypt following a number of skirmishes in the first decade following annexation. The 14-year census was instituted, which in part assisted in the strict segregation of social classes and privileges for ethnic groups. The existing Ptolemaic taxation system was modified with the introduction of some new taxes, such as the poll tax. The segregation of social classes played out in taxation, as Greeks were exempt from the poll tax, and people who lived in the *metropoleis*, or cities, could be taxed at a lower rate than those in the *chora*, or countryside.

Egypt's dry climate has preserved exceptional amounts of material and textual evidence, especially surviving in papyri, making it the best documented region of the Roman world. This can create a skewed perception of Egypt's status and the apparent uniformity of other provinces. In keeping with the traditional policy of the expansionist republic, there was an overall decision by the Augustan administration to impose Roman rule with minimum disruption and maximum utilization of existing local institutions. Generally, the systems put in place in the Augustan period remained during Egypt's Roman Period, with a number of gradual processes toward fundamental social, religious, economic, political, and legal transformation. While Egypt was an imperial province before in the Persian Period, the length and stability of Roman rule in Egypt fostered strengthened and new interregional networks in the ancient world, and as Monson (2012, 15) summarizes, "nearly two centuries of population expansion, urbanization, agricultural intensification, and economic growth."

Like other foreign rulers before them, including the Persians, Libyans, and Assyrians, the Romans did not rule from within Egypt itself. Yet, Roman emperors traveled extensively in the empire, and in addition to Augustus, four other emperors made trips to the Egyptian province: Vespasian (69–79 CE), Titus (79–81 CE), Hadrian (117–138 CE), and Marcus Aurelius (161–180 CE). Vespasian was declared emperor in Egypt upon entering Alexandria after subduing the Jewish revolt. Even with this monumental visit, Hadrian's two visits in 117 CE and 130 CE overshadowed Vespasian's visit in the literary sources of the ancient world and in modern popular legend. In the second trip, in 129–130 CE, the emperor visited the capital at Alexandria, attended the installation of the new Apis bull at Memphis, hunted lions in the desert, and sailed to major cities on a Nile cruise. A large retinue accompanied the emperor on this cruise, on which they also stopped at major tourist attractions, such as the "colossi of Memnon"—two colossal statues of the Eighteenth Dynasty pharaoh Amenhotep III still standing on the West Bank of modern Luxor. The group included the emperor's wife, Sabina, and court poet, Julia Balbilla, a Roman noblewoman of Syrian origin. Balbilla was commissioned to commemorate their visit, for which she wrote four Greek epigrams to be inscribed on the legs of the colossal statues.

Just a month prior to the Luxor visit, the imperial party lost one of their number, Hadrian's Greek companion, Antinous. At a site to the north, Antinous supposedly fell off the boat and drowned in the Nile. Following Egyptian beliefs recorded by Herodotus (2.90), the Egyptians believed death by drowning in the Nile to be the most severe of punishments, because without a body, the deceased was lost for eternity. To combat this fate, a person drowned would be deified after death and associated with Osiris as an honored or favored one. Antinous was given similar honors and deified as a god, Osir-Antinous. Hadrian founded a city at the site called Antinoupolis, the city of Antinous. Antinous's cult gained great favor in the eastern provinces and is an example of the kind of careful and purposeful combination of tradition and innovation visible throughout the ancient world, and especially evident in Roman Egypt.

Egypt was multicultural and multilingual, even in pharaonic times, and as technology developed to encourage improved connectivity, there is continued evidence of combined and adapted identities, language, religion, and images and objects. Some of the most famous images that survive from Roman Egypt are funerary panel portraits that link millennia-old funerary traditions in Egypt with contemporary classical imagery, complete with hair and fashions popular at the imperial court at Rome. These panel portraits are strikingly naturalistic and diverge from more abstract and schematic renderings of the human form in earlier periods. At the same time, the formational funerary beliefs and rituals are essentially the same as those practiced for millennia in Egypt. Evidence survives from visual arts and textual sources that indicate beliefs and rituals for the mummification, burial, and remembrance of the dead relate to earlier traditions. In addition to a careful balance of tradition and innovation, funerary beliefs and practices were also tied to regional variation, and although there are general traits that are distinctive to the Ptolemaic and Roman Periods, many of the core practices retain the practices of Pharaonic times and show more resistance to change than in other areas of culture in Roman Egypt.

Visual evidence from mummy portraits, tombs, and coffins demonstrates the continued importance of ritual and procession in funerary rites—funerary processions with traditional *sem* priests, or funerary priests, continue to make appearances in the visual record in first century CE tombs. Furthermore, tomb imagery continues to depict the Opening of the Mouth Ceremony—an essential part of the funerary rites for previous millennia that took place in front of the tomb. There, the mummy was stood up in front of the tomb, and a priest "opened" all orifices for senses, including eyes, nose, mouth, and ears. These kinds of traditional practices continued to thrive alongside contemporary developments that linked the deceased to current roles as part of a global Mediterranean in Egypt's Roman Period.

Erin A. Peters

See also: Colossi of Memnon; Hawara; Opening of the Mouth; Ptolemaic Egypt

Further Reading

Alston, R. 2002. *The City in Roman and Byzantine Egypt*. London: Routledge.

Bowman, A. K. 1986. *Egypt after the Pharaohs 332 B.C.–A.D. 642: From Alexander to the Arab Conquest*. London: British Museum Publications.

Bowman, A. K. 2007. "Egypt in the Greco-Roman World: From Ptolemaic Kingdom to Roman Province." In H. Crawford, ed. *Regime Change in the Ancient Near East and Egypt: From Sargon of Agade to Saddam Hussein*. Oxford: Oxford University Press, pp. 165–181.

Capponi, L. 2005. *Augustan Egypt: The Creation of a Roman Province*. New York: Routledge.

Capponi, L. 2011. *Roman Egypt*. London: Bristol Classical Press.

Frankfurter, D. 1998. *Religion in Roman Egypt: Assimilation and Resistance*. Princeton, NJ: Princeton University Press.

Monson, A. 2012. *From the Ptolemies to the Romans: Political and Economic Change in Egypt*. Cambridge: Cambridge University Press.

O'Connell, E., ed. 2014. *Egypt in the First Millennium AD: Perspectives from New Fieldwork*. British Museum Publications on Egypt and Sudan 2. Leuven: Peeters.

Riggs, C. 2005. *The Beautiful Burial in Roman Egypt: Art, Identity, and Funerary Religion*. Oxford: Oxford University Press.

Riggs, C., ed. 2012. *The Oxford Handbook of Roman Egypt*. Oxford: Oxford University Press.

Royal Regalia

In ancient Egypt, almost every element on or around the body of the king would be considered regalia. The most obvious are the crowns, but pharaoh also sported special dress, carried various staffs, used particular chairs, and was surrounded by exclusive emblems. Regalia conveyed royalty and divinity, and it also transmitted information about *who* the king was and *what* he was doing.

Regalia played a central role in constructing the identity of the king. The increasing density of royal symbolism through Egyptian history reflected the increasing complexity of the king's role. As pharaoh's functions evolved over time, so too did his accoutrements. The king was given a series of crowns upon accession. This emphasizes the variety of roles inherent in the office of kingship, all of which were related to various deities, desirable characteristics, or aspects of the cosmic cycle. Pharaoh could only present himself as master of the cosmos if he symbolically appeared as such. The term used for "crowns," *khaw*, also referred to "forms of appearance." With crowns and other insignia, the king was transformed from human into a "supernatural" being.

Kingship theology in Egypt developed in accretion layers. From the beginnings of Egyptian history, the king was iconographically associated with the god Horus. With the rise of the solar cult in the Fourth Dynasty (2613–2494 BCE), pharaoh was further identified as a son of the sun god Ra. Later, in the Middle Kingdom (2055–1650 BCE), the king was directly linked with the god Amun. This tendency to acquire new symbolic layers on top of previously established significance is also noted in the development of many other aspects of Egyptian culture.

The concept of "cultural memory" played a part in this layered development of royal iconography. Personal attire, which often expressed status, would also have been considered part of the collective knowledge that helped create the normative self-image of the group. Royal regalia distinguished the most important member of that group, properly identified his various aspects, and transmitted that data to those who viewed his image. Regalia functioned in an emblematic role, almost like hieroglyphs forming "sentences" that could be read and altered by varying the elements.

Although there was an increase in the complexity of royal regalia over ancient Egypt's history, this did not occur steadily. As pharaoh acquired more roles, the iconography expanded. However, there was a noticeable wax and wane in the pace. Certain periods are characterized by the king typically being depicted in the most basic regalia. These are often periods of contraction or reemergence, such as the early Eighteenth Dynasty, beginning in 1550 BCE, when the country became unified again under one Egyptian king. After a period of Hyksos rule, it may have been important to "remind" the Egyptians who their proper ruler was and to portray him as a legitimate descendant of ancient kings. As Egypt's power increased in the Eighteenth Dynasty, the regalia became more complicated, and the end of the era is characterized by an almost baroque increase in costume intricacy.

Upper part of a granite statue of Ramses II, found on the island of Elephantine at the First Cataract. Ramses wears an elaborate wig, with the double crown on top. The *uraeus* is at his forehead. The king's beard is tied on his chin, and he holds the crook and flail, the symbols of kingship. (The Trustees of the British Museum/Art Resource, NY)

Elements of regalia were combined in ways that related to the role the king was fulfilling, whether warrior, chief ritualist, or protector. Some elements and combinations occur with great regularity, while others are quite rare. Recent statistical research has identified specific patterns of regalia that almost never appear together being intentionally combined for certain types of scenes. Studies like this indicate an underlying complexity to regalia selection that has yet to be fully understood by modern scholars.

On and around the king's body, almost every item was distinctly royal, and most elements of regalia were used by no other humans. However, a number of elements were variations of items used by the entire population. For example, almost everyone wore linen sashes and kilts in Egypt. Those of the king, however, were tied differently or brightly colored in a way that set them apart. Wigs were another democratic sort of regalia, but the king's wigs were colored differently or had unusual details. Most elite individuals sat on chairs, but only the king had chairs with the particular decorations that made them *thrones*. These similarities conveyed that the king was part of the population while simultaneously being distinct.

There are three large classes of royal regalia: items worn on the body, items carried in the hand, and items associated with the king. Regalia is often thought of only in terms of the king's costume or what is carried in the hand, but it also includes the king's throne, footstools, palanquins, boats, and architectural elements, in addition to items held in association with the king, such as sunshades and other fans.

The body of the king was covered in regalia. Headgear included many types of crowns, two primary wig types, embellishments such as horns, and diadems. One of the most distinct elements was the upraised cobra, or uraeus, almost invariably found on the king's brow. Symbolic of the fiery eye of the sun, Pharaoh could be easily identified from its presence, even if he wore no other regalia. Conversely, much of the jewelry worn by the king was not exclusive.

Pharaoh also wore colorful shirts, the most common of which showed a pair of falcons with their wings wrapped around the body or a bright red field covered with blue and yellow diamonds. Wide belts decorated with detailed chevron or feather patterns and lines of text generally sported a large buckle at the front, some of which, such as those from the tomb of Tutankhamun, were quite elaborate. Hanging from the front of the king's belt was often an element referred to as a *sporran*. These bold, and distinctly royal, regalia elements were brightly colored, covered with patterns and text, and usually had cobras at the base. At the top of the sporran, there are sometimes small leopard heads or even tiny skins. Hanging from the back of the belt, the king often wore another distinctly royal element—a bull's tail that trailed down past the knees.

The king wore various configurations of white linen kilts and garments. Some of these were quite similar to garments worn by the populace, but the presence of the cobra at the brow, sporran, and bull tail transformed even the simplest outfit into a royal costume. While most people used sashes to tie their kilts, pharaoh had a special sash, which was almost always bright red and uniquely tied. Many wore sandals, but the king's sandals ranged from the simple woven papyrus used by everyone to ornate examples covered in embossed leather, carved stone beads, or gold embellishments; King Tutankhamun was buried with at least 42 pairs. One of the most beautiful pairs has bound foreign enemies represented on the sole. By wearing and walking in these sandals, pharaoh was symbolically crushing Egypt's enemies.

There were royal scepters and staffs the king carried in his hands. Many were derived from professional tools and were variations of those used by the general population. The crook and flail was only carried by the king, Osiris, and a few other gods; by holding these implements, the king was identifying with those divine beings. However, their origins can likely be traced to shepherding tools. Ceremonial weapons, such as the scimitar, mace, and bow, were used to convey the king's "strong arm" as protector of Egypt, but mace-like scepters were also used during festival processions. Kings did carry some staves that were used by the general population, such as the *mks*-staff carried by officials, but kings also carried the potent *was*-staff, with its forked base and animal head, that was otherwise only carried by gods. The *was*, whose hieroglyphic meaning was "dominion," represented the pillars holding up the sky. Another element frequently shown in the king's hand is the *ankh*, a powerful symbol that stood for "life." When the king holds it, it indicates divine and eternal existence.

Often when he is shown processing in festival or interacting with other humans, the king was shielded by large semicircular sunshades or long ostrich-plume fans known as *khu*. These not only served for shade and moving the air but also indicated a divine presence. The king was regularly shown as guarded by divine protectors—vultures, falcons, and sun disks—hovering overhead.

The king's thrones and footstools, carrying chairs, boats, and architecture were usually decorated in such a way that they became regalia. Thrones often bore symbols of the unified Egypt. Footstools and ceremonial pathways were decorated with the bound figures of the enemies of Egypt so that they could literally be "under the feet" of the king as he walked. Carrying chairs and Windows of Appearance, both venues where the king interacted with the people, were designed to link the living king directly with the gods.

Regalia played an integral role in visually distinguishing the king and providing the attributes and divinity needed for different situations. The range and variety of regalia that developed over the span of Egyptian history indicates a complex language of symbols. By combining those symbols in specific ways, the king acquired the traits needed for particular contexts while conveying important information to those who viewed the royal image.

Amy Calvert

See also: Crowns; Jewelry; Kingship; Royal Titulary; Sticks and Staves

Further Reading

Gregory, Steven. 2008. "Observations Regarding the Symbolism of the Blue and Cap Crowns as Used in Iconographic Motifs of the Ramesside Period." In K. Griffin, ed. *Current Research in Egyptology 2007.* Oxford: Oxbow Books, pp. 83–96.

Patch, Diana Craig. 1995. "A 'Lower Egyptian' Costume: Its Origin, Development, and Meaning." *Journal of the American Research Center in Egypt* 32: 93–116.

Shaw, Garry. 2012. *The Pharaoh: Life at Court and on Campaign.* London: Thames and Hudson.

Valbelle, Dominique. 2002. "Pharaonic Regality. The Nature of Power." In C. Ziegler, ed. *The Pharaohs.* London: Thames and Hudson, pp. 95–111.

Vandenbeusch, Marie, Aude Semat, and Margaret Maitland, eds. 2016. *Pharaoh: King of Ancient Egypt.* New Haven, CT: Yale University Press.

Vogelsang, G. M. 1999. *Tutankhamun's Wardrobe: Garments from the Tomb of Tutankhamun.* Rotterdam: Barjesteh van Waalwijk van Doorn & Co.

Wilkinson, Richard. 1992. *Reading Egyptian Art: A Hieroglyphic Guide to Ancient Egyptian Painting and Sculpture.* London: Thames and Hudson.

Wilkinson, Richard. 1994. *Symbol and Magic in Egyptian Art.* London: Thames and Hudson.

Royal Titulary

At his coronation, a new king took four specific names in addition to the one he was given at birth. Known as the royal titulary, this set of five names was not used systematically until the Eleventh Dynasty, beginning around 2055 BCE, but from then on, the practice endured for more than 2,000 years. The fourth and fifth names were written in oval-shaped hieroglyphic signs called *cartouches*. The king's birth name is the one to which we add a Roman numeral to distinguish similarly named rulers within a single dynasty, for example, Thutmose III or Ramses II. The Egyptians called this full set of five names "the Great Name" (*ren wer*) and took great care in choosing these names.

When the various parts of the Nile valley were amalgamated into a single country in the late fourth millennium BCE, the king and his court wanted to find powerful symbols to establish the authority of the new ruler and differentiate him from his subjects. They also tried to integrate—rather than force—the formerly independent city-states into the newly formed central administration to secure their future cooperation. The titulary has its origins in these efforts.

The king and the court cleverly looked to the priesthoods, who put forward an elaborate system that incorporated the institution of kingship into the realm of the gods (Goebs 2007, 275). Associating the king directly with the gods also put him under their protection. The famous Palette of King Narmer, one of the earliest known rulers in ancient Egypt in Dynasty 0 (3200–3000 BCE), was found in a temple deposit at the site of Hierakonpolis in southern Upper Egypt, a discovery most probably indicating that he originated from that city. As the falcon god Horus was the local divinity of Hierakonpolis, Narmer embraced the identity of his local god by calling himself "the Horus Narmer." This name was written with the word "Narmer" inside a vertical rectangular hieroglyph that represented a palace facade and with a falcon on top of the palace. The design represents King Narmer inside his palace under the protection of the god Horus. This is the earliest example of the first name in the royal titulary, the "Horus name." *Narmer* means "the Menacing Catfish" (Leprohon 2013, 22); it was possibly not the king's original name but may have been deliberately chosen at his coronation to let his subjects know that he would be a ruler whose authority would not be challenged. The Horus names of other early kings—such as Aha ("The Fighter"), Djer ("The One Who Repulses Enemies"), Djet ("The Cobra"), and Den ("The (head) Severer)"—demonstrate a similar aggressive quality.

Other names in the titulary reflect the steps to unification. One of Narmer's immediate successors, King Aha, added two other divinities to his titulary, the goddesses Nekhbet and Wadjet, from the cities of El Kab and Buto, respectively. El Kab was across the river from Hierakonpolis, and Buto was an important site in Lower Egypt during the Predynastic Period. This second name in the royal titulary, the "Two Ladies name," was adopted by Aha to honor these cities and thus also their chieftains. The third name of the royal titulary, the "Golden Horus name," honored the ancient city of Nubet ("Gold Town"), modern-day Naqada, another highly important Predynastic site. The fourth name in the royal titulary, *ny-su-bity*, literally "He Who Belongs to the Sedge Plant and the Bee," was a reference to two symbols of Upper and Lower Egypt, respectively, and reflected the unification of these two parts of the Nile valley. The name is often rendered, "the King of Upper and Lower Egypt." In the final name in the royal titulary, the king's birth name was introduced by the phrase "the Son of Ra." This phrase not only honored the sun god Ra and his priesthood but was a reminder of the king's subordinate status to the gods.

Cartouche

The name *cartouche* was given in the late 18th century by Napoleon's soldiers to the oval rings they saw in hieroglyphic texts, which resembled a gun cartridge, or *cartouche* in French. The actual hieroglyphic sign, an elongated shape made by a double rope tied at one end, was called *shenu* by the ancient Egyptians, which came from the verb *shen*, "to encircle," and referred specifically to what the sun surrounded—that is, the entire world. In ancient Egyptian symbolism, it meant that the sun god encircled and thus protected the king as well as all his domains. This protection also applied to the other world, because many royal sarcophagi, and even the tombs' burial chambers, were cut into oval cartouche-like shapes.

The cartouche helped the Frenchman Jean-François Champollion (1790–1832) in his efforts to decipher the ancient Egyptian language. He recognized the names Ptolemy and Cleopatra in the hieroglyphic text, which he knew from Greek histories of ancient Egypt and which were written inside royal rings on the famous Rosetta Stone. He went on to identify other royal names, such as Thutmose, which he also knew from Greek sources, and Ramses, which was well known from the book of Exodus. This increased recognition of hieroglyphic signs further facilitated his eventual decipherment of Egyptian hieroglyphs.

Ronald J. Leprohon

The royal titulary was shrewdly used to announce a king's policy or his accomplishments. King Mentuhotep II (2055–2004 BCE) of the Eleventh Dynasty, whose Theban armies defeated northern forces to end a civil war, changed his Horus name to the newer designation, "the One Who United the Two Lands," to announce this victory. The first king of the next dynasty, the Twelfth, Amenemhat I (1985–1956 BCE), heralded his family's ascent to the throne by taking "the One Who Has Repeated Births" (an expression that designated a renaissance period) as his Horus name and "the One who Unites" as his Golden Horus name. His son, Senusret I (1956–1911 BCE), used the phrase "the One Who Has Lived the (re) Birth" in three of his five names to emphasize the continuation of his father's policies.

King Ahmose (1550–1525 BCE), the founder of the Eighteenth Dynasty, repeated this theme. He had fought a war of liberation against a foreign occupying army and wished to be remembered as "the (very) Image of (re)Birth" and "the One Who Has Bound the Two Lands" in his Two Ladies and Golden Horus names, respectively. One of Ahmose's immediate successors, Thutmose I (1504–1492 BCE), a great warrior king, used the designation "the Victorious Bull" as his Horus name and "the One who is Great of Strength" as his Golden Horus name. Subsequent kings of the Eighteenth Dynasty, a family known for its conquest of foreign territories, used equally belligerent phrases in their titularies for the benefit of their contemporaries.

Kings also borrowed from their predecessors to show their connections to the past. The armies of King Piankhy (747–716 BCE), a ruler from the far south, in what is today the modern-day Sudan, moved north and defeated a divided Egypt to form what is referred to as the Twenty-Fifth Dynasty. Originally, Piankhy called himself "the Horus, the Victorious Bull who Has Appeared in Napata," the last word being the name of his hometown. This Horus name was a direct appropriation of that of Thutmose III, which Piankhy knew from a monument left in his homeland almost eight centuries earlier by that king. After his conquest of Egypt and proclaiming himself the legitimate pharaoh of Egypt, Piankhy changed "Napata" to "Thebes" in his new Horus name, a reference to the famous Egyptian city.

The king's titulary was most probably composed between the selection of the next ruler and his coronation. Accounts differ on the manner in which the titulary was devised. Queen Hatshepsut (1473–1482 BCE) stated that the learned men of the court "were brought in to inscribe her Great Names," which were said to have actually come about through divine inspiration. Surpassing this, Thutmose III (1504–1458 BCE) asserted that it was the great god Amun-Ra himself who "set a titulary for me" (Leprohon 2013, 9).

Ronald J. Leprohon

See also: Horus; Kingship; Personal Names

Further Reading

Brewer, D. J., and E. Teeter. 2007. *Egypt and the Egyptians*. 2nd ed. Cambridge: Cambridge University Press.

Clayton, P. A. 1994. *Chronicle of the Pharaohs: The Reign-by-Reign Record of the Rulers and Dynasties of Ancient Egypt*. London: Thames and Hudson.

Goebs, K. 2007. "Kingship." In Toby Wilkinson, ed. *The Egyptian World*. London and New York: Routledge, pp. 275–295.

Leprohon, R. J. 2010. "The Royal Titulary in the 18th Dynasty: Change and Continuity." *Journal of Egyptian History* 3: 7–45.

Leprohon, R. J. 2013. *The Great Name. Ancient Egyptian Royal Titulary*. Atlanta: Society of Biblical Literature.

Quirke, S. 1990. *Who Were the Pharaohs? A History of Their Names with a List of Cartouches*. London: British Museum Publication.

S

Sakkara

The site of Sakkara, located just to the west of Memphis, was the main cemetery for the capital city of Memphis from its beginning, but particularly in the Old Kingdom, composed of the Third to the Sixth Dynasties (2686–2181 BCE). There are large mastabas in North Sakkara along the edge of the plateau that date to the First Dynasty (3000–2890 BCE). Originally thought to be the tombs of the kings of the First Dynasty, they are now considered to be tombs for the royal family and certain high officials, and the kings were all buried at Abydos.

Sakkara has the oldest pyramid, which is also the oldest stone monument in the world, the Step Pyramid Complex of King Djoser (667–2648 BCE) of the Third Dynasty. This complex was built of local limestone and faced with the beautiful white limestone quarried at Tura, directly across the river. There is only one door in the southeast corner, which leads into a huge rectangular enclosure with niched walls, imitating the walls of the king's palace. Inside is the Step Pyramid, where King Djoser was buried, which dominates the complex, as well as other structures tied to the funerary cult of the king or to the symbolic reenactment of the Sed festival to renew the king's reign. The large open court south of the pyramid was where the king would circle markers symbolizing the boundaries of Egypt and taking control of his realm. Then in the Sed festival court to the east, the king would be crowned in the presence of all the gods, each placed in one of the shrines lining the court. The actual Sed festival would have been celebrated at Memphis after the king had ruled for 30 years; the structures here are for the king's soul to celebrate this festival eternally.

In addition to royal pyramids, Sakkara has many Old Kingdom mastabas, which were the tombs of the high officials who served the king in Memphis. One of the most famous mastabas is that of Ti, the overseer of the sun temples of the Fifth Dynasty (2494–2345 BCE) kings, Nyuserra and Neferirkara. In the offering chamber with the false door are relief scenes of work on his estate with a very famous register of cattle walking through water while following a workman carrying one of the cow's calf.

A well-known mastaba of the Sixth Dynasty is that of Mereruka, the vizier of King Teti (2345–2323 BCE), who was also married to one of his daughters. Because of Mereruka's importance, his mastaba was constructed right near the Pyramid of King Teti. The mastaba is very large and is arranged in three sections. The largest part of the mastaba is decorated for Mereruka. There are scenes of daily life on Mereruka's estate, but farther into the tomb, the scenes are more personal and depict life in his household. Approaching the innermost part of the tomb, there are many offering bearers depicted, carrying offerings toward the

Apis Bull

The Apis bull, the sacred bull of the god Ptah at Memphis, was known since the First Dynasty (3000–2890 BCE). The Apis lived with its mother in the temple at Memphis, and when it died, it was mummified and buried in the catacomb at Sakkara, known as the Serapeum. An embalming area for the Apis bull, possibly dating to the end of the Thirtieth Dynasty (343 BCE) was found in the southwest corner of the Ptah temple; this was probably part of the structure in which the Apis lived as well. The mother of the Apis was regarded as a manifestation of the goddess Isis and was buried in a separate set of catacombs farther north at Sakkara.

Lisa K. Sabbahy

false door where the *ka*, or soul, of Mereruka appears in the shape of a standing statue to partake of the food and drink he needs to live forever. A smaller area in the front of the mastaba is for his wife, and the smallest section at the very back is for their son.

The Pyramid of King Teti is not terribly large, about one-third the height of the Great Pyramid at Giza, so the descending corridor down to the burial chambers is not terribly long. The last part of the corridor is horizontal, with three spaces for the great blocks that were lowered into place to seal the king's burial. The chamber you finally enter into as well as the actual burial chamber on the right are decorated with Pyramid Texts, religious spells to protect the dead king and make sure that he ascends to heaven and joins the gods. The third and undecorated chamber on the left was probably for storing offerings for the king. The sarcophagus in the burial chamber is basalt, and the chamber wall behind it is decorated like the wall of the king's palace. South of the Step Pyramid Complex is another pyramid with Pyramid Texts, that of King Unas (2375–2345 BCE) of the Fifth Dynasty, who ruled right before Teti. Unas is actually the first king to have had Pyramid Texts cut inside his pyramid. The pyramid of Unas is somewhat smaller than that of Teti.

Sakkara becomes important again in the late Eighteenth Dynasty and early Nineteenth Dynasty, roughly from the reign of Akhenaten to that of Ramses II (1352–1213 BCE), when high officials serving the king at Memphis were buried in rock-cut tombs in North Sakkara and temple-style tombs in the area south of the Unas causeway. One of the tombs in North Sakkara belongs to Maia, the wet nurse of King Tutankhamun; there is a scene preserved in the tomb showing the young king sitting on her lap. Perhaps the most important tomb south of the Unas causeway is that of Horemheb, who was the general for Tutankhamun. When Horemheb became king, he cut a tomb in the Valley of the Kings, but his wives, both of whom predeceased him, were buried in the Sakkara tomb. In the Late Period, important officials again cut tombs in the area of the Unas Pyramid, and catacombs were cut for the burial of mummies of baboons, cats, falcons, and ibises, as well as the large catacomb known as the Serapeum, which was for the burials of the Apis bull, the animal manifestation of the god Ptah of Memphis. This catacomb was used from the reign of Amenhotep III (1390–1352 BCE) in the Eighteenth Dynasty until the Roman Period (30 BCE–495 CE).

Lisa K. Sabbahy

See also: Animals, Sacred and Mummies; Pyramid Texts; Pyramids; Tombs, Private

Further Reading

Kanawati, Naguib, Alexandra Woods, Sameh Shafik, and Effy Alexakis. 2011. *Mereruka and His Family*, Part III, 2. *The Tomb of Mereruka*. Oxford: Aris and Phillips.

Lauer, Jean-Philippe. 1976. *Saqqara*. London: Thames and Hudson.

Lehner, Mark. 1997. *The Complete Pyramids*. London: Thames and Hudson.

Martin, Geoffrey. 1989. *The Memphite Tomb of Ḥoremḥeb, Commander-in-Chief of Tutankhamūn*. London: Egypt Exploration Society.

Martin, Geoffrey. 1991. *The Hidden Tombs of Memphis*. London: Thames and Hudson.

Zivie, Alain. 2007. *The Lost Tombs of Saqqara*. Cara Edition. Toulouse: Cara.

Sarcophagi. See Coffins and Sarcophagi

Scarab

Scarabs are representations of the Egyptian dung beetle (*Scarabaeus sacer*) found in the Western Desert of Egypt. As the largest object group known from Ancient Egypt, they appear as amulets, seals, parts of jewelry design, and other artifacts. The scarab presents various levels of stylization of the beetle's anatomy. The back and the sides are more or less naturalistically presented, showing the head and folded wings on the back and the legs on the side. The so-called scaraboids show other animals or human faces on the back, following the overall ovoid shape. The base can show manifold inscriptions and decorations (e.g., geometric designs; anthropomorphic and zoomorphic scenes; inscriptions ranging from generic hieroglyphs to names and titles of gods, kings, or officials; or mottos and formal texts). Equally diverse are the materials used: steatite (soapstone), which could be glazed; faience; metals; glass; stones (agate, amethyst, carnelian); and many more. Decorations and materials can be used for dating purposes, but this is difficult without archaeological context. Even royal names inscribed on a scarab provide no absolute basis for dating, as they were used after a ruler's death, commonly done with the name of Thutmose III, and thus only give a terminus post quem.

The specific reproductive cycle of the beetle lent itself as the perfect representation of solar cycles and their mythological interpretation of death and rebirth. The Egyptian subspecies forms dung balls that they roll standing on the front legs while pushing with the hind legs over large distances and obstacles, just like the sun moving over the horizon. The beetles lay their eggs in this ball in underground nest holes. The young seem to appear spontaneously out of dead matter (dung). The dung beetle as a metaphor of overcoming death was expressed in its Egyptian name. *kheperer*, derived from the verb *kheper*, meaning "to come into being" or "to become."

Small faience scarab with the name of King Ramses II of the Nineteenth Dynasty, as well as possibly cryptographic hieroglyphs giving the name of the god Amun. (Los Angeles County Museum of Art)

It is not clear when the scarab was first equated with the god Khepri as the morning aspect of the sun god as the solar disk is rising in the eastern horizon and being reborn by the sky goddess Nut. Khepri's name is translated as "he, who comes into being." He did not receive a formal cult of his own, but colossal stone scarabs—one of Amenhotep III in Karnak (Amun Temple) or the example in the British Museum (EA74), possibly from the Temple of Ra in Matariya—show incorporation in other temples.

There are several scarab types. The most common is the scarab amulet. Nearly all objects classified as scarab fall into this category. They are small (1–5 cm) and ovoid in shape. Such scarabs are often pierced longitudinally to be worn as necklaces, bracelets, or part of rings, expressing its bearer's personal piety. Because of their small size, scarab amulets were affordable and easy to transport. During the Middle Kingdom, they were used as seals by nonroyal officials, while during the New Kingdom, they connected Egypt with the wider Mediterranean through gift exchange and trade. Other common forms are the heart scarab—a larger amulet often inscribed with chapter 30B of the Book of the Dead to avoid the heart speaking against the deceased in the Final Judgment—and the group of larger commemorative scarabs inscribed with royal announcements during the Eighteenth Dynasty.

Katharina Zinn

See also: Art

Further Reading

Andrews, C. 1994. *Amulets of Ancient Egypt*. London: British Museum Press.

Ben-Tor, D. 1989. *The Scarab: A Reflection on Ancient Egypt*. Jerusalem: Israel Museum.

Cooney, K. M. 2008. "Scarab." In W. Wendrich, ed. *UCLA Encyclopedia of Egyptology.* http://escholarship.org/uc/item/13v7v5gd.

Hornung, E., and E. Staehelin, eds. 1976. *Skarabäen und andere Siegelamulette aus Basler Sammlungen.* Mainz: Philipp von Zabern.

Minas-Nerpel, M. 2006. *Der Gott Chepri: Untersuchungen zu Schriftzeugnissen und ikonographischen Quellen vom Alten Reich bis in griechisch-römische Zeit.* Leuven: Peeters.

Ward, W. A. 1987. "Scarab Typology and Archaeological Context." *American Journal of Archaeology* 91, no. 4 (October): 507–532.

Ward, W. A. 1994. "Beetles in Stone: The Egyptian Scarab." *Biblical Archaeologist* 57, no. 4 (December): 186–202.

Wilkinson, R. H. 2008. *Egyptian Scarabs.* Oxford: Shire.

Scribes and Scribal Equipment

In a time when most people can read and write, the occupation of the scribe seems outdated, but scribes were much more than their name implies. The Egyptian scribe's job description included tasks that are now assigned to accountants, lawyers, secretaries, and priests. Their specialized skills enabled them to keep important economic records, produce valid legal documents, and record the mysteries of the divine. The work of the scribe was difficult to master. It required specialized tools and years of formal education, but the reward for their efforts was a secure living, free of the constant burden of taxes and other misfortunes. In ancient Egypt, writing was the key to the proper maintenance of society and the order of the cosmos, and scribes were the masters of this sacred art.

Today, hieroglyphs survive on temples and in tombs, where they are often carved in stone, but ancient Egyptian scribes did most of their writing with ink on papyrus. Instead of using the ornate, brightly painted characters seen in inscriptions, most scribes wrote using a simplified handwritten version of the hieroglyphic script. At its most detailed, this script is known as *cursive hieroglyphs*, and it was used for high-quality religious documents, such as the Book of the Dead. The handwritten signs of cursive hieroglyphs look very similar to their engraved equivalents, but this method was too slow and cumbersome for everyday tasks. During the Old Kingdom (ca. 2686–2160 BCE), this detailed method of drawing hieroglyphs gradually morphed into a more abbreviated script, known as *hieratic*, in which signs only vaguely resemble their hieroglyph counterparts.

Over time, the hieratic script developed more or less independently, which allowed the signs to change without being tied to their hieroglyphic antecedents. To simplify the task of writing frequent combinations of hieratic signs, scribes began to link them together with a single stroke of the pen, as in modern cursive handwriting. Eventually, these *ligatures*, or groups of separate signs written with one continuous curve, became independent signs in their own right and could no longer be decomposed into their hieroglyphic components. In Lower Egypt, hieratic eventually evolved into an entirely new script, known as *Demotic*, which became the standard method for writing nonreligious texts. The Demotic script bears no obvious similarity to hieroglyphic writing, and even specialists in

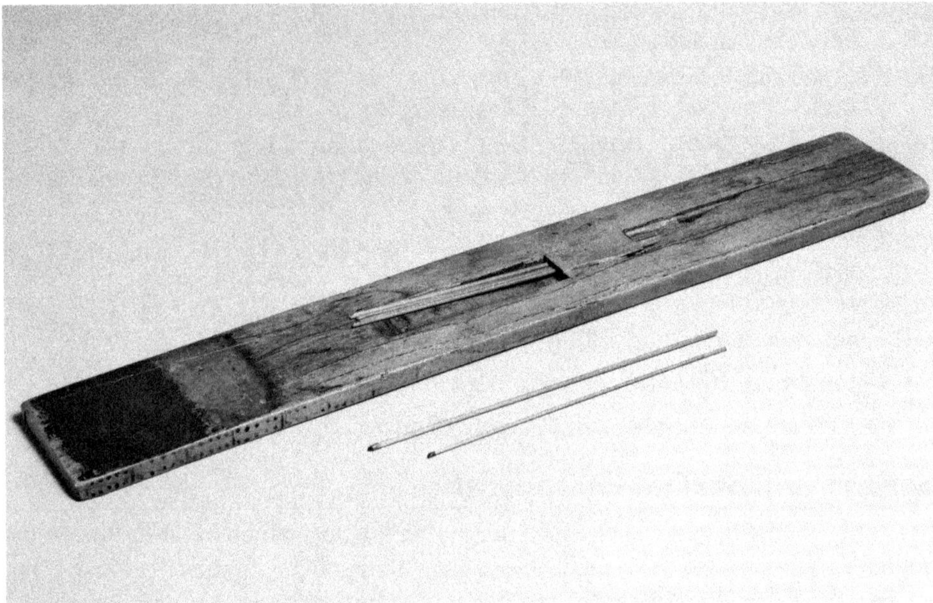

A palette like this was an important part of the equipment used by an ancient Egyptian scribe. Palettes were usually wood and had two round holes cut at the end to hold discs of powder, one of black ink and one of red. A slot cut in the middle held the small brushes with which they wrote. (Harris Brisbane Dick Fund, 1947/The Metropolitan Museum of Art)

Demotic have difficulty determining the relationship of these two distinct writing systems.

These simplified cursive scripts made it easier for scribes to record information quickly in everyday settings, but their development was primarily driven by the tools used to produce them. The basic equipment for a scribe consisted of a cylindrical wooden pen case, a small leather bag for pellets of dried ink, and a wooden palette with two shallow depressions for wet ink. Scribes used black ink to write the main body of a text, but they switched to a different pen and used red ink to write headings and to make corrections; so they routinely needed a palette with two separate spaces, a small bag for both colors of dry ink pellets (along with sundry other materials), and a case for their various pens. This equipment was so standard that it was depicted in a common hieroglyph, used in the Egyptian words for "scribe" and "to write." For most of Egyptian history, scribes wrote using thin pieces of rush (2–3 mm in diameter), which they turned into brushes by chewing the ends to separate the fibers. The Greeks introduced reed pens in the last centuries before the Common Era, but this technology was adopted slowly and intermittently, probably because the traditional brushes were better suited to writing the flowing Egyptian scripts on textured surfaces.

Scribes wrote on papyrus, the predecessor of modern paper, and on ostraca, which were pieces of stone or pottery with a flat surface suitable for writing. In rare cases, scribes wrote on a variety of other surfaces, including leather, linen, and plastered writing boards. The Egyptians made papyrus from a native plant for thousands of years and even exported it to the Greco-Roman world later in their history. The process of making papyrus, which is still imperfectly understood, involved cutting thin slices from the stalk of the papyrus plant, layering them together at right angles, hammering the pieces together into a single sheet, and drying the finished papyrus in the sun. Several sheets were glued together end to end and then rolled up to form a scroll, also known as a *book* when referring to ancient writing. The manufacture of papyrus was a time-consuming and labor-intensive task, and the exact method seems to have been a closely guarded trade secret. By comparison, flat stones and bits of broken pottery could be found lying on the ground and were therefore much easier to come by, making them the ideal writing surface for everyday tasks. Today, thousands of ostraca found in archaeological excavations offer an intimate view of the lives of ordinary people.

By contrast, texts written on costly papyrus were usually the property of the wealthy elite. Official scribes used accounting books of papyrus to record the income and maintenance of temples and other state-sanctioned businesses. Papyrus books also include mathematical treatises, hymns to the gods, and esteemed works of literature and poetry. These texts are often highly calligraphic, even when written in the hieratic script, revealing a deliberate attention to detail commensurate with their rare and elevated status. Egyptian scribes believed that writing offered a path to immortality, as a great work of literature would be read long after its author's tomb had fallen into ruin. Numerous Egyptian texts praise the wisdom of past scribes and exhort the young student to achieve similar immortality in writing, an opportunity afforded only to those with the education required to use the difficult Egyptian scripts.

Most Egyptians could not read and write or could do so only to a limited degree. Instead, they hired scribes to do their writing for them. Like a modern attorney, scribes produced important documents concerning inheritance, marriage, divorce, and other legal matters, but they were also employed to write personal letters and to keep economic accounts. The importance of writing in Egyptian civilization made scribes essential and valuable components of society. As a result, Egyptian scribes belonged to a highly educated literate class. Parents seeking a secure future for their children sent young boys (as far as we know, all Egyptian scribes were male) to scribal schools, where they would study for more than a decade to learn the hundreds of different signs, formulas for letter writing, and accounting methods for detailed bookkeeping. Students first learned the handwritten scripts by repeatedly copying standardized texts on erasable writing boards. Some of these student exercises have survived to the present day and even include mistakes with the teachers' corrections in red ink. In a few cases, close analysis of the handwriting reveals that these corrections were made by the same scribe who wrote the main text, indicating that scribes took their work seriously and actively strove to achieve accuracy and fine penmanship.

Though scribes rarely held political office, they were crucial to the functioning of society and the state, a situation that afforded them a great deal of power within their own arena. A mistake, intentional or not, in the calculation of a farmer's taxes could destroy his yearly profits, and a forged will could rob rightful heirs of their inheritance. In many cases, a single stroke of the scribe's pen could be the difference between wealth and poverty. Thus, the proper order of life depended on precise record keeping. As a result, numerous texts emphasize the importance of the honesty and attention to detail in the character of a good scribe. These qualities were incorporated into the nature of the god Thoth, usually depicted as a man with the head of an ibis. As the god of writing and counting, Thoth embodied the scribal arts in deified form, and the scribes were his emissaries among human beings. Texts addressed to young scribes emphasize the sacred nature of their office, and there is evidence that scribes included a devotional prayer to Thoth as part of their daily routine.

Because scribes had direct access to the bureaucracy and priesthood, they were often privy to secret information. Egyptian temples were not fully open to the average Egyptian citizen. Within the inner sanctum, priests performed mysterious rituals away from the public eye, but scribes, who were needed to manage the temple's affairs, recorded and cataloged this information in the House of Life, a private temple library. Egyptian stories reveal that the House of Life was considered a place of wonder, filled with arcane knowledge of this world and the supernatural. With their important administrative and economic roles, along with their access to the most confidential information, scribes were held in high regard and formed an integral component of Egyptian society for all of its long history.

Christian Casey

See also: Education; Language and Script; Literacy and Orality

Further Reading

Allen, J. P. 2010. "Languages, Scripts, and Literacy." In A. B. Lloyd, ed. *A Companion to Ancient Egypt 2*. Malden, MA: Blackwell, pp. 641–662.

Allon, Niv, and Hana Navrátilová. 2017. *Ancient Egyptian Scribes: A Cultural Exploration*. London: Bloomsbury.

Černý, Jaroslav. 1976. *A Coptic Etymological Dictionary*. Cambridge: Cambridge University.

Gardiner, A. H. 1935. *Hieratic Papyri in the British Museum*. Plates Ser. 3. Vol. 2. London: British Museum.

Parkinson, R. B., and Stephen Quirke. 1995. *Papyrus*. Austin: University of Texas Press.

Simpson, W. K., ed. 2003. *The Literature of Ancient Egypt*. 3rd ed. New Haven, CT: Yale University Press.

Primary Document—Excerpt from a Text Encouraging Scribes in Their Work

The following excerpt is from a New Kingdom text, which encourages scribes to excel in their task. The excerpts reveal a conception of immortality radically different from the expected Egyptian attitude. The writer claims that the scribal arts provide an opportunity to be remembered, which was usually only available to those with the means to construct monuments.

Be a scribe, place it in your mind that your name may become likewise (remembered).
A book is more effective than a tombstone in every respect, than a chapel wall made firm.
These chapters make a pyramid in the mind of the one who pronounces their names,
For truly a name in the mouth of the people is effective in the necropolis.
When a man has perished, his corpse is dirt, and all of his neighbors go to the earth,
But writings cause him to be remembered in the mouths of those who recite.
A book is more effective than the house of a builder, than a chapel upon the West.
It is better than an established villa, than a stela in a temple.

Source: Translated by Christian Casey from P. Chester Beatty No. IV, verso 2, 13-3, 5 from Gardiner, A. H. 1935. *Hieratic Papyri in the British Museum*. Plates Ser. 3. Vol. 2. London: British Museum.

Script. See **Language and Script**

Sculpture and Sculptors

Sculpture in ancient Egypt dates as far back as the Predynastic Period (5300–3000 BCE). From the Early Dynastic Period (3000–2686 BCE), the objective of sculpture became clear: it was not to convey a reality but an ideal. This was constant in all periods of Egyptian history that followed, with the exception of the Amarna Period (1352–1336 BCE), during the latter part of the Dynasty 18 (1550–1295 BCE). Statues are the most common type of ancient Egyptian sculpture, and they represented gods, pharaohs, royal family members, high officials, members of the elite, and even servants.

With the Old Kingdom (2686–2160 BCE), the production of statues began to be in high demand. Statues of deities were produced for temples. Statues started being used in funerary contexts, both in royal and in private tombs. Sculpture appeared with standardized norms as early as the Third Dynasty. During the Fourth Dynasty IV (2613–2494 BCE), the existence of two approaches to style are noticeable, one that followed a more severe representation and another that preferred a softer approach to the facial expressions of the pharaohs. Different approaches in all time periods will be a constant, with the revitalization of old schools of art in later periods and the creation of new ideals. Despite these steps forward and sometimes back, some aspects eventually become standard.

CRAFTSMEN, TOOLS, AND MATERIALS

The materials for statues were procured by workers accompanied by sculptors or master sculptors to guarantee quality. Once found, the right material would be sent to the workshops associated with temples, tombs, or palaces to be worked to its final form. As in all Egyptian social groups, one of the craftsmen was the overseer, and the tasks that each worker carried out were well defined within each group. A master sculptor did not work in the quarry, but in many cases, he would start cutting the form of the statue there to ease the amount of weight being transported. Work in stone required specific tools and was mainly performed in groups, with each individual having a specific job that he fulfilled. A soft stone, like limestone, could be worked simply with a copper or, later, bronze chisel by a trained sculptor, and at the same time, there could be workers polishing another part of the statue. A harder stone, like granite, required pounding with a piece of an even harder stone, making the sculpting an arduous process. Many kinds of stones were used for sculpture, such as limestone, granite, alabaster, sandstone, quartzite, diorite, gneiss, and basalt. Also, precious wood, ivory, and casting with metal were used to produce smaller statues.

Statues were mainly present in temples and their surroundings and inevitably in tombs. No other culture seems to have produced such a number of statues as the ancient Egyptians did. This is, perhaps, intrinsically linked with the belief that the *ka* (the double) of the deceased could inhabit a statue, so *ka* statues were produced for the tomb and also placed in temples for offerings and so that a god could inhabit and manifest on earth in a statue.

FUNCTION, FORM, AND PRINCIPLES

The function of a statue defined its form. In all, there were two principles: the principle of frontality, in which the statue would always be looking to the front, the proper way to receive offerings, and the *twt ankh* ("perfected likeness"), which was extremely important for recognition of whom the statue represented. Although statues tended to represent an individual in the prime of life, they still needed to be recognizable. To this effect, the sculptors either produced a statue that looked very similar to whom they wanted to represent or the name was simply written on the statue; in some periods, the demand for statues tended to produce more standardized ones or the fashion was to follow a pharaoh's likeness.

It is possible to establish several characteristics of representation used during the Dynastic Period. A standing statue of a man would have an advanced left foot, while a statue of a woman would have, at most, a slightly forward foot, but usually both feet were together. The arms were usually parallel to the torso. If seated, the left hand of a man would rest on his thigh. The hands of a woman were held at the sides or, in paired statues, with one arm put around the husband. From the Old Kingdom, statues of dyads and triads became common. During this period, with the increase of individual social importance, many private statues appeared. One of the most recognizable types of nonroyal statues from this time is the one of the scribe, sitting with legs crossed and writing, whose features became the rule for the next millennia. Other officials tended to follow the principles used in the statues of the pharaohs, seated or standing.

The statues of pharaohs tended to appear in three main positions. In a seated position to receive offerings or standing or kneeling to give offerings. One of the most well-known statuettes of a pharaoh kneeling is that of Pepy I (2321–2287 BCE), carved in green slate, presenting two round libation vessels.

TYPES AND STYLES OF STATUES

One type of statue from the Old Kingdom was the falcon-king statue, the most famous being the one of King Khafre (2558–2532 BCE), which was found at the valley temple of his pyramid complex at Giza. This type of statue transmitted a clear message of the legitimacy of the king. It presents the king seated with a falcon, a representation of the god Horus, sitting behind Khafre's head and protecting him with its wings. It also symbolically states the merger of Horus with the king, as they are one. Statues of the pharaoh being accompanied by a god was not unusual during the Fourth Dynasty. Finally, the most recognizable type of statue, the sphinx, representing a head of a pharaoh with a *nemes* headdress, was created during this period. All these types of statues would continue to appear in both the Middle and the New Kingdoms.

By the Middle Kingdom (2055–1650 BCE), after the First Intermediate Period, a renaissance took place. New types of statues of the king appeared, such as the ones represented with the Sed garments or the standing Osiride statues, where the king was represented in the form of the god Osiris. The number of sculptures produced for each pharaoh of the Twelfth Dynasty (1985–1733 BCE) was substantial, and the scale of the statues was impressive. Senusret I, in particular, had colossal statues cut.

During this period, a new loyalty to the king developed that brought about a phenomenon where the elite statues mimicked the facial features of the pharaohs they served. For the first time in Egyptian history, private statues of elite were commonplace in temples. With the creative momentum of the Twelfth Dynasty, new forms of statues were created in what can be called the private sculpture world. The block statue is such a case. It represented an elite official squatting with arms crossed upon the knees. It is theorized that this is the position such a man would be in when carried in a litter by his servants, and so the block statue becomes symbolic

Limestone block statue of Ankhwennefer, a priest of the cat goddess Bastet, from the Late Period. Block statues first developed in the Middle Kingdom as a form of statuary for elite officials. (Purchase, Lila Acheson Wallace Gift and Rogers, Fletcher, Harris Brisbane Dick, and Louis V. Bell Funds and Joseph Pulitzer Bequest, 1993/The Metropolitan Museum of Art)

of being elite. The block shape also allows for extensive inscriptions on its surface. These statues were present in temples and elite tombs and were produced all the way to the end of the Late Period (664–332 BCE).

The New Kingdom brought about the development of a Thutmoside style, seen clearly in the reign of Hatshepsut (1479–1458 BCE) and Thutmose II, with limestone statues showing a softness and almost a femininity. Massive amounts of statuary were produced for the queen's temple at Deir el-Bahari: sphinxes, seated statues, kneeling and offering statues, and standing Osiride statues in front of the pillars on the topmost level. Hatshepsut's steward of Amun, Senemut, also had quite a bit of statuary produced for himself, a number of which portray him with the royal daughter Neferurra on his lap.

The statue program of Amenhotep III (1390–1352 BCE) at his mortuary temple on the West Bank of Thebes is becoming well known because of the ongoing excavations at the site. Colossal seated pairs sat in front of all three pylons on the east-west axis, and standing pairs were outside the northern door. Hundreds of Sakhmet statues were inside, perhaps one for each day of the year, to offer protection to the pharaoh.

The Amarna Period that followed under his son, Amenhotep IV or Akhenaten, completely revolutionized the norms of scale and appearance of royal sculpture. The pharaoh and his family were represented with elongated faces and heads and wide hips with rounded abdomens. Although it was a short-lived period, the two decades of his reign created a subsequent reaction to erase what was considered as a heretical time, and there was a return to pre-Amarna sculpture norms, although some stylistic changes remained.

The Reserve Head

A reserve head sculpture is very peculiar for several reasons. For one, reserve heads were only produced during the Old Kingdom, mainly in the Fourth Dynasty (2613–2494 BCE). Only 33 of these sculptures are known. The majority were found in Giza, with several others found in Abusir, Dahshur, and Abu Roash. They all have the same characteristics: they have life-sized, closely shaved hair, and most have damaged ears and vertical grooves cut on the back of the head. The head ends with the neck, which has a flat, straight bottom so that the head can be stood up. For the most part, they were not painted, although traces of paint have been found on two of them. They were mostly sculpted in limestone; only two were made in siltstone.

The heads were found inside mastaba tombs, but probably none of them were in their original position because the tombs had all been plundered. It is not clear whether the heads had been placed in the burial chamber or the shaft. It is also not clear what their purpose or meaning was. Numbers of ideas have been put forth: the head was an extra in case the head of the deceased was damaged; the heads were used as the model on which to mold a death mask for the deceased; or they served as a kind of *ka* statue. It is clear that they served some kind of funerary purpose, but as to what, and why there was such limited use of reserve heads, remains unclear.

André Patricio

The Ramesside Period (1295–1069 BCE), notably the reign of Ramses II, set the tone for the types of statues to be used in the last dynasties of the New Kingdom, reinforcing the use of all possible sculpture positions and types of statues. Two types of statuary from the Eighteenth Dynasty became more common, the naophorous, in which a naos containing a statue of a god or goddess is offered, and a stelophorous statue, in which a stela is offered. Interestingly enough, the Late Period (644–332 BCE) saw a resurgence of Old Kingdom styles and forms; this is referred to as *archaism*. The use of dark hard stone was also common.

André Patricio

See also: Art; Quarrying; Temples, Mortuary

Further Reading

Hartwig, M. 2015. "Sculpture." In M. Hartwig, ed. *A Companion to Ancient Egyptian Art*. Hoboken, NJ: John Wiley & Sons, pp. 192–218.

James, T., and W. Davies. 1983. *Egyptian Sculpture*. London: British Museum Press.

Nuzzolo, M. 2011. "The 'Reserve Heads': Some Remarks on Their Function and Meaning." In N. Strudwick and H. Strudwick, eds. *Old Kingdom, New Perspectives: Egyptian Art and Archaeology 275–2150 BC*. Exeter: Short Run Press, pp. 200–215.

Robins, G. 2007. "Art." In T. Wilkinson, ed. *The Egyptian World*. New York: Routledge, pp. 355–365.

Robins, G. 2008. *Egyptian Statues*. London: Shire Books.

Russmann, E. 2001. *Eternal Egypt: Masterworks of Ancient Art from the British Museum*. Berkeley: University of California Press.

Schulz, R. 2008. "Small but Beautiful: The Block Statue of Khaemwaset." In S. D'Auria, ed. *Probleme der Ägyptologie* 28. Leiden: Brill, pp. 216–222.

Teeter, E. 2007. "Temple Cults." In T. Wilkinson, ed. *The Egyptian World*. New York: Routledge, pp. 310–324.

Sea Peoples

Although probably not a single battle, the repulsion of the "Sea Peoples" in the Twentieth Dynasty (1190–1077 BCE) is recorded in scenes and inscriptions at Medinet Habu, the memorial temple of Ramses III (1187–1157 BCE), in modern-day Luxor. In the eighth year of his reign, Ramses III faced the threat of an invading coalition of foreign peoples, who are described as coming to Egypt "from the sea." The battle narrative is illustrated with scenes that separately depict a land battle and a naval battle, alongside scenes of the Egyptian army preparing before battle and celebrating victory afterward. These scenes immortalize the king's triumphs on a monumental scale on the outer wall of the temple.

The invading coalition, collectively known as Sea Peoples in modern scholarship because of their island and coastal homelands, included five people groups named in the year eight inscription at Medinet Habu: the Peleset, Tjeker, Shekelesh, Danuna, and Weshesh. Speculations regarding the historical identities of these ethnic groups have frequently been made, often through the study of ethnonym cognates in other ancient texts, with some designations less agreed upon than others. The Peleset's equation to the biblical Philistines has been widely accepted. By contrast, almost nothing is known of the origins or identity of the Weshesh. The artists' detailed renderings of the military equipment and the dress of the foreign soldiers tantalize, but they hardly aid scholars' attempts to identify individual ethnic groups. Many scholars agree that the Sea Peoples originated in the Balkans and areas around the Aegean Sea, but how and why they formed this coalition and began a southward journey toward Egypt is greatly debated, although it may have been caused by severe climactic changes. Their coalition was composed of a plethora of ethnically varied soldiers and seemingly also their families and livestock, who were intent on migrating permanently from their homelands to settle in Egypt. Based on the presence of several ox-drawn carts filled with women and children in the scenes, this event has traditionally been interpreted as a large-scale, destructive migration of displaced peoples.

Scholars primarily rely on two lengthy hieroglyphic inscriptions in the first and second courts of Medinet Habu for reconstructing the narrative of the battle against the Sea Peoples. Their use as historical sources, however, has been critiqued, as no archaeological evidence has yet corroborated the event. The inscription from year five of Ramses III's reign preserved on the southern interior wall of the second court briefly references an event in which the Peleset and Tjeker came to Egypt by land and sea and were defeated at the Nile mouths. The inscription from year eight, on the western interior wall of the first court of the same temple, contains a much longer narrative of the Sea Peoples' invasion. Most scholars agree that the text of the year five inscription primarily narrates the events of an earlier war against invading "Libyans," but it also includes reference to the later Sea Peoples invasion of year eight, not of a separate incursion.

The inscriptions inside the temple are supported by monumental scenes on the northern outer wall of the temple of a naval battle and land battle fought between the Egyptian army and this invading coalition. These scenes were once interpreted as battles fought simultaneously by the Egyptian army against a coordinated land and sea assault from the Sea Peoples; however, their separation by an unconnected and unmilitary scene in which the king hunts lions may indicate that they took place on separate days at different, perhaps proximal, locations. The full pictorial narrative consists of five scenes, the first of which illustrates the distribution of military equipment to the Egyptian army. Ramses III stands overseeing the distribution of quivers, bows, spears, and sickle swords, pronouncing, "Bring out weapons! Send out archers to destroy the rebellious foreign lands who do not know Egypt, by the strength of my father Amun!"

After the preparations, Ramses III is shown in his war chariot, pulled by horses resplendent in feathers and tassels, setting out with his army "for *Djahi*, like the image of Montu, to crush every foreign land that violates his frontier." His marching army consists of Egyptian infantry and charioteers as well as foreign battalions of Sherden soldiers wearing distinctive, horned helmets. Their march culminates in the land battle, in which Egyptian and enemy soldiers fight in a colorful, chaotic mass, embellished with falling and fleeing enemy soldiers. Ramses III charges into battle on his chariot, bow drawn and horses rearing. The Sea Peoples in the scenes carry round shields and long spears, and they ride in chariots as well as oxcarts. From the limited topographical information, it is difficult to determine where this land battle took place—the only toponym that appears in the texts is *Djahy*, an unspecific name for the Levant. The scene of the king celebrating his victory over the Sea Peoples by receiving war captives at his Window of Appearances contains the image of a fort identified as "Migdol-of-Ramses-Ruler-of-Heliopolis," the location of which may have been in northern Sinai.

The scene of the naval battle, the oldest illustration of a naval battle in history, contains reliefs of five foreign war vessels after "they entered the channels of the river mouths," manned by two distinctly portrayed types of foreign peoples, differentiated by their dress. The texts name three types of Egyptian war vessels that oppose them in the scene, filled not only with Egyptian soldiers but with bound foreign soldiers who were captured in the course of the battle. Ramses III is represented on a colossal scale, standing on the shore surrounded by his archers, firing volleys of arrows at the enemy ships. The enemy soldiers are shown falling from their ships in the disarray of inevitable defeat while "their weapons are scattered in the sea." Aside from the mention of the "river mouths" located in the delta region, no attempt was made in the texts or reliefs to specify the exact location of the battle along the Mediterranean coast.

The Egyptians recorded the battles that repulsed the Sea Peoples as overwhelming victories; in the following scene, Ramses III presents rows of captive Sea Peoples to the Theban triad: Amun, Mut, and Khonsu. The Great Harris Papyrus, a document composed by his son Ramses IV (1156–1150 BCE) in honor of Ramses III's reign, records that great numbers of Sherden and Weshesh captives were settled in Egypt as prisoners of war. While the land of Egypt was spared a direct attack by the Sea Peoples, the ancient Anatolian and Levantine states, Qode, Carchemish, and Arzawa, as well as the kingdom of Hatti, a powerful ally of Egypt since the reign of Ramses II (1279–1213 BCE), and Alayshia, on the island of Cyprus, succumbed to their destructive migration.

Despite facing the formidable threat of the Sea Peoples in the first decade of his reign, Ramses III ruled Egypt for over 30 years and is considered the last great king of the New Kingdom.

Taylor Bryanne Woodcock

See also: Foreigners; Weapons and Armor

Further Reading

Ben-Dor Evian, Shirly. 2016. "The Battles between Ramesses III and the 'Sea-Peoples': When, Where and Who? An Iconic Analysis of the Egyptian Reliefs." *Zeitschrift für ägyptische Sprache und Altertumskunde* 143: 151–168.

Cline, Eric H., and David O'Connor. 2012. "The Sea Peoples." In Eric H. Cline and David O'Connor, eds. *Ramesses III: The Life and Times of Egypt's Last Hero.* Ann Arbor: University of Michigan Press, pp. 180–208.

Oren, Eliezer D., ed. 2000. *The Sea Peoples and Their World: A Reassessment.* Philadelphia: University of Pennsylvania.

Redford, Donald B. 1992. *Egypt, Canaan, and Israel in Ancient Times.* Princeton, NJ: Princeton University Press.

Sandars, Nancy K. 1985. *The Sea Peoples: Warriors of the Ancient Mediterranean, 1250–1150 BC.* London: Thames and Hudson.

Primary Document—Account of the Sea Peoples' Attack on Egypt

According to this text, the Sea Peoples marched to attack Egypt by land from the east, and they also sailed in boats up the mouths of the Nile River. To meet this assault, King Ramses III (ca. 1186–1155 BCE) prepared his defenses.

> The foreign countries made a conspiracy in their isles. The lands were moving and scattering in battle at one time. No land stood before their arms, beginning with Hatti, Qode, Carchemish, Arzawa, and Alashiya, cut off at one time. A camp was laid down in one place in Amurru. They slayed its people; its land was like that which never existed. They were coming, while the flame was readied before them, forward to Egypt. Their confederation consisted of the Peleset, Tjeker, Shekelesh, Danuna, and Weshesh, lands united. They laid their hands upon the lands to the circuit of the world; their hearts were approving and confident: "Our plans will succeed!" Now, the heart of this god, the Lord of the Gods, was prepared and ready to ensnare them like birds. He caused my strength to exist and my plans to succeed. My . . . goes out, coming forth like a miracle. I organized my border in Djahi, prepared before them with chiefs, garrison commanders, and maryannu-warriors. I caused the river mouths to be prepared like a strong rampart with fighting ships, warships, and freighters, equipped and completely manned from front to back with brave warriors possessing their weapons, and infantry consisting of every choicest man of Egypt—they were like lions roaring upon the mountain-tops.
>
> Source: Translated by Taylor Bryanne Woodcock from Epigraphic Survey. 1930. *Medinet Habu.* Vol. 1, *Earlier Historical Records of Ramses III.* Oriental Institute Publications VIII. Chicago: University of Chicago Press, plate 46, lines 16–21.

Seals and Sealing

The ancient sealing practice may be described broadly as the process of securing an object with mud or other malleable substance, which was then impressed with a distinctive pattern or design, as a visible guarantee that the sealed object had not been opened or otherwise disturbed. The ancient practice of sealing may be compared, for instance, with the European use of signet rings to secure wax seals on letters. However, it is important to note that ancient Egyptian sealing practice does not usually provide a definitive "signature" for specific individuals. The earliest seals discovered in Egypt were imported from Mesopotamia and date to the Naqada II Period (3500–3200 BCE), although sealing practice itself did not become widespread in Egypt until the First Dynasty, about 3000 BCE, at the cemeteries of Abydos and Sakkara. The first seals manufactured in Egypt imitated the cylinder-shaped forms of contemporary Mesopotamian seals and were typically inscribed with royal names and titles and less often with the titles of private (nonroyal) officials, the names of estates, or purely figural designs. In tomb contexts, cylinder seals probably served as a less expensive alternative to more costly funerary stelae. As objects of daily use, seals might have been worn as amulets or employed for sealing practice.

Objects sealed in the First and Second Dynasties (3000–2686 BCE) primarily included jars and bags, the contents of which were deposited as mortuary offerings in royal tombs. By the Old Kingdom (2686–2160 BCE), private names had ceased to appear on cylinder seals; at the same time, new types of objects were also being sealed, such as boxes tied with string. In addition, evidence for deliveries of goods from royal storehouses to private, nonroyal tombs at Giza, in northern Egypt, and Buhen, in Nubia, has been uncovered in the form large quantities of seal impressions, which is to say, preserved lumps of sealed mud without the object to which it was originally affixed.

Already by the late Old Kingdom, stamp seals had begun to replace the Mesopotamian-inspired cylinder seal forms. The earliest stamp seals take the form of pyramid-shaped amulets with a design on the base, which developed later into circular, button-shaped stamps and design amulets/stamps with animals or human figures on the back. By the late First Intermediate Period and early Middle Kingdom, around 2055 BCE, design amulets in the form of a stylized scarab beetle emerged as the most popular seal type as well as one of the most widely attested, iconic, and characteristically "Egyptian" artifacts. Scarab seals originally bore decorative motifs, S- and C-shaped scroll borders, and amuletic or protective hieroglyphs, often arranged in symmetrical patterns. By the end of the Twelfth Dynasty, roughly contemporary with a major restructuring of the Egyptian administration under the reign of King Senusret III (1870–1831 BCE), scarab seals began to also incorporate the names and titles of nonroyal individuals.

In terms of chronology, seal designs from scarab bases, as well as impressions of those designs, do not by themselves constitute a particularly accurate dating criterion. However, base designs can be classified broadly as characteristic of the First Intermediate Period and early Middle Kingdom (before Senusret III, 1870 BCE), late Middle Kingdom (Senusret III–Dynasty 13, 1870–1650 BCE), or Second Intermediate Period (1650–1550 BCE). As an added caveat, royal names inscribed on many scarab bases provide only a terminus post quem (earliest possible date), because seals were frequently used as heirlooms long after the king whose name they bore had died. Furthermore, mass-produced royal name scarabs were employed most often as amulets, rather than seals, and cannot necessarily serve as evidence for ancient sealing practice.

Along similar lines, individually produced scarabs bearing the names and titles of private individuals, which might have been used as amulets or seals, cannot always be linked with certainty to the individuals themselves, as such objects might have been plundered from tombs for later reuse. Further complicating matters, scarabs with "funerary" epithets need not have been originally designed for use in the tomb, as such epithets might also be interpreted as wishes for a still-living individual, who might then have employed the amulet as an administrative seal. Fortunately, while scarab bases alone lack precision as a dating criterion, an analysis of the whole object, taking into consideration the back, depicting the beetle's carapace, and sides, depicting its folded legs, can produce a workable, albeit complex, system for dating such objects. Of course, these methods work only when the scarab itself is present. In the vast majority of cases, where only the mud seal impression survives, a reliable date may be obtained only in conjunction with other archaeological data, such as pottery analysis.

The basic techniques for the analysis of mud seal impressions, which today form an important part of any archaeological excavation where such objects have been uncovered, were first outlined with regard to impressions from the Egyptian fortress of Uronarti, in Nubia (see Reisner, 1955). With regard to designs on the "front" or "top" of mud seal impressions, we may assign approximate dates, based on the design itself, as outlined above. However, a more important source of data, with regard to sealing practice at a given site, may be found on the "back" or "bottom" of the mud seal impressions, where it was affixed to the sealed object. From the patterns impressed on the back of the mud, it is possible to determine the general identity of the originally sealed objects, which typically do not survive. Distinctive back types attested during the Middle Kingdom include boxes secured with string to a wooden peg, ceramic jars, fabric bags, reed or wicker baskets, papyrus documents, and door bolts.

The practice of administrative sealing reached its peak during the late Middle Kingdom and early Second Intermediate Period. From the New Kingdom, beginning in 1550 BCE, and later, administrative seal impressions occur in substantially smaller quantities and disappear entirely in many cases. However, sealing practice did continue in mortuary contexts, including the use of official necropolis seals, which were impressed onto the mud plaster covering a tomb entrance after burial or upon resealing of an opened monument, as found, most famously, on the sealed tomb of Tutankhamun; so-called funerary cones, made of clay, impressed with the name and titles of the deceased individual and inserted into the wall above their tomb entrance; and, less frequently, mudbricks stamped with the name and title of the tomb owner and used in construction of parts of the funerary monument itself. At the same time, while sealing fell out of favor as a tool for day-to-day administration, the seal—in form, if not function—remained popular as a mortuary amulet, most notably in the case of "heart scarabs," which were inscribed with Spell 30B from the Book of the Dead and placed over the heart of a mummy to ensure proper function in the afterlife. During the reign of Amenhotep III (1390–1352 BCE), scarabs were even issued as mass-produced memorabilia, commemorating, for example, the king's marriage, construction projects, and animal hunts.

Joshua Aaron Roberson

See also: Amulets; Book of the Dead; Scarab; Tomb of Tutankhamun

Further Reading

Ben Tor, Daphna. 1994. "The Historical Implications of Middle Kingdom Scarabs Found in Palestine Bearing Private Names and Titles of Officials." *Bulletin of the American Schools of Oriental Research* 294: 7–22.

Ben Tor, Daphna. 2004. "Two Royal-Name Scarabs of King Amenemhat II from Dashur." *Metropolitan Museum of Art Journal* 39: 17–33.

Ben Tor, Daphna. 2007. *Scarabs, Chronology, and Interconnections: Egypt and Palestine in the Second Intermediate Period.* Orbis Biblicus et Orientalis Series Archaeologica 27. Fribourg and Göttingen: Academic Press and Vandenhoeck & Ruprecht.

Johnson, Janet. 1977. "Private Name Seals of the Middle Kingdom." In McGuire Gibson and Robert D. Biggs, eds. *Seals and Sealing in the Ancient Near East.* Bibliotheca Mesopotamica 6. Malibu: Undena, pp. 141–145.

Reisner, George. 1955. "Clay Sealings of Dynasty XIII from Uronarti Fort." *Kush* 3: 26–69.

Teeter, Emily, and Terry G. Wilfong. *Scarabs, Scaraboids, Seals, and Seal Impressions from Medinet Habu.* Oriental Institute Publications 118. Chicago: Oriental Institute. https://oi.uchicago.edu/sites/oi.uchicago.edu/files/uploads/shared/docs/OIP118.pdf.

Ward, William. 1994. "Beetles in Stone: The Egyptian Scarab." *Biblical Archaeologist* 57, no. 4: 186–202.

Wegner, Josef. 2007. *The Mortuary Temple of Senwosret III at Abydos.* New Haven, CT: Yale University Press.

Williams, Bruce. 1997. "Aspects of Sealing and Glyptic in Egypt before the New Kingdom." In McGuire Gibson and Robert D. Biggs, eds. *Seals and Sealing in the Ancient Near East.* Bibliotheca Mesopotamica 6. Malibu: Undena, pp. 135–40.

Sed Festival

Unlike the Khoiak and Min festivals that were celebrated for certain gods, the Heb Sed ("Sed festival"; meaning and etymology uncertain) was intended strictly for the king. Its primary purpose was his rejuvenation and the renewal of his powers. On this occasion, he wore a characteristic short cloak that wraps around his body, sometimes revealing his shoulders, with his hands protruding out of it in front of his chest. The festival is attested from the dawn of Egyptian history, the First Dynasty (3000–2890 BCE), and even earlier for kings such as Narmer (no confirmed dates available). Also unlike other feasts, the Sed was not an annual celebration that fell on or around the same date each year.

On what basis the Sed festival was celebrated has been the subject of great debate. The most commonly held belief is that it consisted of a jubilee marking a king's 30th regnal year and that it was celebrated at shorter intervals of three to four years thereafter. The 30-year rule is based on sources from the Ptolemaic Period (332–30 BCE), when Egypt was ruled by the descendants of Alexander the Great's general, Ptolemy. For example, in the Demotic (a term denoting both a later phase of the ancient Egyptian language and the script used to write it) section of the text in the Memphis Decree of Ptolemy V Epiphanes (204–180 BCE), more famously known as the Rosetta Stone, one of the titles of this king is "Lord of Sed Festivals," which is translated as "Lord of the Thirty Years Festivals" in Greek. Much evidence of Sed festivals, however, has survived from reigns that did not last 30 years.

This has led to the formulation of alternative explanations for when they were celebrated. One proposed solution is that it was organized every 30 years, independently of the reigns of individual kings and regardless of length of reign. This could account for a possible Sed festival by Mentuhotep III (2004–1992 BCE) in his second regnal year, but it does not explain celebrations that were less than 30 years apart, as with Hatshepsut (1473–1458 BCE) and Thutmose III (1479–1425 BCE). It has also been suggested that the Heb Sed marked the king's 30th birthday. This, however, is refuted by the two most famous instances, those of Amenhotep III (1390–1352 BCE) and Ramses II (1279–1213 BCE), which were celebrated in their respective 30th regnal years. Another suggestion has been that Sed festivals took place three decades after a king's designation as coregent, when he was directly elevated to kingship during his predecessor's reign, or royal heir.

Ramses II, however, celebrated his first Sed festival in his 30th year as king, even though his father, Seti I (1294–1279 BCE), had named him as his successor. In the end, it cannot be expected that this festival was celebrated according to the same criteria over the course of more than 3,000 years of ancient Egyptian history.

The exact rituals of the Sed festival are unknown, as is the order of their performance, but it must similarly be assumed that its regular procedure changed over time. Matters are further complicated by the fragmentariness of the surviving pictorial evidence and the differences exhibited by them. Even when faced with an intact source, one must still assume a summary representation of the constituent rituals and actions. The Heb Sed was preceded by preparations needed for its celebration, such as the construction of palaces, temples, shrines, and pavilions; the erection of obelisks; and the restoration of existing temples. The festival itself seems to have begun with a procession, following which the king, wearing the Sed cloak, eventually sat under a pavilion on a raised platform, receiving homage from all those present, making land endowments to temples, and rewarding officials. This is the most iconic episode, one that can stand in for the whole festival, so much so that this pavilion, equipped with two thrones back-to-back, symbolizing the ruler's kingship over both Upper and Lower Egypt, in combination with the hieroglyph for "festival," is used to write "Heb Sed." Later on, the king visited the chapel of Wepwawet, "the Opener of Ways," a funerary jackal deity, whose standard then accompanied him in the other most characteristic episode of the festival, the king's ritual run, which was both a demonstration of his power and its regeneration and also symbolic of his assumption of kingship.

It must be borne in mind that a lot of evidence from ancient Egypt, both pictorial and textual, does not necessarily reflect reality but expressed an ideal outcome, if not in one's lifetime then in the afterlife, both of which were considered just as "real." Amenhotep II (1427–1400 BCE) and Thutmose IV (1400–1390 BCE), neither of whom reigned for 30 years, inscribed the columns of their respective monuments in Karnak Temple in Luxor with "First occasion of the Sed Festival" or "First occasion and repetition of the Sed Festival." The first of these common generic phrases is attested for rulers who did indeed celebrate jubilees, but instead of recording actual events after the fact, it often represents wish fulfillment and anticipation. Furthermore, no confirmed subsequent Sed festival for a single ruler is ever referred to with the second phrase. With no mention of specific dates and in the absence of any other evidence, it follows that neither king celebrated a jubilee. Supporting this notion is that Thutmose III, who probably did celebrate at least one, had columns in his *Akhmenu*, or Festival Hall, in Karnak, inscribed with the first phrase; this structure, however, was constructed before he ever celebrated a Sed festival.

Depictions of kings participating in the Sed festival or, more commonly, reliefs that show a deity presenting them with a, or many, Heb Sed hieroglyph(s) are attested as well. In a case similar to Thutmose III's, Ramses II depicted himself in such a scene well before his own festival of renewal. Djoser (2667–2648 BCE) of the Third Dynasty not only depicted himself performing the iconic ritual run, but he also included an arena for the celebration of this festival inside his pyramid complex in Sakkara in the afterlife. There is no evidence supporting that he celebrated a jubilee, however; neither did he reign for 30 years. As with the above column inscriptions, the evidence from his reign expresses the desire to celebrate an infinity of Sed festivals, stretching his kingship into eternity.

The historicity of a given Heb Sed is determined through a combination of factors. These include contemporary sources mentioning preparations for, or giving accounts of, the festival; royal officials bearing titles indicating their roles in it; exact dates; and numbered festivals in the case of a king who celebrated several, for example, 3 for Amenhotep III and 14 for Ramses II. Vessels used to store food and drink to be consumed during the Sed festival with inscriptions listing their contents constitute proof of historicity. Unfortunately, this applies only to Amenhotep III, the survival of whose palace in Malqata, on the West Bank of Luxor, where his Heb Sed was celebrated, also meant the preservation of rare material evidence of this kind. Ultimately, based on relevant sources from the reigns of around 70 kings, consisting of statues, wall reliefs, and textual evidence (Hornung and Staehelin 2006, 13–32), only a handful seem to have celebrated their 30-year jubilees. Amenhotep III and Ramses II are the only certain cases. Pepi I (2321–2287 BCE), Pepi II (2278–2184 BCE), Amenemhat III (1831–1786 BCE), Thutmose III, and Ramses III (1184–1153 BCE) are very likely candidates. And Senusret I (1956–1911 BCE), Hatshepsut, and Akhenaten (1352–1336) are less likely (Hornung and Staehelin 2006, 36–37). Of these, Pepi I, Senusret I, Amenemhat III, Thutmose III, Amenhotep III, and Ramses II celebrated their Sed festivals in or around their respective 30th regnal years, but Pepi II's is unknown, thus supporting the notion that the Heb Sed was a celebration marking the 30th year since a king's accession to the throne.

Arto Belekdanian

See also: Karnak; Kingship; Opet Festival; Palaces; Pyramids

Further Reading

Galán, José. 2000. "The Ancient Egyptian Sed-Festival and the Exemption from Corvee." *Journal of Near Eastern Studies* 59, no. 4: 255–264.

Gohary, Jocelyn. 1992. *Akenaten's Sed-festival at Karnak*. London: Kegan Paul International.

Hornung, Erik, and Elisabeth Staehelin. 2006. *Neue Studien zum Sedfest*. Aegyptiaca Helvetica 20. Basel: Schwabe.

Nuzzolo, Massimiliano. 2015. "The *Sed*-Festival of Niuserra and the Fifth Dynasty Sun Temples." In P. der Manuelian and T. Schneider, eds. *Towards a New History for the Egyptian Old Kingdom*. Leiden: Brill, pp. 366–392.

Stadelmann, Rainer. 2011. "The heb-sed Temple of Sneferu at Dahshur." In M. Bárta, F. Coppens, and J. Krejčí, eds. *Abusir and Saqqara in the Year 2010*. Vol. 2. Prague: Charles University in Prague, pp. 736–746.

Uphill, Eric. 1965. "The Egyptian Sed-Festival Rites." *Journal of Near Eastern Studies* 24: 365–383.

Seth

The cult of the god Seth dates back to the Naqada I Period of the Predynastic, around 4000–3500 BCE, at Ombos, or Nubt, in the fifth nome of Upper Egypt. Among the Egyptian gods, Seth is probably one of the most intriguing in relation to his manifestations and different roles he played in mythological accounts, ritual and royal scenes, and relationships to other gods. In a pivotal monograph on this deity that appeared decades ago, Te Velde (1967) defined Seth mainly as a "god of confusion," and so a negative interpretation has dominated the modern view on this ancient god for decades.

Thanks to more recent studies and discoveries, it is now clear that Seth was worshipped as a normative deity and respected for his strength and protective character through the whole course of the ancient Egyptian civilization. The considerable number of sources according to which this god went under a serious proscription in the later periods, which then led to its rather negative image by Plutarch, who identified him with the Greek *Typhon*—a deadly serpentine giant in Greek mythology—therefore need to be reconsidered according to each specific context and by taking in account the new evidence. As a matter of fact, Seth's cult is attested until the Roman Period (30 BCE–395 CE) in the temples of the Dakhla Oasis, and a peculiar image of the god as a winged falcon-headed warrior spearing the snake Apophis is found in the temple of Hibis in the Kharga Oasis, which dates to the Persian Period (525–404 BCE), but was still in use until the Roman Period.

The demonization of Seth as an opponent of creation and assimilated to Apophis is instead attested in religious texts from the Twenty-Fifth Dynasty (747–656 BCE) onward and originates from his negative role in the mythological accounts about Osiris, killed by Seth, who then contends for his throne with Horus, the son and legitimate heir of Osiris. The fight between Horus and Seth is narrated in a literary tale, *The Contendings of Horus and Seth*, in Papyrus Chester Beatty I of the Ramesside Period (1295–1069 BCE). Seth's role as evil brother and jealous uncle contrasts with the function of the god as protector of the Ra, the sun god, against the archenemy Apophis, the giant snake attacking the solar boat daily during the journey in the underworld. Despite these two contrasting functions, "Great of Power" is a main epithet of this god, who was protector of the sun god and slayer of Apophis while at the same time vilified in relation to his conduct toward Osiris and Horus.

Seth also played a role in the ancient Egyptian personal piety; on some votive stelae of the New Kingdom, Seth is clearly worshipped as a sort of personal patron and benefactor of the devotees. This positive role of the deity is also connected to the idea of a cosmic reconciliation of Horus and Seth as "companions" who maintain the kingship and the order of creation after a period of chaos; hints and allusions to this idea can be found in some religious texts, such as the Book of the Dead and the Memphite Theology. Moreover, Nemty, a local deity from Nubt (Ombos), was represented as having two faces; the same deity was also called "He with Two Faces" and depicted on funerary papyri of the Third Intermediate Period—a falcon-Horus head and a Seth-animal head, acknowledging the reconciliation among the two gods. Depictions of Seth as falcon-headed god are also known from a series of sources from the New Kingdom.

Seth may manifest in different animal forms, but his main animal symbol is a very peculiar one whose identification is still controversial and therefore it is just called the "Seth animal." His body resembles a mix between a greyhound and a wild pig, characterized by tall rectangular ears, a slightly curved snout, and an erect tail ending in an arrow. It is not clear whether this was considered a fantasy animal by the ancient Egyptians or if it corresponded to an animal belonging to the local Egyptian fauna in antiquity, such as the oryx antelope, the greyhound, the okapi, the orycterope, or the ass. When referring to the ancient Egyptian terminology, the so-called *sha*-animal, as depicted and mentioned in the Middle Kingdom tombs of Beni Hasan, together with other fantastic creatures of the desert and including the griffin, closely resembles the Seth animal. The god is actually also strongly associated with the desert, the "Red Land," as opposed to the Nile valley, the fertile "Black Land." The Seth animal is also a hieroglyph that in two main variants—Gardiner List E 20 and 2, sitting and laying down—functions not only as an ideogram for name of the god but also as a classifier/determinative for words indicating "rage" and "suffering," especially in texts dated to the First Intermediate Period (2160–2055 BCE) and Middle Kingdom (2055–1650 BCE). The Seth deity is also used as determinative for other similar words connected to misfortune. Very interestingly, from the New Kingdom, beginning in 1550 BCE, onward, the Seth hieroglyphs are still used as word classifiers, but not only with a negative meaning.

Seth can also manifest as hippopotamus; in particular, in the already mentioned *Contendings of Horus and Seth*, it is narrated how he transforms into a hippopotamus to fight Horus. Seth also can appear as a pig or as an ass. His donkey's manifestation becomes especially popular in the magic spells of the "Greek-Egyptian magical papyri," where Seth or Typhon is summoned up to help the magician to obtain the desired results in what very often are spells of aggressive magic. As a hippopotamus, Seth appears mainly in the ritual scenes of the Ptolemaic-Roman temples (332 BCE–495 CE), where Seth is chained up and speared by Horus. In these rituals, Seth incarnates "the enemy" of order and creation, similar to the giant snake Apophis, who he is depicted spearing from the boat of Ra in earlier scenes occurring on papyri and on tomb walls. The manifestation as hippopotamus, an animal that was known—similar to Seth—as a symbol of strength and aggressive behavior, also occurs on the already mentioned votive stelae of the Ramesside Period. In the latter, the hippopotamus of Seth is not speared, as in the temple scenes, but rather worshipped, while standing on a shrine, by a kneeling devotee in a clearly protective function toward the latter. In a peculiar scene occurring in a royal tomb of the Ramesside Period (1295–1069 BCE) and corresponding to the fifth division of the "Book of Gates," a pig whose caption names "the swallower" is depicted within a boat beside an enthroned Osiris in front of a scale; the scene has been recognized as a very significant variant of the last judgment, where the pig represents Seth.

Seth has been also assimilated to the Canaanite god Baal and with the epithet of "the Asiatic"; he appears then as an anthropomorphic male figure with a conical cap and two short horns in the front, as in its representation on the 400-Year Stela. The association between the two gods derives from their common character as storm gods and gods of the foreign lands. In relation to Baal, Seth's cult in the northeastern delta is attested in the Second Intermediate Period (1650–1550 BCE), at the time of the Hyksos, and speaks of the important role that this god had in relation to the foreign lands. Under the Ramessides, Seth is also important as god of royalty; some of the Ramesside pharaohs are named "Seti," namely "the One of Seth," and a statue of Ramses III of the Twentieth Dynasty (1186–1069 BCE) depicts the pharaoh being crowned by Seth and Horus.

Recent studies have also revealed how the veneration of Seth was present in religious centers far from the Nile valley during the early New Kingdom, beginning in 1550 BCE, such as in Mut al-Kharab, in the Dakhleh Oasis. These kinds of studies have also shown how the earlier assumption, based on the already mentioned Te Velde's study on the proscription of the god's cult after the New Kingdom, does not really stand on solid ground, as it is only based on evidence coming from the Nile valley. Moreover, the areas where the cult of Seth is attested should not be considered as peripheral to the main religious centers of the valley as previously believed; the images of the gods in the major temples of the oases—such as the one, already mentioned, in the Hibis Temple in the oasis of El-Kharga—speak of the recognition of the god within the royal sphere that controlled the administration of the oases as well.

Rita Lucarelli

See also: Demons; Deserts; Funerary Books, Royal; Horus; Isis; Osiris

Further Reading

Allon, Niv. 2007. "Seth Is Baal: Evidence from the Egyptian Script." *Ägypten und Levante* 17: 15–22.

Cruz-Uribe, Eugene. 2009. "Stx aA pHty 'Seth, God of Power and Might.'" *Journal of the American Research Center in Egypt* 45: 201–226.

Gardiner, Alan Henderson. 1931. *The Library of A. Chester Beatty: Description of a Hieratic Papyrus with a Mythological Story, Love-Songs, and Other Miscellaneous Texts; the Chester Beatty Papyri, no. 1*. London: Privately printed by J. Johnson at the Oxford University Press and published by E. Walker.

Hope, Colin A., and Ashten R. Warfe. 2017. "The Proscription of Seth Revisited." In Camilla Di Biase-Dyson and Leonie Donovan, eds. *The Cultural Manifestation of Religious Experience: Studies in Honour of Boyo G. Ockinga*. Münster: Ugarit, pp. 273–283.

Kooyman, Milena. 2017. "Always on the Periphery? Seth and Personal Piety in New Kingdom Egypt." In Camilla Di Biase-Dyson and Leonie Donovan, eds. *The Cultural Manifestation of Religious Experience: Studies in Honour of Boyo G. Ockinga*. Münster: Ugarit, pp. 365–376.

McDonald, A. 2007. "A Metaphor for Troubled Times: The Seth Deity Determinative in the First Intermediate Period." *Zeitschrift für Ägyptologie* 134: 26–39.

Te Velde, Herman. 1967. *Seth, God of Confusion: A Study of His Role in Egyptian Mythology and Religion*. Probleme der Ägyptologie 6. Leiden: Brill.

Sex. See **Gender and Sex**

Ships and Shipping

The towns and villages of Egypt were tied together by the Nile and with the outside world by the shipping lanes of the Mediterranean and Red Seas. Watercraft sustained these connections, supporting communication, exchange, distribution, ritual activities, and the imposition of power. Nilotic watercraft ranged from simple papyrus rafts to giant barges. They operated as platforms for hunting, fishing, fowling, and sport. More efficient than overland travel, watercraft supported agricultural redistribution as well as local and foreign trade. The construction of Egypt's iconic monuments was facilitated by robust barges. Boats were essential for the imposition of state control and served as mechanisms for collecting taxes, policing river traffic, and deploying armies. They were vectors for information exchange, and during inundation, they were the means of maintaining social connections between isolated villages. Watercraft acquired prominent roles in mythology and ritual activity; magical boats conveyed the deceased from this world to the next, while celestial barques transported the gods across the heavens and through the netherworld.

EARLY BOATS

The earliest watercraft on the Nile were papyrus rafts. They ranged from simple floats to large vessels capable of transporting animals. Papyrus rafts were used throughout Egypt's history and were the basis of transport for common people. They are depicted in scenes of hunting, fishing, and stick-fighting, and they retained a sacred, archaic association with the gods, royalty, and funerary rituals. The earliest wooden boats discovered in Egypt are from the First Dynasty (3000–2890 BCE), though it is probable that Egyptians were building plank-built boats by the Gerzean/Naqada II Period (3500–3200 BCE), when new crescent-shaped vessels with dual deckhouses appear in pottery and petroglyphs and woodworking tools (e.g., axes, adzes, chisels) appear as burial components.

CARGO VESSELS AND BARGES

Cargo vessels sustained Egypt, transporting grain, bread, cattle, oil, beer, and all varieties of agricultural products to market. Old Kingdom (2686–2160 BCE) freighters had flat bottoms and transom ends. They frequently had a sloped-roof stern shelter for the crew and different configurations of enclosed deckhouses, animal pens, and cargo stowage amidships. By the Middle Kingdom, starting in 2055 BCE, round-bottomed, spoon-shaped vessels became the predominate form. In iconography, cargo vessels are shown with goods stacked precariously on their roofs, though this may also be a convention to show internal storage. Monumental architecture required barges capable of hauling massive stones. Papyrus fragments from Wadi al-Jarf document boat crews transporting stone to the Great Pyramid building site. Barges were outfitted with hogging trusses (massive cables that ran from bow to stern) to provide longitudinal support and prevent hull deformation under heavy loads. New Kingdom barges achieved enormous proportions. Ineni built a 120-cubit (206 foot) barge to transport obelisks for Thutmose I (1504–1492 BCE). Hatshepsut's (1473–1458 BCE) obelisk barge was larger, with three layers of through-beams and five hogging trusses. It was towed by a fleet of 30 boats. Numerous timbers from working boats were integrated into the pyramid causeway of Senusret I (1956–1911 BCE) at Lisht. They demonstrate that cargo boats were heavily built with short, thick, joggled planks, curved hulls, and massive internal framing. Traveling boats conveyed high-status individuals along the Nile. Convoys might have included dedicated cooking, supply, and escort vessels. Kings would have traveled in imposing ships of state, like the one depicted on Sahura's (2487–2475 BCE) pyramid causeway.

SEAGOING BOATS

Egyptians engaged in seaborne trade during the Early Dynastic (3000–2686 BCE), but the earliest primary evidence of seagoing ships comes from Wadi al-Jarf, where harbor facilities, anchors, ship timbers, and pottery all indicate that ships were regularly sailing across the Red Sea to Sinai during the reign of Khufu (2589–2566 BCE). Seagoing ships are depicted on the walls of Sahura's mortuary complex as well as the causeway of Unas (2375–2345 BCE). Seagoing ships had to endure greater dynamic forces than Nilotic boats and probably stimulated advances in ship construction. Sahura's ships were equipped with hogging trusses and truss-girdles, bipod masts, and three steering oars per side. The ships of Hatshepsut's Punt expedition were more advanced, with improved hogging trusses, through-beams (instead of truss-gridles), pole masts with wide sails, and quarter rudders with tillers. Fragments of Middle Kingdom ships were found at the Red Sea harbors of Ayn Soukna and Mersa Gawasis. Between voyages, the ships were disassembled and stored in long rock-cut galleries, along with coils of rope and sailing tackle.

WARSHIPS

Watercraft likely played a role in early interregional conflict and the unification of Egypt. The Gebel el-Arak knife handle (Naqada II) depicts a naval battle and corpses floating in the water. Boats are associated with conquest imagery from the Narmer Palette, Gebel Sheikh Suleiman Monument, and Heirakonpolis Tomb 100. Boats generally served as troop transports instead of fighting platforms. The Tomb of Intef at Thebes of the Eleventh Dynasty (3000–2686 BCE) depicts three rowed warships manned by archers and marines. The Medinet Habu reliefs illustrate a naval battle between the fleet of Ramses III (1479–1425 BCE) and the Sea Peoples. Ramses's warships were equipped with a rowing bulwark, bow and sterncastles, brailed sails, lion figureheads, and the first examples of fighting tops. Archers and slingers fire on their opponents, marines prepare to board, and sailors use grapnels to capsize the Sea Peoples' ships.

FUNERARY AND PILGRIMAGE VESSELS

Boats were buried alongside tombs during the Early Dynastic, Old, and Middle Kingdoms. They were demonstrations of power, mobility, and access to resources. While often referred to as "solar boats," they likely represent funerary barges (used to transport the deceased to the burial site) or pilgrimage boats (used for making afterlife journeys to sacred locations). Scenes of postmortem pilgrimages depict a mummy or statues aboard a towed vessel. Funerary barges and pilgrimage boats are typically papyriform vessels, that is, wooden boats designed to evoke the form of archaic papyrus rafts. Some hulls were painted green (associated with resurrection and papyrus). They had steering oars mounted on their quarters and traditionally had ornate bow and stern finials.

Early Dynastic boat burials were found at Sakkara (4), Helwan (19), Abu Rawash (6), and Abusir North (including a sacrificed helmsman). A fleet of 14 First Dynasty vessels was discovered at Abydos (encased in boat-shaped superstructures). Unlike other Early Dynastic boat burials, they were associated with a royal funerary enclosure instead of an elite tomb. A funerary boat associated with a Third Dynasty elite tomb was recently excavated at Abusir South.

Two disassembled boats were discovered in boat pits on the south side of Khufu's pyramid. One is undergoing conservation; the other has been reassembled. The 143-foot papyriform vessel is made of long cedar planks and has an ornate cabin in the stern. The vessel would have been towed; the oars lashed to its side are steering oars and should be located at the stern. It is unclear whether the vessel was ever used. Empty boat pits are associated with several other Old Kingdom pyramids. Additionally, six funerary boats were found at the Dahshur pyramid complex of Senusret III (1870–1831 BCE). They had spoon-shaped hulls and once had papyriform finials. A boat vault was also found at Senusret III's mortuary complex in South Abydos. The walls had a nautical tableau depicting 120 vessels.

BOAT MODELS

Boat models appear from the Predynastic Period on. Early wood, clay, and ivory models portray both papyrus rafts and plank-built boats. Models became increasingly prevalent during the Sixth Dynasty (2345–2181 BCE) and included paddles, spars, and steering oars. Substantial model fleets were associated with the tombs of Niankh-Pepy-Kem (8), Queen Neith (16), and Kaemsenu (11). By the First Intermediate Period, boat models were painted and included carved figures, equipment, and rigging. The finest examples come from the Middle Kingdom tomb of Meketre at Deir el-Bahari, dating to the late Eleventh Dynasty. Tomb 10A (Djehutynakht, late Eleventh/early Twelfth Dynasty) contained a flotilla of 58 boat models, including cargo vessels, traveling boats, kitchen barges, hunting skiffs, a military transport, funerary barques, and pilgrimage boats. The tomb of Tutankhamun contained 35. Boat models provide a unique glimpse of shipboard life, portraying the owner, crew, servants, hunters, fishermen, mourners, and priests.

SOLAR BARQUES

Ra voyaged across the sky in his day barque (*mandjet*) and through the Duat in the night barque (*mesktet*). Funerary vessels are often referred to as "solar barques," but there is debate over this designation. Solar barques carried cultic objects associated with Ra, and not coffins or deckhouses. These icons are known from tomb iconography, boat models, and the Book of the Dead. Two models of solar barques were found outside the tomb of Imhotep at el-Lisht (high priest of Ra at Heliopolis). One of the most unique representations is a detailed plan and profile on the ceiling of the tomb of Ramses VI. A 30-meter-long mudbrick model of a solar barque lies south of Nyuserra's sun temple at Abu Ghurob.

CULTIC VESSELS

Just as gods traversed the sky in celestial barques, their cultic images were taken on ritual processions in portable barques—large, extravagant models with an enclosed shrine for the icon. Tomb biographies describe the commissioning of portable barques, which were crafted from precious woods, plated in gold and silver, and ornately decorated. Portable barques could be carried on the shoulders of priests or dragged. Between journeys, they resided in dedicated barque sanctuaries. During the Opet festival, the sacred barques of Amun, Mut, and Khonsu traveled between Karnak and Luxor. They were ferried across the river in sacred ships, which constitute a second category of cultic vessel. The most famous of these ships is the *Amun-Userhet*, first attested to in Ahmose's Karnak Stela. The *Userhet* had crowned ram-head finials and a gilded shrine that housed the portable barque of Amun. The version constructed by Ramses III was 130 cubits in length. Other important sacred ships include the Neshmet-barque of Osiris and the *henu* barque of Sokar.

SHIP CONSTRUCTION

The hulls of Egyptian boats were fastened together with rope ligatures. Watercraft were designed so they could be disassembled, transported overland, and reassembled; thus, they did not employ fixed fasteners like pegged tenons or nails. Early boats were laced along plank seams, while Khufu's *Royal Ship* was fastened with ropes that ran transversely across the hull. Later period cargo vessels and seagoing ships relied on discrete point-to-point lashings. The Dahshur boats are fastened with dovetail joints. Initially, tenons were used for aligning planks. By the Middle Kingdom, they were large and closely set, helping to stiffen the hull. Seagoing ships used paired tenons. Nilotic vessels were typically constructed from short lengths of local wood, while seagoing ships and prestigious vessels (e.g., Khufu's *Royal Ship*, *Amun-Userhet*) were built from long planks of imported cedar. Old Kingdom vessels were flat-bottomed, but by the Middle Kingdom, most vessels had rounded hulls, exploiting the structural strength of the arch. Ship construction scenes appear in many tombs, for example, the Fifth Dynasty (2494–2345 BCE) tomb of Ti), and construction techniques were later described by Herodotus (484–425 BCE).

PROPULSION AND STEERING

Early rafts and boats were punted or paddled. Rowing (mechanically more effective) appears by the Old Kingdom. The earliest depictions of sails are on the

Qustul incense burner and a Naqada II jar (both dated 3200–3000 BCE). Both show single pole masts with rectangular sails. Sails enabled fast, efficient upriver travel and represent an enormous leap in nautical technology. It is perhaps not coincidental that sails, amplifying mobility, appear just prior to Egyptian unification. Old Kingdom vessels carried tall and narrow boom-footed sails on bipod masts. The rig began to evolve at the end of the Old Kingdom; the boom was hung in lifts, sails dramatically increased in width, and the bipod was replaced by the pole mast. This form was refined through the New Kingdom.

Brailed sails appear in Egypt during the Eighteenth Dynasty. While it is unclear where they developed, their introduction marks a dramatic technological leap. Brailing lines, attached to the loose foot of the sail, allowed sailors to adjust the sail shape to tack more effectively. Old Kingdom vessels often had numerous steering oars, each directly held by a helmsman. This inefficient design was replaced in the Fifth Dynasty, when tillers and rudder stanchions appear, greatly reducing the work of helmsmen. Quarter rudders remained in use through the New Kingdom, though in the Middle Kingdom, many Nilotic vessels were outfitted with axially mounted steering oars.

Douglas Inglis

See also: Barque, Sacred; Furniture and Woodworking; Nile River; Punt; Sea Peoples; Tomb Models

Further Reading

Jones, Dilwyn. 1995. *Boats*. Austin: University of Texas Press.

Landström, Björn. 1970. *Ships of the Pharaohs: 4000 Years of Egyptian Shipbuilding*. Garden City, NY: Doubleday.

Tallet, Pierre. 2012. "Ayn Sukhna and Wadi el-Jarf: Two Newly Discovered Pharaonic Harbours on the Suez Gulf." *British Museum Studies in Ancient Egypt and the Sudan* 18: 147–168.

Vinson, Steve. 1998. *The Nile Boatman at Work*. Mainz am Rhein: Philipp von Zabern.

Wachsmann, Shelley. 1998. *Seagoing Ships & Seamanship in the Bronze Age Levant*. College Station: Texas A & M University Press.

Ward, Cheryl A. 2000. *Sacred and Secular: Ancient Egyptian Ships and Boats*. Archaeological Institute of America Monographs New Series 5. Philadelphia: University Museum, University of Pennsylvania.

Silver

Silver was used in ancient Egypt at least as early as the Predynastic Period, as the oldest silver objects in Egypt are beads dating from the Naqada II Period 3500–3200 BCE). Silver is found in the Fourth Dynasty (2613–2494 BCE) in the tomb objects of Queen Hetepheres at Giza. Silver leaf was used to cover the bottom part of her headrest, and she had a set of silver anklets inlaid with semiprecious stones. It is also in the Fourth Dynasty when silver gets a separate name from gold, *nbu hedj*, "white gold," rather than just *nbu*, "gold."

Silver can be found in Egypt as part of galena ores or occurring in gold deposits, but not in large amounts. As silver was rare in ancient Egypt, it was considered more valuable than gold, indicated by the fact that silver items precede gold in lists of valuables from the Old and Middle Kingdoms (2686–1650 BCE). Silver was more common and more readily available in the New Kingdom (1550–1069 BCE) when Egypt had an empire in Nubia and Southwest Asia and gained new sources for this metal. The ancient Egyptians mostly used silver to manufacture personal possessions such as jewelry or small vessel and bowls. The most fabulous silver objects from ancient Egypt date to the rulers of the Twenty-First (1069–945 BCE) and Twenty-Second (945–715 BCE) Dynasties, who were buried at Tanis in the northeast Delta. The inner anthropoid coffins of kings Psusennes I and Sheshonq II were of silver, and there were silver vessels and small canopic coffins found as well.

The ancient Egyptian records do not present evidence related to the source of silver until the New Kingdom. One of the most common opinions about the source is that there was no local silver ore in Egypt, and all silver was received from outside, either by trade with the Mediterranean area or as tribute from conquests in Syria and Palestine. Others have suggested, by analyses and experimental processes, that the earliest Egyptian silver was a natural alloy of silver and gold and could be found in Egyptian and Nubian gold mines. Lucas concluded that the gold, electrum, and silver used in ancient Egypt, and probably elsewhere, were all varieties of the same alloy and only differed in the relative proportions of the principal constituents (1926, 317–318).

The well-known Treasure of Tod, found buried in a copper chest below the floor of the Temple of Tod north of Luxor and carrying the name of King Amenemhat II of the Twelfth Dynasty, contained numbers of silver ingots and vessels. An analysis of its silver shows that it was "almost certainly imported and a northern Greek or south Anatolian origin is possible" (Ogden 2000, 170).

Mahmoud Ahmed Emam

See also: Beads; Gold; Jewelry; Tanis

Further Reading

Brier, B. 2005. "Treasures of Tanis." *Archaeology* 58: 18–25.

Gale, N. H., and Z. A. Stos-Gale. 1981. "Ancient Egyptian Silver." *Journal of Egyptian Archaeology* 67: 103–115.

Lucas, A. 1926. *Ancient Egyptian Materials and Industries.* London: Edward Arnold & Co.

Ogden, J. 2000. "Metals." In Paul T. Nicholson, and Ian Shaw, eds. *Ancient Egyptian Materials and Technology*. London: Cambridge University Press, pp. 148–176.

Petrie, W. M. F. 1915. "The Metals in Egypt." *Ancient Egypt* Part I: 12–23.

Schorsch, Deborah. 2001. "Precious Metal Polychromy in Egypt in the Time of Tutankhamun." *Journal of Egyptian Archaeology* 87: 55–71.

Wachsmann, S. 2010. "Ahhotep's Silver Ship Model: The Minoan Context." *Journal of Ancient Egyptian Interconnections* 2, no. 3: 31–41.

Sledge

A sledge is a simple overland vehicle made of wood, normally with two parallel runners that turn upward on the front end. It was generally used in ancient Egypt for hauling heavy cargo, not for transporting people or animals. Ropes were attached to a horizontal bar on the front part of the sledge and pulled by a team of men, oxen, or both. Pictorial evidence shows that liquid was poured over the ground to facilitate its movement, and archaeologists have documented ancient mud-paved paths with drag marks on the surface. On softer sand, Egyptians created a track by laying a series of wooden planks to prevent the sledge from digging into the ground. To tow the load up to a higher level, solid ramps were built with mudbricks and compacted soil.

Egyptians frequently used the sledge to haul masonry blocks, columns, obelisks, and statues in construction of large buildings like pyramids and temples. They also employed it in agriculture, mining and quarrying, and boat transportation. The 14-foot-long sledge discovered next to the pyramid complex of Senusret III (1870–1831 BCE) in Dahshur, and now exhibited at the Egyptian Museum in Cairo, is the largest extant example of an ancient Egyptian sledge, and it was likely used to move the boats that were found buried nearby.

Pictorial evidence indicates that the sledge was often used in funerary processions to transport coffins and burial goods, and actual sledges have been discovered inside tombs. From the Eighteenth Dynasty (1550–1295 BCE), the sledge-shaped base was incorporated into the design of funerary equipment, such as canopic chests and coffins. In the tomb of Tutankhamun, there was a shrine of Anubis, a game board, and many boxes of different types that feature this motif. These sledges were not functional, but they were added for symbolic and religious reasons.

The sledge was also frequently employed in ritual processions of sacred emblems and divine images, including statues of deified kings. Portable shrines, often in the form of sacred barques, commonly featured the sledge-shaped base, although these shrines were generally lifted with carrying poles by priests, not dragged on the ground. Some gods and goddesses, including Wepwawet, Hathor, the Apis, Hatmehyt, and Mehyt, had close association with the sledge iconography when they were depicted in their animal manifestations.

The two most common ancient Egyptian words for "sledge" were *temet* and *wenesh*. The textual contexts of these words may indicate that the former usually designated sacred sledges while the latter referred to mundane tools.

Kei Yamamoto

See also: Obelisk; Pyramid Construction; Tomb of Tutankhamun

Further Reading

Arnold, Dieter. 1991. *Building in Egypt: Pharaonic Stone Masonry*. Oxford: Oxford University Press.

Arnold, Dieter. 2003. *The Encyclopedia of Ancient Egyptian Architecture*. New York: Princeton University Press.

Partridge, Robert. 1996. *Transport in Ancient Egypt*. London: Rubicon Press.

Yamamoto, Kei. 2011. "The Sledge-Shaped Base in Ancient Egyptian Sculpture: Interpreting an Unusual Late Period Statuette Base from North Abydos." *Journal of American Research Center in Egypt* 47: 279–292.

Yamamoto, Kei. 2015. "Iconography of the Sledge in Ancient Egyptian Funerary Art." *Bulletin of the Egyptological Seminar* 19: 665–674.

Sphinx, Great

The main features of royal pyramid complexes are a pyramid, a pyramid temple, and a valley temple, but the second of three complexes at Giza includes the significant additions of the Great Sphinx and a neighboring "Sphinx Temple." Although a minority opinion groups the Sphinx with the Great Pyramid as part of King Khufu's (2589–2566 BCE) complex, overwhelming consensus regards it as a product of King Khafra's (2558–2532 BCE) reign. Either way, construction of the Sphinx is confidently dated to the Old Kingdom, or "Pyramid Age," of Egyptian history. Originally sculpted from a high area of natural rock on the Giza Plateau, its current form also includes stone blocks from multiple later restorations. It stands at an imposing height of almost 66 feet.

A sphinx is a composite form, which means it is the combination of parts from different organisms. Ancient Egyptian art and religion abound with such composite beings. Although a basic sphinx draws from just two sources—a lion for the body and a human for the head—the Egyptians often assembled parts from three or even more bodies for composite deities, demons, or symbols. The association of the pharaoh's strength specifically with a lion's power and ferocity was prominent throughout history. The human face of the Great Sphinx is understood as that of King Khafra, presumably with idealized features.

About a millennium after the Old Kingdom, New Kingdom (1550–1069 BCE) art and architecture experienced a major increase in the use of sphinxes. For the Great Sphinx, this was also an era of rebirth, prompting alterations to the monument itself and its immediate surroundings. The Sphinx was by that time reinterpreted as a manifestation of the sun god Horemakhet, or "Horus-in-the-Horizon." It thus became the central focus of a religious zone where pharaohs, officials, and others erected buildings and set stelae as expressions of devotion. Amid this activity, a royal statue was likely added in front of the Sphinx's chest. Likewise, delineation of a false beard from stone below the Sphinx's face may date to this period, possibly along with some painted polychrome detailing, traces of which still remain.

King Thutmose IV (1400–1390 BCE) of the Eighteenth Dynasty erected the Dream Stela between the Sphinx's forelegs. The inscription on this massive, 12-foot-tall granite stela commemorates his own reign as the fulfillment of a promise from the god, which was conveyed in a dream when Thutmose was still a prince. Supposedly, if he unburdened the Sphinx of sand that had blanketed it for many centuries, kingship would be his reward. Thutmose's efforts also may have included the first major post–Old Kingdom restorations of the Sphinx. Further masonry repairs have followed periodically, most notably from the Ptolemaic-Roman Period (332 BCE–395 CE), and even into very recent decades.

Part of modern lore surrounding the Great Sphinx relates to its missing nose. Many theories have been conjured, including one that suggests troops of Napoleon Bonaparte used it for target practice during the French military expedition to Egypt. However, trends in the preservation of figural sculpture confirm that noses, along with ears, are facial features most vulnerable to loss over the millennia that separate ancient Egyptian and modern times. The true fate of the Great Sphinx's nose remains unknown.

Nicholas Picardo

See also: Giza; Pyramids

Further Reading

Lehner, Mark. 1997. *The Complete Pyramids*. London: Thames & Hudson.

Lehner, Mark, and Zahi Hawass. 2017. *Giza and the Pyramids*. Cairo: American University in Cairo Press.

Zivie-Coche, Christiane. 1997. *Sphinx: History of a Monument*. Ithaca, NY: Cornell University Press.

Sports and Games

Sporting activities occupied an important role in the daily lives of ancient Egyptians. By *sports* is meant running, archery, jumping, different styles of fighting, and swimming. Some of these sports had quite a relevant role in the pharaonic ideology that considered the pharaoh as a personification of state. The vitality and force of the state was directly linked to the vigor and energy of the king himself and needed to be constantly exercised and renewed.

Running is one of those sporting activities that serves royal ideology. One of the most significant royal rituals, the *ḥb-sd*, also known as the Sed Festival, usually took place after 30 years of reign and was intended to renew the vitality of the king and, through him, the vitality of the monarchy itself. It consisted of offerings to deities, a recrowning of the king, and a ritual run by the pharaoh himself. This was an expression of the force of the pharaoh and the institution he headed. The Step Pyramid complex of King Djoser (2667–2648 BCE) of the Third Dynasty in Sakkara had a large open court with markers to run around so that the king's soul, or *ka*, could renew his kingship forever.

Although running is perhaps one of the easiest sporting activities to practice in any society, aside from the ritual that was mentioned, there is only one other reference of running from the Twenty-Fifth Dynasty, a stela from the reign of King Taharqa (690–664 BCE), describing a foot race by the king's soldiers from Memphis to Dahshur and back.

Another sporting activity closely linked to royalty and the elites was archery, standing on the ground or while riding in a chariot, something that only started being practiced from the New Kingdom onward. The composite bow, as well as horses and chariots, were introduced into Egypt by the Hyksos during the Second Intermediate Period (1650–1550 BCE). There is a famous stela of King Amenhotep II (1427–1400 BCE) in the Luxor Museum that depicts the king in his galloping chariot shooting arrows through copper ingots set up on stands. On a stela of Amenhotep II that he set up in a small chapel just northeast of the Great Sphinx at Giza, the king not only brags about shooting these targets but also of rowing heavy boats and galloping in his chariots (see Lichtheim 1976, 39–42).

Concerning the sports for the general public, there is the high jump, attested by two representations, in the Tomb of Ptahhotep, the vizier of King Djedkara (2414–2375 BCE) of the Fifth Dynasty, and in the Tomb of Mereruka, the vizier of King Teti (2345–2323 BCE), of the Sixth Dynasty, both of which are located in Sakkara.

Fighting seems to have been the most popular sport among the ancient Egyptians, and it is attested in iconographic representations from Predynastic times

This scene of pairs of men wrestling is part of the decoration in the Beni Hasan tomb of Amenemhat, an important provincial official of the early Twelfth Dynasty. These men were probably soldiers taking part in training, as Amenemhat was also commander of the province's army. (DEA/G. Sieon/De Agostini/Getty Images)

(5300–3000 BCE) to the end of the New Kingdom (1550–1069 BCE), although the majority of representations are dated to the Middle Kingdom (c. 2055–1650 BCE). In particular, there are many fighting and wrestling scenes in the tombs of Beni Hasan.

Stick-fighting seems to have been particularly popular in the New Kingdom, probably in preparation for war. Many of these scenes can be found at Medinet Habu, the mortuary temple of Ramses III (1184–1153 BCE). There are two examples of stick-fighting or fencing during royal celebrations. One is found in the tomb of Kheruef, the steward of Queen Tiye, the wife of Amenhotep III (1390–1352 BCE), on the West Bank of Thebes. As part of the Sed festival of the king, pairs of men are fighting with papyrus reeds or stalks of papyrus. The other example is from the tomb of the high priest of Aton, Meryra II, in Tell el-Amarna, showing soldiers both fencing and wrestling during the great *Durbar,* a ceremonial state reception held by King Akhenaten in regnal year 12.

A rich variety of games are known from ancient Egypt. Various ball and board games were played, and both kinds are attested by depictions in relief scenes in tombs, textual references, and from the survival of actual games and their pieces in tombs. Naturally, some of these games were more exclusive, but others would have been played by all social groups.

In ball games, there was a separation between those that were played only with a ball and those that used a ball and a bat. There seems to have been a game just played by girls, where two girls, riding on the backs of two other girls, throw balls back and forth. Many of these balls, which were made with leather, wood, clay, papyrus, or palm tree, have been found.

Apophis

When the sun god set at night and traveled through the underworld to rise again in the morning, he faced evil forces who wanted to stop him. The most evil and dangerous was Apophis, the underworld snake that symbolized not only evil but chaos. The evil Eye of Apophis symbolized this evil snake, and it could only be defeated by the Eye of Ra. That was the point of the ritual showing the king "batting" the Eye of Apophis.

Lisa K. Sabbahy

There is a very unusual representation of the pharaoh Thutmose III (1479–1425 BCE) at the temple of Deir el-Bahari hitting a ball with a bat. The texts that follow the scene indicate that the ball was "the Eye of Apophis"; by hitting the ball with the bat, which represented the Eye of Ra, the king would symbolically win over evil forces. This is the earliest example of this scene, but it occurs again twice with King Amenhotep III (1390–1352) at Luxor Temple and then not again until Ptolemaic times (332–30 BCE), when there are a number of examples in temples. Thutmose hits the ball in the presence of the goddess Hathor, but Sakhmet can be shown as well.

There were four different types of board games, with three of them documented since the time of the First Dynasty (3000–2890 BCE). The most popular board game was *senet*, "passing," a game that represented going into the underworld and avoiding all the dangers until arriving in the world of the afterlife. This game was played by two players and had the form of a rectangular box made in stone, wood, or terracotta. The top of the box was divided in 30 squares, separated in three rows of 10 squares each. Both players had five or seven pieces, generally made in faience, cone-shaped or flattened at the top, that would advance along the squares, as determined by tossing small sticks or wood or bone. At the beginning of the game, the pieces were placed alternately on the first squares of the board. Some of these squares had inscriptions, and some at the end were marked with deities. The player that first crossed all the squares with all his pieces would be the winner. Some tomb scenes depict the tomb owner playing senet, but no opponent is shown. It is assumed that they are playing against the forces of evil to enter into the afterlife. The most famous scene is probably the one in the Tomb of Nefertary, the chief queen of Ramses II (1279–1213 BCE).

The second game was *men*, "resistance," and this too was for two players. The equipment consisted of a long and narrow plaque that had 13 or more sections, and each player had five pieces that would be moved according to the result of the "dice." In its original form, this game disappeared by the Old Kingdom, but a very similar one appeared in the First Intermediate Period and can be found until the Late Period.

The third game, *mehen*, "snake," could be played by six players on a circular surface in the form of a coiled snake, usually made out of stone. The snake's body was divided in sections. Each player had six pieces in the form of lions and six balls of different colors that would determine the movement of the pieces. The objective of the game was also funerary. The player, who symbolizes the dead, would protect himself from the serpent and in doing so would win the game. Despite its popularity, this game disappeared at the end of the Old Kingdom.

The fourth game, *tjau*, "thieves" or "the game of the twenty houses," entered Egypt during the Seventeenth Dynasty (1580–1550 BCE), probably imported by the Hyksos. It involved two players and a board divided into 20 squares. The players had five pieces that each had to move around, with the goal of being the first off the board.

Maria Helena Trindade Lopes

See also: Chariot; Giza; Sed Festival; Weapons and Armor

Further Reading

Borghouts, J. F. 1973. "The Evil Eye of Apophis." *Journal of Egyptian Archaeology* 59: 114–150.

Decker, W. 1993. *Sports and Games of Ancient Egypt*. Cairo: American University.

Kendall, T. 2007. "Mehen: The Ancient Egyptian Game of the Serpent." In I. L. Finkel, ed. *Ancient Board Games in Perspective: Papers from the 1990 British Museum Colloquium, with Additional Contributions*. London: British Museum, pp. 33–39.

Lichtheim, Miriam. 1976. *Ancient Egyptian Literature: A Book of Readings*. Vol. 2, *The New Kingdom*. Berkeley: University of California Press.

Piccione, P. 1999. "Sportive Fencing as a Ritual for Destroying the Enemies of Horus." In E. Teeter and J. Larson, eds. Chicago: Oriental Institute of the University of Chicago, pp. 335–350.

Piccione, P. A. 2007. "The Egyptian Game of Senet and the Migration of the Soul." In I. L. Finkel, ed. *Ancient Board Games in Perspective*. London: British Museum, pp. 54–63.

Tyldesley, J. A. 2008. *Egyptian Games and Sports*. Shire Egyptology. London: Shire.

State Formation

The emergence of a territorial state in Egypt, around 3,200 BCE, under a divine king marks the beginning of a new sociopolitical structure that resulted in the first nation-state, but it also highlights a change in the interaction between human culture and biology. Egyptian state formation is often correlated with the unification of Upper Egypt and Lower Egypt in the Naqada IIIC Period. This unification is seemingly depicted on the Narmer Palette, where the king is shown wearing the Red Crown of Lower Egypt in one scene and the White Crown of Upper Egypt in another, thereby showing his rule over the two lands. However, the process of state formation can be traced back to the ranked societies of the Neolithic, beginning in 5300 BCE, when mixed farming first started to be practiced in Egypt, and continued into the consolidated state of the Old Kingdom in 2686 BCE. In the Predynastic Period (5300–3200 BCE), distinct cultural complexes, the Lower Egyptian (Maadi-Buto) and the Upper Egyptian (Badari-Naqada), have been identified, but by the First Dynasty in 3000 BCE, there was a near homogeneous culture, albeit with regional differences.

The point at which Egypt changed from a prestate to a state is usually regarded as being the change from the Protodynastic and Dynasty 0 (Naqada IIIB) to the

Dynastic. However, the theoretical concept of prestate and state is not this simple, and there are many stages in statehood, from the developed chiefdom, through the proto-state and incipient state phases, to the consolidated state. There was not a ranked social development from one stage to the other, but more of an organic process that was not necessarily contemporaneous in all regions of Egypt, that is, patchwork not linear. Therefore, when there were proto-states in the Naqada and Hierakonpolis regions, there may have been developed chiefdoms in the Memphite region and areas of the delta. This is also seen with the Badarian, for while this Neolithic culture was still present in Middle Egypt, the Naqada I stage had already started in places such as Abydos. There was no linear evolutionary trajectory that led to the formation of the first nation-state, but there was a more syncopated phenomenon, characterized by periods of political experimentation and shifting social boundaries with overlapping clusters of development, the location and nature of which ebbed and flowed.

Many early theories pertaining to state formation used the unification of the kingdoms of Upper and Lower Egypt as their stating point and were based on the royal and religious iconography occurring from Naqada II onward and also on later texts. During the 1970s, new approaches developed around the emergence of complex society, putting forward prime movers or monocausal theories, such as warfare, trade imperatives, hydraulic or Oriental despotism, geographic circumscription, agricultural intensification and surplus, and population increase leading to heightened social competition, as causes of state formation. Access to prestige goods not only enhanced the power and prestige of the elite but provided essential raw materials.

Although the majority of research into this period has been conducted in the Nile valley, with its more accessible and better-preserved remains, over the last 25 years, a steady flow of information on Lower Egypt and the surrounding deserts has broken the traditional fascination with Upper Egypt, allowing more inclusive interpretative theories. Excavation has now been conducted at several delta sites covering the period of state formation, such a Kafr Hassan Dawood, Kom el-Khilgan, Minshat Abu Omar, Tell el-Fara'in (Buto), Tell el-Farkha, Tell Ibrahim Awad, and others. These sites have now joined the traditional Upper Egyptian sites of Abydos, Adaïma, el-Amra, Elephantine, Hierakonpolis, Koptos, Naga ed-Dêr, and Naqada. Several sites in the Memphite to Faiyum region also have Naqada III remains, including Abu Ghurab, Abu Roash, Gerza, Helwan, and Tarkhan.

Armed with a fuller set of archaeological data, a new generation of researchers has started to question the text-based image of state formation and tried to give a view based more on archaeological evidence, looking at the role of ideology, local and regional geography and interregional contacts, economic modeling, and social stratification in the rise of social complexity. Most researchers now favor a complex multicausal explanation. State formation is a symbiosis of many factors: (1) a sufficient number of people to form a complex stratified society; (2) controlling a specific territory and having centralization and urbanism; (3) containing a productive system capable of yielding surplus to maintain craft specialists and privileged classes; (4) having an ideology that explained and justified a hierarchical administrative organization and sociopolitical inequality; and (5) the agency of dominant individuals, where their actions and choices determined the way certain polities acted.

The changes from small-scale farmers to marked social hierarchy is different in the Nile valley and delta; it appears that greater social differentiation, as displayed in the mortuary record, began in Upper Egypt. The Predynastic graves of Lower Egypt are characterized by few, if any, grave goods, whereas the contemporaneous graves in Upper Egypt show a temporal trend toward increased amount, quality and variety of grave goods, some of which seem to have been made specifically as funerary offerings. However, up to 15 grave goods have been found in graves at Merimde Beni Salama belonging to this period. The role of Lower Egypt in the process of state formation has been a long-debated question; Wilkinson (1996; 2000) suggests there was "cultural unification" during the Naqada IIC Period (3500 BCE) and "political unification" under the Upper Egyptian Thinite kings during the Naqada IIIC Period (3000 BCE).

The term *cultural unification* refers to the supposed uptake of Naqada culture during the Naqada IIC/D phase by Lower Egyptians and preceded a near homogenous pan-Egyptian culture and ideology (Upper Egyptian) by Naqada IIIA (3200 BCE). This is sometimes referred to as the "Naqada expansion." Both phrases should be abandoned, as they infer a binary opposition between Upper and Lower Egypt and are heavily influenced by the later ideology of kingship, in which the two lands form a core principle of royal action. Moreover, the Lower Egyptians did not take up wholesale the culture of the Upper Egyptians during this period; rather, certain forms of ceramic and stone vessels as well as lithics were introduced into Lower Egypt from Upper, as demonstrated by the admixture of Maadi-Buto and Naqada II forms of pottery at the delta sites of Minshat Abu Omar and Tell el-Fara'in (Buto) from about 3400 BCE. This gradual change in materiality, as shown in settlement sites, argues against large-scale diffusion, whereby people from Upper Egypt migrated to Lower Egypt and displaced the indigenous delta population. More possibly, there was acculturation of individuals or groups as the Lower Egyptian culture came into continuous firsthand contact with those from the Upper Egyptian culture. This contact resulted in changes in both regions and led to the appearance of a syncretic or mixed culture. Over time and due to various processes, this contact culminated in assimilation of southern traits by the north. Moreover, there was no uniformity of culture in either Upper or Lower Egypt. The two regions did show great affinity with each other in Naqada IIIA, but there was not one homogeneous culture throughout.

Regional development seems to have been dependent on access to resources and lines of communication. The heterogeneous environments of the Nile valley, delta, and the surrounding deserts—as well as their various resources, such as water, alluvium, flora, fauna, minerals, and stone—were all contributing factors in the formation of the first nation-state. Environmental change, population pressures, economic developments, competition for resources, and Egypt's position at the juncture of Africa and Asia all helped in the transition from the Neolithic to the early state. In the second half of Naqada II, there seems to have been conflict between communities, coinciding with increased aridity as the various elites attempted to monopolize prestige goods and raw materials. There was also the growth of urban centers as a result of processes of population concentration. Several small polities, including the Upper Egyptian entities of Hierakonpolis (Nekhen), Naqada (Nubt) and Abydos (Thinis), arose during Naqada II, resulting in the two large polities of Hierakonpolis and Abydos being ruled by hereditary chiefs, crystallizing in Naqada IIIA–B (3300 BCE).

The Protodynastic Period (Naqada IIIA–B) saw many of the major developments associated with the process of state formation, such as expansion of power of the hereditary lineages, growth of population, territorial control and expansion, development of royal iconography, and the conspicuous consumption of wealth, often of exotic objects. These rulers were engaged in long-distance exchange networks, which allowed the privileged classes to attain prestige goods from places such as Southwest Asia, Nubia, and farther afield, and they engaged in hosting feasts to forge political alliances. The building of large tombs filled with copious amounts of objects, such as Tomb U-j at Umm el-Qa'ab, dating to Naqada IIIA, is a good example of this conspicuous consumption, although it is not representative of this early period. Other large tombs of Naqada III also existed at Hierakonpolis, Naqada, and other locations. The iconography of this period was focused on religion and power, often showing smiting scenes and control over the forces of chaos. Claims of military superiority are closely tied to and support the special relationship of chieftains with the deities, of whom they were the earthly representatives, each giving legitimacy to the other and thus maintaining authority and the social order. However, there was a change in the items that carried the iconography. The decorated C-ware and D-ware pottery of Naqada I and II disappeared and was replaced by the largely undecorated pottery of Naqada III. Items such as knife handles, palettes, mace-heads, and monumental architecture were the media that now carried the ideology of these rulers.

The rulers of the southern Upper Egyptian polity of Abydos (Thinis) expanded their political control during the period directly preceding Dynasty 1, possibly through warfare or alliances, and this process eventually resulted in their controlling the region from Elephantine to the Nile Delta under the reign of Narmer. The capital of this newly formed nation-state, Memphis, was located where the delta meets the Nile valley, the optimal position for maintaining control over both Upper and Lower Egypt and utilizing their natural and human resources while also cementing control of the flow of goods from the Levant. The location of Memphis was therefore strategic from a specifically political and economic point of view and was regarded as symbolic of the formulation of the Egyptian territory.

However, the burial place of the first kings of Egypt remained at Abydos, where their tombs are located in Cemetery B. The tombs of the kings of the First Dynasty at Umm el-Qa'ab, just slightly to the southeast, grew large and more complex. It was not until the Second Dynasty that the kings started to be buried at Sakkara, away from their ancestral burial ground, finally breaking their kinship ties and allowing them to more effectively rule the state and establish fuller connections between previously unrelated kinship groups.

Geoffrey John Tassie

See also: Abydos; Hierakonpolis; Lower Egypt; Memphis

Further Reading

Hassan, F. A. 1988. "The Predynastic of Egypt." *Journal of World Prehistory* 2, no. 2: 135–185.

Köhler, E. C. 2008. "Interaction between and the Roles of Upper and Lower Egypt in the Formation of the Egyptian State, Another Review." In B. Midant-Reynes and Y. Tristant, eds. *Egypt at Its Origins 2: Proceedings of the International Conference "Origin of the State, Predynastic and Early Dynastic Egypt," Toulouse (France), 5th–8th September 2005.* Orientalia Lovaniensia Analecta 172. Leuven: Peeters, pp. 515–543.

Köhler, E. C. 2010. "Theories of State Formation." In W. Wendrich, ed. *Egyptian Archaeology.* Oxford: Wiley-Blackwell, pp. 36–54.

Midant-Reynes, B. 2000. *The Prehistory of Egypt: From the First Egyptians to the First Pharaohs.* Oxford: Blackwell.

Petrie, W. M. F. 1920. *Prehistoric Egypt.* London: British School of Egyptian Archaeology.

Stevenson, A. 2016. "The Egyptian Predynastic and State Formation." *Journal of Archaeological Research* 24, no. 4: 421–468.

Teeter, Emily, ed. 2011. *Before the Pyramids: The Origins of Egyptian Civilization.* Chicago: Oriental Institute of the University of Chicago.

Wengrow, D. 2006. *The Archaeology of Early Egypt: Social Transformation in North East Africa, 10,000 to 2,650 BC.* Cambridge World Archaeology Series. Cambridge: Cambridge University Press.

Wilkinson, T. A. H. 1996. *State Formation in Egypt: Chronology and Society.* Oxford: BAR.

Sticks and Staves

The stick, or staff, in ancient Egypt was one of many different kinds of insignia used to outwardly show an individual's social and economic status. Kings, gods, and some elite persons used sticks to express and enforce their divine status. Sticks also had a practical function as walking aids, tools for farmers, batons for disciplining by police, and weapons for soldiers. Throughout Egyptian history, there were many different kinds of sticks that were depicted in tomb and temple decoration as well as the physical examples that are found within burials. By studying these, one can gain a deeper understanding into ancient Egyptian culture as expressed in iconography and physical objects.

The most common type of staves were the straight staff and the *medu* staff, both of which appear as early as the Early Dynastic Period (3000–2686 BCE). The high elite most often used these two sticks, although kings are sometimes shown carrying either staff as a badge of status as well. The *was* scepter and *djam* staff are both divine sticks, used primarily by male deities, sometimes by goddesses, and occasionally by divinized kings or elite persons. Both sticks have a mythical creature's head as the pommel of the staff, with a U-shaped fork at the bottom. The *was* scepter is characterized by a straight shaft, while the *djam* scepter's shaft undulates. The four cardinal deities use either stick as they support the heavens, and the *was* scepter is often shown flanking tomb and temple scenes supporting the heavens. Modern scholars consider the *was* and *djam* scepters as two variants of the same object, which explains why they are both used interchangeably.

Some sticks are only used by the king, one example being the *mekes* staff, which has a lotus or lily bud in the middle of the shaft. The king holds this stick in the presence of the gods, and sometimes the king carried this staff when making public appearances, possibly as a way to emphasize his position as mediator between the people and the gods. Additionally, there is the *ames* staff, consisting of a straight body with a flail projecting out of the side at an oblique angle. In the Pyramid Texts of the Old Kingdom (2686–2160 BCE), this stick is associated with Horus and the newly transfigured king. Throughout the Middle (2055–1650 BCE) and New Kingdoms (1550–1069 BCE), the *ames* staff is still part of the royal regalia and has royal connotations. However, during the New Kingdom, select elite persons were able to use the *ames* staff as well, as a transfigured deity in the Book of the Dead or in funerary procession scenes in Theban tombs, where the staff served as a funerary offering.

Other staves include the *abet* staff, a stick with a straight body ending with either a U-shaped or V-shaped projection at the bottom. Minor characters frequently use the *abet* staff in tomb scenes, particularly those that depict agricultural activities. Excavated examples exhibit signs of wear and use, suggesting that this stick served as a walking aid or support in life for the staff owner. Sticks with a curved end are known as the *awet* staff. One type of *awet* staff has a rounded top and is shaped like the modern shepherd's crook; this *awet* staff has association with Osiris, as he is sometimes depicted carrying this staff instead of the *heka* scepter. The other type of *awet* staff has a gradually curved end and is often shown being held by minor figures or by soldiers and the king in military dress, suggesting it served as a weapon rather than a walking aid. The forked staff has a straight body with a forked projection at the top and was used extensively in tomb decoration during the Eighteenth Dynasty. High officials are depicted using this stick as an emblem of status throughout the New Kingdom. However, physical examples of this staff are known from as early as the late Middle Kingdom, and they frequently appear in New Kingdom burials as an offering. The lotiform staff is a stick with a straight body and a pommel shaped like a lotus blossom or lily flower. Goddesses are most often shown carrying this staff, rather than the divine *was* or *djam* scepters. Sometimes, though rare, queens or elite women are shown carrying the lotiform staff as a badge of status.

In the Old Kingdom, sticks appear in burials of both commoners and royalty and were most often placed on the left-hand side of the mummy. The examples of sticks that survive appear to be the daily life objects that were then interred with the deceased for use in the afterlife. Starting in the Middle Kingdom, object friezes decorate the interiors of coffins, depicting religious tools and royal regalia. Included in the friezes are sets of staves, meant to be used by the deceased to travel from this world to the next, to assist with their transformation into a deity, and to help them function effectively in the afterlife. At this time, it was also common to have a set of "ceremonial staves" interred with the deceased, along with weapons such as bows and maces. This set of staves included the *pedj-aha* emblem, which was placed on the right side of the mummy, along with the *was* and *djam* scepters; the *medu*, *abet*, and *awet* "shepherd's crook" staves were all placed together on the left-hand side of the mummy. Sometimes the sticks that were buried with the deceased were broken to ritually "kill" the object so it could not be used against the deceased in the afterlife.

In the New Kingdom, physical staves are still interred with the deceased, some as daily life objects and others as funerary ritual objects. New Kingdom sticks found in burials often have inscriptions along the shaft of the staff and instruct the stick to assist the deceased in the afterlife. In tomb decoration at this time, funerary procession scenes show offering bearers carrying various sticks as offerings, while priests and the "nine companions" of the deceased carry ritual staves for the funerary rites. By the Third Intermediate Period (1069–664 BCE), sticks still functioned as funerary offerings for the deceased, as examples of staff pommels and butt-ends were found within the royal burials at Tanis, along with many examples of forked bronze ends from private burials. During the Ptolemaic-Roman period, sticks still served as religious and social insignia, used by the gods, the king, or the elite to express their social or religious status.

Nicholas R. Brown

See also: Furniture and Woodworking; Royal Regalia; Tomb of Tutankhamun; Weapons and Armor

Further Reading

Dothan, T. 1976. "Bronze Butts from Palestine and Egypt." *Israel Exploration Journal* 26, no. 1: 20–34.

Fischer, H. G. 1978. "Notes on Sticks and Staves." *Metropolitan Museum Journal* 13: 5–32.

Gordon, A. H., and C. W. Schwabe. 1995. "The Egyptian *wAs*-Scepter and Its Modern Analogues: Uses as Symbols of Divine Power or Authority." *Journal of the American Research Center in Egypt* 32: 185–196.

Hassan, A. 1976. *Stöcke und Stäbe im Pharaonischen Ägypten.* Munich: Deutscher Kuntsverlag.

Jéquier, G. 1921. *Les Frises d'Objets des Sarcophages du Moyen-Empire.* Cairo: IFAO.

Mace, A. C., and H. E. Winlock. 1916. *The Tomb of Senebtisi at Lisht.* New York: Metropolitan Museum of Art Press.

T

Tanis

The ancient Egyptian name for Tanis, in the northeast delta, was *Djanet*. It was the site of an important temple for the god Amun, meant to be the equivalent of Karnak Temple in Thebes. It was built, beginning in the Third Intermediate Period, by Psusennes I, the first king of the Twenty-First Dynasty (1039–991 BCE). During the Third Intermediate Period, rule over Egypt was divided between the kings in the north and the High Priests of Amun in the south. The kings ruled the delta from Memphis, and the important religious site, and site of the royal burials, was Tanis.

For the most part, Tanis was built with reused blocks from the Ramesside (1295–1069 BCE) royal city of Per-Ramses to the southwest. Per-Ramses (modern Tell el-Daba) had been built on the Pelusiac branch of the Nile, which had silted up and been abandoned by the end of the New Kingdom (1069 BCE). Avaris, the old capital of the Hyksos (1650–1550 BCE) in the Second Intermediate Period, is right next to Per-Ramses. The Hyksos had taken a large number of Middle Kingdom (2055–1985 BCE) statues to Avaris, and these, along with statues Ramses II (1279–1213 BCE) moved from Heliopolis to Per-Ramses, were taken to Tanis as well. The blocks were taken to Tanis, for the most part by Psusennes I, who constructed a large enclosure wall and temple of Amun. There were five pairs of obelisks, all belonging to Ramses II, that were brought to Tanis and have been found there. Inside the southeast corner of the enclosure, there were also seven tomb structures for the kings of the Twenty-First and Twenty-Second Dynasties.

Tomb 3, the tomb of Psusennes I, was found intact by Pierre Montet in 1939. Although organic materials had been destroyed by groundwater, many objects of gold and silver were found. King Psusennes I had a gold mask and was placed into an anthropoid coffin of silver. This was then put into a large anthropoid coffin of black granite, which was then placed into a much larger outer rectangular-shaped coffin of pink granite. The lid of this coffin still carried the name of King Merneptah (1213–1203 BCE) of the Nineteenth Dynasty. There was nothing left on the surface to indicate what kind of superstructure was over these tombs, but the underground, chambers built of limestone and granite had the walls decorated with texts from the Book of the Dead and the Book of Night.

Little is known about Tanis after the Twenty-Second Dynasty (945–715 BCE), although in the Late Period (664–332 BCE), the temple enclosure was enlarged and a small temple of Horus was added to the southeast end of the enclosure; it was completed in Ptolemaic times. So far, no settlement site or royal residence has been found at Tanis, but large areas of the site have yet to be excavated.

Lisa K. Sabbahy

See also: Mummies, Royal; Tell el-Dab'a; Valley of the Kings

Further Reading

Coutts, Herbert, ed. 1988. *Gold of the Pharaohs: Catalogue of the Exhibition of Treasures from Tanis*. Edinburgh: City of Edinburgh Museums and Art Galleries.

Hill, Marsha. 2015. "Later Life of Middle Kingdom Monuments: Interrogating Tanis." In A. Oppenheim, D. Arnold, D. Arnold, and K. Yamamoto, eds. *Ancient Egypt Transformed: The Middle Kingdom*. New York: Metropolitan Museum of Art, pp. 294–299.

Verner, Miroslav. 2013. *Temple of the World: Sanctuaries, Cults and Mysteries of Ancient Egypt*. Cairo: American University in Cairo Press.

Tattoos

In traditional societies, permanent body decoration has a psychological or practical purpose, or sometimes both. Sending out a range of social signals, body decoration plays an important role in expressing and reinforcing social relationships, values, and society itself, but they may also have medical and protective properties. Unlike temporary body modifications, such as makeup or hairstyles, the permanence of tattoos (and scarification) demonstrate permanent social relationships between an individual and society. Permanent body decoration is often applied when an individual goes through a rite of passage and attains a new social status, such as adulthood or motherhood. There are several lines of evidence that can be used, such iconographic depictions of tattooed people, tattooing needles, and, most importantly, tattooed mummies.

Some Predynastic (5300–3000 BCE) figurines have geometric and zoomorphic designs painted on them, similar to designs on contemporary pottery. However, this in itself is not conclusive evidence of extensive tattooing. The recent findings of a tattoo of an ovicaprine and below it one of a bovine on the upper arm of a mummified man and others on a woman, four S-like signs on her shoulder and another throw-stick-like design on her upper arm, provide the earliest physical evidence for tattooing in the Nile valley, if not the world. The tattoos on these Naqada IID/IIIA Period, about 3325 BCE, mummies from Gebelein were identified using infrared photography.

The earliest evidence for the practice of tattooing in pharaonic Egypt are three Eleventh Dynasty (2125–2055 BCE) female mummies found at Deir el-Bahari, if the women are accepted as being culturally Egyptian rather than Nubian. The tattoos mainly consist of dots and dashes, probably made with an uneven number of needles dipped in soot. These dots were often grouped into geometrical patterns, such as lozenges, consisting of 16 dots and were usually placed on the chest, the abdomen, the arms, or the legs. These women were Hathoric dancers, the most famous being Amunet, a priestess of Hathor. The tattoos on the human remains resemble the patterns found on figurines from contemporary domestic and funerary contexts, such as footless faience figurines, which usually depict a nude woman wearing just a cowrie shell girdle and bead necklace (Musée du Louvre, E10942). Paddle doll figurines also sometimes had lozenge shapes painted on

Faience female figurine found at the site of Lisht, from the Middle Kingdom. This figurine might represent a woman who was a dancer in the cult of the goddess Hathor, and serve as a symbol of fertility. (Rogers Fund, 1908/The Metropolitan Museum of Art)

them consisting of 16 dots or an image of Taweret placed by the genitals (Egyptian Museum Cairo JE 43088b).

Based on current evidence, it appears that only women were tattooed in pharaonic Egypt. A similar practice was also observed in Nubia, as originally only C-Group women were tattooed, but by the Meroitic Period, both men and women were tattooed and scarified. Many tattooed bodies were found in various Nubian cemeteries during the archaeological rescue surveys. These mummies, belonging primarily to the C-Group, contemporary with the Middle Kingdom (2055–1650 BCE), had dotted and lozenge-shaped tattoos on their abdomens, chests, arms, and legs. Some tattooed mummies even had tattooed figurines placed in the grave with them, suggesting that patterns on figurines are representations of tattoos. C-Group mummies have also been found at Hierakonpolis, found in Tombs 9 and 10. The tattoos on the woman in Tomb 9 included a diamond of short dashed lines on her left hand and a pattern of dots and dashes running down the back of her left arm. On her torso was a dotted zigzag with a more elaborate lattice pattern of dotted squares running across the abdomen, up and over the hip, and onto her back.

Four tattooed mummies have been found in a New Kingdom tomb (1550–1069 BCE) at Deir el-Medina. The first of these mummies to be examined using infrared photography revealed that she had 30 tattoos running across her hips, arms, back, and neck. Unlike the previous Middle Kingdom examples, these tattoos were figurative, many being sacred symbols. A group of symbols consisting of two baboons flanking a wadjet, surmounting a pair of sacred eyes separated by a *nefer* sign, were tattooed on the woman's neck. Other symbols so far identified include lotus blossoms on the mummy's hips, cows on her forearms, and snakes on her upper arms. Additional images of wadjet eyes were placed on her back and shoulders. The cows were symbolic of the goddess Hathor, and the placing of the wadjet and *nefer* symbols on her neck may have been protective, so that she was good of voice, possibly invoking ritual power. Like the previous Eleventh Dynasty mummies, this woman may have been in the service of the priesthood of Hathor and was probably a singer.

Scenes on certain objects from the New Kingdom, such as a faience bowl (National Museum of Antiquities, Leiden AD 14), show as a female musician with a tattoo of the god Bes tattooed on her thigh. Tattoos of Bes were also found on the thighs of two wooden statues of naked women (Philadelphia Museum of Art, cat. no. 10349), originally found in a tomb in the Egyptian town of Buhen, Nubia.

Tattooing continued in both Nubia and Egypt in the first millennium BCE, although the Ptolemaic (332–30 BCE) tattoos were usually dotted patterns on the face and hands, sometimes on wrists and arms. The Meroitic female mummies show tattoos of a similar type and in analogous positions to those of the C-Group mummies, but also with facial and hand tattoos. A few male mummies also have dotted facial and hand tattoos. Tattooing continued into the Coptic era, with religious symbols being tattooed on wrists and hands. One mummy in the British Museum, who died 1,300 years ago, has the symbol of the Archangel Michael tattooed on her inner thigh.

These tattoos all had a polyvalent symbolism, and many had phylactic properties. It seems that the tattooing of women in Middle Kingdom Egypt and in the C-Group and Meroitic periods in Nubia may have indicated physiological changes, reproductive capacity, and sexuality. However, the figurative tattoos of the New Kingdom had magico-religious significance, possibly displaying their piety, and some, such as the Bes tattoos, offering protection during childbirth.

Geoffrey John Tassie

See also: Childbirth; Deir el-Medina; Female Figurines; Hathor; Nubia

Further Reading

Austin, A., and C. Gobeil. 2016. "Embodying the Divine: A Tattooed Female Mummy from Deir el-Medina." *Bulletin de L'Institut Français d'Archéologie Orientale* 116: 23–46.

Bianchi, R. S. 1988. "Tattoo in Ancient Egypt." In A. Rubin, ed. *Marks of Civilization: Artistic Transformation of the Human Body*. Los Angeles: Museum of Cultural History, University of California, pp. 21–28.

Bianchi, R. S. 1996. "Tattooing and Skin Painting in the Ancient Nile Valley." In T. Celenko, ed. *Egypt in Africa*. Indianapolis: Indianapolis University Press, pp. 81–83.

Friedman, R. 2004. "Seeking the C-Group: Excavations in the Nubian Cemetery, 2003." *Nekhen News* 16: 24–26.

Friedman, R. 2017. "New Tattoos from Ancient Egypt: Defining Marks of Culture." In L. Krutak and A. Deter-Wolf, eds. *Ancient Ink: The Archaeology of Tattooing*. Seattle: University of Washington Press, pp. 11–36.

Tassie, G. J. 2003. "Identifying the Practice of Tattooing in Ancient Egypt and Nubia." *Papers from the Institute of Archaeology* 14: 85–101.

Watson, T. 2016. "Sacred Tattoos Found on Egyptian Mummy." *Nature* 533: 155.

Winlock, H. E. 1942. *Excavations at Deir el-Bahri, 1911–1931*. New York: Macmillan.

Taxation

The land of Egypt belonged to the king, which was made clear in the Sed festival, which was celebrated after 30 years of reign to renew the king's rule. The king held on to a small object, a papyrus document proclaiming his inheritance of the country, granted him by the gods, while running around curved stones representing the boundaries of Egypt. While land was granted to and owned by private individuals and institutions, like temples and funerary cults, it technically all belonged to the crown, and taxes were collected to support the running of the state, building projects, military needs, the royal palace, and so forth.

It is not absolutely clear at the beginning of pharaonic history how taxes were assessed and collected. In the Early Dynastic Period (3000–2686 BCE), the king and his retinue made a tour through the country, known as the "Following of Horus," which was done on an annual basis. This has been interpreted as a trip for the king to examine his kingdom and collect taxes, but there really is no proof of taxes being part of this. By the Second Dynasty, a biannual "count" or "census" started, which is sometimes mentioned in connection to gold or to cattle, but, again, there is no evidence of a collection or that it was for the king. What there is evidence of, however, are royal decrees that land, produce, and people the king has set aside for a cult, either temple or funerary, cannot be touched, and this is interpreted as an exemption from any and all taxation. For example, King Pepy I of the Sixth Dynasty set up a stela with a decree for the chapel of his mother, stating that he has commanded an exemption, and no official, not even belonging to the royal retinue, can take anything belonging to this chapel, including "serfs and

Scene from the Sixth Dynasty tomb of Mereruka, who was vizier to King Teti and married to one of his daughters. It shows farm managers being brought in to give an accounting of their harvest to the vizier's scribes. (DeAgostini/Getty Images)

large and small cattle" (Lichtheim 1973, 28). Warden has suggested that these decrees "detail a murky, un-systematized collection of labor, for the most part, -not goods-, which appears to have been sporadic, and collection authorities which were varied and haphazard" (Warden 2015, 489). In the Sixth Dynasty, administrative changes did take place, with the assignment of a vizier to Abydos in Upper Egypt, and one of his responsibilities was tax collection (Kanawati 1980, 128–129). There are a number of scenes in Sixth Dynasty mastabas, for example, that of Mereruka, the vizier of King Teti I, showing the "overseers of the estates" being brought in by force and some of them being beaten because the taxes have not been paid (Sakkara Expedition 1938, pls. 37–38).

With the Middle Kingdom, there is clearly more organization to tax collecting. Amenemhat, the nomarch of Beni Hasan, states in the autobiographical text in his tomb that he spent 16 years ruling his nome "with all the dues for the king's house being in my charge. . . . I was praised for it in the king's house in every year of the cattle tax. I delivered all their dues to the king's house, and there was no shortage against me in any bureau of his" (Lichtheim 1988, 138–139). From the late Middle Kingdom is a very broken but interesting papyrus document. The scribe who wrote it made a list of specific dates, along with a list of officials and helpers, "the clerk of the land," "the holder of the cord," and "the stretcher of the cord," who went out to measure fields for determining the rate of tax that would be taken from the crop (Smither 1941).

The Wilbour Papyrus, dating to regnal year four of Ramses V, is undoubtedly the most important tax document preserved from ancient Egypt. It lists 2,800 plots of land, spread over a distance of 87 miles in Middle Egypt, from the Fayum down to the modern city of Minya. It lists the owner, the size of the plot, and the percentage of the crop that would be paid in taxes, if taxes are to be paid. Many temples, from all over Egypt, are listed among the landholders. Small plots of three to five arouras (an aroura being 0.66 of an acre) were expected to pay one and a half sacks of the harvest per aroura, whereas larger portions of land were taxed at 30 percent of their harvest (Katary 2007, 194).

There is a genre of Late Egyptian writing that includes descriptions of various professions, all of which are made to sound terrible, except for the profession of scribe. Young scribes would practice writing these and, at the same time, be convinced they wanted to be professional scribes. The text about the farmer starts out, "Have you not recalled the condition of the cultivator faced with the registration of the harvest-tax after the snake has carried off one half and the hippopotamus has eaten up the rest? The mice abound in the field, the locust descends, the cattle devour." It goes on to describe the farmer being beaten and tied up and thrown into his well because he could not pay. It ends with, "He who works in writing is not taxed, he has no dues to pay. Take note of this" (Caminos 1954, 247).

Lisa K. Sabbahy

See also: Agriculture; Labor; Law; Nile River

Further Reading

Caminos, Ricardo. 1954. *Late Egyptian Miscellanies*. London: Oxford University Press.

Kanawati, N. 1980. *Governmental Reforms in Old Kingdom Egypt*. Warminster, UK: Aris and Phillips.

Katary, Sally. 1989. *Land Tenure in the Ramesside Period.* London and New York: Kegan Paul International.

Katary, Sally. 2007. "Land Tenure and Taxation." In T. Wilkinson, ed. *The Egyptian World.* London and New York: Routledge, pp. 185–204.

Lichtheim, Miriam. 1988. *Ancient Egyptian Autobiographies Chiefly of the Middle Kingdom.* Freiburg: Universitätsverlag.

Sakkara Expedition. 1938. *The Mastaba of Mereruka.* Part I. Chicago: University of Chicago Press.

Smither, Paul. 1941. "A Tax-Assessor's Journal of the Middle Kingdom." *Journal of Egyptian Archaeology* 27: 74–76.

Tell el-Amarna

Tell el-Amarna, known during the New Kingdom as Akhet-Aten, or "Horizon of the Aten," was an urban center established by the pharaoh Akhenaten (1352–1336 BCE) as a capital city and cult center of the god Aten during the Eighteenth Dynasty. The contemporary name, Tell el-Amarna, is often shortened to just "Amarna" and is also used to denote the time period during and immediately after the reign of Akhenaten, the Amarna Period. The site is located in the present-day Minya governorate in Middle Egypt and was part of the ancient 15th Upper Egyptian nome, or administrative district, approximately 300 kilometers south of Cairo. There was no substantial activity or occupation at the site prior to the Amarna Period, and it was abandoned after the end of Akhenaten's reign, approximately 12 years after it was first occupied. Archaeological evidence suggests a substantially smaller reoccupation occurred during the Late Period (664–332 BCE) and then again in the Roman Period (30 BCE–395 CE).

Amarna is one of the most extensively excavated sites in Egypt. The first recorded European visitor to the site was Father Claude Sicard in 1714, who published a drawing of one of the Boundary Stelae found at Tuna el-Gebel. It was visited and recorded by the Napoleonic scientific expedition in 1799, and their publication of the adjacent modern village of el-Till in the *Description de l'Égypte* in 1817 heralded the beginnings of interest in the site. During the 1820s to 1840s, travelers such as John Gardiner Wilkinson and Richard Lepsius's Royal Prussian Expedition visited Amarna to plan, draw, and make copies of the monuments, art, and texts found there.

The first modern excavations of the site were carried out by William Matthew Flinders Petrie from 1891 to 1892. A German team led by Ludwig Borchardt worked at the site in the early 1900s and is credited with the discovery of the now famous painted bust of the queen Nefertiti. The Egypt Exploration Society carried out work at the site from 1901 to 1907 and 1921 to 1936. Contemporary work on the site has been carried out for the past 40 years by the Amarna Project, which was originally affiliated with the Egypt Exploration Society and is now with the McDonald Institute for Archaeological Research.

The layout, major structures, and founding ideology of the city are explained on the inscriptions found on the rock-cut Boundary Stelae that line the cliffs on the east and west banks of the settlement. There are 16 positively identified stelae,

13 on the east and 3 on the west. The stelae were given letter designations by Petrie during his excavations, although he left gaps in the order in anticipation of new discoveries. The purpose of these monumental inscriptions was partly to delineate the limits of the new city, although construction extended beyond their perimeter into the Eastern Desert plain. The stelae also provided a medium for Akhenaten to describe his vision for the city. He claimed the previously unoccupied land for the sole worship of the Aten, and he listed a series of monuments, temples, and estates that he would build for the god. Several of these structures have been located in the archaeological record, while others are known from administrative documents and depictions in the elite rock-cut tombs at the city.

There are two variations of the proclamation text on the stelae; the first, which dates to year five of Akhenaten's reign, can be found on three of the stelae, while the remaining stelae were inscribed with a later text dating to year six. Several of the stelae are topped with lunettes featuring images of Akhenaten, Nefertiti, and their daughters worshipping the Aten before an offering table. Statues of the royal family carved into the living rock are present at the base of some of these stelae. It is possible that these monuments were intended to be visited, as remains of access paths have been found.

The archaeological remains of the city lie on the east bank of the Nile and are generally divided into areas of occupation with modern designations. There were several roadways across the city that ran north to south, the most prominent one being the "Royal Road," which linked the North City palaces to the administrative buildings in the Central City and the Main City. The desert to the east of the city also shows evidence of a network of ancient roads.

There are several different mudbrick structures that have been identified as either royal residences or administrative buildings. The North Palace and North Riverside Palace are conventionally believed to have been the actual residences of most of the royal family, while the Great Palace in the Central City and the "King's House" served a more formal function for the court. One building in the Central City has been identified as "the Bureau of Correspondence of Pharaoh" and was the location of the discovery of the collection of clay cuneiform tablets now known as the "Amarna Letters." These documents contained detailed diplomatic correspondence from the late Eighteenth Dynasty. The "House of Life," a scholarly archive, also appears to have been located as part of the same complex. A series of planned, standardized houses were also excavated near these administrative buildings and likely served as residences for the governmental employees.

Aside from the governmental buildings required for a functioning capital city, Amarna also contains the remains of several major religious structures. The known temples at Amarna do not follow the conventional layout of New Kingdom cult buildings. Open-air courtyards were often a feature of major temple complexes, but the traditional design of New Kingdom sanctuaries favored enclosed, dark spaces using large blocks of stone. The temples at Amarna appear to have been primarily open-air structures that were built using the smaller stone *talatat* blocks, which were the ubiquitous building material of the Amarna Period. This would have allowed for direct access to the Aten, manifested in the physical sun

Talatat

A talatat is a somewhat small, low, and long block of sandstone that was used for building during the reign of Amenhotep IV (Akhenaten). It is thought that they were cut in this size so that workmen were able to carry these blocks on their own, making the building faster. During the first five years of his reign, Amenhotep IV built eight structures at Karnak, four of them temples. They were destroyed by Horemheb, who took the talatat and used them to build the foundations of the Second and Ninth Pylons at Karnak. Archaeological work at these two pylons and in the floor of the hypostyle hall discovered 45,000 decorated or inscribed talatat blocks (Redford 1984, 67–68). Talatat blocks were also used to build at Tell el-Amarna, and Ramses II had large numbers of talatat blocks removed from there and reused in buildings at Hermopolis.

Lisa K. Sabbahy

Reference

Redford, Donald. 1984. *Akhenaten: The Heretic King*. Princeton, NJ: Princeton University Press.

disk, during religious rituals as well as for much more rapid construction than that of traditional temples.

Two sites in the Central City have been identified as cult temples dedicated to the Aten. These have been designated as the Great Aten Temple and the Small Aten Temple by archaeologists. The Great Aten Temple enclosure includes two distinct buildings, designated as the Long Temple and the Sanctuary, within a larger expanse of land. This whole complex has been tentatively identified as the "House of the Aten" mentioned in the list of buildings planned by Akhenaten in the Boundary Stele inscriptions, although inscriptions found at the site have not confirmed this. Two gateway pylons accessed the enclosure, with an ascending ramp constructed of mixed sand and plaster. The Long Temple, the structure closest to the pylons, consisted of a series of open-air courtyards, divided into six sections either by pylons or by a series of columns. Temple ritual activity appears to have been focused in the sixth courtyard, which features the remains of a large offering table, although rows of smaller offering tables filled the preceding courtyards. The Sanctuary was located to the east of the Long Temple and was surrounded by a low perimeter wall. It has a layout that appears to have been a compressed version of the Long Temple. These structures have been partially lost due to the encroachment of the modern cemetery adjacent to the village of el-Till.

The Small Aten Temple has been identified as the "Mansion of the Aten" temple from the Boundary Stelae inscriptions. Similar to the Sanctuary, it was an enclosure that consisted of three open-air courtyards containing rows of offering tables as well as a central dais in the second court that may have supported a central altar.

Two smaller buildings have been identified as "sunshade" temples, associated with women from the royal family. The first building, now known as Kom El Nana, was located southeast of the Main City. Inscriptional evidence reconstructed from the site identifies it as the "Sunshade of Ra of the Great Royal Wife" mentioned in the Boundary Stelae, and iconographic evidence shows an emphasis on images of Queen Nefertiti. Similarly, the Maru Aten was identified as a "Sunshade of Ra" dedicated to the princess Meritaten. This enclosure appears to have contained two structures consisting of gardens and pools, with an artificial island containing an open-air shrine and offering table. This particular temple was not mentioned in the Boundary Stelae inscriptions.

A complex known as the Desert Altars is located near the North Tombs, although it is built on the desert floor rather than cut into the limestone cliffs. It consists of three foundations oriented north to south. The northernmost structure appears to have been a mudbrick altar, which was accessed via four ramps. The central structure had three altars, a large central construction flanked by two smaller ones. A building with a colonnade appears to have stood on the southernmost foundation. The specific purpose of these structures remains unclear, although their proximity to the cemeteries suggests they may have played a role in private funerary religion.

While some residential areas of the city appear to have been organized methodically, many of the larger residential zones do not show evidence of strict urban planning. Archaeologists have identified three central residential zones. The northernmost, called the North Suburb, extended northward from the Central City. There is evidence of reoccupation at this site during the Roman Period, although part of the site has been lost under cultivation and the modern village of el-Till. The Main City and South Suburb contained dense residential areas south of the Central City, which appear to have been oriented around three roads that ran north-south. This area also housed a series of sculptor's workshops, including the workshop of Thutmose, where the painted limestone bust of Nefertiti was discovered in 1912.

Two additional settlements were located on the eastern desert plain and appear to have been formally planned housing areas. The larger of the two has been identified as a workmen's village and was likely a counterpart to the Theban village of Deir el-Medina. This settlement is believed to have housed the craftsmen who excavated and decorated the royal and elite rock-cut tombs at Amarna. The second settlement, designated as the "Stone Village" by archaeologists, may have served as temporary housing for workers from the main workmen's village or for individuals of a less prestigious social group.

The Royal Tomb was located in the bedrock of the limestone cliffs in what has been designated as the Royal Wadi and follows the design and layout of royal tombs found in the Valley of the Kings. This tomb was unfinished, although it likely contained the burials of Akhenaten, Tiye, and princess Meketaten. The traditional royal funerary texts and imagery are absent; instead, the decoration features scenes of the royal family worshipping the Aten as well as an unusual scene depicting the death of Meketaten.

The nonroyal tombs are traditionally divided into two major groups, the North Tombs and South Tombs, located in the limestone cliffs on the northern and southern ends of the settlement, respectively. These elite tombs are notable for containing iconography depicting monuments at the city of Amarna and depictions of the royal family as well as variations of the "Hymn to the Aten," rather than the traditional funerary scenes and texts commonly found in New Kingdom elite tombs. The North Tombs are a collection of six principal tombs, although none of these were finished prior to the abandonment of the site. Three extensive nonelite cemeteries have been identified on the desert plain adjacent to the North Tombs. The South Tombs consist of 19 numbered tombs. The *wadi* between Tombs 24 and 25 is the site of another nonelite cemetery, designated by excavators as the South Tombs Cemetery. There is evidence that the South Tombs were reoccupied in the Late Period and the North Tombs during the Coptic period, with the tomb of Panehsy being used as a Coptic church.

Megan Paqua

See also: Aten; Cities and Villages; Temples, State; Tombs, Private

Further Reading

Amarna Project. www.amarnaproject.com.

Kemp, Barry. 2014. *The City of Akhenaten and Nefertiti: Amarna and Its People*. London: Thames & Hudson.

Murnane, William, and Charles Van Siclen. 1993. *The Boundary Stelae of Akhenaten*. Abingdon-on-Thames, UK: Routledge.

Seyfried, Friedericke. 2013. *In the Light of Amarna: 100 Years of the Nefertiti Discovery*. Petersburg: Michael Imhof Verlag.

Stevens, Anna. 2015. *The Archaeology of Amarna*. Oxford Handbooks Online. doi:10.1093/oxfordhb/9780199935413.013.31.

Primary Document—Akhenaten's Oath from the Boundary Stelae at Tell el-Amarna

King Akhenaten (1352–1336 BCE) moved to a new city he had built at Tell el-Amarna in year five of his reign. He set up at least 14 boundary stelae on both sides of the Nile, the majority being placed on the east side around his city. He repeats an oath in each direction that he will never pass the boundary stelae. Some scholars accept that he is actually saying he will never leave his city.

> My oath, truly which is my wish to say, which I will not say falsely, forever and ever. As for the southern stela (which is upon) the eastern mountain of the horizon of the disk, it is the stela of the horizon of the disk, the one which I made to stand in its position. I will not pass it to the south forever and ever.

Source: This text is from stela U; translated by Lisa K. Sabbahy from Sandman, Maj. 1938. *Texts from the Time of Akhenaten*. Bibliotheca Aegyptiaca VIII. Bruxelles: Fondation Égyptologique Reine Élisabeth, 126, line 11–127, line 3.

Tell el-Dab'a

Tell el-Dab'a, also known as Avaris and *Hut-waret* in ancient Egyptian, is located in the northeastern delta along the Pelusiac branch of the Nile. It is best known for serving as the capital of the Hyksos kings during the Second Intermediate Period (1650–1550 BCE). Its location made Tell el-Dab'a an important point for trade and cultural contact with the Near East and Aegean. The site includes settlement and cemetery remains, all of which have provided important information about Egyptian history and chronology, trade and foreign contact, acculturation, urbanism, and warfare. Different areas of the site have been identified with more precise names derived from nearby modern settlements or with alphabetic designations for archaeological area and strata (e.g., Area H, the palatial district, also called Ezbet Helmi).

Although it was an important center and the capital of the Hyksos state, only a limited amount of textual material has been found, for the most part monumental fragments and seal impressions. Excavations at the site have focused on its stratigraphy and material culture, especially pottery sequences. The archaeological evidence from Tell el-Dab'a serves as a balance to the Upper Egyptian monumental inscriptions describing the Theban-Hyksos conflict, providing on-the-ground evidence substantiating some elements of the textual record.

Work at Tell el-Dab'a is ongoing and continues to provide information that updates our understanding of the site and Egyptian history during the Late Middle Kingdom and Second Intermediate Period. As such, the dating and identification of different areas has changed over the years. It is a site that exemplifies the dynamic nature of Egyptian archaeology and the necessity of engaging with current scholarship.

FOUNDATION AND MIDDLE KINGDOM OCCUPATION

The earliest occupational evidence is of planned, orthogonal, Twelfth Dynasty (1985–1773 BCE) settlements. A reference to an estate of Khety suggests the presence of an earlier First Intermediate Period foundation in the area; however, no archaeological remains have been found. In Ezbet Rushdi, excavators found portions of a mortuary temple for Amenemhat I dating to the reign of Senusret III (1870–1831 BCE). All indications are that these were purely Egyptian foundations.

The nature of the settlement changed in the later Twelfth Dynasty (1985–1773 BCE), when non-Egyptian traits emerge in the architectural and burial records, indicating a mixed Egyptian and non-Egyptian immigrant population. A residence of the Syro-Palestinian middle-room type first dates to this time, but middle- and broad-room style houses do not become common until later. Burials included both Egyptian and non-Egyptian elements. Distinctly foreign aspects include burial location and orientation as well as funerary goods, particularly weapons and pottery. Three fragments of a large statue found in the cemetery exemplify the blending of Egyptian and non-Egyptian traditions. The statue shows a seated man in a traditionally Egyptian pose. His garb and hair, however, are in traditionally Asiatic, that is Syro-Palestinian, fashion.

Temples exhibit Egyptian and non-Egyptian architecture and characteristics. Both Egyptian and non-Egyptian cults were celebrated locally. The chief local god, Seth, was syncretized with the Canaanite god Ba'al. Tripartite Egyptian chapels were found, but the largest construction, a broad-room temple, has direct parallels in the ancient Near East. Tree pits in front of one of the temples contained oak trees, sacred to the Near Eastern goddess Asherah. A house used for funerary meals and pits for the burial of meal remains were also excavated, demonstrating the active practice of non-Egyptian religious activities. Burials contained mixed-culture goods surrounded the temples.

The site continued to expand in the Thirteenth Dynasty (1773–1650 BCE), when more foreign characteristics emerged. Egyptian-style houses continued to be predominant, but Syro-Palestinian forms become more common. Significant portions of the pottery corpus are non-Egyptian, including local imitations of foreign pottery forms, resulting in a mixed material culture. Funerary traditions continue to exhibit foreign practices and goods, including donkey burials. An abundance of what appear to be emergency mass and pit burials during this period may suggest that an epidemic took place at this time.

THE SECOND INTERMEDIATE PERIOD

The site is best known for serving as the political base for the Hyksos. Tell el-Dab'a continued to expand during this time, with its architecture and material culture becoming increasingly non-Egyptian, although Egyptian elements are still present. Notably, the material culture remains mirror the political events of the Second Intermediate Period (1650–1550 BCE); Upper Egyptian pottery is relatively rare, and foreign pottery is abundant.

Two palaces dating to this period have been excavated. The first can be dated by seal impressions to the reign of Khayan, around 1600 BCE. Small fragments of an Old Babylonian cuneiform tablet were found in the palace, evidencing the extent of the Hyksos' international contact. Architecturally, this palace is non-Egyptian, finding parallels at Ebla in northwest Syria. Monumental blocks associated with the second, larger palace, often called "the citadel," name the Hyksos kings SekerHer, Khayan, and Apepi.

Evidence from the site speaks to the conflict of the Second Intermediate Period. Pits in the Khayan palace included the skeletal remains of severed right hands in what appears to have been the throne room. Additional pits were found elsewhere in and around the palace complex. These remains echo the Egyptian practice of "taking hands" to document achievements in battle. In his autobiography, the naval commander Ahmose son of Ibana of el-Kab boasts of taking hands while campaigning with King Ahmose, around 1550 BCE, against the Hyksos. Weapons in burials include a form of non-Egyptian Middle Bronze Age axe, which appears to match the wounds on the mummy of the Theban king Seqenenra Taa. Ahmose son of Ibana's inscription, as well as royal inscriptions of kings Kamose and Ahmose, describe the conquest and plunder of Tell el-Dab'a, including descriptions of architectural elements attested archaeologically at the site.

THE NEW KINGDOM AND LATER

Tell el-Dab'a was not completely razed and abandoned after the Theban conquest. The population decreased in the early Eighteenth Dynasty, beginning in 1550 BCE, but it continued to be occupied due to its strategic position. Pottery and burials suggest the presence of Nubian soldiers, demonstrating its continued use as a military base. A new citadel and palace, with architectural parallels at Deir el-Ballas, was constructed in the same area as the late Hyksos palace by Thutmose III/Hatshepsut (1479–1458 BCE). The facility, perhaps to be identified as the naval base *Peru-nefer*, was used as a trade and campaign base. The palace was abandoned during the reign of Amenhotep II (1427–1400 BCE), but the site was reoccupied under Amenhotep III (1390–1352 BCE) and continued to function through the New Kingdom.

Foreign contact and interaction at this time is further evidenced through the presence of Minoan-styled wall frescoes in the Eighteenth Dynasty palaces (Palaces F and G). Many of the fresco remains were found in rubbish dumps, but small sections were in situ. These frescoes include scenes of a bull leaping and labyrinth motifs similar to those found at the palaces of Knossos, Crete. The technique of the frescoes, along with locally produced Minoan-style pottery, are indicative of Minoans being present at Tell el-Dab'a.

During the Ramesside Period (1295–1069 BCE), Tell el-Dab'a was absorbed into the southern part of Per-Ramses. Many Ramesside period burials were excavated in Ezbet Helmy. Later remains are largely denuded from the site; however, recent excavations have found casemate foundations for tower-houses and objects dating to the Twenty-Sixth (664–525 BCE) and Twenty-Seventh (525–405 BCE) Dynasties.

Kathryn E. Bandy

See also: Ethnicity; Foreigners; Palaces; Seth

Further Reading

Bader, Bettina. 2013. "Cultural Mixing in Egyptian Archaeology: The 'Hyksos' as a Case Study." *Archaeological Review from Cambridge* 28, no. 1: 257–286.

Bietak, Manfred. 1996. *Avaris: The Capital of the Hyksos. Recent Excavations at Tell El-Dab'a*. London: British Museum.

Bietak, Manfred. 2012–2013. "Report on the Excavations of a Hyksos Palace at Tell El-Dab'a/Avaris." *Ägypten und Levante* 22/23: 17–53.

Bietak, Manfred. 2016. "The Egyptian Community at Avaris during the Hyksos Period." *Ägypten und Levante* 26: 263–274.

Bietak, Manfred. 2017. "A Thutmosid Palace Precinct at Peru-Nefer/Tell El-Dab'a." In Manfred Bietak and Silvia Prell, eds. *Palaces in Ancient Egypt and the Ancient Near East*. Vol. 1, *Egypt*. Vienna: Verlag der Österreichische Akademie der Wissenschaften, pp. 231–257.

Bietak, Manfred, and Irene Forstner-Müller. 2011. "The Topography of New Kingdom Avaris and Per-Ramesses." In Mark Collier and Steven Snape, eds. *Ramesside Studies in Honour of K. A. Kitchen*. Bolton: Rutherford Press, pp. 23–50.

Bietak, Manfred, Marinatos Nanno, and Palivou Clairy. 2007. *Taureador Scenes in Tell El-Dab'a (Avaris) and Knossos*. Vienna: Österreichischee Akademie der Wissenschaften.

Lehmann, Manuela. 2012. "The City of Avaris after the New Kingdom." *Egyptian Archaeology* 40: 29–31.

Schiestl, Robert. 2006. "The Statue of an Asiatic Man from Tell El-Dab'a, Egypt." *Ägypten und Levante* 16: 173–185.

Temples, Mortuary

Mortuary temples, sometimes referred to as memorial temples or funerary temples, were a standard part of the royal funerary complex from the beginning of Egyptian history, although their form changed significantly as concepts of kingship developed. The mortuary temple served a vital function for the royal cult and played an important role in the king's deification after his death. This transformation was achieved through cyclical rituals that occurred at the temple. Development of this monument type occurred over a long span of time, changing significantly in size and plan. These temples were not used for funerary rites but instead for divine cult and royal rejuvenation, providing a framework for performing rituals that changed the human king into an immortal god.

The earliest such structures appear at the dawn of kingship at Abydos. Massive mudbrick enclosures, separated from the royal tomb by more than a kilometer, were designed for performing rituals that supported the king in his rebirth. Intended as the counterpart to the tomb, the interior was almost entirely open for ritual and festival activities. At Sakkara in the Third Dynasty (2686–2613 BCE), King Djoser created the first stone mortuary complex and brought together the enclosure and tomb into one unit. He was also responsible for the transformation from the earlier low, bench-shaped royal tomb to the prominent pyramid, showing an increased demand for monumentality in royal mortuary expression.

The mortuary complexes of the Fourth Dynasty (2613–2494 BCE) were a radical change. Establishing a pyramid as the focal point, a cult chapel was added on the east side of the pyramid. This chapel was connected by a stone causeway to a second cult chapel some distance east. The complex was symmetrical, aligned on an axis dominated by the pyramid, perhaps indicating an evolution in the concept of the deceased king as he became connected to the sun god Ra and, in death, joined the daily solar cycle. Texts found in later Sixth Dynasty (2345–2181) pyramids, but likely dating much earlier, specifically state that the pyramid's function was to facilitate the union of the deceased king and sun god.

The two types of temples associated with pyramid complexes, the one at the base of the pyramid and the other at some distance, were conceptually connected, with both serving different aspects of the cult, as well as being physically connected by long covered stone causeways. The pyramid temple included pillared courts and statue niches to house cult images of the divine king. The valley temple was used for the active cult of the deceased king and was where his image met with those of the gods during divine festivals. The pyramid complex continued to develop, but all included royal cult temples as a central component.

First ruler of the Middle Kingdom, Nebhepetra-Mentuhotep (2055–2004 BCE), who reunified Egypt after the decentralization of the First Intermediate Period, constructed his complex at Thebes, far south of the pyramid plains. Building on earlier plans, he made additions to accommodate significant changes in beliefs related to the king. Nebhepetra-Mentuhotep's mortuary complex included divine shrines as well as the tomb and royal mortuary chapel. This was a site of joint cult, where the king and the gods united. Unlike the Old Kingdom pyramid complexes, where the king was viewed as divine, scenes here show the king only being allowed long rule through the gift of the gods.

Nebhepetra-Mentuhotep established the procession where the cult image of Amun was carried from his shrine at Karnak and brought to the west bank to visit the king's mortuary temple. This annual reaffirmation of the union between the king and the gods grew into the "Beautiful Festival of the Valley," which in the late New Kingdom lasted 27 days. Other Middle Kingdom rulers built their mortuary complexes in the north, following late pyramid complex plans, but in the New Kingdom (1550–1069 BCE), Thebes became the primary location for royal mortuary monuments.

The specific locations of the royal mortuary temples were directly influenced by the existing processional routes. They appeared along the series of canals at the edge of the floodplain that ran the length of the necropolis south to a small temple at Medinet Habu, which the cult statue of Amun visited on a regular basis in an important ritual.

Unlike Old and Middle Kingdom mortuary temples, New Kingdom tombs and mortuary temples were separated by several miles. This was functional in the Theban landscape, as temples needed to be accessible to the divine cult statues as they processed, while the tombs needed to remain hidden and secure and thus were cut into valleys behind the impressive cliffs that dominate the landscape.

At the mortuary temples, there is a continued linkage between the royal cult and the divine cult. These temples were basically large, elaborate bark stations for the cult statues of Amun and other gods to visit on their regular journeys. Sections of these temples were dedicated to the solar god Ra, and to the goddess Hathor. These joint cults were meant to last "millions of years," bringing a type of immortality to the king by directly connecting his worship to that of the gods.

Architecture in mortuary temples played a role in the ritual. Like most New Kingdom temples, mortuary temples were designed as a microcosm of the universe. The gateway, called a pylon, was actually a huge hieroglyph: "Horizon." Beyond the gateway, lying along a symmetrical central axis, are open courtyards, followed by roofed columned halls, chapels, and finally a small sanctuary, usually with a raised floor, where the cult image was housed. Conceptually, these structures embodied the act of creation itself. Beginning in the sanctuary and processing along the central axis out of the temple, the cult statue moved from the dark sanctuary, representing the mound of creation, through the emerging swamp of the columned hall, out into the brilliant sunlight of the open courtyards, and then passed through the pylon out into the living world. By processing along this path, ritual participants aided in the renewal of the cosmos.

Most mortuary temples were constructed of sandstone, while the support buildings, including storehouses and living quarters for priests, were made of mudbrick. At some sites, these outbuildings have been preserved enough to give a sense of their daily functioning. These temples also had economic purpose and were used as wealth repositories as well as venues for redistribution. At least 30 royal mortuary temples were constructed at Thebes during the New Kingdom, but most of them are in very poor condition. The few examples that remain largely intact are key to aiding our understanding of the function of these monumental structures that each king felt essential to their afterlife survival.

An unusual mortuary temple is *Djeser-Djeseru*, "Holiest of Holies," that Hatshepsut (1473–1458 BCE) constructed at Deir el Bahri, right next to the earlier temple of Nebhepetra-Mentuhotep. Hatshepsut was obviously influenced by the earlier structure in the general architectural form and the choice of location. By placing her mortuary temple here, she gained connection with an earlier revered ruler as well as with the existing Hathor shrine at the site that had already been a festival destination for more than 500 years. Her temple has a unique plan, significantly different from most New Kingdom temples, with a series of ramps and porticos, but it has the same functions and components; it was simply arranged differently to fit the space.

The mortuary temple of Amenhotep III (1390–1352 BCE) was the largest temple ever built in Egypt. The central axis, from the first pylon to the rear wall, was nearly a half mile long. Almost completely leveled in subsequent millennia, partially by an earthquake, its primary remaining visual elements are the two colossi that were placed in front of the main gate, known as the Colossi of Memnon. Each gigantic statue was cut from a single block of an extremely hard quartzite and weighs more than 1000 tons, giving a hint of the incredible wealth and exceptional effort that was expended in constructing this monument. Excavations are ongoing at this temple and changing our understanding of this enormous temple complex.

The mortuary temple of Seti I (1294–1279 BCE) at the northern end of the necropolis lies directly across the river from Karnak. Quite well-preserved, this temple was the first to include a small palace in the plan. These palaces, which became standard, included a "Window of Appearance" through the facade into the first courtyard for the king to use in festival activities. The most complete example, and possibly the last complete mortuary temple built at Thebes, is the temple of Ramses III (1184–1153 BC) at Medinet Habu, at the southern end of the necropolis. Ramses III took advantage of the fact that there was already a small temple at the site that was the destination for cultic processions; by building his mortuary temple right next to this temple, which was visited by the cult statue of Amun every 10 days, his royal cult gained extra attention.

Little remains of the mortuary temple complexes of later kings. In the millennia that followed, the structures were reused, quarried, had pieces hauled off as trophies, and were left to the ravages of time. The most complete examples surviving today give us the barest hint of their original splendor, but in essence, their function lives on: the monuments are enduring, and their kings are remembered, as was intended.

Amy Calvert

See also: Colossi of Memnon; Pyramids; Temples, State; Valley of the Kings

Further Reading

Arnold, Dieter. 1979. *The Temple of Mentuhotep at Deir el-Bahari.* New York: Metropolitan Museum of Art.

Haeny, Gerhard. 1997. "New Kingdom 'Mortuary Temples' and 'Mansions of Millions of Years.'" In B. Shafer, ed. *Temples of Ancient Egypt.* Ithaca, NY: Cornell University Press, pp. 86–126.

Lehner, M. 1997. *The Complete Pyramids.* London: Thames & Hudson.

Murnane, W. 1980. *United with Eternity: A Concise Guide to the Monuments at Medinet Habu.* Chicago: University of Chicago.

Wilkinson, R. 2000. *The Complete Temples of Ancient Egypt.* London: Thames & Hudson.

Temples, Ptolemaic-Roman

The Greek Ptolemies and Roman emperors expanded the form and function of cult temples established in the Pharaonic Period after adopting the Egyptian kingship system under Ptolemy I (305–285 BCE). In the Ptolemaic (332–30 BCE) and Roman periods (30 BCE–395 CE), new cultic activities and more rituals were added to the calendar of cult temples. In addition, more laypeople were allowed in the temple's precinct than in earlier periods of Egyptian history. To promote this expansion, the Ptolemies enlarged the layout of cult temples to include new forms for such purposes. Continuing into the Roman Period, the Roman administration (emperors, prefects, and priests in Egypt) designed space for temple cultic practice to continue and thrive. While becoming increasingly complex in architectural form and layout, with theology recorded in relief carving and painted decoration, temples in the Ptolemaic and Roman Periods are deeply immersed in pharaonic traditions, particularly of the New Kingdom (1550–1069 BCE).

The form and function of cult temples in Egypt was standardized in the New Kingdom. In this standard, the sanctuary—the home of the god and center of the microcosm of the universe—was built in the middle of the temple's core. This core was the most sacred part of the temple and located in the back part of the temple and surrounded by a number of rooms. In the New Kingdom, pharaohs generally extended the temples lengthwise, so there were a limited number of rooms around the main sanctuary; new buildings were added to the front and back of the temple. New Kingdom cult temples are characterized by their spatial grandeur and light, as seen in the high clerestory windows of the hypostyle hall at Karnak. The Ramesside kings began experimenting with space, so areas around the sanctuary were "tomblike and narrow" as early as the Nineteenth Dynasty (1295–1186 BCE).

Similar experimentation continued into the Ptolemaic Period. Dieter Arnold has identified three chronological phases of style in the form of cult temples during the Ptolemaic Period. The first style, during the reigns of Ptolemies I to V (305–180 BCE), is characterized by a continuance of projects and forms begun by the Thirtieth Dynasty (380–343 BCE) kings. The second style, from the reigns of Ptolemies VI to IX (180–80 BCE), is the "classic" Ptolemaic style, in which forms are ordered and calm. In the last style, from the reigns of Ptolemy X to Cleopatra

VII (80–30 BCE), there is continued exploration with complex forms. The most deeply carved and modeled reliefs come from this period. Further, the regular use of nontypical colors, such as pink, purple, gold, and silver, along with colors in the traditional color palette, and the most experimentation with column capitals comes from this period. Generally, column capitals are organic in form, usually palm, lily, and papyrus buds. Hathor heads and sistra, ritual shaking musical instruments, are also added to the repertoire.

Continuing the expansion of form and function, the Ptolemies built cult temples farther lengthwise and widthwise, so there were a greater number of rooms around the sanctuary. Less light was let in, as the simpler pronaos, or front room, was preferred over the clerestories and spacious hypostyle halls of the New Kingdom. Building on Late Period (664–332 BCE) precedents, more rituals and processions were added to the ritual calendar at Ptolemaic temples in comparison with their New Kingdom counterparts, so new forms were added to the many-structured temple precincts. These include the birth house, the wabet, pronaos, entrance porch, kiosk, entrance kiosk, cult terrace, an increased column capital repertoire, screen walls, and broken-door lintels. The birth house celebrated the birth of the child god of the site's main deity; for instance, Hathor's son Ihy is honored at the temple of Dendera. Rites associated with the child god were added to the ritual calendar in addition to rituals that associated the king with the child god. Purification rites, especially associated with the New Year festival, were conducted in the wabet, or pure hall. The entrance porch was a secular resting spot for festival participants, and the entrance kiosk was a sacred resting spot, where traveling gods in their barque (sacred boat) shrines rested during processions.

After Augustus annexed Egypt into the Roman Empire in 30 BCE, the Roman emperors took on the role of Egyptian king and continued to build cult temples. Augustus was one of Egypt's most prolific temple builders and added to or began the construction of at least 24 temples, significantly more than Cleopatra VII (51–30 BCE), who is known to have built at four sites. The Romans continued the general expansion of areas where cultic activities that involved public participants could be carried out. There was a proliferation of adding cult terraces at the front of temples and contra temples at the rear of temples. These contra temples functioned as counterpoints to the publicly inaccessible and sacred interior areas. Furthermore, beginning with Augustus, structures for the worship of the imperial cult were integrated into venerable temple precincts like those of Amun at Karnak and Isis at Philae. Later emperors also added classical structures to long-standing cult temples. The remarkable example of Luxor is twofold, with the addition of an Iseum, a temple dedicated to Isis in her pan-Mediterranean form, in front of the entrance pylon in the reign of Hadrian (117–138 CE), and the renovation of the interior to an imperial cult chamber under the Tetrarchs (284–324 CE).

Like the expansion of temple form and function, there was significant development in color palette and placement of colors in temple painting in the Ptolemaic and Roman Periods. An excellent example of temple painting from this period is Hathor's temple at Dendera. The general appearance of the polychromy at Dendera shows the same color categories used in earlier periods, all against a white background. Vivid and luminous colors in the black, white, red, and green/blue

Detail of decoration from the ceiling of the outer hypostyle hall of the Ptolemaic-Roman temple of the goddess Hathor at Dendera. The middle register depicts the solar boat crossing the heavens, and the register above and below show the *bas,* or souls, of people adoring the sun god. (Mikhail Kokhanchikov/Dreamstime.com)

categories are present, with the additional variegated category visible in the detailed patterns of the birds' plumage. Yet, new complex patterns, especially in crowns, regalia, and thrones of deities, are different than earlier periods—such as a blue crown adorned with circles worn by the goddess Isis that is in the traditional shape of the White Crown of Upper Egypt. Similar variation in decoration can be seen at the cleaned temple of Isis at Deir Shelwit. In numerous scenes in the interior, Osiris's *atef* crown is painted yellow with red plumes; this crown is similar to the yellow crown of Upper Egypt. Although an unusual choice, the use of yellow for this crown has been documented with frequency from the reign of Ptolemy I and is commonly recorded at the Augustan temple of Dendur, now in the Metropolitan Museum in New York.

Although it at first seems that the Ptolemies and Romans caused great change in cult temples as compared to the New Kingdom, even many of the experiments in form and decoration discussed above had pharaonic precedents. For instance, while the color pink is generally thought to be a Ptolemaic development, it was used as early as the Nineteenth Dynasty in the mortuary temple of Seti I at Abydos. There are also examples of nonnaturalistic uses of green/blue to reference the freshness of the object colored, such as deities' skin and the White Crown of Upper Egypt in Middle Kingdom coffin texts. Regarding temple form, the birth house can be traced to the Nineteenth Dynasty Ramesseum, the wabet is a form of the New Kingdom solar complexes, the entrance kiosk is similar to the way station popular in New Kingdom temples, screen walls are first seen in the Third Dynasty (2686–2613 BCE), and broken-door lintels were popular in the Amarna period.

It can be concluded that although there was change in the form of the Ptolemaic and Roman temples, this change occurred within the acceptable realms of the canon of art and architecture in Egypt. The Ptolemies and Romans expanded on the projects of earlier pharaohs, just as millennia of pharaohs before them, thereby preserving the purpose and potency of cult temples in Egypt.

Erin A. Peters

See also: Dendera; Edfu; Philae Island; Ptolemaic Egypt; Roman Egypt; Temples, State

Further Reading

Arnold, Dieter. 1999. *Temples of the Last Pharaohs*. New York: Oxford.

Baines, John. 2001. "Colour Use and the Distribution of Relief and Painting in the Temple of Sety I at Abydos." In W. V. Davies, ed. *Colour and Painting in Ancient Egypt*. London: British Museum Press, pp. 145–157.

Clarysse, W. 2010. "Egyptian Temples and Priests: Graeco-Roman." In A. Lloyd, ed. *A Companion to Ancient Egypt*. Malden, MA: Wiley-Blackwell, pp. 274–309.

Finnestad, R. B. 1997. "Temples of the Ptolemaic and Roman Periods: Ancient Traditions in New Contexts." In B. E. Shafer, ed. *Temples of Ancient Egypt*. Ithaca, NY: Cornell University Press, pp. 185–237.

Heidel, J. B., and W. R. Johnson. 2015. "The Tetrarchic Architectural Renovation of Luxor Temple: Context, Significance, and the Amun Cult." In M. Jones and S. McFadden, eds. *Art of Empire: The Roman Frescoes and Imperial Cult Chamber in Luxor Temple*. New Haven, CT: Yale University Press, pp. 39–59.

Kaper, O. E. 1998. "Temple Building in the Egyptian Deserts during the Roman Period." In O. E. Kaper, ed. *Life on the Fringe: Living in the Southern Egyptian Deserts during the Roman and Early Byzantine Periods*. Leiden: Research School CNWS, pp. 139–152.

Klotz, D. 2012. *Caesar in the City of Amun: Egyptian Temple Construction and Theology in Roman Thebes*. Turnhout, Belgium: Brepols.

McKenzie, Judith. 2007. *The Architecture of Alexandria and Egypt, c. 300 B.C. to A.D. 700*. New Haven, CT: Yale University Press.

Peters, E., and D. C. Patch. 2017. "Living Color: The Met Museum's Temple of Dendur." *Egyptian Archaeology* 50: 5–10.

Temples, State

The designation "state temple" is a category assigned by modern scholars to the temples of Egypt that were site of worship for a deity. This term is meant to differentiate them from the "mortuary temples" built to sustain the souls, or *kas*, of deceased kings and prominent individuals. Unfortunately, the boundaries between the two are rather nebulous. Many mortuary temples contained shrines dedicated to the worship of major deities, and some state temples, such as the temple of Luxor, operated as temples to the cult of the royal *ka*.

Hieroglyphic and pictorial representations of shrines or temples from the Pre- and Protodynastic Periods (5300–3000 BCE) suggest that the designs of the temples of Upper Egypt were distinct from those of Lower Egypt. The *Per-Nu* style of shrine, which became symbolic of Lower Egypt, consisted of a rectangular building, built either of wood and woven mats or mudbrick, with a barrel-vaulted roof and a large post at either corner. The *Per-Wer* shrine type, the prototypical Upper Egyptian shrine, was likewise a barrel-vaulted rectangular structure, although this version slanted downward toward the rear of the building, lacked corner posts, and most likely was adorned with cattle horns at the front. This style might have evolved from a king's tent. Nonfunctional versions of the *Per-Wer* and the *Per-Nu* shrines can be found in the mortuary temple complex of King Djoser (2267–2648 BCE) at Sakkara.

Very little is known about the state temples of the Old and Middle Kingdoms, although their existence is recorded in the titles of courtiers and royal annals, such as the Palermo Stone. Fragments of inscriptions dating to the Old Kingdom (2686–2160 BCE) have been found at several later temples, including Tell Basta and Heliopolis, indicating the presence of Old Kingdom religious structures at these sites, although little is known of their architecture. Beginning in the reign of Userkaf (2494–2487 BCE) and continuing until the reign of Menkauhor, (2421–2414 BCE), the kings of the Fifth Dynasty constructed a series of sun temples near their pyramid complexes. Although only two sun temples, those of Userkaf and Niuserra, have been located and excavated, they are believed to have consisted of a large squat obelisk within an open courtyard with an offering table in front of it. Reliefs are preserved from two ritual spaces on the south side of the obelisk, a Sed chapel and a space containing scenes of nature during the varying seasons, likely a reference to the role of the sun in bringing about natural abundance. A causeway led from the courtyard of the sun temple to a valley temple.

It is believed that the construction of state temples increased dramatically during the Middle Kingdom (2055–1650 BCE), although very few remain, as most were torn down and rebuilt by later pharaohs. The extant evidence, including the foundations for a temple of Montu built by Senusret I (1956–1911 BCE) at el-Tod,

Hypostyle Hall

The hypostyle hall was an essential component of the standard Egyptian state temple. Although the earliest excavated hypostyle halls date to the Middle Kingdom, the large number of reused Old Kingdom columns in later structures points to their presence in Old Kingdom state temples. The extensive use of columns in hypostyle halls, though necessary to support the roof of such a large space, also possessed symbolic value. Egyptian literature referred to temple columns as the posts that hold up the sky, evoked by celestial imagery on the ceilings of hypostyle halls. Likewise, the columns, designed to mimic plants, evoked the primordial swamp with its tall plants that surrounded the mound of creation in Egyptian mythology.

Some of the columns display *rekhyt* birds, symbols of the Egyptian populace, instructing temple visitors where to stand during ceremonies, which indicates that the hypostyle hall was restricted to temple personnel except for special occasions. Noblemen often commissioned statues of themselves to be placed in the hypostyle hall as a sign of their devotion to the god. Some of these statues, such as those at Karnak of Amenhotep, son of Hapu, developed cults of their own and acted as intermediaries between petitioners and the gods.

Patrick Salland

indicates that these temples usually included a courtyard followed by a columned hall and then a shrine, often tripartite, to accommodate the worship of a triad of gods. The temple of Amun at Karnak, also built by Senusret I, appears to have utilized a similar plan. This Middle Kingdom temple would serve as the core of the Karnak complex throughout most of its history, although little survived the restoration efforts of later pharaohs.

By the Eighteenth Dynasty (1550–1295 BCE), the state temple took on a standardized plan that would dominate until the advent of Christianity. This plan consisted of an entrance pylon, a column courtyard, a hypostyle hall, and an inner sanctuary, usually arranged in this order along a north-south axis. All of these elements would have been surrounded by a high mudbrick wall, which not only protected the temple from intrusion but also separated the sacred space from the profane world beyond. Several temples, including the temple of Khonsu at Karnak and the temple of Horus at Edfu, preserve this temple plan in its most perfect and complete form. Others show variations. The temple of Amun at Karnak, the largest surviving state temple in Egypt, while mostly adhering to the plan, was expanded by multiple pharaohs over the course of some 2,000 years and shows significant alterations to the basic plan.

The entrance to the prototypical state temple of the New Kingdom would have been through a pylon, a pair of monumental towers with slightly sloping sides with a portal in the center. These pylons were designed to not only intimidate and astonish visitors but also to mimic the shape of the hieroglyph for horizon—two mountains flanking the sun disk—thus telling visitors that the space beyond was sacred. The pylon could be augmented with colossal statues of the king, pairs of granite obelisks, and large cedar flagpoles set into the face of the pylon. Scenes found on pylons typically depict the king smiting enemies or engaging in battle in the presence of the gods. These apotropaic scenes symbolized the king's power over *isfet*, the dangerous chaotic pollution that existed outside the sacred precinct. Similar scenes are displayed on the exterior walls of other portions of the temple.

Continuing along the east-west axis, one would next enter the outer courtyard, a large rectangular space surrounded by a peristyle. Under normal circumstances, this was the farthest that the majority of the population could go within the temple. Certain areas of the courtyard were set aside as spaces where all Egyptians could make petitions to the gods of the temple, usually separated from the rest of the temple by wooden walls or a curtain.

Beyond the courtyard was the hypostyle hall, a rectangular structure dominated by multiple rows of columns. These columns, like most others utilized in state temples, were designed to mimic the shapes of plants or organic posts used to support the roofs of less permanent buildings. The most common types of columns imitate a stalk of papyrus, a lotus flower, or palm branches lashed to a wooden pillar. Beginning in the New Kingdom, composite columns, utilizing design elements inspired by several different plants, became common.

Although referred to as a "hall," in most instances, the hypostyle was wider than it was long, often only two or three rows of columns deep. The hypostyle hall was centered on a wide aisle along the east-west axis of the temple. The columns flanking this aisle were taller than those on either side and supported a clerestory,

Naos

The naos, meaning *temple* in Greek, was the main shrine of a temple or tomb where a cult statue was housed. Due to their association with the statue, naoi were usually located in the inner sanctuary of a temple or offering chamber of a tomb. Three times a day, temple priests would open the shrine's double doors and remove the statue of a god so that it could be presented with offerings, dressed, and anointed. The archetypal naos is a freestanding rectangular structure with gently sloping sides placed upon a plinth. At the top of the naos was usually a cavetto cornice, often adorned with rearing uraei, upon which rested a squat pyramid. The design of the naos evolved from the predynastic *Per-Wer* and the *Per-Nu* shrines, made of perishable materials. Although naoi continued to be made of wood throughout most of pharaonic history, stone appears to have been the most commonly used material. By the Late Period (664–332 BCE), naoi made of particularly hard stone and bearing long texts and complex figural decoration became the norm. Some of these naoi, such as the naos of Wadjet at Buto, which was said to be 70 feet in height, reached monumental proportions.

Patrick Salland

whose windows provided the only light in this section of the temple. The scenes on the walls of hypostyle halls often represent the king in the presence of the gods and priests carrying the divine barque.

At the rear of the hypostyle hall was the entrance to the sanctuary, the inner chamber of the temple where the statue of the god resided, usually within a *naos* shrine. Here the high priest and his attendants would perform offerings to the cult statue of the god three times a day, corresponding with the day's three meals. Although it was believed that only the king could perform these rituals, a fact that was reinforced by scenes on the walls depicting the king alone before the gods, the tasks were carried out by priests as royal proxies. Surrounding the sanctuary were spaces for the storage of offerings, the ritual barque, and other temple furniture. The inner sanctuary featured a low ceiling and was raised on a platform, thereby mimicking the mound of creation that rose above the primordial swamp.

In addition to these main elements, some state temples utilized other components, either as part of the temple itself or immediately adjacent to it. Temples dedicated to solar deities often included sun courts, large open courtyards similar to the outer courtyard. *Mammisi*, or birth houses, are shrines dedicated to the birth of the god and are found inside the precincts of some temples, such as the Temple of Hathor at Dendera. Other temple precincts contain barque shrines, places for the barque of the god to rest during festival processions.

In addition to these main components of the temple proper, the temple complex included a number of support structures, such as granaries, workshops, butcher shops, bakeries, sacred lakes, and homes for priests. The sacred lake was of particular importance, as this was where the priests would bathe before entering the ritually clean temple. The storerooms and centers of production point to the role these state temples played as centers of the Egyptian economy. Temples often owned large tracts of land, farmed by tenant farmers, across much of the country.

The temple of Karnak, for instance, owned lands from Pi-Ramses in the delta to Napata in Nubia, employing some 8,760 farmers and producing, among other things, 1.75 million sacks of grain annually. The granaries of the Ramesseum in western Thebes could hold 226,328 sacks of grain, enough to feed 3,400 families for a year. Although it was a mortuary temple, the storage capacity of the Ramesseum is most likely similar to that of state temples of the same size and importance.

Patrick Salland

See also: Dendera; Edfu; Temples, Mortuary

Further Reading

Arnold, Dieter. 1999. *The Temples of the Last Pharaohs*. New York: Oxford University Press.

Blyth, Elizabeth. 2007. *Karnak: The Evolution of a Temple*. Hoboken, NJ: Taylor & Francis.

Shafer, Byron, ed. 2005. *Temples of Ancient Egypt*. New York: I. B. Tauris.

Teeter, Emily. 2012. *Religion and Ritual in Ancient Egypt*. Cambridge, MA: Cambridge University Press.

Wilkinson, Richard. 2017. *The Complete Temples of Ancient Egypt*. New York: Thames and Hudson.

Thebes, East and West

Thebes was known in ancient Egypt as *Waset*. It was also often referred to as "Southern Heliopolis," as Thebes was a comparable religious center to Heliopolis in the delta. Thebes encompassed a broad floodplain that was inundated annually with the Nile flood. Inhabited from the Paleolithic Period on, this fertile region rose to prominence during a height of Egyptian civilization and was the royal capital for generations during an era of great wealth and stability. This resulted in a landscape covered with thousands of structures—tombs, temples, shrines, and chapels—many of which are related in some way to other local monuments and linked by regular festival processions, which became a prominent feature in the local culture that continues to this day. Due to the incredible density of monuments, Thebes is sometimes referred to as the largest open-air museum in the world.

The fields of Thebes are framed by large limestone cliffs, and Paleolithic tools were discovered in the western hills. There are Old Kingdom 2686–2160 BCE *mastaba* tombs on the west bank, and the ritual landscape of Thebes dates back to the first constructions at Karnak on the east bank of the Nile. The first certain evidence of an Amun Temple at Karnak dates from the First Intermediate Period (2125–2055 BCE). In the Middle Kingdom, the region rose in prominence with the Theban rulers, beginning with Nebhepetra-Mentuhotep (2055–2004 BCE), who reunited Egypt after the political breakdown of the First Intermediate Period. These rulers built extensively at Karnak and around Thebes, and the area increased significantly in importance. There was a strong connection between the cult of Amun and the royal cult, a relationship firmly established by Nebhepetre-Mentuhotep. His monumental mortuary temple in the western hills at Deir el-Bahri included his tomb, royal cult shrine, and shrines to Amun and Hathor.

The temple at Deir el-Bahri became the primary destination for the east-west processional route from the Amun Temple at Karnak. Processional routes were the paths the bark, or boat, with the sacred image of Amun traveled on cyclical bases in festivals. Such festivals were common in the New Kingdom (1550–1069 BCE), allowing the populace to engage with the gods. The festival courses also molded the architectural development of the region, as structures arose along their paths. Nebhepetra-Mentuhotep's later successor, Senusret I (1956–1911 BCE), likely established the north-south processional route from Karnak, suggested by the position of his bark shrine. The logical destination of this route is Luxor Temple, but little evidence of a Middle Kingdom temple at Luxor survives. The later Luxor Temple was dedicated to a primordial version of Amun and the royal cult. This site was used for rituals related to divine kingship and the renewal of the god Amun, all of which were considered essential to the continued functioning of the cosmos.

There is some evidence of a Middle Kingdom small temple at Medinet Habu on the west bank that was ritually connected with the primeval mound of Djeme, the ancient name for the area of Medinet Habu. A later Eighteenth Dynasty structure, standing on top, was the destination for the Decade Festival, which occurred every 10 days. During this festival, the cult statue of Amun-Ra from Karnak traveled to Medinet Habu and visited this small temple associated with the mound of creation to be reborn. There is no direct Middle Kingdom evidence for this festival, but the presence of an existing structure under the later temple used for this purpose is suggestive.

During the New Kingdom, Thebes was the political capital during a period of military expansion and exceptional wealth and was the royal seat for generations of kings. Amun-Ra; his consort, Mut; and their child Khonsu—a grouping known as the Theban Triad—became the supreme deities of Egypt. During this era, hundreds of structures were added to the landscape.

On the east bank of the Nile lay the major temples of Karnak and Luxor and the New Kingdom city. Buried under the modern city of Luxor, the ancient city likely had a population of approximately 50,000 people, but it is virtually unexplored.

The royal mortuary temples on the west bank stretched by the end of the New Kingdom from the Temple of Seti I (1294–1279 BCE) at Gurna in the north to the Temple of Ramses III (1184–1153 BCE) at Medinet Habu in the south. There were nearly 30 such royal temples, although many are largely destroyed. Locations of the mortuary temples were inspired by the processional routes. During the annual "Beautiful Festival of the Valley," the statues of Amun and the royal cult visited each mortuary temple and the Hathor shrine at Deir el-Bahri. Their procession followed a series of canals carved into the edge of the floodplain, and kings constructed their mortuary temples along this path. Linkages between royal and divine cults became standard in New Kingdom Thebes. Mortuary temples are elaborate bark stations for the cult statues, and parts of the Mortuary Temples are also dedicated to Hathor and Ra. These were structures dedicated to the joint cult of the king and the gods, meant to last "Millions of Years"—a phrase many of these temples included in their names.

In the low desert hills behind these large temples, nonroyal tombs were cut into the limestone. Some of these were little more than pits; others were multichambered, columned complexes covered in magnificent decoration. These nonroyal sites stretch the length of the hills west of the mortuary temples, their location allowing vicarious participation in festivals.

Against the western cliffs at Deir el-Bahri lies the memorial temple, royal tomb, and Hathor shrine of Nebhepetra-Mentuhotep and the later Eighteenth Dynasty mortuary temples of Hatshepsut (1473–1458) and Thutmose III (1479–1425). Behind these cliffs, in the shadow of a pyramidal peak, lies the Valley of the Kings, a deep natural wadi that was used for royal burials for five centuries. The fantastic scenes within the tombs, referred to as the Books of the Dead, were intended to aid the king on his journey through the Netherworld.

The artisans who cut and decorated the royal tombs of western Thebes did not live in eastern Thebes with the majority of the population. For nearly 500 years, generations of artisans lived in a desert village close to the monuments. Called *pa demi*, "the Village," this walled town contained approximately 70 houses, with perhaps a total of 400 people living in the village. Finds from this site include thousands of limestone chips, or ostraca, covered in short texts that provide insight into their daily lives. Footpaths connect sites throughout the Theban Hills from the village, along the ridge, to the Valley of the Kings, and north to the bay of Deir el-Bahri. One path from the village leads south to the Valley of the Queens, *Ta set neferu*, "the Place of Beauty," established by Seti I, which contains approximately 90 tombs, including some exceptional ones for royal women and children.

Cyclical festivals connected monuments across the Theban landscape and focused on the procession of divine barks or cult images from one sacred location to another, allowing the general public to directly encounter their deities. Most of these rituals relate to regeneration of the kings, gods, and the blessed dead while supporting the sun god on his nightly voyage through the Netherworld. Two primary annual festivals were the "Beautiful Festival of the Valley" and the "Beautiful Festival of the Opet." Both were designed to reaffirm the relationship between the king and the gods.

The Valley Festival occurred during the second month of harvest season. This festival was focused on regeneration, rejuvenation, and the connection between the living and the dead. The procession included cult statues of Amun-Ra and deified kings, who emerged from Karnak, crossed the Nile, and visited the Deir el-Bahri shrines of Hathor as well as each of the royal mortuary temples. The population also accompanied the procession to the west bank, visiting family tombs and making offerings for their ancestors.

The Opet Festival took place during the second month of the flood season. During this festival, the barks of Amun-Ra, Mut, and Khonsu traveled from Karnak to Luxor Temple. Both the Opet Festival and the structure and function of Luxor Temple were focused on the royal cult. The goal of the ritual was to reaffirm ties between Amun-Ra and the king as the living Horus and to renew royal authority. The procession in the early New Kingdom paraded for more than a mile via a canal carved along the east bank, but this was later turned into a sphinx-lined route. There were six bark shrines along the way. Over time, this festival got longer, indicating its increasing importance; originally, it was 11 days, but it eventually lasted 27 days.

Even today, festival processions are part of Theban culture. During the three-day-long annual festival of Abu el-Haggag, a model bark filled with children dressed in bright clothing is paraded through town. The modern cities on the floodplain live surrounded by a maze of thousands of ancient structures whose presence continues to influence local life. The long development of this sacred landscape resulted in a complex web of interconnected monuments we are only beginning to understand.

Amy Calvert

See also: Deir el-Medina; Karnak; Temples, Mortuary; Valley of the Kings; Valley of the Queens

Further Reading

Bierbrier, Morris. 1982. *The Tomb Builders of the Pharaohs*. Cairo: American University in Cairo Press.

Dorman, P., and B. Bryan, eds. 2007. *Sacred Space and Sacred Function in Ancient Thebes*. University of Chicago Studies in Ancient Oriental Civilization 61. Chicago: University of Chicago Press.

Murnane, W. 1980. *United with Eternity: A Concise Guide to the Monuments at Medinet Habu*. Chicago: University of Chicago.

Nims, Charles. 1965. *Thebes of the Pharaohs*. London: Elek Books.

Strudwick, Nigel, and Helen Strudwick. 1999. *Thebes in Egypt: A Guide to the Tombs and Temples of Ancient Luxor*. Ithaca, NY: Cornell University Press.

Thoth

The ancient Egyptians believed that writing was invented and given to them by Thoth, whom they called *Djehuty*. He is generally recognized as a god of writing, wisdom, and also of the moon, but these associations hardly exhaust the plurality of his roles or the complexity of his nature, which are already apparent in his first appearance in textual sources.

He is primarily depicted as an ibis, an ibis-headed man, or a baboon, sometimes wearing the lunar crescent and disk on his head. His consort, or alternatively daughter, was Seshat, the goddess of writing and literature. The realm of the gods was believed to be mirrored in human society, and the king and his main representative and secretary, the vizier, had their parallels in Ra and Thoth. This is intimately connected with Thoth's identity as the moon: as the delegate of the sun god Ra, he governed the world in his absence, after sunset.

Thoth is generally depicted traveling with Ra in his solar barque with *Maat*, the goddess personifying the ancient Egyptian conception of the natural world order, truth, and justice. This ties in with Thoth in his capacity as vizier and judge. In funerary religion, according to Spell 125 of the "Book of Going Forth by Day" (or Book of the Dead), the weighing of the heart of the deceased against an ostrich feather, the symbol for *Maat*, is supervised by Thoth, whose fairness made him the one who writes down and announces the verdict.

In mythology, too, Thoth is a staunch supporter of justice: after Seth killed Osiris, the king of Egypt, to usurp the throne, Horus, the latter's son and rightful heir, had Thoth's unwavering loyalty. The new moon's regeneration into the full moon made Thoth a god of medicine. He is the one who healed the Eye of Horus after Seth damaged it. This Eye, called the *Wadjet* (from *wadja*, "to be hale, uninjured"), is itself none other than the full moon after it was healed from its "waned" state. Through a complex web of mythological associations, his role here parallels the part he plays in a version of another fundamental Egyptian myth, the *Myth of the Solar Eye*, in which the eye of the sun god, his daughter, leaves him in anger to go Nubia, but she eventually returns after being placated by Thoth.

Thoth was the god of writing and the patron of scribes. He was generally shown with the head of an ibis, although the baboon was also considered one of his forms. Thoth's cult center was located at Hermopolis. (Amanda Lewis/Dreamstime.com)

Thoth was also a creator god. According to one creation myth, the world emerges out of the Ogdoad, four couples of deities that embody the chaotic characteristics of precreation, and who, in a later version of this myth, are begotten by Thoth. This myth originates from Thoth's main cult center, Hermopolis, called *Khemenu* in Egyptian, which was also the word for "eight."

Arto Belekdanian

See also: Cosmology; *Maat*; Myths, Creation

Further Reading

Bleeker, C. J. 1973. *Hathor and Thoth: Two Key Figures of the Ancient Egyptian Religion.* Leiden: Brill.

Boylan, Patrick. 1922. *Thoth, the Hermes of Egypt: A Study of Some Aspects of Theological Thought in Ancient Egypt.* London: Oxford University Press.

Meeks, Dimitri, and Christine Favard-Meeks. 1997. *Daily Life of the Egyptian Gods.* London: John Murray.

Tomb Models

Tomb models, also known as models of daily life or servant statues, are depictions in three dimensions of people engaged in activities like brewing and baking, butchery and cooking, and bearers bringing supplies as well as boats for transport along and across the Nile, storehouses, and workshops. Other types of models made especially for the tomb are miniature or dummy offering vessels, food offerings, weapons, tools, sacred emblems, and royal regalia. The ancient Egyptians believed that what was depicted magically came into being. Just as the tomb owner would need food, drink, shelter, and transport in life, models provided these for a well-fed and happy afterlife, in some cases complementing carved and painted scenes on tomb walls and in others substituting for them in undecorated tombs.

The earliest tomb models are found in graves of the Predynastic and Early Dynastic Periods (Naqada II to Third Dynasty, 3500–2686 BCE). Predominantly in pottery are model boats, offering bearers, brewers, and domed granaries. It is not until the Old Kingdom (late Fourth Dynasty, 2613–2494 BCE) that tomb models of servants performing tasks begin to appear in numbers. Found in the tombs of high-ranking state officials between the Fourth and Sixth Dynasties at Giza and Sakkara, tomb models comprise single figures carved in limestone, the most common type being that of a woman grinding grain on a quern. Other food preparation models include bakers with ovens, brewers straining beer mash into jars, butchering of a calf, and a person attending a cooking pot. Manufactured goods are represented by potters throwing on a wheel, finishing the interior of storage jars, and heating a forge. Dome granaries in stone or pottery provided storage, while domestic life is represented by wet nurses and harpers and transport by a range of wooden model boats. Usually, only two or three models were included in the tomb, but there are instances of large groups of models; at Giza, the tomb of Djasha contained 16 models, and that of Nykau-Inpu contained more than 20. Some servant models are inscribed with the names of the sons and daughters of the tomb owner. It is unlikely that the tomb owner's family members would have performed menial tasks like food preparation themselves, but they chose to be depicted this way to show their dedication to the mortuary cult of their deceased relative (for which they were responsible) and to ensure their own participation in the afterlife. As such, Old Kingdom models may properly be termed "serving statues" because they depict the servicing of the mortuary cult.

By the end of the Sixth Dynasty (2181 BCE), tomb models are also found in the tombs of provincial officials. At the same time as this social change is the choice of wood as the medium for models, sometimes with elements such as jars and quern stones added in limestone and often comprising pairs of servants on the same baseboard. Wooden models were produced in larger numbers and greater variety than those of limestone; the tomb of Nyankh-Pepi-kem at Meir contained 17 servant models and 8 boats.

Most tomb models date to the late First Intermediate Period and early Middle Kingdom, or the Tenth, Eleventh, and early Twelfth Dynasties (about 2025–1956 BCE). During this period, the increased wealth of the provincial officials and their local courts is reflected in the tomb model repertoire by an increase in model

Particularly in the Middle Kingdom, wooden models were put into tombs along with, or instead of, wall scenes. This wooden model portrays the deceased in a boat, probably traveling across the Nile to the cemetery. Two women, acting as Isis and Nephthys, stand at the foot and head of the mummy. Two lector priests wearing leopard skins stand at the head and recite funerary spells. (Gift of J. Pierpont Morgan, 1912/The Metropolitan Museum of Art)

types, complexity, and numbers. A typical elite Middle Kingdom burial could include a pair of model boats, a granary structure, one or two offering bearers, and a food preparation scene arranged on a single base, which may have included figures of men and women baking, brewing, cooking, and butchering. Some wealthy Middle Kingdom tombs contained duplicates of scenes, perhaps to ensure a plentiful supply of offerings. The tomb of Djehutinakht and his wife at el-Bershah contained at least 45 model scenes, including 12 offering bearers and 8 granaries as well as a flotilla of 58 boats, and the tomb of Karenen and his wife at Sakkara contained 14 scenes, a procession of 20 offering bearers in two rows, and 8 boats. It is likely that the number and range of activities represented reflects the tomb owner's aspirations in the afterlife rather than a reflection of a living reality.

By the Twelfth Dynasty, food preparation and manufacturing scenes are increasingly depicted as taking place within a low walled structure developing to entirely enclosed structures, like those from the tomb of Meketre at Thebes and Gemniemhat at Sakkara.

Geography appears to have played a part in the choice of certain subjects depicted in tomb models. Agriculture and animal husbandry, such as ploughing with cattle, force-feeding cattle, and hoeing the soil, appear in models found at Asyut, el-Bershah, Meir, and Beni Hasan, reflecting the agricultural wealth of this region where the Nile valley was at its widest. However, in contrast, the large

Soul Houses

In 1906–1907, Flinders Petrie (1853–1942) excavated the Middle Kingdom cemetery at Rifeh, where he found a range of pottery tomb models called soul houses and offering trays. They had been placed on the ground to mark the position of tomb shafts instead of built tomb chapels.

There are three basic types:

- simple pottery plates, called offering trays, with modeled food offerings and drainage channels
- pottery trays with modeled food offerings, drainage channels, and a single-story domed hut-like structure or shrine
- pottery model houses, sometimes multistoried, with domestic architecture elements such as columns, doors, windows, stairs, vents, and roof terraces

Found throughout Egypt, all three types of offering trays and soul houses feature drainage channels or grooves in their upper surface, which converge on a centrally placed spout. Liquid offerings, perhaps water or beer, would be poured over the surface of the tray and drain through the spout. The modeled food offerings are varieties of bread, meat cuts such as a haunch of beef or even an entire trussed ox, and vegetables such as onions. Offerings to the dead made in this way ensured that the deceased received the nourishment wished for in the funerary prayer of bread and beer, oxen and fowl. The house structure itself would have provided shelter and domestic comforts as well as substituting for a tomb chapel (a house for the soul).

Angela M. J. Tooley

Theban model of Meketre inspecting a herd of cattle reflects his elevated social position as chancellor and high steward. Manufacturing processes on the other hand, such as spinning and weaving, carpentry, metalworking, and brickmaking, appear to have no geographical significance but reflect the increased complexity of the model repertoire at its zenith during the early Middle Kingdom.

Model boats appear most frequently in pairs rigged for rowing or sailing, for traveling north or south. Besides traveling boats, they are models imitating papyrus skiffs, fishing craft, cargo boats, and ritual craft for ferrying the mummified deceased to the necropolis and others that are solar boats for sailing with the sun god Ra in the afterlife. Of all the model types, offering bearers are the most significant. Frequently larger in scale than other tomb models and better made, they are often found in pairs carrying different offerings in their baskets and hands, and they may represent the estates or domains from which the offerings were drawn, either real landholdings within the tomb owner's estate or idealized estates for provisioning the tomb owner in the afterlife.

By the reign of Senusret III (1870–1831 BCE), the wealth of provincial officials had declined, which is reflected in a decrease in the number and variety of tomb models. By the New Kingdom (1550–1069 BCE), tomb models had all but died out, but not entirely. Model boats continued to be placed in some tombs, and the tomb of Tutankhamun even contained a large model granary divided into 16 compartments filled with barley and emmer wheat.

Not all Middle Kingdom elite burials included servant models. A different a kind of burial that placed a greater importance on the funerary texts inscribed on coffins, Coffin Texts, also included model ritual objects like scepters, staves, weapons, and ritual garments as a means of attaining the afterlife. These types of models were designed to protect the deceased and safeguard passage to the afterlife, something that servant models could not provide. By the end of the Middle Kingdom, early shabti figures, probably inspired by the mummiform figurines placed on Twelfth Dynasty model funerary boats, began to appear and be inscribed with chapter 6 of the "Book of Going Forth by Day," or the Book of the Dead. Taking over many of the functions of tomb models, shabtis remained ubiquitous throughout Egyptian history.

Angela M. J. Tooley

See also: Afterlife; Animals; Beer; Bread; Food; Ships and Shipping

Further Reading

Breasted, James H., Jr. 1948. *Egyptian Servant Statues.* Washington, D.C.: Pantheon Books.

D'Auria, Sue., Peter Lacovara, and Catharine H. Roehrig. 1988. *Mummies and Magic. The Funerary Arts of Ancient Egypt.* Boston: Museum of Fine Arts.

Freed, Rita E., Lawrence M. Berman, Denise M. Doxey, and Nicholas S. Picardo. 2009. *The Secrets of Tomb 10A: Egypt 2000 BC.* Boston: Museum of Fine Arts.

Roth, Ann M. 2002. "The Meaning of Menial Labor: 'Servant Statues' in Old Kingdom Serdabs." *Journal of the American Research Center in Egypt* 39: 103–121.

Tooley, Angela M. J. 1995. *Egyptian Models and Scenes.* Princes Risborough, UK: Shire Egyptology 22.

Winlock, Herbert E. 1955. *Models of Daily Life in Ancient Egypt from the Tomb of Meket-Re at Thebes.* Cambridge, MA: Harvard University Press.

Tomb of Tutankhamun

The tomb of Tutankhamun is the most exceptional discovery ever made in Egypt: the first ancient Egyptian royal burial found intact. Tutankhamun's tomb was discovered in the center of the Valley of the Kings in 1922 by the English archaeologist Howard Carter (1874–1939) under the sponsorship of George Edward Stanhope, the 5th Earl of Carnarvon (1866–1923). Although it was robbed and resealed twice not long after his burial, Tutankhamun's tomb was found with more than 5,000 objects and an undisturbed gold sarcophagus containing the mummified body of the king inside.

In 1905, Lord Carnarvon, an English aristocrat with a passion for Egyptian archaeology, arrived in Luxor searching for a warm climate that would help his recovery from an illness. He decided to finance some excavations, and the Egyptian Antiquities Service told him that he should work with an experienced archaeologist. Finally, on February 8, 1915, Carter and Carnarvon were allowed to excavate in the Valley of the Kings. Carter explored areas in the Valley of Kings that had been neglected by other archaeologists and spent seven years in search of Tutankhamun's tomb. Thanks to Carter's determination and intuition, the research came to success: an entrance to a previously unknown tomb was discovered.

The tomb of Tutankhamun (KV 62, with KV meaning the Kings' Valley) remained undetected because of a water course that carried and deposited sand and rubble that covered the entrance. Also, it was found right below the tomb of Ramses VI (KV 9), and its entrance was hidden by the dumping of material from the work in KV9.

After years of searching, on November 4, 1922, a workman uncovered a stone step, the first of a descending stair into the mountain. Carter sent a telegram to England informing Lord Carnarvon about the find: "At last made wonderful discovery in Valley; a magnificent tomb with seals intact; recovered same for your arrival; congratulations" (Malek 2009, 27). He then asked Carnarvon to come back to Egypt immediately.

Sixteen descending steps cut into the bedrock led to a sealed doorway. The royal seal of Tutankhamun and the seal of the guardian of the necropolis stamped in the mud at the entrance indicated that this tomb was sealed and that no one had entered inside since the burial. However, in the doorway, there were signs of it having been opened and reclosed, suggesting that the contents might have already been plundered in antiquity. A descending corridor, filled with sand and rubble, led to a second sealed door leading to a room that Carter named the antechamber. A candle was introduced in a small opening made in the top left corner of the door. Despite hot air escaping that almost blew out the light, Carter was able to see inside, and Carnarvon asked him, "Can you see anything?" Carter replied, "Yes, it is wonderful!" (Malek 2009, 28–29).

The small size and simple plan of the tomb have led to the suggestion that it was originally a nonroyal tomb that, after the early death of the king, would have been converted into a royal tomb, but this is not certain. The tomb consists of the descending corridor with stairs, antechamber, annexe, treasury, and burial chamber. Only the four walls of the burial chamber had been decorated with painted scenes.

King Tutankhamun

Tutankhamun (1336–1327 BCE) ascended to the throne at the age of 10 years, taking the crown name of Nebkheperura, "Lord of the forms of Ra." He may have been the son of Pharaoh Akhenaten (formerly Amenhotep IV, 1353–1336) and his queen Nefertiti, who also had six daughters, but this is still debated.

Tutankhamun was born in Akhet-Aten (Tell el-Amarna), the new capital dedicated to the Aten founded by his father in Middle Egypt, and he probably lived there until the third year of his reign. Tutankhamun's name means "Living image of Amun," although his original name at birth was Tutankhaten, "Living image of Aten." The change of his name to Tutankhamun reflects the return to religious orthodoxy described in his Restoration Stela, when the royal residence moved back to Memphis.

Tutankhamun married his half sister Ankhesenpaaten, later Ankhesenamun, and had two daughters who were stillborn or died shortly after birth. After Tutankhamun's early death, his widow tried to marry a Hittite prince, but he was killed on the way to Egypt; two Egyptian military men ascended the throne: first Ay (1327–1323 BCE) and then Horemheb (1323–1295 BCE), the last king of the Eighteenth Dynasty.

Maria Rosa Guasch-Jané

The thieves were mostly interested in metal and the fat-based cosmetics, and they had entered the antechamber and annexe, which was completely ransacked. The second group of thieves had access to the whole tomb and took a great deal of jewelry from the treasury, but they did not disturb the actual burial.

The antechamber was the main storage area of the tomb; it contained chairs and a golden throne, alabaster vases, wooden boxes, and also chariots. On the long west wall of the antechamber, "we found the whole of the wall-space occupied by the three animal-sided couches" (Carter 1923, 112): the first was lion-headed, the second cow-headed, and the third was half hippopotamus and half crocodile. By the north wall of the antechamber, two life-sized wooden statues protected the king's eternal rest in the chamber behind them.

The annexe was a storeroom at the south end of the antechamber, and the contents were oils and fats, unguents, wines, baskets of fruits, nuts, and seeds. It also included personal objects of the king: furniture, such as beds and stools; model boats and archery equipment. The doorway of the annexe was left unsealed after the robberies.

On February 17, 1923, Carter officially started the opening of the burial chamber, in which four gilded wooden shrines, a granite sarcophagus, and three mummiform coffins were found. The walls of the burial chamber are decorated with scenes of the Book of the Amduat ("What is in the Other World"), and a unique scene showing Ay carrying out the Opening of the Mouth ceremony on Tutankhamun's mummy. By doing so, Ay openly claimed to be the king's legal son and heir. The doors of the second shrine of gilded wood that contained the royal sarcophagi still had the necropolis seal, which was a sign that the pharaoh's mummy was still intact inside. A delicate linen pall with golden stars and wooden supports completely covered the second shrine. After opening the second anthropoid coffin of gilded wood, a third coffin entirely made of gold was found. Inside, the mummified king wearing a gold mask remained untouched since his burial more than 3,000 years before. The mummy, wrapped with linen bands, was covered with different kinds of jewelry: bracelets, collars, amulets, and rings.

Between the wall and the outermost shrine on the north, 11 oars were found, and, to the south, there was a wine jar. To the west, there were mainly funerary objects, such as bouquets of flowers and pottery jars, and, to the east, a sacred goose of Amun, a lamp with traces of oil, and a silver trumpet. To the east was the treasury. The door leading to the treasury was not sealed; however, the room was found relatively undisturbed compared to the annexe and antechamber. The treasury held Tutankhamun's internal organs removed during mummification and placed in a golden canopic shrine, guarded by four goddesses. Two embalmed female fetuses, the stillborn daughters of Tutankhamun and Ankhesenamen, were placed inside coffins in a wooden box. Other religious objects were also in the room, such as a shrine of Anubis in the form of a jackal for the king's protection, as well as little boxes with shabtis, figures that served as "substitutes" when the king was asked to carry out manual tasks in the afterlife.

Howard Carter documented with great accuracy each stage of emptying Tutankhamun's tomb, and it proceeded rather slowly, not finishing until 1939. This made possible the recovery and preservation of these exceptional objects and their context.

Maria Rosa Guasch-Jané

See also: Chariot; Cosmetics and Toiletries; Food; Furniture and Woodworking; Mummies, Royal; Music and Musical Instruments; Royal Regalia; Weapons and Armor; Wine

Further Reading

Carter, H. 1923. *The Tomb of Tut.ankh.Amen.* Reprinted (2003) by N. Reeves. *The Tomb of Tut.ankh.Amen.* Vol. 1, *Search, Discovery and Clearance of the Antechamber.* Bath, UK: Duckworth Egyptology.

Carter, H. 1927. *The Tomb of Tut.ankh.Amen.* Reprinted (2001) by N. Reeves. *The Tomb of Tut.ankh.Amen.* Vol. 2, *The Burial Chamber.* Bath, UK: Duckworth Egyptology.

Carter, H. 1933. *The Tomb of Tut.ankh.Amen.* Reprinted (2000) by N. Reeves. *The Tomb of Tut.ankh.Amen.* Vol. 3, *The Annexe and Treasury.* Bath, UK: Duckworth Egyptology.

Griffith Institute. 2017. "Tutankhamun Anatomy of an Excavation." http://www.griffith.ox.ac.uk/gri/carter.

Malek, J. 2009. *Tutankhamun: The Story of Egyptology's Greatest Discovery.* London: Carlton Books.

Reeves, N. 1990. *The Complete Tutankhamun: The King, the Tomb, the Royal Treasury.* London: Thames and Hudson.

Tomb Robbery

Tomb robbery in Egypt has a long history, for as long as there were tombs equipped with vast amounts of funerary goods, there were people willing to rob them for personal gain. The topic of tomb robbery, however, is more complex than groups of bandits raiding tombs in the night. First, there is both ancient and modern tomb robbery. The earliest tomb robbers were the ancient Egyptians themselves. This robbery continued into the modern era, with looters of all nationalities robbing Egypt of its antiquities. Second, there is a gradient of legality regarding tomb robbery. During ancient times, it was not unheard of for a pharaoh to reuse the tomb equipment of a predecessor or for a relative to take over the tomb and funerary objects of an ancestor. In these cases, the line is blurred between outright theft and sanctioned reuse of funerary materials. In the modern era, ongoing debate persists regarding the acquisition of certain funerary objects from ancient Egyptian tombs, particularly before strict antiquities laws developed in the 1970s.

Evidence for tomb robbery exists in tandem with the development of socially stratified burials containing grave goods. With the knowledge that people were burying the dead with funerary goods—and in particular luxury goods—tomb robbery developed into a means of gaining additional wealth, albeit illicit. There are burials at the site of Naga ed-Der dating to around 3500 BCE that have evidence they were plundered soon after internment. As tombs grew into larger marked graves, looters knew exactly where to dig to find the buried objects that accompanied the body. The remains of these robbers' holes are a common feature of many Egyptian tombs and archaeological sites.

There are many famous examples of tomb robbery throughout ancient Egypt's history. This form of outright theft was punished by ancient the Egyptian legal system, and many documents from the resulting court cases survive in the archaeological record. The majority of these documents date to the Ramesside Period (1295–1069 BCE) of the New Kingdom, and the most important records for studying tomb robbery are Papyrus Amherst, Papyrus Abbott, the Mayer Papyri, and Papyrus Ambras. Papyrus Amherst (see sidebar) details the interrogation and torture of eight suspected tomb robbers. After corroborating all confessions, the thieves were sentenced to death by means of impalement. However, the harsh Egyptian judicial system did not find all suspects guilty. The Mayer Papyrus finds five suspected robbers innocent of all crimes and details their exoneration and release.

The ancient Egyptians took several preventative measures to ensure their tombs would not be robbed. One of the main ways the Egyptians protected their tombs was by hiding the location of the burial. This protection is cited as one of the reasons the New Kingdom pharaohs utilized the Valley of the Kings as the royal necropolis. Their predecessors' burials were marked with monumental structures, such as pyramids, which made the location of the tomb extremely visible on the landscape. While this visibility was a mark of power, it was also a point of vulnerability, as tomb robbers could easily locate the burial and the funerary goods contained inside. The Valley of the Kings featured subterranean tombs, many of which did not have clearly marked entrances. This new method of royal burial made robbery a more challenging task. In addition, this grouping of tombs, hidden in a desert wadi, was easily patrolled by police forces whose presence increased the protection of the burials.

Similar methods of hiding the location of the burial were used by elites. Bodies were often cached in large groups in a single hidden tomb that could be guarded. During times of crisis, when instances of tomb robbery were prevalent, some portions of the Egyptian population resorted to burying their dead within temple precincts with large enclosure walls, which provided an added layer of protection for the burial. Of course, the Egyptians also tried to protect their tombs with the deterrent of punishment. As seen in the excerpt from Papyrus Amherst, there were harsh interrogation methods and a punishment of death for anyone convicted of tomb robbery.

In addition to outright theft, there was also sanctioned reuse of funerary equipment that occurred at all levels of Egyptian society. Textual evidence suggests that elite families tracked ownership of family tombs via inheritance patterns and ancestry. The purpose of this tomb ownership was to maintain control over the burial goods inside to be able to reuse these goods legally. This emphasis on tomb ownership occurred most often when Egypt was in political and economic crisis. When trade materials and goods were scarce, new funerary objects, such as coffins, could not be made. Thus, families often reused such objects by repainting older coffins or reinscribing names on funerary objects. The ancient Egyptians did not view this as outright theft, but rather the sanctioned reuse of funerary objects that were inherited by the descendants of the dead.

Even the king reused objects of his predecessors. For example, several Middle Kingdom (2055–1650 BCE) kings used stone blocks from the mortuary complex of King Khufu's (2589–2566 BCE) Great Pyramid of the Old Kingdom. Stone was not in short supply, nor were the laborers needed to cut the stone. Rather, these kings probably reused these blocks because they believe they rightfully owned the material of previous kings, and there was a justified continuity of divine kingship in being able to make a physical connection to the past. Many of King Tutankhamun's (1336–1327 BCE) funerary materials were reinscribed for him, having originally belonged to other Amarna Period rulers. Even entire royal tombs could be reused; for example, the tomb of Nineteenth Dynasty ruler Tawosret (1188–1186 BCE) was usurped by the Twentieth Dynasty king Setnakht (1186–1184 BCE).

In more modern times, tomb robbery persisted, with the goal of fueling a growing antiquities trade. One of the most famous instances of tomb robbery in the modern era involves the Abd al-Rassul brothers, who were part of a notorious family in the Sheikh Abd al-Qurna antiquities market community on the Theban West Bank. In the 1870s, these brothers flooded the antiquities market with funerary objects that, connected by style and date to one another, were, as a group, uniquely different from other antiquity market objects. This drew the attention of Egyptologists, who imprisoned one of the brothers until he revealed the location of the tomb. These actions resulted in the proper 1881 discovery of TT 320, commonly known as the Royal Cache, which contained more than 50 internments of kings, queens, royals, and elites from the Seventeenth to the Twenty-First Dynasties.

Tomb robbery both in Egypt and worldwide continues to the modern day. Illicit digging and the resulting black-market antiquities trade helps fuel many illegal activities. It is because of such violating acts that both national and international laws have been put in place to safeguard ancient sites of national heritage and stop the illegal trade of antiquities. The first milestone in world heritage protection was the 1972 UNESCO Convention, which prompted an international dialogue about antiquities law. Egypt most recently updated their Antiquities' Protection Law in 2010, stating in Article 35 that

> any discovered antiquities by either Egyptian or international excavation missions are the property of the Egyptian state. Penalties for illegally removing antiquities from Egypt are explained in following articles, with Article 42 stating that the punishment for antiquity theft is a maximum of seven years in prison and an extensive fine. With these and other internationally sanctioned laws, there is hope that tomb robbery and other illegal excavations will be prevented and many of stolen antiquities from Egypt will be returned to their country of origin.

Marissa Stevens

See also: Crime and Punishment; Law; Mummies, Royal; Valley of the Kings

Further Reading

Aldred, Cyril. 1979. "More Light on the Ramesside Tomb Robberies." In J. Ruffle, G. A. Gaballa, and K. A. Kitchen, eds. *Glimpses of Ancient Egypt*. Oxford: Aris & Phillips Ltd, pp. 92–99.

Bierbrier, M. L. 1993. *The Tomb-Builders of the Pharaohs*. Cairo: American University in Cairo Press.

Capart, J., A. H. Gardiner, and B. van de Walle. 1936. "New Light on the Ramesside Tomb-Robberies." *Journal of Egyptian Archaeology* 22, no. 2: 169–193.

"Law No. 117 of 1983 as Amended by Law No. 3 of 2010: Promulgating the Antiquities' Protection Law." *Official Gazette: Ministry of Culture Supreme Council of Antiquities* (February 14, 2010).

Peet, T. E. 1930. *The Great Tomb-Robberies of the Twentieth Egyptian Dynasty*. Oxford: Oxford University Press.

Primary Document—Confessions of Eight Tomb Robbers

Papyrus Amherst is a legal document dating to year 16 of Ramesses IX's reign (1126–1108 BCE) and details the confessions of eight men who robbed the tomb of Sobekemsaf II, a Seventeenth Dynasty (1580–1550 BCE) king. These eight men were tortured during their confession, which calls into question the authenticity of their claims. Yet, the detail of their accounts makes it likely that these eight men were a ring of professional tomb robbers. One man recounted the following:

> We took our copper tools and broke into the tomb of this king through its innermost chambers. . . . We opened [the king and queen's] sarcophagi and their coffins in which they were, and we found the great mummy of this king fashioned with a great quantity of amulets and jewelry upon his neck, and his crown of gold was still upon him. . . . We collected the gold we found on the great mummy of [the king]. . . . We collected all that we found upon [the queen] likewise, and set fire to their coffins. We took their furniture which we found together with them, containing articles of gold, silver, and bronze, and we divided them between ourselves. (Papyrus Amherst 2, 7–18)

After each of the eight men recounted a similar story, the papyrus states the following:

> Total of people who had been in the tomb of this [king]: eight men. Their examination was administered by beating with sticks, and there was performed contortion of their feet and hands. They told the same story. (Papyrus Amherst 3, 16–17)

Source: Translated by Marissa Stevens. Capart, J., A. H. Gardiner, and B. van de Walle. 1936. "New Light on the Ramesside Tomb-Robberies." *Journal of Egyptian Archaeology* 22, no. 2: 169–193.

Toiletries. *See* Cosmetics and Toiletries

Tombs, Private

The vast majority of ancient Egyptian burial places belonged to private individuals, that is, those who were not rulers or their immediate families. As such, they embraced the whole range of options, from simple graves to elaborate monumental structures. Where resources permitted, they comprised two distinct elements, an offering place open to the public, with a stela or statue to act as the conduit

False Door

A false door is a symbolic door in a private tomb or royal funerary temple through which the deceased could pass to partake of offerings. The ancient Egyptians believed that the dead had the same need for sustenance as the living, and so a priest would approach the false door each day, offer food and drink, and recite the offering formula, or the *hotep-di-nesu*, "offerings which the king gives," to feed the deceased. The same offering formula is also carved on the false door, and a scene referred to as the "table of bread scene" is usually represented in the top middle of the door, showing the deceased eating from an offering table. In this way, if the priest did not come, the formula and the scene could magically feed the deceased.

Lisa K. Sabbahy

between the world of the living and the dead, and a sealed burial place, the substructure.

During the Early Dynastic Period (3000–2686 BCE), the latter was at many sites initially a cutting in the bedrock or desert gravel roofed with wood; in others, it was wholly rock-cut, an arrangement that became more general as burial chambers came to be placed more deeply underground. Above this, a low bench-shaped structure of brick was erected, its sides adorned with deep ornamental niches. The niche at the southern end of the eastern facade (i.e., facing west, toward the abode of the dead) was the offering place, and by the end of the First Dynasty, about 2890 BCE, began to be equipped with a stela, representing the dead person in front of a table of offerings. This not only provided a concrete focus for those bringing offerings to the deceased but could also magically generate such offerings if no real ones were provided.

As time went by, the simple niche and stela evolved into a room built into the body of the mastaba, a chapel with the stela at the rear. The stela itself also developed into a "false door," the original core image being surrounded by stylized paneling, making more concrete its role as a portal between the worlds. The chapel itself came to be adorned with further depictions of offerings, their presentation to the dead, and also scenes of the production of food and drink that made up the principal offerings. Later on, the decorative repertoire was enlarged to include scenes of recreation and aspects of the dead person's career. As the Old Kingdom (2686–2160 BCE) progressed, in more wealthy tombs, the chapel was enlarged by the addition of further rooms, with the false door in the innermost directed toward the west. In some Sixth Dynasty tombs (2345–2181 BCE), the chapel had expanded into a dozen or more rooms, some pillared and of truly monumental proportions. The Old Kingdom also saw the addition of closed rooms, known as "serdabs," linked to the main chapel only by narrow slits, within which were placed statues of the deceased, apparently as additional conduits between the worlds.

The mastaba had generally lost its paneling by the beginning of the Old Kingdom, and from the Fourth Dynasty, beginning 2613 BCE, onward, they began to also be built in stone; indeed, at some sites (e.g., the Fraser Tombs near Tihna), they were actually carved from the living rock. Also during the Fourth Dynasty, the first examples are found of rock-cut tomb chapels, where the mastaba was omitted and the chapel cut into a rock face. Such tombs were generally constructed at sites, particularly in Upper Egypt, where the topography was not suitable for the construction of conventional mastabas.

Another type of tomb was to be found in the Nile Delta, where conditions were very different from the valley. Here, rock, or even desert gravel, was deeply buried under alluvial layers, meaning that from the earliest times, tomb substructures had to be built from brick, or on occasion stone, in shallow cuttings in the surface of sandbanks that lay above the level of the Nile inundation. The forms of the superstructures of such sepulchers are obscure, but they are likely to have been some form of mastaba, at least until the New Kingdom, beginning in 1550 BCE.

Where resources did not permit a mastaba or rock-cut tomb chapel, a false door might be simply erected on the desert surface or carved into a convenient stone surface adjacent to the substructure. During the Second and Third Dynasties (2890–2613 BCE), the latter was generally approached by a stairway, but during the Fourth Dynasty, the stairway was replaced in mastabas by a vertical shaft, which was usually entered from the roof of the mastaba, cutting through its core down into the bedrock. Rock-cut tomb chapels generally retained a stairway or sloping passage approach to the substructure. The underground burial installation itself was normally a single undecorated room, sometimes with a protective portcullis slab, or slabs, sealing the access from the approach shaft or corridor. From the end of the Fifth Dynasty (ca. 2345 BCE), some burial chambers began to be decorated with depictions of offerings, although most remained plain.

The basic pattern of mastabas and rock-cut tomb chapels continued into the Middle Kingdom (2055–1650 BCE), although in some cases there was a significant elaboration of substructures to improve security, something also found in contemporary royal tombs. Decoration of offering places continued to follow the patterns established during the Old Kingdom, while, although the vast majority of substructures remained undecorated, the repertoire was expanded to embrace the formerly royal Pyramid Texts.

Rock-cut tomb chapels of the early New Kingdom continued to follow earlier practice as far as decoration was concerned, with the principal addition of vignettes, such as representations of the funeral and the posthumous pilgrimage to Abydos. However, at Thebes, a new basic floor plan was introduced, with a broad but shallow forehall, beyond which lay a narrow but deep inner room, at the end of which lay the false door or the statue that had begun to appear as a substitute focus for offerings during the Middle Kingdom. This basic plan could be expanded or elaborated by the addition of columns to a deepened forehall or widened inner room as well as by inserting additional rooms along the main axis. Outside Thebes, rock-cut tomb chapels more often centered on rectangular halls, with a simpler overall plan.

During the earlier part of the Eighteenth Dynasty, beginning in 1550 BCE, access to the substructure in such tombs was normally via a vertical shaft in the forecourt of a rock-cut tomb chapel, but from the middle of the dynasty, a sloping passage or stairway started to be used instead, which soon started to be placed at

Mastaba

A mastaba in Arabic is a bench, and it is used to describe the superstructure of elite tombs built in the Old and Middle Kingdoms, which have a rectangular shape. The mastaba had to fulfill two specific functions: protect the body and provide a cult place for the deceased. A vertical shaft went down from inside the mastaba to a burial chamber just large enough for the sarcophagus and accompanying objects. This shaft was filled up with rubble and closed after the burial. The cult for the deceased focused on the false door with an offering table out in front. The false door, a stylized door carved in stone, was provided for the soul, or *ka,* to pass through and receive offerings every day.

The scenes that were carved on the walls of the rooms inside the mastaba fall roughly into two groups: scenes of daily life on the estate of the deceased and scenes of offerings for the cult of the deceased. Because the agricultural pursuits on the estate provided the offerings for the cult, the two types of scenes are naturally interrelated.

Lisa K. Sabbahy

the southern end of the forehall of the chapel. Substructures also began to be made more elaborate, with the addition of vestibules and pillared halls in some of the most elaborate examples. However, decoration remained rare, and where it was found was usually based on the recently developed Book of the Dead, which replaced earlier schemes.

The mastaba tomb disappeared almost entirely during the New Kingdom and was replaced by the "temple tomb," whose layout closely resembled a contemporary cult temple, with the most elaborate having one or more pylons fronting what could be multiple courtyards before culminating in a built offering place. The latter often had a small pyramid built on top of or behind it. Such pyramids were also sometimes built on the slope above the entrances of rock-cut tomb chapels from the beginning of the New Kingdom, coinciding with their no longer being employed as part of royal tombs. They would continue to be part of private tombs to the end of the New Kingdom, and in some cases they incorporated a niche containing a stela dedicated to the sun.

In some small private tombs, in particular those built for members of the tomb-builders' community at Deir el-Medina, the actual chapel, with a vaulted ceiling, was built into the core of the brick-built pyramid, while some larger rock-cut tomb chapels had a "secondary" chapel inserted into their pyramids.

The Amarna Period in the later Eighteenth Dynasty saw major changes in private tomb decoration. In keeping with the period's religious revolution, all the decorative motifs developed since the Old Kingdom were abolished in favor of a scheme built around the activities of the royal family. The tomb owner was largely reduced to a subsidiary figure in scenes focused on the royal family, the only exceptions being where he might be shown at the entrance to the chapel, adoring the sun, or on occasion in the one icon carried over from the traditional scheme, that of the deceased's funeral.

When orthodoxy was restored during the reign of Tutankhamun (1336–1327 BCE), there was, curiously, no return to the ancient prerevolutionary "core"

Burial chamber of the family tomb of the workman Sennedjem, at Deir el-Medina on the West Bank of Thebes. These workmen cut and painted the royal tombs in the Valley of the Kings, and they themselves had beautiful tombs. Sennedjem and his wife are shown adoring the gods of the underworld, while on the right is the god Osiris. (DeAgostini/Getty Images)

decorative scheme focusing on the production of offerings in private tombs. Instead, with the exception of those relating to the career and funeral of the deceased, a wholly new approach was adopted built around mythological icons, particularly taken from the Book of the Dead, a composition formerly restricted to the substructure. This intrusion of the underworld into the offering place reversed its previous strict exclusion from this part of the tomb and marked a beginning of an erosion of various other distinctions between parts of the private tomb, and also between royal and private tombs, that would be all but complete by the end of the Third Intermediate Period in 664 BCE.

This latter breakdown was seen in the appearance of motifs previously restricted to New Kingdom royal tombs in the substructures of the rock-cut tomb chapels of certain highly placed individuals at Thebes. These substructures, whether decorated or undecorated, in some cases became exceptionally large, those of the first half of the Nineteenth Dynasty, beginning in 1295 BCE, having the curious feature of a 360-degree spiral descent between the entrance to the substructure and the burial chamber itself. At the other end of the scale, the artisans' tombs at Deir el-Medina had small vaulted burial chambers that were richly decorated with elements primarily from the Book of the Dead but executed in a way heavily influenced by royal tombs—not a surprising occurrence, given that the same people were decorating both groups of sepulchers.

As the condition of Egypt declined during the Twentieth Dynasty (1186–1069 BCE), the number of monumental private tombs known also reduces significantly, and by the beginning of the Twenty-First Dynasty in 1069 BCE, the construction of them seems to have ceased almost entirely. A few reused blocks attest to some decorated tombs at Tanis, the new northern capital, but at Thebes, just one rock-cut tomb chapel can be securely dated to the dynasty. The vast majority of burials seem to have been made in simple undecorated burial chambers accessed by shafts or sloping passages and often reused from earlier periods. Nothing is known of any associated offering places, and a fundamental shift in funerary culture is indicated by the fact that many of the coffins of the period were not only reworkings of coffins made in earlier periods but were also reused within the dynasty, apparently sometimes in successive generations.

The handful of small decorated offering places known from the Twenty-Second Dynasty (945–715 BCE) at Thebes suggest some revival in funerary culture at this time, which is also indicated by a comprehensive revision of the design of coffins at the same time and a cessation of the endemic reuse of such material. However, the troubles of the late ninth and early eighth centuries were certainly not conducive to any revival of monumentality.

It was the reunification of Egypt under the Twenty-Fifth Dynasty (747–656 BCE) that permitted monumental tombs to be built by the highest of the private elite. On the other hand, midranking individuals seem generally buried in unmarked family vaults, a number of Theban examples of which were cut under the floors of the ancient memorial temple of Hatshepsut at Deir el-Bahari; others reused parts of New Kingdom tomb chapels, in particular their substructures.

In contrast, however, certain senior officials were able to construct vast partly rock-cut temple tombs on the Asasif at Thebes, with the offering places and expansive substructures decorated with an eclectic mix of texts, ranging from the Pyramid Texts to the Book of the Dead and the Books of the Underworld originally composed for the royal tombs of the New Kingdom. Such tombs continued through the Twenty-Sixth Dynasty (664–525 BCE), examples also being found in the Memphite necropolis. The latter also hosted a new form of shaft tomb, with the burial protected by an ingenious use of sand to both close sarcophagi and render the tomb all but impervious to robbers. Such tombs seem generally to have had minimal superstructures, essentially a surrounding wall, with one or more stelae as foci for offerings.

Monumental private tombs disappear from the record following the Persian takeover in 525 BCE, with the final known examples being known from the end of the Late Period and beginning of the Ptolemaic in 332 BCE. At Sakkara, these comprise small stone-built chapels standing above shafts leading to the burial chamber.

Aidan Dodson

See also: Afterlife; Book of the Dead; Pyramid Texts

Further Reading

Arnold, Dieter. 2008. *Middle Kingdom Tomb Architecture at Lisht*. New York: Metropolitan Museum of Art.

Clark, Reg. 2016. *Tomb Security in Ancient Egypt from the Predynastic to the Pyramid Age*. Oxford: Archaeopress.

Dodson, Aidan, and Salima Ikram. 2008. *The Tomb in Ancient Egypt: Royal and Private Sepulchres from the Early Dynastic Period to the Romans*. London and New York: Thames & Hudson.

Kanawati, Naguib. 2001. *The Tomb and Beyond: Burial Customs of Egyptian Officials*. Warminster, UK: Aris & Phillips.

Manniche, Lise. 1988. *City of the Dead*. London: British Museum Press.

Manniche, Lise. 1988. *The Tombs of the Nobles at Luxor*. Cairo: American University in Cairo Press.

Martin, Geoffrey T. 1991. *The Hidden Tombs of Memphis: New Discoveries from the Time of Tutankhamun and Ramesses the Great*. London: Thames and Hudson.

Reisner, G. A. 1936. *The Development of Egyptian Tomb Down to the Accession of Cheops*. Cambridge, MA: Harvard University Press.

Roeten, Leo 2016. *Chronological Developments in the Old Kingdom Tombs in the Necropoleis of Giza, Saqqara and Abusir: Toward an Economic Decline during the Early Dynastic Period and the Old Kingdom*. Oxford: Archaeopress.

Strudwick, Nigel, and John H. Taylor, eds. 2003. *The Theban Necropolis: Past, Present and Future*. London: British Museum Press.

Swinton, Joyce. 2014. *Dating the Tombs of the Egyptian Old Kingdom*. Oxford: Archaeopress.

Transportation

The impressive monuments of ancient Egypt would not have been possible without its people's mastery of various methods of transportation. Gathering and transporting the workforce and resources for the construction of the Great Pyramid of King Khufu (2589–2566 BCE) in the Fourth Dynasty, for example, would have required highly sophisticated and integrated land and water networks of travel and transportation.

Egypt has a unique geography consisting of a narrow corridor of habitable land along the Nile valley, bordered on either side by inhospitable deserts. Settlements were thus all located along a single river, clearing the way for easy contact, both in terms of cultural exchange as well as warfare. The cultural homogeneity achieved during the Naqada II/Gerzean Period, about 3500–3200 BCE, ultimately resulting in the unification of Upper and Lower Egypt into history's first nation-state around 3000 BCE, soon after the earliest attestations of images of boats with sails, can scarcely be ascribed to mere chance. The central administration could thereafter easily exert its influence by simply moving up and down the Nile. Fluvial transportation also had the added benefits of protection from robbery and smoother passage than movement on land with its inherent difficulties, such as rough terrain or Egypt's intricate system of irrigation canals and basins.

Boats were made of either wood or papyrus. It was quickly realized that tightly tying bundles of papyrus plants together formed a floating platform that could be used to catch more fish farther from the shore, and that enabled short-distance transportation. Larger vessels were made of wood, mostly cedar imported from the Levant due to the rarity of native Egyptian wood suitable for construction. Already from the Old Kingdom (2686–2160 BCE), wooden ships appear in both textual and representational sources. Furthermore, actual examples have survived due to Egypt's ideal climate for the preservation of archaeological material. The most famous is King Khufu's boat, one of two discovered buried in a disassembled state in separate pits on the south side of his pyramid. One was reconstructed and is currently in the Solar Boat Museum next to his tomb. This impressive cedar ship, 43 meters long, could certainly have sailed and was probably used to transport the king's mummy and burial goods to his final resting place.

Ships were used for long-distance transport of all manner of cargo, most notably stone and grain. Moderate quantities of stone blocks could be hauled from quarries to a construction site on any cargo ship. However, the transportation of large cargoes, such as obelisks, had to be undertaken with ships built specifically for this purpose. A unique relief dating to the reign of Hatshepsut (1473–1458 BCE) in her temple in Deir el-Bahari in Thebes (modern Luxor) depicts the transportation of two obelisks to Karnak temple in Thebes on board a massive ship that would have been about 60 meters long.

Ships were employed for military purposes as well. The ornate ivory handle of the flint Gebel el-Arak knife, dated to the Naqada II/Gerzean Period, depicts war scenes in which ships figure prominently. Unlike cargo ships, which relied on sails for locomotion, warships, which required reliable speed, were propelled with oars or paddles, as were the ceremonial/official vessels of the king and his dignitaries. The most famous depiction of watercraft being used for war are Ramses III's (1184–1153 BCE) reliefs of his naval battle with the Sea Peoples in his temple in Medinet Habu in Thebes.

Given that water transportation was the fastest way to travel long distances, kings used this method to travel for administrative and religious purposes. In the Early Dynastic Period (3000–2686 BCE), for example, the king went "Following of Horus," when he and the leading figures of his administration traveled the length of the land every two years, presumably amid much pomp, to make visible the power of central government at a time when Egypt had only recently become a nation-state. These processions were also occasions on which the country's economic wealth was documented. In the New Kingdom (1550–1069 BCE), kings attended the annual Opet festival in honor of Amun in Thebes, the leading deity at the time. The king's travels along the length of the nation were mirrored in religious belief in the sun god's daily celestial journey in his solar barque.

Travel was not restricted to just the Nile. Expeditions were certainly being sent to a place called Punt via the Red Sea as early as the Old Kingdom. The most famous was that of Hatshepsut, depicted on the walls of her temple in Deir el-Bahari. Punt was probably located on the eastern coast of modern Sudan and Eritrea, and expeditions were sent there to obtain exotic goods like frankincense, ebony, and ivory. There was no canal linking the Nile with the Red Sea at the time, and its western coast was not suitable for permanent settlement. Ships were therefore constructed in the city of Coptos in Upper Egypt, which was connected to the Red Sea through a desert valley called the Wadi Hammamat. Then they were dismantled and transported to sites on the coast that served as points of departure for expeditions by sea, where they were reassembled. No nails were used in ship construction; rather, planks were sewn together with rope or attached to each other with joints. Mersa/Wadi Gawasis is one such site, used mostly in the Twelfth Dynasty (1985–1773 BCE) of the Middle Kingdom, and it has revealed a wealth of information on Egyptian seafaring expeditions. Shrines, partially made of limestone anchors, have been discovered, along with cargo boxes that would have contained goods brought from Punt; numerous stelae; and around 30 coils of rope, each 20–30 meters long, that were stored in a manmade cave.

The donkey was the main mode of transporting cargo on land. Camels were not introduced, or at least domesticated, in Egypt until the first millennium BCE. The transportation of ship parts, trade with the oases, and land-based mining or quarrying expeditions to the desert were undertaken with donkey caravans. This was the case with Harkhuf's exploratory expeditions in Nubia during the reign of Pepi II (2278–2184 BCE) in the Sixth Dynasty. Donkeys were also used to transport agricultural produce (as well as other products, such as salt and natron, as is the case in the Middle Kingdom *Tale of the Eloquent Peasant*) from fields to granaries near embarkation points, whence they would be collected by state officials and transported by boat on the Nile.

While donkeys could be used to transport relatively light loads of stone, these were generally moved with sledges dragged by oxen or people. A scene painted in the tomb of a Middle Kingdom official named Djehutyhotep, in Deir el-Bersha in Middle Egypt, depicts a colossal royal statue being transported on a sledge dragged by a large number of workers. Although the wheel was known as early as the Old Kingdom, it was not used extensively: the land was unsuitable, and cart axles could break under the load of heavy weights. Due to the suitability of the donkey and the sledge to their respective tasks, there was simply no need for wheeled vehicles. Depictions of oxcarts exist, but they are rare; such wheeled vehicles became more common in the Ptolemaic-Roman Period (332 BCE–495 CE).

Palanquins were used by royalty and the elite, but they were quickly replaced by the horse-drawn chariot after its introduction at the end of the Second Intermediate Period (1650–1550 BCE). Egyptian chariots were sophisticated marvels of engineering. This is especially apparent in the construction of their wheels: they had to be light to allow for greater speed and both flexible and hard to withstand shock while traveling on unprepared ground, as situation would have often obtained. To this end, wheels were of a composite construction, consisting of several types of wood glued together and chosen for their natural qualities. Chariots revolutionized warfare in the ancient Near East; they acted as elevated mobile firing platforms, allowed commanders to travel quickly and keep contact with their subordinates on the battlefield, and were effective against a fleeing or disorganized army.

Rough terrain, which would have been damaging to wheels, kept chariots from being used for long-distance travel. Paved roads are poorly attested but not absent from the archaeological record. Many were made to facilitate stone transportation for construction projects. One paved road, for example, linked the Fifth Dynasty pyramids at Abusir with quarries almost a mile away.

Arto Belekdanian

See also: Chariot; Nile River; Punt; Ships and Shipping; Sledge

Further Reading

Adams, Colin. 2007. *Land Transport in Roman Egypt.* Oxford: Oxford University Press.

Bard, Kathryn A., and Rodolfo Fattovich. 2011. "The Middle Kingdom Red Sea Harbor at Mersa/Wadi Gawasis." *Journal of the American Research Center in Egypt* 47: 105–129.

Fabre, David. 2004. *Seafaring in Ancient Egypt.* London: Periplus.

Jones, Dilwyn. 1995. *Boats. Egyptian Bookshelf.* London: British Museum Press.

Köpp, Heidi. 2016. "Wagons and Carts and Their Significance in Ancient Egypt." *Journal of Ancient Egyptian Interconnections* 9: 14–58.

Partridge, Robert. 1996. *Transport in Ancient Egypt.* London: Rubicon.

Vinson, Steve. 1994. *Egyptian Boats and Ships.* Princes Risborough, UK: Shire Publications.

Treaties. See **Foreign Relations and Treaties**

Tutankhamun, King of Egypt. See **Tomb of Tutankhamun**

U

Unification of Egypt. *See* State Formation

Upper Egypt

Ancient Egypt was divided into two main regions, namely, Upper Egypt, the Nile valley, in the south, and Lower Egypt, the delta of the river, in the north. This duality was present in the royal title "King of Upper and Lower Egypt," or "He of the Sut-Plant and the Bee." The modern terminology *upper* and *lower* derives from the flow of the Nile from the highlands of East Africa northward to the Mediterranean Sea.

GEOGRAPHY, DIVISIONS, AND RESOURCES

Upper Egypt is a narrow, fertile strip of a land along the Nile River surrounded by deserts and mountains. It extends between the First Cataract in the south, south of the modern city of Aswan, to el-Ayyat, about the latitude of the pyramid of Lisht, in the north. The width of the river valley variates from 1.5 to 25 kilometers. The modern term "Middle Egypt" covers the area from el-Ayyat to Sohag. An important feature of Middle Egypt is the Bahr Yussef, in Arabic, called "the canal of Joseph," which was possibly inaugurated in the Middle Kingdom (2055–1650 BCE). It is a canal parallel to the Nile that connects the river with the Fayum lake.

The ancient Egyptian name of Upper Egypt was *Ta-Shemaw*, literally "the Land of Reeds." The royal symbol of Upper Egypt was the *hedjet*, the White Crown of Upper Egypt. The fertile part of the Nile valley was called *Kemet*, the "Black Land," referring to the dark color of the fertile soil, and the Eastern and Western Deserts were known as *Deshret*, the "Red Land."

Upper Egypt was traditionally divided into 21 administrative units termed "nomes" in Egyptological literature, from the Greek word meaning a district, although their number and borders varied in different periods. The first certain attestation of nomes comes from the Fifth Dynasty (2494–2345 BCE). In the Old Kingdom, nomes in the south were grouped together to form bigger administrative entities, but this form of the organization is poorly known. The area from Elephantine in the south to present-day Nag Hammadi was called *Hen-Nekhen*, which indicated the seven southernmost nomes of Upper Egypt. The sector between Elephantine and Abydos was designated "the Head of the South" (*Tep-Resi*), which may reflect some kind of administrative entity. During Ptolemaic times (332–30 BCE), there was reform of the administrative divisions, which changed the number and the borders of nomes.

Upper Egypt has important natural resources—various stones and minerals—especially in the Eastern Desert. Basalt was quarried near Coptos, and gold came from the Eastern Desert at the latitude of Kom Ombo and El Kab. The landscape of the northern part of Upper Egypt is dominated by limestone hills, but from about Esna to the south, sandstone is the dominant rock. The important sandstone quarries were located at Gebel el-Silsila. Granite occurs in the area of Aswan and makes up the rocks of the First Cataract.

HISTORY

As a region isolated by deserts to the east and west, Upper Egypt developed its own individual culture from the time of the Predynastic Period (5300–3000 BCE). The inhabitants were culturally distinct from the inhabitants of Lower Egypt to the north and Nubia to the south. After Egypt was united, the early kings chose the city of Memphis as the capital of the whole of Egypt, about 3000 BCE. The post of "Governor of Upper Egypt" was created, perhaps as early as the Fifth Dynasty (2494–2345 BCE), but by the end of the Sixth Dynasty, the significance of title had waned.

During the First Intermediate Period (2160–2055 BCE), nomarchs gained more independence, and some of them established local dynasties and expanded their territories. Upper Egypt was divided into two kingdoms at the end of this period. The northern kingdom was ruled by a dynasty based at the city of Heracleopolis. In the south, the local Eleventh Dynasty (2055–1985 BCE) emerged at Thebes and ultimately gained control over the whole country, thus ending the First Intermediate Period. Thebes had not been an important city before the First Intermediate Period, so this new dynasty changed the situation. But the following Twelfth Dynasty moved the royal residence north to Itja-tawy, near the pyramid site of Lisht.

During the Second Intermediate Period (1650–1550 BCE), Egypt was again divided, this time between the Hyksos in the north and another dynasty that emerged in Thebes. A little-known group of kings emerged in Thinite nome at that time as well. The new Theban Seventeenth Dynasty (1580–1550 BCE) launched wars against the Hyksos, which were successfully concluded by the first ruler of the Eighteenth Dynasty, which began in 1550 BCE. Thebes became the capital of the newly unified Egypt, and from that time onward, the glory of Thebes grew, as did that of its chief god, Amun. Memphis was still very important as the administrative center and traditional capital, but Thebes became the religious center of the empire.

Pharaohs of the Nineteenth and Twentieth Dynasties (1295–1069 BCE) were spending more time in the north of the country, but Thebes remained the administrative center of the south, and the High Priests of Amun played an important political role. The dynasty of priest-kings at Thebes ruled most of Upper Egypt. The Third Intermediate Period (1069–664 BCE), as well as the Late Period (664–332 BCE), was a time of unrest, including military invasion by the Assyrians and the sacking of Thebes in 664 BCE. Revolts broke out in late Ptolemaic times in

Thebes, which were put down by the kings in Alexandria. A Roman garrison was installed in Thebes after the Roman conquest of Egypt.

Wojciech Ejsmond

See also: Lower Egypt; Nile River; Nomes and Provincial Administration

Further Reading

Baines, John, and Málek Jaromír. 2005. *Atlas of Ancient Egypt*. Cairo: American University in Cairo Press.

Gardiner, Alan. 1947. *Ancient Egyptian Onomastica*. Oxford: Oxford University Press.

Jeffreys, David. 2007. "The Nile Valley." In T. Wilkinson, ed. *The Egyptian World*. Abingdon, UK: Routledge, pp. 7–14.

Porter, Bertha, and Rosalind Moss. 1991–2004. *The Topographical Bibliography of Ancient Egyptian Hieroglyphic Texts, Statues, Reliefs and Paintings*. Vols. 1–3 & 6. Oxford: Griffith Institute.

Wilkinson, Toby. 2010. *The Rise and Fall of Ancient Egypt*. London: Bloomsbury.

V

Valley of the Kings

Down to the beginning of the Eighteenth Dynasty, around 1550 BCE, kings' burial chambers usually lay close to the monumental public element of the burial complex, the mortuary temple, often with an adjoining pyramid. However, the founder of the Eighteenth Dynasty, King Ahmose I, placed his burial chamber a kilometer to the west of his mortuary temple and pyramid at Abydos, inaugurating a spatial separation of offering place from the burial itself that would endure until the beginning of the Third Intermediate Period, about 1069 BCE.

Ahmose I's successor, Amenhotep I (1525–1504), moved the royal mortuary complex back to Thebes, placing his tomb in a wadi behind Dra Abu'l-Naga, which had been the royal necropolis during the Seventeenth Dynasty (1580–1550 BCE). However, his successor, Thutmose I (1504–1492 BCE), had his cut in a hitherto virgin complex of wadis now known as the Valley of the Kings. They together occupy an area of over three and a half square miles and are grouped into the "Kings' Valley" (with one square mile occupied by tombs) and the "West Valley," which is much smaller. A pyramidal peak, el-Qurn, dominates the valley, and may have been regarded as a substitute pyramid.

With the exception of a short break late in the Eighteenth Dynasty, this was to be the location of all kings' burial chambers until the end of the Twentieth Dynasty in 1069 BCE. The associated offering places, of a kind dubbed today "memorial temples," were placed along an almost two-mile stretch on the edge of the cultivated land to the east of the valley. Some queens, royal children, and high officials were also buried in the valley, either in shaft tombs or modestly sized corridor tombs. The officials' interments had associated offering places in the form of tomb chapels on the Sheikh Abd el-Qurna and other hills to the east, overlooking the cultivated land.

The kings' switch from earlier forms of tomb seems likely to have been prompted by a desire for increased security, as the earliest tombs in the valley were so placed as to allow their locations to be obliterated by the flash floods that periodically penetrate it, depositing debris in the process. This is certainly the case with what seems to have been the first tomb constructed in the valley, KV 20. This comprises a sinuous set of corridors leading to two large chambers, the innermost one, lined with limestone blocks, constructed by the female king Hatshepsut (1473–1458 BCE). However, it seems likely that the tomb was originally cut for Thutmose I and taken over and extended by his daughter.

Hatshepsut's chamber was decorated with the Book of Amduat, the first of a series of Books of the Underworld that recounted the sun god's nocturnal voyage through the netherworld, in which the dead participated and shared in the sun's rebirth at sunrise. This would be the key motif found in kings' tombs beyond the end of the New Kingdom, although various additional "Books" would be developed over time to supplement and partly replace the Amduat. Another important decorative work is the Litany of Ra, first found in the tomb of Thutmose III (1479–1425 BCE) (KV 34).

The latter was the first tomb in the valley for which there is no doubt as to its original author (questions remain over the burial place of Thutmose II (1492–1479 BCE), to whom KV 42 is sometimes attributed). KV 34 featured an oval burial chamber, recalling the shape of the cartouche that enclosed hieroglyphically written royal names, preceded by an antechamber, a deep pit (probably both a conceptual and actual protective feature), and then a pair of corridors and stairways leading from the surface. The tomb's plan turned through a right angle at the midpoint, a feature to be found in all kings' tombs down to the reign of Amenhotep III (1390–1352 BCE). The Amduat covered the walls of the burial chamber, and an illustrated version, the Litany, adorned the antechamber.

Amenhotep II (1427–1400) (KV 35) introduced some changes, omitting the Litany of Ra, adding representations of the king in the company of the gods, and recasting the shape of the burial chamber, which was henceforth rectangular, with six pillars, and a sunken crypt at the far end to hold the sarcophagus. This basic scheme continued to the reign of Amenhotep III (WV 22), by which time an additional right-angled turn had been incorporated, plus additional chambers for his wives—a feature unique to his tomb as far as the Valley of the Kings is concerned. This was also the first tomb to be cut in the West Valley, a move perhaps prompted by the exhaustion of the kinds of tomb sites hitherto used for royal tombs, and possibly by the increasing number of nonkingly individuals now being buried in the East Valley. These included the king's parents-in-law, Yuya and Tjuiu (KV 46).

Under Akhenaten (1352–1336 BCE), the royal necropolis was moved to Tell el-Amarna, but it returned to the Valley of the Kings under Tutankhamun (KV 62), who was interred in what seems to have been cut as a tomb for nobility or minor royalty and enlarged and decorated on the king's premature death. Restricted to the small burial chamber, the decoration included motifs not otherwise found in a burial chamber (royal or private), coupled with the king and gods, and the first hour of the Amduat, apparently standing for the whole.

A similar, but different, mix of traditional and nontraditional motifs were also placed on the walls of the burial chamber of Ay (1327–1323 BCE) in WV 23, the last tomb to be cut in the West Valley. In contrast to earlier tombs, it had no right-angled turn in its axis: an essentially straight axis would be standard in all later tombs. The plan of the Ay's tomb was truncated, presumably because of his short reign, but the tomb of Horemheb (1323–1295 BCE) (KV 57) was cut to its full extent, showing a plan broadly similar to earlier tombs, except for a straight axis. A major change, however, was in the mode of decoration, which was now in painted raised relief rather than simply painted on plaster, as had previously been the case. The decorative scheme was also new, the burial chamber being adorned with a new composition, the Book of Gates, the Amduat being omitted altogether; the rest of the decoration was made up of depictions of the king and the gods.

The tomb of Seti I (1294–1279 BCE; KV 17) marked a further advance in the development of the royal tomb, as rather than having decorated chambers linked by plain corridors, all walls and ceilings of his sepulcher were decorated from the outer doorway onward. The Litany and Amduat were now reinstated and supplemented by elements from the Book of the Dead alongside the gates and usual depictions of the king and gods. This conception was carried over into the tomb of Ramses II (1294–1279 BCE; KV 7) but with some architectural changes, most importantly changing the form of the burial chamber, which henceforth would have eight pillars, with the crypt in the center of the chamber, rather than at the far end.

The basic tomb layout seen in KV 7 formed the prototype for all later kings' tombs in the valley, although every tomb possessed some unique features, with no two having the same combination of decorative elements. The latter included the introduction of yet more Books of the Underworld, including the Books of the Earth and of Caverns. A number of tombs also had truncated plans caused by the king's premature death or other circumstances, for example, civil unrest and banditry. Other issues included subterranean collisions, most notably that between KV 11, being cut for Twentieth Dynasty founder Sethnakht (1186–1184 BCE), and the late Nineteenth Dynasty rebel king Amenmeses (1203–1200? BCE; KV 10). This led to KV 11 being temporarily abandoned and Sethnakht being buried in KV 14, intended for the female king Tawosret (1188–1186 BCE). The latter had been begun when she was the wife of Seti II as one of the small number of dedicated queens' tombs in the Valley of the Kings.

From the reign of Seti II (1200–1194 BCE) onward, the angle of descent of the tombs became increasingly shallow, and it appears that attempts to conceal the entrance after the burial were dropped in favor of reliance on police patrols. Indeed, entrances became increasingly large, reflecting corresponding expansions of the underground elements. The last two kings' tombs begun in the valley were never occupied by their owners, that of Ramses X (1180–1099 BCE) (KV 18) being far from completion and that of Ramses XI (1099–1069 BCE) (KV 4) being structurally almost complete but with the decoration hardly begun; neither showed any evidence of a royal burial.

The tombs in the valley were subject to robbery from at least the latter part of the Eighteenth Dynasty onward, but this became endemic during the latter part of the Twentieth Dynasty. As a result, many mummies required restoration and were gradually concentrated in a smaller number of tombs for greater security. Eventually, all those that survived, save those secreted in the tomb of Amenhotep II, were removed from the valley altogether and, eventually, placed together in what seems to have originally been the tomb of Ahmes-Nefertiry, the wife of Ahmose I, near Deir el-Bahari (TT 320), early in the Twenty-Second Dynasty, beginning in 945 BCE.

Subsequently, a number of tombs were reused for the burial of female members of the clergy of Amun during the Twenty-Second Dynasty, some of which then survived intact until modern times, including KV 64, found in 2012. By the early centuries CE, only a few tombs remained visible, some of these being frequented by Coptic monks, who left extensive texts in, for example, KV 2 (Ramses IV, 1153–1147 BCE).

Aidan Dodson

See also: Deir el-Medina; Funerary Books, Royal; Mummies, Royal

Further Reading

Dodson, A. 2016. *The Royal Tombs of Ancient Egypt*. Barnsley, PA: Pen and Sword.

Hornung, E. 1990. *The Valley of the Kings: Horizon of Eternity*. New York: Timken.

Reeves, N., and R. H. Wilkinson. 1990. *The Complete Valley of the Kings*. London and New York: Thames and Hudson.

Weeks, K., ed. 2002. *The Valley of the Kings*. Vercelli: White Star.

Wilkinson, Richard H., and Kent Weeks, eds. 2016. *The Oxford Handbook of the Valley of the Kings*. Oxford and New York: Oxford University Press.

Valley of the Queens

Throughout Egyptian history, it was generally the practice to bury members of the royal family in separate structures from kings; joint monuments for kings and queens, as found in many cultures, were quite rare and at a few specific points in time. These included the reign of Amenemhat III (1831–1786 BCE) in the Twelfth Dynasty; the Seventeenth Dynasty (1580–1550 BCE); the late Eighteenth Dynasty, roughly 1350 BCE; and the Third Intermediate Period (1069–664 BCE). During the Old and Middle Kingdoms, royal family tombs were often placed within or just outside the enclosures of kings' pyramids, and in the cases of most queens, and some princesses, surmounted by pyramids.

However, following the beginning of the Eighteenth Dynasty, which started in 1550 BCE, kings abandoned pyramids, and their spouses followed suit. In addition, kings' tombs began to be separated from their offering places by a significant distance, soon becoming concentrated in the Valley of the Kings. In parallel with this, the tombs members of the royal family also began to be placed in remote locations. Some were placed alongside those of kings in the Valley of the Kings, but a considerable number were placed in and among the numerous wadis of the southern part of the Theban necropolis. While some particularly remote ones were employed, for example, in the Wadi Siqqat Taqa el-Zeide for the tomb of Queen Hatshepsut as regent, and for members of the later Eighteenth Dynasty royal family in the Wadi Bariya, a number were from the outset concentrated in a rather more accessible valley, which is now known as the Valley of the Queens.

Among the very earliest tombs is the shaft tomb of Ahmes (QV 47), a daughter of Seqenenre Taa, of the late Seventeenth Dynasty, which comprised a simple undecorated chamber, its ownership being determined by the princess's mummy shroud. A large number of very similar tombs exist in the same area, most so thoroughly robbed as to make their ownership impossible to determine, although certainly dating to the Eighteenth Dynasty. However, QV 46 belonged to the vizier

Imhotep (reign of Thutmose I), QV 30 to the probably contemporary stable master Nebiri, and QV 88 to a titular prince Ahmose. The latter three were all probably associated with tomb chapels on the Sheikh Abd el-Qurna, a kilometer to the north (see Tombs, Private).

During the middle of the Eighteenth Dynasty, a significant number of royal family members were interred in the Valley of the Kings, some in independent tombs, some in communal tombs, and some in the tomb of the king himself; under Amenhotep III and Akhenaten, dedicated additional chambers were provided in the kings' sepulchers. However, with the advent of the Nineteenth Dynasty in 1295 BCE, a significant enhancement in the profile of members of the royal family was accompanied by, for the first time, extensively decorated rock-cut tombs for senior members, which were in almost all cases cut in the Valley of the Queens.

The first tomb of this sequence was provided for Sitre, the wife of Ramses I (QV 38), although only the first room was ever fully cut, and even then the decoration was only sketched out. As with later tombs in the valley, this was based on depictions of divine beings of the underworld, in some cases interacting with the deceased. Some vignettes were derived from the Book of the Dead, but no extensive texts or depictions were employed. This overall scheme differed fundamentally from that found in contemporary kings' tombs, whose decoration primarily comprised the Books of the Underworld.

The next tomb constructed in the Valley was QV 80, the sepulcher of Tuy, the wife of Seti I and mother of Ramses II. This comprised an antechamber and a stairway leading to a four-pillared burial chamber with a sunken crypt, although the tomb has been badly damaged by flooding and only traces of the original very fine decoration survive.

In contrast, the tomb of Ramses II's wife Nefertary (QV 66), which was built to an almost identical plan to that of Tuy, is extremely well-preserved, with decoration in painted relief of the highest quality. A granite sarcophagus was provided in the center of the burial chamber, although only the lid has survived, the coffer probably having been removed for reuse in antiquity. Various pieces of funerary equipment were found, including many shabtis and pieces of funerary furniture, together with parts of the legs of the queen's mummy. A somewhat simplified version of the tomb's design was provided for Ramses II's sister-wife Henutmire (QV 75). She had a granite anthropoid coffin, the trough of which was later reused for the burial of the ninth century BCE Theban king Horsieset I.

Other tombs in the valley were constructed for a number of the daughters of Ramses II (1279–1213 BCE), who received the title of queen from their father. All were of less elaborate plan than those of Tuy, Nefertary, and Henutmire, but they followed same basic scheme of decoration as earlier tombs. They included the tombs of Nebettawy (QV 60), Meryetamun (QV 68), and Bintanat (QV71). A rectangular granite sarcophagus was provided for Meryetamun (coffer missing), while a reused granite anthropoid coffin was found in the tomb of Bintanat. QV 73 belonged to Ramses's daughter, Henttawy; this tomb seems to have been originally constructed and decorated with the name left blank and then allocated to the princess.

A number of other tombs were similarly constructed, but no name was ever added, although a string of titles had been included. QV 31 and QV 40 were thus intended for queens who were also king's daughters, QV 36 and QV 73 a king's daughter. One assumes that these tombs were "mass produced," with the intent that the name of the deceased would be added when allocated, but this was never done.

No tombs datable to the latter part of the Nineteenth Dynasty have been positively identified, although certain tombs decorated during the Twentieth Dynasty (1186–1069 BCE) appear architecturally to belong to the previous period and may have been left unfinished in light of the upheavals affecting the royal family during the last years of the Nineteenth Dynasty. In particular, QV 42, containing a granite coffin made for a queen and with a plan different from that seen under Ramses II, and ultimately redecorated for Prehirwenemef, son of Ramses III, would seem to belong to just this troubled period.

Another earlier tomb decorated for a son of Ramses III (1184–1153 BCE) is QV 55, belonging to Amenhirkepeshef. Like QV 42 and a series of bespoke tombs for the king's sons, the decoration is very different from that seen in the tombs of the womenfolk of Ramses II. Although figures of deities and vignettes derived from the Book of the Dead are present, the key tableaux in all feature Ramses III introducing his dead son to the gods. The phraseology of the dedication texts suggests that all the princes' tombs were commissioned/usurped at the same time. Four original tombs seem to have been cut for Ramses III's sons: QV 41 (never decorated), QV 43 (Sethhirkopeshef, possibly later Ramses VIII?), QV 44 (Khaemwaset), and QV 53 (Ramses, later Ramses IV). One other anonymous prince had a tomb begun in the Valley of the Kings (KV 3). Such Twentieth Dynasty tombs can be easily distinguished from Nineteenth Dynasty sepulchers by their simple axial plans and shallow angle of descent. Apart from the reused coffin in QV 42, a granite coffin was found in QV 55, and the lid of a granite sarcophagus in QV 43.

The tombs of two wives of Ramses III are known in the valley: Tyti, mother of Ramses IV (QV 52), and Iset, mother of Ramses VI (QV 51). However, as can be seen from the titles quoted in the tombs, both were decorated under their sons. A broken granite coffin was found in QV 51, which is recorded as having been robbed under Ramses IX. QV 74, one of the tombs clearly originally cut under Ramses II, was possibly redecorated for Duatentopet, wife of Ramses IV (1153–1147 BCE), making it the latest certain original burial in the valley.

However, a number of the tombs, robbed out during the late Twentieth and early Twenty-First Dynasties were reused during the Twenty-Fifth and Twenty-Sixth Dynasties (747–525 BCE) for the mass burial of members of a number of local middle-class artisan families. Large groups of coffins were found in QV 43 and QV 44, apparently marking the last ancient usage of the valley. The open tombs were first explored from the early 19th century onward, with large-scale excavations carried under the direction of Ernesto Schiaparelli during 1903–1905, when many important tombs, including QV 66, were found. Further extensive work has been undertaken under the direction of Christian Leblanc since the 1980s.

Aidan Dodson

See also: Coffins and Sarcophagi; Queens; Valley of the Kings

Further Reading

Dodson, Aidan. 2016. *The Royal Tombs of Ancient Egypt*. Barnsley, PA: Pen & Sword.

Dodson, Aidan, and Salima Ikram. 2008. *The Tomb in Ancient Egypt: Royal and Private Sepulchres from the Early Dynastic Period to the Romans*. London and New York: Thames & Hudson.

Donadoni Roveri, Anna Maria. 1988. "The Valley of the Queens." In Anna Maria Donadoni Roveri, ed. *Egyptian Civilization: Religious Beliefs*. Milan: Electa; Turin: Istituto Bancario San Paolo, pp. 146–161.

Lecuyot, Guy. 2000. "Ta set neferu: The Valley of the Queens—A Brief History of Its Excavations." *KMT* 11, no. 2: 42–55.

McDonald, John K. 1996. *House of Eternity: The Tomb of Nefertari*. Los Angeles: Getty Conservation Institute/J. Paul Getty Museum.

Villages. See **Cities and Villages**

Vizier

"Vizier" is an etymologically Arabic word that is the standard translation of the ancient Egyptian title *tjaty*, chosen for its perceived similarity with the Grand Vizier of the Ottoman Empire. Since its earliest attestation, at least as early as the Fourth Dynasty (2613–2494 BCE), it designates the pharaoh's second in command, his chief executive.

In the Old Kingdom (2686–2125 BCE), viziers often held an additional title, "overseer of all the works of the king," and as such were in charge of royal construction projects, including the royal tombs. In the Fourth Dynasty, these positions were largely occupied by the royal sons, or at least by individuals closely related to the royal family (Haring 2010, 221). Hemiunu, Khufu's vizier (2589–2566 BCE), who directed the construction of the Great Pyramid, was also the son of prince Nefermaat, the son and vizier of (most likely) Khufu's father Sneferu (2613–2589 BCE). From the Fifth Dynasty (2494–2345 BCE), members of the royal family could no longer hold the most prestigious offices, including the vizirate (Haring 2010, 221). In the New Kingdom (1550–1295 BCE), the title of "overseer of all the works of the king," the incumbent of which was in charge of temple construction, was no longer held by the *tjaty*. The royal tomb, however, was still his responsibility: the workmen who built the royal tombs in Valley of the Kings being under his charge, at least in the Nineteenth (1295–1186 BCE) and Twentieth Dynasties (1186–1069 BCE).

There was only ever one vizier at a time, except in the New Kingdom, when, aside from the reigns of Akhenaten (1352–1336 BCE) and Ramses III (1184–1153 BCE), Upper and Lower Egypt were each under the charge of a vizier (Haring 2010, 221). The heyday of the vizirate came during the Thirteenth Dynasty (1773–after 1650 BCE): it had become hereditary, and powerful viziers such as Ankhu and his family guaranteed stability at a time when the king's power had declined (van den Boorn 1988, 346, 358). At the end of the New Kingdom, however, the title and privileges of the vizier were acquired by the High Priests of Amun in

The vizier was the highest official in Egypt under the king. This is a seated statue of the vizier Zamont of the later Middle Kingdom. Notice the high gown with two straps in the front. This particular piece of clothing was worn only by viziers. (Egyptian National Museum, Cairo, Egypt/ Bridgeman Images)

Luxor. The title is still attested in the Third Intermediate (1069–664 BCE) and Late Periods (664–332 BCE), but the role of the incumbent of the office is unclear (Haring 2010, 221–222).

The most important source of information on the vizier and his responsibilities is the *Duties of the Vizier*. There are four known copies, all found in viziers' tombs, that of Rekhmire, who served under Thutmose III (1479–1425 BCE), being the most complete. The *tjaty*'s responsibilities had three main aspects: he was the king's deputy, the director of the *per-nesu* "royal palace," and the head of civil administration (van den Boorn 1988, 310–324). As the king's deputy, the vizier gave him daily reports on the country's condition and, conversely, was also the one who heard every royal decree. Some royal powers were delegated to him, and he could thus assign officials state-owned fields or rescind them or allocate war booty to administrative districts.

As the director of the palace, the vizier was mostly, but not exclusively, in charge of its security and relationship with the outside world: for example, he ordered the opening of all the doors to the palace every day; received daily reports on the opening and closing of all sealable rooms inside; was kept equally abreast of all movements in and out of the palace and of the condition of the palace guard posts; appointed the overseer of policemen; received local officials; and organized the troops that would accompany the king when he journeyed and those that would stay behind and garrison the city.

As the chief civil official of the Egyptian state, the vizier controlled the civil administration through the dispensation of justice, operational control of the central government's departments and of local dignitaries, and the appointment of officials. Offending central government functionaries in departments outside of the vizier's did not receive punishment from their own direct superiors; they were judged and punished by the vizier, as were local officials. The vizier appointed these local administrators, who answered directly to him and to whom they delivered the taxes they gathered from their respective provinces. Departments of the central administration, on the other hand, were controlled by the vizier through an intermediary, the "great prison": its scribes composed documents detailing inquiries its officials had carried out that were then submitted to the vizier along with previous pertinent documentation that was available in the great prison's archives. These were thus not actively directed by the vizier, but they had a certain degree of freedom to act; their actions, however, were ultimately supervised by him through the great prison (van den Boorn 1988, 318–319). He did take an active part in two areas, however, agriculture and hydraulics, in that he sent out officials to dig canals and cultivate fields (van den Boorn 1988, 319). While this could indicate state participation in irrigation projects on a local level, it is believed that this was only for temple or state-owned lands (Haring 2010, 224–225).

The *Duties of the Vizier* has been generally thought to have been composed during the Thirteenth Dynasty (van den Boorn 1988, 334). Van den Boorn, however, argues for the early Eighteenth Dynasty reign of Ahmose (1550–1525 BCE), who reunified the country after the Second Intermediate Period (1650–1550 BCE), describing the text as "a propagandistic text stressing and describing the prime position, preeminent role and wide-ranging tasks of the vizirate," in which it "reoccupies its paramount position of the late MK [Middle Kingdom] but now under the command of a powerful kingship" (van den Boorn 1988, 359).

Arto Belekdanian

See also: Officials

Further Reading

Boorn, G. P. F. van den. 1988. *The Duties of the Vizier: Civil Administration in the Early New Kingdom*. Studies in Egyptology. London and New York: Kegan Paul International.

Haring, Ben. 2010. "Administration and Law: Pharaonic." In Alan B. Lloyd, ed. *Companion to Ancient Egypt*. Chichester, UK: Wiley-Blackwell, pp. 218–236.

James, T. G. H. 2003. "The Vizier and His Role." In T. G. H. James, ed. *Pharaoh's People: Scenes from Life in Imperial Egypt*. London: Tauris Parke.

Votive Offerings. *See* Offerings, Votive

W

Weapons and Armor

To better understand Egyptian military weapons and armor, a brief overview of some key characteristics about ancient Egyptian warfare must be given. As previously mentioned, Egypt did not employ a standing army until the New Kingdom (1500–1070 BCE). Prior to this time, Egypt conscripted the needed military force from the local populace and augmented it by employing elite foreign mercenaries. Two of the most notable groups of mercenaries used by the Egyptians were the Medjay and the Sherden. The Medjay were Nubians and were recognized as superior archers and light infantry. A model of 40 armed Nubian archers was found in the tomb of Mesehti, a governor in central Egypt, and dates to the Eleventh Dynasty, near the beginning of the Middle Kingdom. The Nubian archers in this model do not carry shields but hold their bows in one hand while carrying clumps of arrows in the other. The Sherden, on the other hand, were Libyan in origin, or they were possibly related to the invasion of the so-called Sea Peoples, and their involvement with Egyptian military campaigns is normally associated with Ramses II during the New Kingdom. The Sherden are identified in battle reliefs by their unusual helmets, which were topped with horns and a disk. They seem to have been close-quarter combat experts, as their weapons usually included a knife or dagger and a spear along with a circular shield.

There is no evidence prior to the New Kingdom that the Egyptians who were conscripted into, or those who volunteered for, military service were given extensive combat training. This is partially evidenced by the lack of sophisticated weapons designed specifically for military use. Nearly all of the weapons utilized by the Egyptians could double as tools used in craft production or were extremely simple in their function. The mace could be used as a pounding implement; the axe was used extensively in carpentry; knives were used in butchery and leatherworking; and all ranged weaponry used in military campaigns were primarily hunting implements. Each of these tools were modified to be more effective when engaging enemy soldiers, but their initial purpose and use in other activities meant that conscripted soldiers were familiar with them and could wield them as weapons with some degree of success. Only the *khepesh*, a curved blade commonly, and incorrectly, viewed as an Egyptian sword, was strictly a military weapon.

The dangerous ends of early weapons, as well as those designed to inflict crushing or bludgeoning damage, were usually constructed of stone. With the development of metallurgy, bladed weapons could be effectively crafted in copper or copper alloys like bronze. Egypt did not begin extensively producing iron weapons until the Roman Period, by which point they had been conquered in turn by the Libyans, Nubians, Persians, and the Macedonians and were thus no longer viewed as a serious military threat. Most of the Pharaonic weapons discussed below made use of a combination of copper-based metals, wood, and leather in their construction. Variations in production and materials will be addressed in the individual sections.

MACE

The mace is among the most simple of weapons. Composed of a fist-sized disk or pear-shaped blunt rock or stone attached via leather thongs or straps to the end of a wooden shaft, these weapons are little more than hammers wielded with the intension of causing bodily harm. Maces were designed to be used in one hand and therefore allowed soldiers to also use shields. Ceremonial maces have been preserved that contain relief carvings on their stone heads commemorating important events or battles. One of the most famous of such maces is the Scorpion macehead found at Hierakonpolis (ca. 3000 BCE), which depicts a Predynastic king, identified as Scorpion, performing an irrigation ritual to bring fertility to the Nile valley. Maces are also the traditional weapon used in smiting scenes, which represent the king's conquering power, although during the New Kingdom, the khepesh began to be substituted in such scenes.

AXE

The axe was possibly the earliest attested bladed weapon used by the Egyptians, with clear examples dating to the Old Kingdom. The earliest examples of axe blades are crafted out of stone. Once metal began to be used to craft the blades, they took on a semicircular shape and could be attached to a wooden or horn haft by threading leather cord through small holes placed in the blade running parallel to the haft. During the Middle Kingdom, several different forms of axes were used, including a "scalloped" or "tanged" design that expanded the cutting edge of the blade into a larger yet shallower semicircular pattern. At the same time, some of the material on the inside of the blade was removed to reduce the weight and need for more metal. The result was three thick prongs that extended toward the haft and allowed the elements to attach together. By the New Kingdom, the blade of the axe was commonly trapeziform with a convex cutting edge and large extended lugs, which allowed for easy attachment of the blade to the haft using leather thongs. This style of axe is prevalently seen in depictions of warfare as a common weapon wielded by soldiers of the Middle and New Kingdoms.

Axes used in combat were likely to have shorter hafts than woodcutting axes. These hafts had elliptical cross-sections that allowed for a more comfortable grip and increased the military effectiveness by limiting the chance that a glancing blow might disarm the soldier wielding the axe. The blade design used in the New Kingdom allowed the wielder to reach over or around shields used by the enemy by extending the blade in a perpendicular direction from the haft. The cutting design also increased the penetration ability, thereby making the enemies' shields and armor potentially less effectual. Shallow axe blades were occasionally attached to longer hafts and operated in a similar manner to a polearm. The length and weight of such weapons meant the wielder was required to use two hands and was thus restricted from using a shield. Such designs could have been useful when wielded from a chariot, but it is unclear if they were used in such a manner. There are also several axes of ceremonial design dated to the New Kingdom. These axe blades often have openwork designs displaying figures or scenes. The open design would have greatly reduced the weight of such axes, but it would also have made them less effective in combat. No matter the style, a cross-sectional view of an axe blade has a wedge-shaped design. This ensured maximum force was applied to the cutting edge of the blade by providing additional weight and increasing the penetrating ability of the weapon.

KHEPESH

The khepesh is a sickle-shaped bladed weapon somewhere between 14 and 24 inches in length. It is sharpened along the leading convex edge and is designed to be wielded in one hand. Tutankhamun's funerary goods had two excellent examples of such weapons. The khepesh is commonly depicted in present-day media as an Egyptian sword. However, this representation is flawed in two ways. First, the khepesh is Asiatic in origin. Many examples have been found in Anatolia and Syria that predate Egyptian examples. Second, due to its wedge-shaped cross-section, the khepesh is more closely related to the axe than to a sword.

In the New Kingdom, it became the weapon most often held by the king in smiting scenes, but it is also commonly seen in battle scenes carried by the king while he rides into battle in his chariot. It is possible that this is due to the advantages granted to the wielder of this type of weapon as they attack from an elevated or mounted position. As an attacker swings the blade down while riding by in a chariot, the curved blade slashes through the enemy and is simultaneously pulled out as the attacker continues passing the target without becoming stuck in the enemy. This ability is well-documented, and nearly all cavalry swords contained some curve to them all the way through the 20th century, when mounted armed combat ceased. The use of the khepesh by regular ancient Egyptian infantry is attested in battle depictions of the New Kingdom, but the king's use of the khepesh is extensive.

KNIFE AND DAGGER

Knives can be produced in a variety of materials, but metal double-edged blades with a slightly thicker center proved the most useful in the New Kingdom. The short blade lengths, 12 inches or shorter, ensured that these weapons were reserved for close-quarter combat only, and they would probably have been ineffective against a shielded enemy. The inclusion of a pommel officially changes a knife into a dagger and made the weapon better balanced. Blades extending beyond a foot long are more often classified as swords, but these were rarely used by the Egyptian soldier.

SPEAR

New Kingdom spears were composed of long wooden poles and tipped with straight blades, often made of metal. The blades were often leaf-shaped and not necessarily thin. These design elements kept the blade from becoming trapped inside an enemy or shield and allowed for some degree of slashing in addition to piercing attacks. The profile of spearheads changed little over the course of Egyptian history, but it followed the style of being roughly triangular in shape, with a narrow aft section where they were attached to their poles. In the New Kingdom, the standard method of attaching the spearheads to their hafts was to prepare a socket in the metallic head that wrapped around the pole and allowed either piece to be replaced with relative ease. The spear came in two varieties: the short spear used for stabbing and the long spear used for thrusting. Spears filled the middle ground between melee and ranged weaponry; they could be used for both, as they could be held or thrown with accuracy. Spears can be used quite effectively when paired with a shield, but their piercing style of damage and relatively light weight would have also made shields an effective defense against them. Middle Kingdom models of soldiers show spears and shields were common, possibly the most common, weapons for army personnel.

BOW AND ARROW

Egyptians used two types of bows over the course of the Pharaonic Period. The self-bow was little more than a tapered wooden stave made of acacia wood and measuring between one and two meters. The composite recurved bow was more complex, requiring wood and horn to be laminated together and shaped in opposition to the pull of the string. However, composite bows were much stronger than self-bows and provided greater power to the arrow. Bows were strung with dried, twisted animal gut strings, but if a bow was left strung for long periods of time, it would lose its effectiveness.

Arrows were made of reed and fletched with feathers to ensure accuracy in aiming. Different tips could be applied to the arrows to make them more effective for certain targets. Blunted tips were useful in hunting fowl. Bone tips provided penetrating power. But for military campaigns, bronze tips were the most useful, as they provided the best chance to pierce enemy defenses. One of the greatest examples of the power that could be imparted to an arrow is an account of Amenhotep II, who is depicted as having pierced three sheets of copper with a single arrow. Interestingly, quivers were not extensively used by the Egyptians. In most reliefs and depictions, archers are shown holding their extra arrows in the hand that pulls back the string of the bow.

SHIELDS

The most common piece of protective gear used by the Egyptians was the shield. Nearly all infantry soldiers were equipped with a rectangular shield, peaked on the top and squared on the bottom, that when held extended from their face to their knees. The shields were constructed of wood and covered with cowhide. Ceremonial shields have also been discovered in funerary deposits that include cutaways and relief carvings covered in gold and other precious materials. Such shields would have either been too heavy to wield in combat or ineffective, as their cutouts would have exposed the soldier to unnecessary harm. Some wall reliefs also display shields being used to create makeshift fortifications around temporary encampments.

ARMOR

Normal infantry soldiers did not have body armor. During the New Kingdom, the king could be equipped with armor made of small interconnected pieces of leather or bronze scale that would cover his torso. Only a few examples of such armor exist. It is likely that bronze scale armor would have been quite heavy, unwieldy, and oppressive in the hot desert regions of Egypt and the Near East. As a result, such armor would have been a luxury and only used during the actual fighting of the campaign. Helmets were rarely used by Egyptians, and no example of the blue war crown worn by the king in most battle scenes has ever been discovered.

The Egyptians had and used other types of military equipment, including siege ladders for assaulting fortified locations; naval vessels, which were primarily used as personnel carriers; and, of course, the chariot. For further information on these pieces of equipment, refer to the suggested reading or the entry on chariots in this collection.

Daniel Shay Matthew Johnsen

See also: Army; Chariot

Further Reading

Darnell, John Coleman, and Colleen Manassa. 2007. *Tutankhamun's Armies: Battle and Conquest during Ancient Egypt's Late 18th Dynasty.* Hoboken, NJ: John Wiley & Sons.

Partridge, Robert. 2002. *Fighting Pharaohs: Weapons and Warfare in Ancient Egypt.* Manchester: Peartree Publishing.

Petrie, W. M. Flinders. 1917. "History in Tools." *Science Progress (1916–1919)* 12, no. 45: 71–82.

Shaw, Ian. 1991. *Egyptian Warfare and Weapons.* Shire Egyptology 16. Princes Risborough, UK: Shire Publications.

Spalinger, Anthony J. 2005. *War in Ancient Egypt: New Kingdom.* Malden, MA: Blackwell Publishing.

Weaving and Looms

The production of cloth from plant or animal fibers has its historical background in the plaiting of mats and basketry. In pharaonic Egypt cloth weaving is closely connected with the development of state organization. From this period, two main forms of looms are known: one that spreads out the warp (the threads that are connected to the loom and through which a second set of threads, the weft, is woven at a 90-degree angle) horizontal to the ground and one that is set vertically. Other kinds of looms, mentioned below, were introduced into Egypt in the Late Period (ca. 722–332 BCE).

Unlike regions with higher humidity, the dry Egyptian climate has led to the preservation of a vast number of objects consisting entirely or partly of woven fibers: clothes, napkins, towels, bedding, saddle cloths, cloths used as supports for other types of decoration (such as the gilding on horse harnesses), mummy wrappings, curtains, cushion cases, carpets, tent cloths, cloth filters for liquids, and many more. In a society such as pharaonic Egypt, these objects were produced on a small scale in individual homes, but tomb depictions suggest that mass production would have been done by craftsmen under state-organized supervision. The weavers would be supplied with or would trade for raw materials, which in turn were grown, harvested, and spun as well as dyed on demand. For the first millennium CE, written records point to the production of simple funerary shrouds in hermits' dwellings and monasteries. Other manufacturing centers are not known so far.

Through most of Egyptian history, linen made from flax (*Linum sp.*) was the main plant fiber used for cloth production. Wool yarn was known in Egypt approximately from the time of the introduction of the wooly sheep, which probably came from the Near East in or shortly before the Middle Kingdom (2055–1650 BCE). Most of the preserved polychrome woolen objects, however, have been found in archaeological contexts dating to the first millennium CE. Approximately from the same period, there is evidence for cotton and silk cloth from Egypt, but both are scarce and mostly considered to be produced abroad.

Prior to weaving, the raw fibers had to be spun into yarn. From the pictorial evidence from ancient Egypt, this process seems to have happened in the same room as the weaving. The finished fibers could be dyed using ochreous earths and plant colorants. Through the use of such treated yarns, further decoration could be added to the woven patterns.

In contrast to the rather stiff materials (reeds, long leaves, or coarse plant fibers) from which ropes, mats, and baskets are made, the weaving of soft and flexible threads from linen, hair, wool, or cotton is made easier by the use of a loom. The simplest form of loom consists of two parallel beams that are fixed in the ground by pegs and between which the warp threads are kept taut. During the initial preparation of the long threads—which can be up to about 65 feet in length—for the loom and to keep them from entangling while they are put on the machine, they are prewound around sticks set into the wall or the floor. This process is called *warping*. The warp can then be put in a continuous loop around both weaving beams. To be able to use the whole thread for cloth production, it has to be pulled around the beams. As an alternative, the warp threads can be rolled up on one end beam and released as necessary. The finished cloth can be rolled up onto the beam closer to the weaver.

In the most basic form of weaving, the weft thread runs from one side to the other over the first, third, fifth, and so on, warp thread and under the second, fourth, sixth, and so on. At the far side of the cloth, the weft is guided around the

Scene from a Middle Kingdom tomb at Beni Hasan shows two women on the right spinning thread and two women on the left weaving. The figure in the middle is in charge of the work. The hieroglyphs above the figures are terse captions, saying simply "weaving" and "spinning." (Rogers Fund, 1933/The Metropolitan Museum of Art)

last warp and led back to the beginning, crossing over the threads it previously ran under, and under those it crossed over in the first pass. To simplify this process, the threads are separated (forming a *shed*) by a flat rod (a *warp-spacer*) inserted between the warp threads and then turned on its side, or by the use of *heddles*, long sticks lying outside the warp to which each set of threads is leashed by short strings that can be lifted alternately by hand, thus lifting the connected warp threads with them. By adding more heddles and selecting different groups of threads, patterns can be woven in repeating order. For nonrepeating decoration, shorter threads can be inserted with needles and cross back at the end of the pattern, even if the warp extends further. This turning back often creates small gaps in the garment. The technique is found mainly in textiles from the late first millennium CE. After each passing of the weft, it has to be beaten down toward the previous one with another long flat stick to close the gaps between them and strengthen the cloth. The stick (a *weaving sword*) is inserted in the shed to do this, or it can be replaced by a comb, which is used from the surface. The weft itself is passed through the shed after having been first wound onto a spool, either lengthwise or crosswise. To keep the warp threads evenly spaced, further rods with notches on one side may be inserted at a distance from where the cloth is woven and behind the heddles. While one set of threads runs through the notches, the other is guided underneath the warp-spacer.

The same basic functions and parts are found on the vertical loom, in which the beams are separated by a frame, and the whole is held upright, for example, by a wall. While the horizontal loom is depicted from the Middle Kingdom, the vertical one seems to have been used only from the New Kingdom (1555–1069 BCE) onward. The replacement of one of the beams in a vertical loom by weights (the warp-weighted loom) is attested parallel to the time of the Pharaonic empire mainly for the region of the northeastern Mediterranean. These looms have been found in Egypt only in contexts where military installations were present or a high percentage of non-Egyptian population from the Late Period onward. The use and invention of the treadle-powered opening of the shed in horizontal looms (the treadle loom) is thought to have happened in Egypt. However, so far archaeological evidence provides no clear support for this assumption.

Johanna Sigl

See also: Agriculture; Basketry and Cordage; Clothing; Footwear

Further Reading

Carroll, Diane L. 1985. "Dating the Foot-Powered Loom: The Coptic Evidence." *American Journal of Archaeology* 89: 168–173.

Kemp, Barry J., and Gillian M. Vogelsang-Eastwood, eds. 2001. *The Ancient Textile Industry at Amarna, Memoir of the Egypt Exploration Fund.* London: Egypt Exploration Society.

Schrenk, Sabine, and Nettie K. Adams. 2006. *Textiles in Situ: Their Find Spots in Egypt and Neighbouring Countries in the First Millennium CE, Riggisberg Berichte 13.* Riggisberg: Abegg-Stiftung.

Vogelsang-Eastwood, Gillian M. 2000. "Textiles." In Paul T. Nicholson and Ian Shaw, eds. *Ancient Egyptian Materials and Technology.* Cambridge: Cambridge University Press, pp. 268–298.

Weighing of the Heart

The ancient Egyptian belief in the divine judgment occurring after death and performed during the deceased's journey to the netherworld is represented by the "Weighing of the Heart." This is depicted in a scene showing the deceased's heart being weighed on a scale in front of Osiris and the gods "who hear cases," namely, the 42 judges of the netherworld. Such a scene is the main vignette of Spell 125 of the Book of the Dead, and its main variants are found on papyri, coffins of the first millennium BCE, shabti chests, mummy bandages, and less often on the walls of the tomb chapels of the Late Period (664–332 BCE). The vignette is accompanied by the text of the spell, which includes the "Negative Confession" (or "Declaration of Innocence"), where the deceased denies having committed 42 main sins during her or his life on earth. In one unique case, a variant of this scene occurs on a relief in a temple, namely, in the small Ptolemaic Period temple of Deir el-Medina in Western Thebes, dedicated to Amun, Hathor and *Maat.*

The attention to ethics and to the good and pious deeds to be performed in society is also evident from certain literary and laudatory texts, such as the biographies inscribed on stelae and tomb walls since the Old Kingdom (2686–2160 BCE). The fear of a final judgment if one did not respect the ethical code of society, namely, not acting according to *Maat*, "Truth and Justice," is the reason why magical compositions such as the Book of the Dead needed to help the deceased to

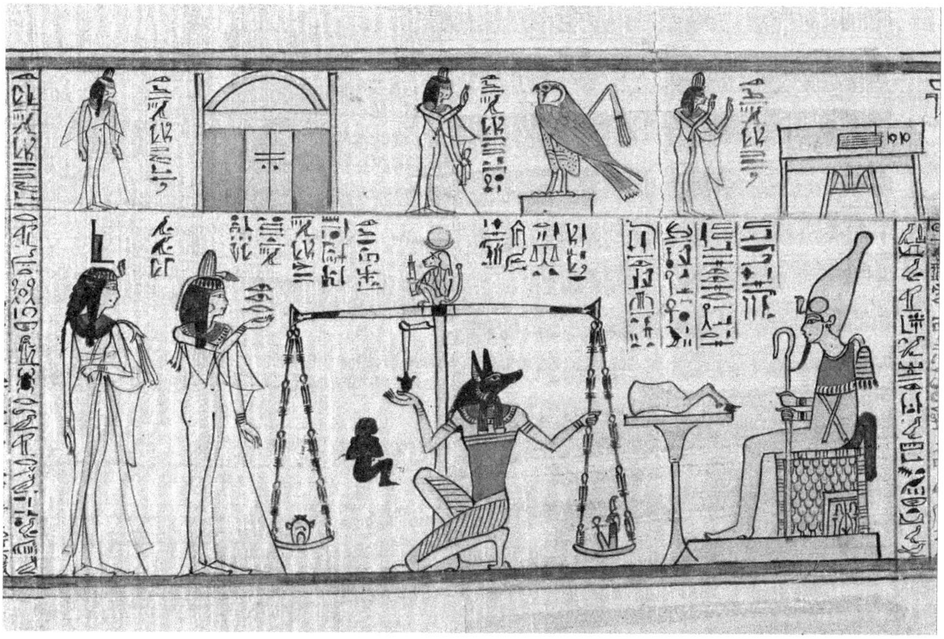

One of the vignettes, or illustrations, in the Book of the Dead is the "Weighing of the Heart," in which the heart of the deceased is weighed on a scale against *Maat*, or truth and justice, in the presence of the god Osiris. If the heart of the deceased was "heavy with sin," they would not get into the afterlife. (The Metropolitan Museum of Art/ Rogers Fund, 1930)

be "justified" by assessing his or her truthful conduct on earth through divine tribunals. These are also mentioned in Spells 18 and 20 of the Book of the Dead as well as in the earlier Coffin Texts of the Middle Kingdom (2055–1650 BCE). However, from the New Kingdom (1550–1069 BCE) until the Ptolemaic-Roman Period (332 BCE–395 CE), the scene of the Weighing of the Heart becomes the most representative and popular symbol of the belief in a final judgment that took place during the deceased's journey to the netherworld.

The ancient Egyptians believed that the heart was the repository of the emotions as well as of the intellect, and therefore it needed special protection after death to survive with the mummy. Spell 30B of the Book of the Dead, which is generally copied near the Weighing of the Heart scene in the papyri or on scarab-shaped amulets to be placed on the breast of the mummy, clearly states that the heart has its own independent will, and therefore the deceased addresses it by saying, "do not oppose me as witness, do not oppose me in tribunal." In the Weighing of the Heart scene, the hieroglyph of the heart, *ib*, is placed on one of the two pans of the scale, while on the other is the hieroglyph of the feather symbolizing *Maat*, the goddess of Truth and Justice, or in some variants the seated goddess herself is shown.

The weighing is generally overseen by Thoth, who appears in the form of a baboon on the scale or as an anthropomorphic god with an ibis head, standing near the scale, holding the scribal palette and pen, ready to record the verdict.

Anubis, the jackal-headed god, can also be shown in the scene, overseeing the two scale pans or accompanying the deceased before it. The "Goddess of the West," or *Maat*, can also be depicted while accompanying the deceased in the Judgment Hall. In some variants, the scale can have a human head or the feather of *Maat* placed on the top of its center pole. The weighing scene takes place in the "Hall of the Two Truths," the columned hall where the 42 deities are housed and Osiris is enthroned. The names of the 42 judges, which the deceased needs to know to pass the judgment, are written above them.

A peculiar but important figure of the scene of the Weighing of the Heart is Ammet (Am-mt), a composite demonic creature whose name literally means "the devourer/swallower of the dead." Her main function is to swallow the deceased who does not pass the judgment. Ammet appears in smaller or bigger dimensions in comparison to the scale and to the other figures, with a body composed of a crocodile head, a lion in the upper body, and a hippopotamus in the rear. She incarnates the idea of punishment in the netherworld and the constant threat that the deceased has to face during his journey in the Realm of the Dead, where it was also possible to "die a second death." Differently from other demonic beings with harmful character, which occur in other spells, Ammet is depicted only in the scene of the Weighing of the Heart, clearly showing the very specific function she has as punisher of the sinners. In some variants, she does not lie on the ground but stands on a shrine, showing a rather divine status.

The judgment hall, in a peculiar variant with an empty personified scale in front of an enthroned Osiris, is also depicted in the fifth division of the Book of Gates, which decorate a number of royal tombs in the Valley of the Kings, such as the tomb of Horemheb, Ramses VI and VII; this peculiar variant relates to the vindication of the sun god Ra, to which the king assimilates in the netherworld, over the enemy of creation, the giant snake Apophis.

Rita Lucarelli

See also: Afterlife; Book of the Dead; Ethics; *Maat*; Osiris

Further Reading

Assmann, Jan. 2005. *Death and Salvation in Ancient Egypt.* Ithaca, NY: Cornell University Press.

Manassa, Colleen. 2006. "The Judgement Hall of Osiris in the Book of the Gates." *Revue d'Égyptologie* 57: 109–150.

Taylor, John. 2010. *Journey through the Afterlife: Ancient Egyptian Book of the Dead.* London: British Museum Press.

Wigs. See **Hair and Wigs**

Wine

One of the world's oldest and most extensive records about viticulture and wine production comes from ancient Egypt. Wine was a luxury drink mainly consumed by the royalty and nobility, but it was also offered to gods in daily temple rituals and used in medicine and in the royal rituals for the afterlife. The archaeological evidence includes painted scenes of wine production and wine offering to gods and also wine jars, some with inscriptions, and organic material (dried grapes and wine remains). From the Predynastic Period, about 5300 BCE, onward, large wine jars, about three feet high and stamped with royal seals, were placed in tombs as offerings for the afterlife of the deceased.

From the Old Kingdom (2686–2160 BCE) through to the Ptolemaic-Roman Period (332 BCE–395 CE) wall paintings in nobles' tombs depicted the harvest of grapes and winemaking, such as the scene from the well-known New Kingdom tomb of Nakht on the West Bank of Thebes. Recent research (Wine of Ancient Egypt 2017) has documented a total of 92 scenes from Egyptian private tombs showing the different steps in the grapes harvest, including vinery, taking care of the vine, harvesting grapes, and counting the baskets. In the winemaking scenes, the steps represented are transporting grapes to a press, pressing grapes, heating and filtering, pressing the remains in a sack press, filling wine jars, fermentation, offerings to the goddess Renenutet, wine tasting, sealing the wine jars, labeling wine jars, counting wine jars, transporting wine jars to a cellar, refrigerating the jars during fermentation, and storing wine jars in a cellar.

During the New Kingdom Period (1550–1069 BCE), amphora-type wine jars with two handles, about two feet high, were inscribed in hieratic, the cursive script of ancient Egyptian, in black ink, indicating the regnal year of the harvest, the name of the product, the quality and sweetness, the provenance, the property (royal or private), and the name and title of the winemaker. Like the labels in the modern wine bottles, these inscriptions give us information about the harvest and wine production, revealing that the ancient Egyptians considered this information relevant and necessary to be able to distinguish between wines.

The symbolism of wine in ancient Egypt was based on its red color, not only because of the relation established between wine and the blood of the resurrection

Winemaking scene from the tomb of Nakht on the West Bank of Thebes, Eighteenth Dynasty. Men are shown picking grapes and crushing them. The wine was stored in the large pottery vessels. (Werner Forman/Universal Images Group/Getty Images)

god Osiris but also because of the reddish color of the Nile River during the annual flood, which was the harvest time for grapes. In Egypt, the grapes harvest started at the end of July. In this period of the year, the Nile waters became reddish due to ferruginous sediments, the naturally occurring material transported in the water that had a high concentration of iron. Both the majority of the floodwater and the sediment was carried down to the Nile by the Blue Nile, originating in Lake Tana in Ethiopia during the summer monsoons.

From the beginning, ancient Egyptian mythology related wine only with the color red. For many years, the only known evidence for wine was the representation of red grapes in tombs and the myths that connected red wine with the blood of Osiris, the god of the underworld. In the papyrus of the royal scribe Nakht in the British Museum, a vine is depicted leading to the nose of the god Osiris as a symbol of resurrection, and this symbolism is still in use in Coptic iconography today. The first mention of white wine in Egypt is from the Greek writer Athenaeus of Naucratis, who lived during the third century BCE, in his book *The Deipnosophistae*, "The Sofists at Dinner," where he explains that Mareotis wine, from the area of Lake Mariut near the city of Alexandria, was "excellent, white and enjoyable, aromatic."

In the burial chamber and the annex of Tutankhamun's tomb (KV62), more than 30 wine jars were found of two main types: two-handled amphorae and single-handled (Carter 1933, 147–149; Holthoer 1993, 43–67). The annex had 23 amphorae with ink-written hieratic inscriptions found together with food for the king's sustenance during the afterlife. One amphorae inscription, for example, reads, "Year 4, wine from the Estate of Aten in the Western River by chief vintner Nen" (Černy 1965, 1); the clay seal is broken, and it is open on the upper part. Years four, five, and nine of Tutankhamun's reign are identified in these amphorae inscriptions. These wines allow scholars to date the length of the king's reign, as no wine produced later than year nine of Tutankhamun can be identified with certainty among the burial furnishings.

Another three wine amphorae with hieratic inscriptions were found in the burial chamber lying on the ground between the walls and the outermost shrine surrounding the mummified body of the king. These amphorae were on the east, west, and south sides. The results of analyzing samples of wine remains inside Tutankhamun's amphorae have revealed that in ancient Egypt, both red and white wines were given the name *irp*, which adds new information to our understanding of the word *wine*. Furthermore, chemical analyses of samples from the three amphorae at the burial chamber revealed that there was a red wine in the western amphora, a white wine in the eastern, and that the southern amphora, which was inscribed *shedeh*, contained a red wine with a different elaboration process.

For almost a century, the meaning and nature of the word *shedeh*, which has no translation, has been a mystery. Some scholars suggested pomegranates or grapes as its raw material. According to Papyrus Salt 825 at the British Museum in London (BM10051), dating to the Late Period (664–332 BCE), the only text found so far that mentions the elaboration of the *shedeh*, it was filtered and heated. Nevertheless, due to damage to the papyrus, the botanical source of *shedeh* remained unknown. The results of analyzing a unique sample of a residue from the southern amphora in Tutankhamun's burial chamber, bearing the inscription "Year 5, *shedeh* of very good quality of the Estate of Aten of the Western River, chief vintner Rer" (Černy 1965, 2), confirmed that *shedeh* was a red grape wine (Guasch-Jané et al. 2006b, 101). Further research has suggested a religious meaning of the use of the three types of wines in Tutankhamun's burial chamber. The western red wine, the eastern white wine and the southern *shedeh* were served in a three-step ritual for the king's resurrection.

Maria Rosa Guasch-Jané

See also: Agriculture; Beer; Language and Script; Tomb of Tutankhamun

Further Reading

Athenaeus. 1927–1941. *The Deipnosophists*. Vol. 1. Translated by C. B. Gulick. 7 vols. London: Harvard University Press.

Carter, H. 1933. *The Tomb of Tutankhamen*. Vol. 3. Reprinted (2000) by N. Reeves. *The Tomb of Tutankhamen*. Vol. 3, *The Annexe of Treasury*. Bath, UK: Duckworth Egyptology.

Černy, J. 1965. *Hieratic Inscriptions from the Tomb of Tutankhamun*. Oxford: Griffith Institute.

Guasch-Jané, M. R., et al. 2006a. "First Evidence of White Wine in Ancient Egypt from Tutankhamun's Tomb." *Journal of Archaeological Science* 33, no. 8: 1075–1080.

Guasch-Jané, M. R., et al. 2006b. "The Origin of the Ancient Egyptian Drink *shedeh* Revealed Using LC/MS/MS." *Journal of Archaeological Science* 33, no. 1: 98–101.

Guasch-Jané, M. R. 2011. "The Meaning of Wine in Egyptian Tombs: The Three Amphorae from Tutankhamun's Burial Chamber." *Antiquity* 85, no. 329: 851–858.

Holthoer, R. 1993. "The Pottery." In John Baines, ed. *Stone Vessels, Pottery and Sealings from the Tomb of Tutankhamun*. Oxford: Griffith Institute, pp. 40–85.

Murray, A. M. 2000. "Viticulture and Wine Production." In P. T. Nicholson and Ian Shaw, eds. *Ancient Egyptian Materials and Technology*. Cambridge: Cambridge University Press, pp. 577–608.

Reeves, N. 1990. *The Complete Tutankhamun*. London: Thames and Hudson.

Wine of Ancient Egypt. 2017. "Copyright *Irep en Kemet*." http://www.wineofancientegypt.com.

Wisdom Literature

Wisdom literature is a conventional umbrella term that has derived from modern biblical scholarship and been applied to bodies of literature from the whole ancient world. In the case of ancient Egyptian literature, this term broadly refers to two long-lived, influential literary genres: *Instructions* (or *Teachings*) and *Discourses*.

INSTRUCTIONS

The *Instructions* were occasionally self-defined as *sebayt*, "teaching" in Egyptian. Their didactic materials were frequently framed by a story or a prologue and epilogue that described the relationship between the speaking wise man and his addressee(s), advertised his status and authority as well as the value of his teachings, and invited his audience to pay attention to what he had to say. The instruction proper comprised principally short sayings and admonitions on a wide range of matters of human conduct. In some cases, as in the *Instruction of Amenemope* or the *Instruction of Papyrus Insinger*, these sayings and admonitions were organized thematically in numbered or titled chapters. In other cases, as in the *Instruction of Ani* or the *Instruction of Hardjedef*, the didactic materials were accumulated in a less organized manner, jumping haphazardly from one theme to another. The most popular themes discussed in the *Instructions* were family and household, conduct before the gods, death, farming, conduct in formal occasions, and public speaking (their style and treatment of various themes is illustrated by the translated texts).

The choice of and extent to which these wisdom works dwelled on specific themes depended on the type of addressee they had in mind. All named addressees were male members of the elite; thus, the issues raised were tailored to their lives and needs. Sometimes such addressees would have a specific status, and so the *Instruction* addressing them would touch upon the particular expectations and requirements of that status: for instance, the *Instruction to Merikare* claimed to have been addressing an active pharaoh and therefore discussed tasks a pharaoh was meant to fulfill. In general, however, one cannot trust the claimed profiles of such addressees, as they seemed to have been pseudepigraphic, that is, that their named addressees were not their real audience. The same probably applied to the celebrity wise men most of these *Instructions* were ascribed to: they were probably not composed by these acclaimed intellectuals. The literary pseudepigraphy of the *Instructions*, which often assigned them to older times, functioned as a guarantee for these wisdom works' reputation, authority, validity, and popularity.

The issue of pseudepigraphic authorship relates to the Egyptian *Instructions*' dates. Their composers generally wanted their audience to think that the wisdom they communicated originated in older, better times, when the popularity of their celebrity speakers and addressees was at its peak. The surviving copies of these texts, however, point in most cases toward later dates, a discrepancy that has caused many (some still unresolved) debates among modern scholars. For example, in the case of the *Instruction of Ptahhotep*, four papyrus copies are extant, with striking differences suggesting radically different scholarly redactions, the earliest of which dates to the Twelfth Dynasty (1985–1773 BCE), while the text's archaizing language and historical references located its production during the Sixth Dynasty (2345–2181 BCE). In general, the current scholarly consensus agrees that the genre of *Instructions* probably began in the Old Kingdom (2686–2160 BCE) and continued to thrive throughout the history of pharaonic and Ptolemaic-Roman Egypt, making it the longest-surviving Egyptian literary tradition. Eventually, around the third century CE, the genre was adopted by Coptic authors and began to promote the Christian ethos.

Another troublesome issue pertaining to our modern reception of *Instructions* is the interpretation and translation of their contents. Specifically, the *Instructions*' thematic versatility and ethical orientation, which resulted in the regular usage of abstract vocabulary rich in cultural connotations, have made these works the hardest to understand and translate in modern languages. Consequently, one may observe significant variation among the ways in which modern scholars have translated them.

The general difficulty in understanding and reconstructing the contents of these wisdom works is also linked, to some extent, to the manner in which they were written down and have survived through the ages. Written mainly in the Egyptian cursive scripts, namely, hieratic and Demotic, copies of *Instructions* have survived often incomplete on papyri, wooden tablets, and potshards; their incomplete state has forced modern scholars to fill in the gaps with their own hypothetical reconstructions. On a positive note, the diversity of writing surfaces on which such works were copied suggests that *Instructions* were popular within multiple contexts, such as scribal schools and private libraries. Finally, one should note this wisdom genre's international affiliations. Specifically, so far it has been proven that Egyptian *Instructions* influenced and were influenced by ancient Near Eastern literature and, from the Greco-Roman era onward, ancient Greek and Roman wisdom.

DISCOURSES

The second genre of Egyptian wisdom literature shared many features with *Instructions*. Like *Instructions*, *Discourses* attempted to communicate versatile wise observations and to promote an ideal lifestyle. They, too, tended to be attributed to seemingly famous Egyptian wise men who lived in a glorified past and whose reputation and authority guaranteed their writings would circulate widely and their life convictions would be persuasive and educational. In the case of the prophetic members of the genre of *Discourses*, the ascription of their speeches to older times also created a safe fictional distance that proved the accuracy of their prophecies. In addition, like *Instructions*, their wisdom text proper was often framed by a fictional story that introduced the setting, the speaker, and his audience. Written in cursive scripts, *Discourses*' extant copies were frequently incomplete, as was the case with *Instructions*; in combination with the fact that they, too, used obscure language, this has resulted in much speculation and variation in their modern editions. Finally, like *Instructions*, the tradition of *Discourses* lasted for almost the whole course of ancient Egyptian history and at times interacted with like-minded international literary traditions, such as Hebrew apocalyptic works.

Unlike *Instructions*, the genre of *Discourses* has been more loosely defined by modern scholars and thus is often considered to include both reflective speeches and dialogues, like the *Dialogue between a man and his Ba*, and pessimistic speeches prophesizing a gloomy, apocalyptic future. In either case, *Discourses* did not include many pedagogical admonitions as *Instructions* did. Instead, their style tended to be more lyrical, depending much on poetic and very often obscure description of symbolic images (their distinctive style is illustrated in the second translated text). Judging, also, from the smaller number of surviving copies and less diversity in writing surfaces, one would assume that *Discourses* did not enjoy the same levels of popularity with *Instructions*. In many cases, the known works have survived in single papyrus copies (e.g., the *Words of Neferti* in a single

Eighteenth Dynasty (1550–1069 BCE) papyrus), a fact that questions not only their contemporary popularity but also even their initial literary success.

Nikolaos Lazaridis

See also: Ethics; Families; Scribes and Scribal Equipment

Further Reading

Hagen, Fr. 2012. *An Ancient Egyptian Text in Context: The Instruction of Ptahhotep.* OLA 218. Leuven: Peeters.

Lazaridis, N. 2007. *Wisdom in Loose Form: The Language of Egyptian and Greek Proverbs in Collections from the Hellenistic and Roman Periods.* Mnemosyne, Supplements 287. Leiden: Brill.

Lichtheim, M. 1983. *Late Egyptian Wisdom Literature in the International Context: A Study of Demotic Instructions.* OBO 52. Freiburg/Schweiz and Göttingen: Universitätsverlag and Vandenhoeck & Ruprecht.

Lichtheim, M. 1996. "Didactic Literature." In A. Loprieno, ed. *Ancient Egyptian Literature: History and Forms.* Leiden and New York: Brill, pp. 243–262.

Vernus, P. 2001. *Sagesses de l'Égypte pharaonique.* Paris: Imprimerie nationale éditions.

Williams, R. J. 1990. "The Sage in Egyptian Literature." In J. G. Gammie and L. G. Perdue, eds. *The Sage in Israel and the Ancient Near East.* Winona Lake: Eisenbrauns, pp. 19–30.

Primary Document—Excerpt from the Instruction of Ptahhotep

The *Instruction of Ptahhotep* (also known as *The Maxims of Ptahhotep*) is an example of wisdom literature that was composed in the 25th or 24th century BCE during the reign of the Fifth Dynasty king Djedkara Isesi by the royal vizier Ptahhotep. The text was discovered in Thebes in 1847 by Egyptologist M. Prisse d'Avennes.

If you are weak, follow a man of excellence,
And all your conduct will be good before the god. . . .
Respect him in accordance with what he has become,
For wealth does not come of its own accord. . . .
It is the god who makes him excellent,
And protects him while he sleeps.
Follow your heart as long as you live.
Do not do more than what is allocated (to you).
Do not waste the time of following the heart,
As wasting time is an offense to the spirit.
Do not lose the hours of daylight
Beyond providing for your household.
As things happen, follow your heart,
For there is no profit in things, when they become a burden.

Source: *Instruction of Ptahhotep* 7,7-10, translated by Nikolaos Lazaridis from Pap. Prisse for Ptahhotep, its best publication being Žaba, Z. 1956. *Les maximes de Ptahhotep.* Prague: Éditions de l'Académie Tchécoslovaque des Sciences.

***Primary Document—Excerpt from the* Words of Neferti**

The *Words of Neferti* is a text that is thought to have been composed at the start of the Twelfth Dynasty in the 20th century BCE.

I shall describe what is before me.
I do not foretell what does not come.
The river of Egypt is dry,
One may cross the water on foot,
One seeks water for ships to sail on. . . .
Strange birds will breed in the Delta marshes,
Having made their nest on the fringes,
Coming close to people because of hunger. . . .
All happiness has departed. . . .
Men of violence have risen in the East,
Asiatics have come down to Egypt.

Source: *Words of Neferti* 26–33, translated by Nikolaos Lazaridis from its only extant copy on Pap. Hermitage 1116B, its best publication being Helck, w. 1970. *Die Prophezierung des Nfr·tj.* Wiesbaden: O. Harrassowitz.

Woodworking. *See* Furniture and Woodworking

Women

There is a great deal of written and pictorial evidence from ancient Egypt that can be used to reconstruct the lives of women in ancient Egypt, from village women to those of the royal court. However, it is questionable how accurately we can understand their role and status in their society. Much of the pictorial evidence is from tombs that only the nobility and royalty were able to have, and the depictions in them do not realistically show everyday life but portray a perfect eternal life, meant to be lived in the afterlife. Royal woman had their own tombs, usually within a complex for their husband, the king, but a nonroyal woman commonly shared the tomb belonging to her husband and was accorded the role of accompanying spouse, not tomb owner and center of attention. It also has to be pointed out that all the craftsmen and artisans who decorated the tomb were male, which might well have affected how women were depicted.

While written documents such as letters have survived as evidence of women's daily lives in ancient Egypt, many if not all appear to have been written down by male scribes. Although scholars assume royal and noble women were literate, there is no direct proof; findings only provide evidence of male children attending school, being trained as scribes, and going on to work in the government. From the top down, from king to petty bureaucrats, the power structure of ancient Egypt

Scene from a banquet celebrating the "Beautiful Festival of the Valley" in a Theban tomb of the Eighteenth Dynasty. One of the female guests is seated in a low chair, while a young servant makes her comfortable, and another servant stands ready to give her a bowl of wine. (Rogers Fund, 1930/The Metropolitan Museum of Art)

was male. We can reconstruct a view of the lives of women in ancient Egypt, but it appears to have been presented entirely from a male perspective.

Because of their relationship with the king, royal women were obviously at a completely different level from nonroyal women and in a position of special status and power. A very important difference between the queen and the king, however, was that while king was considered a god and filled a divine role, the queen was not divine; she could only consort with divinity. The queen passed the divinity and legitimacy of her husband to her son, so he could take the throne. Interestingly enough, she could also rule for him, in his name, if he became king when he was a minor. This type of rule by the king's mother is called a *regency* and is known from as early as the First Dynasty, the beginning of ancient Egypt history.

In unusual circumstances, if the king died without an heir, the queen could take over. This happened at the end of the Twelfth Dynasty when Queen Sobekneferu had a short rule of about four years. This happened again in the Eighteenth Dynasty when Queen Hatshepsut served as regent for her minor stepson following the death of her husband, King Thutmose II. At some point between two and seven years later, Hatshepsut proclaimed herself king along with the young king Thutmose III, and the two of them ruled together in a coregency for 22 years until her death. Although kings of ancient Egypt were male, as they ruled as the god Horus, son of Osiris, Sobekneferu solved her gender problem by proclaiming that she was a female Horus, and she wore the garb of a male king over her own female clothing. When Hatshepsut became king, she simply had herself portrayed as a man for state purposes. It was no secret that she was actually a female, so some texts of the time show confusion in the pronouns. For example, one of Hatshepsut's officials on a military campaign in Nubia states, "I followed the good god, King of Upper and Lower Egypt, may she live! I saw when he overthrew the Nubian bowmen" (Redford 1967, 57). It would seem that Hatshepsut was successful in her long reign with Thutmose III because she had the backing of the royal court as well as the powerful religious establishment of ancient Egypt.

Women in ancient Egypt held many different types of jobs, but they changed through time with changes in ancient Egyptian society. In the Old Kingdom, 2650–2150 BCE, there are women holding titles such as dancer, grinder of grain, food vendor, winnower, domestic servant, singer, overseer of singers, weaver, overseer of weavers, stewardess of the queen's household, overseer of cloth, overseer of ornaments, and seal bearer. Women who held higher status because of the position of their husband could be accepted into the royal court and carry a title, like noblewoman of the king. As for religious positions, women served as mourners at funerals, made offerings in private tombs as a servant of the *ka*, or they could be priestesses of the goddesses Hathor and Neith.

It seems that in the First Intermediate Period that followed, problems of a decentralized government, low Niles and possible famine, and civil unrest and power struggles impacted the role and position of women. When Egypt was reunified and a single king again ruled over all of Egypt in the period of the Middle Kingdom, titles such as overseer or administrator or titles describing work of any importance in the royal palace were no longer held by women. Women in the Middle Kingdom "were not appointed to positions where they held authority over other people, even in private households" (Ward 1989, 37). Also, Middle Kingdom households had labor more clearly divided in terms of gender: on the whole, women tended to work inside while men worked outdoors. Documents excavated from the Middle Kingdom town of Lahun show that women were only valued as laborers in the textile industry.

The majority of the evidence for female titles during the New Kingdom Period (1539–1075 BCE) originates as tomb inscription within the Theban necropolis. Women in the role of common "wife" remained "mistress of the house." Women married to high-ranking political officials were donned with a religious title, *shemayit*, or "chantress," of a deity, as seen with Amun of Thebes and Hathor. A chantress possessed sacred objects of the goddess Hathor, including a rattling instrument called a *sistrum* and an ornate beaded necklace called a *menat*. Chantress seems to be the only known religious title in the New Kingdom that could be held by a woman, other than "God's Wife of Amun," which could only be held by a royal woman. The wives of high-ranking men were also given the title of *menat nesu*, or "wet nurse of the king." A woman holding this title had a path to acceptance within the royal family, garnering royal favor for herself and potential societal advancement for the male members of her family.

From the evidence available, women in ancient Egypt seemed to have enjoyed legal equality with men. Women could inherit property and will it to others as they pleased. There is evidence that they could buy, sell, and trade, although "men were normally the 'public' partners in a marriage and handled business deals and property transactions, sometimes acting in their wife's name" (Johnson 1999, 170). Women were not only arrested, tried, and punished like their male counterparts, but they also initiated court cases when wronged and served as witnesses. Women kept their own personal property during divorce proceedings and also retained one-third of the couple's joint property. In the Late Period (664–332 BCE), marriage contracts are known. They state that a husband has to pay his wife a specified sum to divorce her, and the point of these contracts seems to be to keep the man from marrying a younger woman.

Women of the elite class were immortalized in statues and in images decorating their husbands' tombs. In ancient drawings, women are young, beautiful, and light-skinned to reflect an easy indoor existence. They are depicted in passive poses and are always scaled smaller than their husbands, to stress their inferior position. On the other hand, peasant women depicted on tombs as a part of a tomb owner's estate are drawn active and at work: harvesting, weaving, and serving food and drink. These women are depicted more freely because the purpose of their images is to show a sense of production and service, not the people performing the tasks at hand.

Ancient Egyptian literature portrays women with two different natures: good and bad. As stated in the instructions in the Insinger Papyrus, "It is in women that good fortune and bad fortune are upon earth" (Bryan 1996, 46). On one hand, there is the perfect, virtuous wife and loving mother, and on the other hand, there is the alluring, dangerous woman who can lead a man astray. All ancient Egyptian wisdom literature advises men to stay away from this second type of woman and hints at the consequences he will suffer if he does not. Wisdom literature also stressed how important the ideal wife and mother was and how a man must care for his mother when she is old. A text called the *Instructions of Any* has a lengthy description of the sacrifices a mother makes for her son, and it directs him to give his mother double everything that she gave to him while he was a child.

Lisa K. Sabbahy

See also: Families; Gender and Sex; Marriage and Divorce; Queens; Priestesses

Further Reading

Bryan, Betsy. 1996. "In Women Good and Bad Fortune Are on Earth: Status and Roles of Women in Egyptian Culture." In Anne K. Capel and Glenn Markoe, eds. *Mistress of the House, Mistress of Heaven: Women in Ancient Egypt*. Cincinnati: Cincinnati Art Museum, pp. 25–46.

Fischer, Henry. 2000. *Egyptian Women of the Old Kingdom and of the Heracleopolitan Period*. New York: Metropolitan Museum of Art.

Johnson, Janet. 1999. "Speculations on Middle Kingdom Marriage." In M. A. Leahy, ed. *Studies on Ancient Egypt in Honour of H. S. Smith*. London: Egypt Exploration Society, pp. 169–172.

Quirke, Stephen. 2007. "Women of Lahun (Egypt 1800 BC)." In Sue Hamilton, et al., eds. *Archaeology and Women: Ancient and Modern Issue*. Walnut Creek, CA: Altamira Press, pp. 246–262.

Redford, Donald. 1967. *History and Chronology of the Eighteenth Dynasty of Egypt: Seven Studies*. Toronto: University of Toronto Press.

Robins, Gay. 1993. *Women in Ancient Egypt*. London: British Museum Press.

Robins, Gay. 1994. "Some Principles of Compositional Dominance and Gender Hierarchy in Egyptian Art." *Journal of the American Research Center in Egypt* 31: 33–40.

Toivari-Viitala, Jaana. 2001. *Women at Deir el-Medina*. Leiden: Brill.

Troy, L. 1984. "Good and Bad Women. Maxim 18/284–288 of the Instructions of Ptahhotep." *Goettinger Miszellen* 80: 77–81.

Ward, William. 1989. "Non-Royal Women and Their Occupations in the Middle Kingdom." In Barbara Lesko, ed. *Women's Earliest Records from Ancient Egypt and Western Asia*. Atlanta: Scholars Press, pp. 33–43.

Bibliography

Aldred, Cyril. 1971. *Jewels of the Pharaohs*. New York: Thames & Hudson.

Allen, James P. 2006. *The Art of Medicine in Ancient Egypt*. New York: Metropolitan Museum of Art.

Allen, James P. 2010. *Middle Egyptian: An Introduction to the Language and Culture of Hieroglyphs*. Cambridge: Cambridge University Press.

Andrews, Carol. 1990. *Ancient Egyptian Jewellery*. London: British Museum Press.

Antoine, Daniel, and John H. Taylor. 2014. *Ancient Lives, New Discoveries: Eight Mummies, Eight Stories*. London: British Museum Press.

Arnold, Dieter. 2009. *The Monuments of Egypt*. Cairo: American University in Cairo Press.

Arnold, Dorothea. 1996. *The Royal Women of Amarna: Images of Beauty from Ancient Egypt*. New York: Metropolitan Museum of Art.

Assmann, Jan. 2005. *Death and Salvation in Ancient Egypt*. Ithaca, NY: Cornell University Press.

Brewer, Douglas J., and Emily Teeter. 2008. *Egypt and the Egyptians*. Cambridge: Cambridge University Press.

Capel, Anne K., and Glenn E. Markoe. 1996. *Mistresses of the House Mistresses of Heaven: Women in Ancient Egypt*. New York: Hudson Hills Press.

Cline, Eric H., and David O'Connor. 2009. *Thutmose III: A New Biography*. Ann Arbor: University of Michigan Press.

Darnell, John Coleman, and Colleen Manassa. 2007. *Tutankhamun's Armies*. Hoboken, NJ: John Wiley & Sons.

Dawson, Julie, and Helen Strudwick. 2016. *Death on the Nile: Uncovering the Afterlife of Ancient Egypt*. London: Fitzwilliam Museum.

Donker van Heel, Koenraad. 2016. *Mrs. Naunakhte & Family: The Women of Ramesside Deir al-Medina*. Cairo: American University in Cairo Press.

Edwards, I. E. S. 1975. *The Pyramids of Egypt*. Harmondsworth, UK: Penguin Books.

Forster, E. M. 1986. *Alexandria: A History and a Guide*. New York: Oxford University Press.

Freed, Rita, et al. 2009. *The Secrets of Tomb 10A: Egypt 2000 BC*. Boston: Museum of Fine Arts.

Gardiner, Sir Alan. 1988. *Egyptian Grammar*. Cambridge: Cambridge University Press.

Goddio, Franck, and Aurélia Masson-Berghoff. 2016. *The BP Exhibition: Sunken Cities.* London: Thames & Hudson.

Hawass, Zahi. 2003. *The Treasures of the Pyramids.* Vercelli: White Star Publishers.

Hornung, Erik. 1990. *The Valley of the Kings: Horizon of Eternity.* New York: Timken Publishers.

Hornung, Erik. 1992. *Idea into Image: Essays on Ancient Egyptian Thought.* New York: Timken Publishers.

James, T. G. H. 2003. *Pharaoh's People: Scenes from Life in Imperial Egypt.* London: Tauris Parke Paperbacks.

Jenkins, Nancy. 1980. *King Cheops' Royal Ship: The Boat beneath the Pyramid.* London: Thames & Hudson.

Kemp, Barry. 2007. *How to Read the Egyptian Book of the Dead.* New York: W. W. Norton & Company.

Kemp, Barry J. 1989. *Ancient Egypt: Anatomy of a Civilization.* London: Routledge.

Kemp, Barry J. 2012. *The City of Akhenaten and Nefertiti: Amarna and Its People.* Cairo: American University in Cairo Press.

Kitchen, K. A. 1982. *Pharaoh Triumphant: The Life and Times of Ramesses II.* Warminster, UK: Aris & Phillips.

Lehner, Mark. 1997. *The Complete Pyramids.* London: Thames & Hudson.

Lehner, Mark, and Zahi A. Hawass. 2017. *Giza and the Pyramids.* Cairo: American University in Cairo Press.

Leprohon, Ronald J. 2013. *The Great Name: Ancient Egyptian Royal Titulary.* Atlanta: Society of Biblical Literature.

McDowell, A. G. 1999. *Village Life in Ancient Egypt: Laundry Lists and Love Songs.* Oxford: Oxford University Press.

Moeller, Nadine. 2016. *The Archaeology of Urbanism in Ancient Egypt.* New York: Cambridge University Press.

O'Connor, David. 2009. *Abydos: Egypt's First Pharaohs and the Cult of Osiris.* Cairo: American University in Cairo Press.

O'Connor, David, and Eric H. Cline. 2001. *Amenhotep III: Perspectives on His Reign.* Ann Arbor: University of Michigan Press.

O'Neill, John P. 1999. *Egyptian Art in the Age of the Pyramids.* New York: Metropolitan Museum of Art.

Oppenheim, Adela, et al. 2015. *Ancient Egypt Transformed: The Middle Kingdom.* New Haven, CT: Yale University Press.

Parkinson, Richard. 1999. *Cracking Codes: The Rosetta Stone and Decipherment.* Los Angeles: University of California Press.

Parkinson, Richard. 2008. *The Painted Tomb-Chapel of Nebamun: Masterpieces of Ancient Egyptian Art in the British Museum.* Cairo: American University in Cairo Press.

Patch, Diana C. 2011. *Dawn of Egyptian Art.* New York: Metropolitan Museum of Art.

Pinch, Geraldine. 1994. *Magic in Ancient Egypt.* London: British Museum Press.

Pinch, Geraldine. 2004. *Egyptian Myth: A Very Short Introduction.* Oxford: Oxford University Press.

Quirke, Stephen. 2001. *The Cult of Ra: Sun-Worship in Ancient Egypt.* London: Thames & Hudson.

Redford, Donald B. 1984. *Akhenaten: The Heretic King.* Princeton, NJ: University of Princeton Press.

Reeves, Nicholas. 1990. *The Complete Tutankhamun.* Cairo: American University in Cairo Press.

Reeves, Nicholas, and Richard H. Wilkinson. 1996. *The Complete Valley of the Kings.* London: Thames & Hudson.

Robins, Gay. 1993. *Women in Ancient Egypt.* London: British Museum Press.

Roehrig, Catharine H. *Hatshepsut: From Queen to Pharaoh.* New York: Metropolitan Museum of Art.

Ruffle, John. 1977. *The Egyptians: An Introduction to Egyptian Archaeology.* Ithaca, NY: Cornell University Press.

Sabbahy, Lisa. 1985. *Ramses II.* Provo, UT: Brigham Young University.

Seyfried, Friederike, ed. 2012. *In the Light of Amarna: 100 Years of the Nefertiti Discovery.* Berlin: Staatliche Museum und Papyrussammlung.

Shafer, Byron E. 1991. *Religion in Ancient Egypt: Gods, Myths, and Personal Practice.* Ithaca, NY: Cornell University Press.

Shafer, Byron E., and Dieter Arnold. 1997. *Temples of Ancient Egypt.* Ithaca, NY: Cornell University Press.

Shaw, Garry J. 2013. *The Pharaoh: Life at Court and on Campaign.* London: Thames & Hudson.

Shaw, Ian. 2012. *Ancient Egyptian Technology and Innovation.* London: Bristol Classical Press.

Smith, Mark. 2017. *Following Osiris: Perspectives on the Osirian Afterlife from Four Millenia.* Oxford: Oxford University Press.

Snape, Steven. 2014. *The Complete Cities of Ancient Egypt.* London: Thames & Hudson.

Taylor, John H. 2010. *Journey through the Afterlife: Ancient Egyptian Book of the Dead.* London: British Museum Press.

Vassilika, Eleni. 2010. *The Tomb of Kha.* Torino: Scala Group.

Verner, Miroslav. 2013. *Temple of the World: Sanctuaries, Cults and Mysteries of Ancient Egypt.* Cairo: American University in Cairo Press.

Verner, Miroslav. 2014. *Sons of the Sun: Rise and Decline of the Fifth Dynasty.* Prague: Charles University in Prague, Faculty of Arts.

Wilkinson, Richard H. 1994. *Symbol & Magic in Egyptian Art.* New York: Thames & Hudson.

Winlock, Herbert E. 2010. *Tutankhamun's Funeral.* New York: Metropolitan Museum of Art.

About the Editor and Contributors

EDITOR

LISA K. SABBAHY has a PhD in Egyptian archaeology from the University of Toronto and is an assistant professor of Egyptology at the American University of Cairo and the director of the AUC MA Program in Egyptology and Coptology.

CONTRIBUTORS

KHOLOUD MOHAMED ABDEL MAKSOUD, PhD, is a lecturer in the Department of Natural Resources, Geology, Institute of African Research and Studies, Cairo University, Egypt.

KATHRYN E. BANDY graduated from the University of Chicago with her PhD in 2016. Her research utilizes textual, archaeological, and art historical sources to examine urban and regional administration during the late Middle Kingdom to the early New Kingdom.

ARTO BELEKDANIAN is an Egyptian Egyptologist with a PhD from Oxford University, Queen's College, with a special interest in Egyptian kingship, religion, and festivals.

JOLANDA E. M. F. BOS, PhD, studied Egyptian archaeology at the Rijksuniversiteit Leiden, the Netherlands. During the last 20 years, she has worked at different excavations in Egypt. Her main field of expertise lies in the sphere of archaeological beadwork analysis and human hair research.

NICHOLAS R. BROWN has an MA in Egyptology from the American University in Cairo and is currently a PhD student in Egyptology at the University of California, Los Angeles.

JENNIFER RUTH BUTTERWORTH studied Egyptology at the University of Memphis and received her PhD in art history from Emory University.

AMY CALVERT holds a PhD from the Institute of Fine Arts at New York University. She is the founder and director of the Art of Counting project, which is dedicated to the quantifiable discovery of patterns, trends, and messages in visual material from ancient Egypt and other eras.

CHRISTIAN CASEY is a PhD candidate in Egyptology at Brown University. His research focuses on the study of Egyptian phonology, where he uses novel computational methods to solidify and expand our understanding of the sounds of Egyptian languages.

ALESSANDRA COLAZILLI holds a PhD in Egyptology from the Sapienza University of Rome and has worked at Kom el Ghoraf, in the western delta.

AIDAN DODSON is a senior research fellow at the University of Bristol. He has a master's degree in museum practice and archaeology and a PhD in Egyptology from the University of Cambridge.

NOREEN DOYLE holds dual master's degrees in nautical archaeology from Texas A&M University and in Egyptology from the University of Liverpool. She works as a research specialist at the University of Arizona.

WOJCIECH EJSMOND received his academic degrees from the University of Warsaw in the archeology of ancient Egypt. He is director of the Gebelein Archaeological Project and codirector of the Warsaw Mummy Project.

YASMIN EL SHAZLY is currently an assistant adjunct professor of Egyptology at the American University in Cairo. She earned her MA and PhD in Egyptology from Johns Hopkins University.

MAHMOUD AHMED EMAM is a teaching assistant of ancient African history and archaeology at the Institute of African Research and Studies, Cairo University, Egypt.

KATJA GOEBS is an associate professor of Egyptology in the Department of Near and Middle Eastern Civilizations at the University of Toronto. She holds a master's in Egyptology from the University of Hamburg and a PhD in Egyptology from the University of Oxford.

MARIA ROSA GUASCH-JANÉ obtained her PhD in pharmaceutical sciences from the University of Barcelona. She has a master's degree in Egyptology from the Autonomous University of Barcelona.

LAUREL DARCY HACKLEY has an MA in Egyptology from the American University in Cairo and is a PhD candidate at the Joukowsky Institute for Archaeology and the Ancient World at Brown University.

SANDRA S. HEINZ holds a master's in classical archaeology and a PhD in archaeology from the University of Oxford. She is an adjunct lecturer at Princeton University.

SERGEI IGNATOV, PhD, DSc, is the head of the Bulgarian Institute of Egyptology, New Bulgarian University, Sofia.

SALIMA IKRAM is a distinguished university professor of Egyptology at the American University in Cairo. She has worked as an archaeologist throughout Egypt as well as in Turkey and Sudan and has published extensively.

DOUGLAS INGLIS received his master's in anthropology from Texas A&M University, where he is also a doctoral student, specializing in ancient Egyptian watercraft.

JACQUELINE E. JAY is an associate professor of history at Eastern Kentucky University. She received her PhD from the University of Chicago.

DANIEL SHAY MATTHEW JOHNSEN recently completed an MA in Egyptology at the American University in Cairo, Egypt.

LORETTA KILROE is a PhD candidate at the University of Oxford. Her work specifically focuses on ceramic pilgrim flasks in Egypt and Sudan. She has worked as a field ceramicist on several British Museum excavations in Sudan.

NIKOLAOS LAZARIDIS is an associate professor of ancient Mediterranean history at California State University, Sacramento. He received his PhD from the University of Oxford.

RONALD J. LEPROHON received his PhD from the University of Toronto in 1980. He is currently a professor of Egyptology in the Department of Near and Middle Eastern Civilizations at the University of Toronto.

MARIA HELENA TRINDADE LOPES is a full professor of Egyptology and the executive coordinator of the Department of History in the faculty of Social Sciences and Humanities at the Universidade Nova de Lisboa.

RITA LUCARELLI is an assistant professor of Egyptology at the University of California, Berkeley, and faculty curator of the ancient Egyptian collection of the Phoebe A. Hearst Museum of Anthropology, UC Berkeley.

EMILY RUSSO MACINTOSH is an Egyptologist and ancient art historian. She holds a PhD in Egyptology and Assyriology from Brown University.

CAROLINE ARBUCKLE MACLEOD is a Canadian archaeologist currently based in Los Angeles and is a specialist in the history of technique, woodworking, and production of Egyptian wooden coffins.

ALICIA MARAVELIA is a professor of Egyptology at the People's University of Athens. She holds a PhD in Egyptology from Université de Limoges.

HEATHER LEE MCCARTHY received her PhD in Egyptology from the Institute of Fine Arts at New York University. She is currently the deputy director of the New York University Epigraphical Expedition to the Ramses II Temple at Abydos.

MEGAN PAQUA is a MSc candidate in museums and digital culture at the Pratt Institute School of Information. She previously completed an MA in Egyptology at the American University in Cairo.

ANDRÉ PATRICIO has an MA in clinical psychology and an MA in history, with specialization in Egyptology. He is a PhD fellow in ancient history at Lisbon NOVA University.

ANNA LOUISE PEARMAN is a retired humanities professor who earned her master's in Interdisciplinary Studies from George Mason University.

SIMONE PETACCHI holds a master's in Egyptology from the University of Liverpool and a PhD from the University of Lille III. He is currently a consultant curator for Egyptian antiquities at the Stibbert Museum in Florence.

ERIN A. PETERS holds a PhD in art history from the University of Iowa. She is a joint lecturer of curatorial studies in the Department of History of Art and Architecture at the University of Pittsburgh.

NICHOLAS PICARDO is associate director of the Giza Project at Harvard University. As a specialist in household archaeology and digital humanities, he has worked at the Egyptian sites of Abydos, Giza, Kom el-Hisn, and Sakkara.

JOSHUA AARON ROBERSON holds a PhD in Egyptology from the University of Pennsylvania. He is currently an assistant professor of art history at the University of Memphis, Institute of Egyptian Art and Archaeology.

DANIELA ROSENOW is an Egyptologist with a specialization in Roman, Late Antique, and Early Islamic glass. She is currently an academic research fellow at the German Archaeological Institute Cairo.

CORINNA ROSSI specialized in Egyptology at Cambridge University, where she earned MPhil and PhD. She is currently associate professor of Egyptology at the

Politecnico di Milano and director of the Italian Mission to Umm al-Dabadib (Kharga Oasis).

ARIANNA SACCO has an MA in archaeology with a specialization in Egyptology from the University of Naples L'Orientale; an MA in interdisciplinary approaches to history, archaeology and social anthropology from the University of Thessaly in Volos; and is currently working on her PhD at Leiden University.

PATRICK SALLAND received his PhD in Egyptian art and archaeology from New York University's Institute of Fine Arts. His previous research has focused on palaces of the New Kingdom.

GARRY JOHN SHAW earned his PhD in Egyptology from the University of Liverpool, where he also taught Egyptian history.

JOHANNA SIGL holds a PhD in Egyptology and archaeozoology. She directs an excavation project in the Middle Kingdom settlement on the island of Elephantine on behalf of the German Archaeological Institute Cairo.

MARISSA STEVENS earned her PhD in the Department of Near Eastern Languages and Cultures at the University of California, Los Angeles, in 2018.

LISA SWART is an Egyptologist with a master's degree in ancient Near Eastern studies and a PhD in ancient studies from Stellenbosch University, South Africa.

GEOFFREY JOHN TASSIE earned his PhD at the Institute of Archaeology, University College London, in 2009 and is a postdoctoral research fellow at the University of Edinburgh and also honorary research fellow and associate lecturer at the University of Winchester.

ANGELA M. J. TOOLEY is an independent researcher. She was awarded a doctorate from the University of Liverpool on the subject of Middle Kingdom wooden models.

ANDRÉ JACQUES VELDMEIJER is a visiting research scholar at the American University in Cairo and is specialized in leatherwork and footwear. He codirects several projects, including the Ancient Egyptian Leatherwork Project.

CAROLA VOGEL received her PhD in Egyptology from the Johannes Gutenberg University, Mainz. She has a strong background in ancient Egyptian military history and publishes and lectures extensively in this field.

AMBER LUE WARD obtained her MA in art history with a concentration in Egyptian art and archaeology from the University of Memphis.

TAYLOR BRYANNE WOODCOCK is a doctoral student at the University of Toronto with a research focus on the construction and expression of ethnic identity in Egypt and Nubia. She completed her master's degree in Egyptology at the American University in Cairo.

KEI YAMAMOTO is a research specialist at the University of Arizona. He received his PhD in Near and Middle Eastern civilizations from the University of Toronto.

MOUSTAFA SAID ZAYED is an Egyptologist and holds a PhD in history from the Université du Québec à Montréal and is also a lecturer there.

KATHARINA ZINN is senior lecturer for Egyptian archaeology and heritage at the University of Wales Trinity Saint David, Lampeter. She received both her master's and PhD in Egyptology from the University of Leipzig.

Index

Page numbers in **bold** indicate the location of main entries. Page numbers in *italics* indicate photos.